The Sociology of Economic Life

The Sociology of Economic Life

EDITED BY

Mark Granovetter
State University of New York–Stony Brook

Richard Swedberg
University of Stockholm

Westview Press
BOULDER • SAN FRANCISCO • OXFORD

Copyright © 1992 by Westview Press, Inc.

Published in 1992 in the United States of America by Westview Press, Inc., 5500 Central Avenue, Boulder, Colorado 80301-2847, and in the United Kingdom by Westview Press, 36 Lonsdale Road, Summertown, Oxford OX2 7EW

Library of Congress Cataloging-in-Publication Data
The Sociology of economic life / edited by Mark Granovetter, Richard
 Swedberg.
   p. cm.
Includes bibliographical references and index.
ISBN 0-8133-1032-6. ISBN 0-8133-1033-4 (pbk.).
   1. Economics—Sociological aspects. 2. Capitalism. 3. Economic
history. 4. Industrial sociology. I. Granovetter, Mark S.
II. Swedberg, Richard.
HM35.S64 1992
306.3—dc20   91-25979
                                                                          CIP

Printed and bound in the United States of America

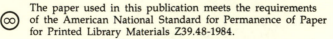 The paper used in this publication meets the requirements of the American National Standard for Permanence of Paper for Printed Library Materials Z39.48-1984.

10   9   8   7   6   5   4   3   2   1

Contents

Introduction

RICHARD SWEDBERG
MARK GRANOVETTER

This book is part of a recent and very exciting development: *the opening up of the academic debate about the economy to include a genuinely social perspective.* To the layperson it might seem obvious enough that the economy is part of the social world and not isolated from the rest of society. In academic economics, however, exactly the opposite opinion prevailed for several decades because during the early twentieth century, economists became convinced that economics could best progress if a series of simplifying assumptions was made that allowed formalization of the analysis with the help of mathematics. And these assumptions usually meant that a radically nonsocial approach had to be used.

We do not mean to imply that mathematical economics has been fruitless. On the contrary, brilliant analyses have been carried out by Paul Samuelson, Gerard Debreu, Kenneth Arrow, and others. What we do argue, however, is that sooner or later the realization was bound to come that it was unwise to make such a sharp separation between what is "economic" and what is "social."

As things turned out, the first ones to challenge this artificial division of labor between economics and the other social sciences were the economists themselves. Often they did this together with social scientists who felt that the economic model would also work on topics other than strictly economic ones. The first attempts in this direction came in the mid-1950s when a few scholars like Gary Becker and Anthony Downs argued that political topics could be analyzed with economic models (see, for example, Swedberg 1990b). In the 1960s this new approach was also extended to several other disciplines, including history, law, and demography. By the mid-1970s it appeared that all of these studies had something in common, and the term *economic imperialism* was increasingly used to identify them. In 1976 Gary Becker published an important programmatic work called *The Economic Approach to Human Behavior*, which more or less became the manifesto for this school of thought (Becker 1976). At this time the new approach was still a bit suspect in the eyes of many established economists. But when James Buchanan received the Nobel Prize for economics in 1986 and Gary

Becker finally became president of the American Economic Association, it was clear to everyone that the attempt to introduce the economic model into other social sciences had become perfectly respectable in the economics profession.

We shall criticize certain aspects of this "economic approach to human behavior," especially the one stipulating that existing economic institutions are to be understood as efficient solutions to certain problems in the market. For the moment, however, we sidestep this issue and instead emphasize that scholars like Becker and Downs were extremely important in being the first to challenge the peculiar division of labor between economics and the other social sciences that had developed in the twentieth century. They showed that one should not assume that certain topics are inherently "economic" (as in: Why does something cost as much as it does?) while others are "social" (as in: Why do people vote as they do?). Spurred on by proponents of "the economic approach," other social scientists have also begun to question the old sharp division of labor and have proposed their own solutions for what a new division should look like. Some of the main such strategies for restructuring the relation between economics and sociology are:

- *Rational Choice Sociology* (James Coleman, Gary Becker, Michael Hechter, and others). The basic idea is that the neoclassical model should be extended to topics that by tradition only sociologists have dealt with.
- *New Economic Sociology* (Mark Granovetter, Harrison C. White, Viviana Zelizer, and many other sociologists). The key notion is that many economic problems that by tradition belong to the economists' camp can be fruitfully analyzed with the help of sociology.
- *Socio-Economics* (Amitai Etzioni and a number of scholars from different social science disciplines). It is here argued that neoclassical economics is not enough to solve economic problems; a much broader perspective— which includes sociology, psychology, political science, and the other social sciences—must be used.
- *PSA-Economics (Psycho-, Socio-, Anthropo-Economics)* (a small circle around George Akerlof). The idea here is that by integrating certain findings from psychology, sociology, and anthropology directly into the economist's model, many problems, which for a long time have baffled economists, may be solved.
- *Transaction Cost Economics* (Oliver Williamson and scholars inspired by his approach). According to Williamson, many problems at the intersection of law, economics, and organization can be solved by assuming that institutions gravitate to forms that efficiently reduce transactions costs.

In a recent book of interviews, *Economics and Sociology: On Redefining Their Boundaries,* one of us (Swedberg) surveyed some of these strategies and interviewed many key proponents for these perspectives, and the reader may want to peruse some of these for an introduction to the issues in contention (Swedberg 1990a; see also the discussion of "socio-economics" in Etzioni 1988). Many positive things, as is clear from these interviews, can be said about each of the different perspectives. Although Akerlof's approach, for example, might not seem very original from the brief description given above, it is in reality both subtle and sophisticated. And although we, throughout this introduction, will criticize the proponents of "the economic approach" rather vigorously, many important ideas can be found in their works. This anthology, however, is first and foremost part of what has become known as New Economic Sociology (or New Sociology of Economic Life), and many—though not all—of the articles are written from this perspective. In order to give the reader more of a sense for economic sociology we shall offer a few words about its history and background before discussing the readings. We shall then give a brief introduction to the way economic sociologists look at things—what intellectual tools are available to economic sociologists and how they use these tools.

A BRIEF HISTORY OF ECONOMIC SOCIOLOGY

At the publication of Adam Smith's *Wealth of Nations* ([1776] 1976), there was no sharp separation between economic topics and social topics (for a more detailed history of economic sociology, see Swedberg 1987). Instead, there was an easy mingling of the two that continued in the nineteenth century, especially in Germany where the local version of this institutional economics soon became known as the Historical School. In England, however, Ricardo and a few other economists soon popularized a much more abstract analysis. These two perspectives—the historical-social one in Germany and the abstract-deductive one in England—had great difficulty in coexisting, and around the turn of the century they clashed very violently with one another. This fight started in Germany and Austria in the 1880s (where it became known as the *Methodenstreit*, or "the battle of the methods") and soon spread to several other countries, including England and the United States. The abstract-deductive approach won a devastating victory over the historically and socially oriented economists. During the twentieth century the claim of the latter even to be known as "economists" was increasingly questioned, and to a large extent they vanished into a new academic category—that of the economic historian.

Some of the historical economists were also attracted to sociology. The reason for this was simple: Sociology had clearly more of an affinity with the Historical School in economics than with the abstract-deductive approach of people like Ricardo and Menger. Indeed, the very first sociologist (or at least the person who coined the term *sociology*), Auguste Comte, had already in the 1830s criticized the economists for being far too abstract and non-empirical. Comte's critique was revived around the turn of the century, by economists as well as by sociologists, as part of "the battle of the methods." Of the sociologists, Emile Durkheim in particular was close to Comte, and when Durkheim formulated his own program for economic sociology, it was very close to what Comte had advocated. The other founder of economic sociology, Max Weber, was not hostile to the economists, as Durkheim had been. Still, Weber's ideas were ultimately closer to those of Comte and the Historical School than to those of the other side.

Durkheim and Weber made an unsuccessful effort to motivate support for economic sociology among sociologists. Durkheim, for example, wrote his major thesis on the division of labor in society, and it contains—like *Rules of Sociological Method* and some of his other writings—a sharp criticism of the economists' tendency to radically isolate their topic from everything "social" (see Durkheim 1915, [1893] 1984). Durkheim also conducted a very imaginative study of how the respect for property has emerged throughout the course of Western history (Durkheim 1983). And in each issue of the journal he had started, *l'Année Sociologique*, he saw to it that a section on *sociologie économique* was included.

Ultimately economics never fascinated Durkheim to the same extent as morality, religion, and education. For Weber, however, economics was one of his major interests. He wrote a thesis, for example, on medieval trading corporations and a major work on the social structure of agriculture in ancient civilizations (Weber 1976a, 1988c). During his lifetime he also wrote on industrial relations and stock exchanges, and he took part in an important discussion on whether economic theory is applicable not only to industrial societies but also to pre-industrial societies (see Weber 1976a, 1988a, 1988b).

Weber's two most important works in economic sociology are *Economy and Society* ([1922] 1978) and *General Economic History* ([1919] 1981). The former is an exceptionally rich work that, among other things, contains an important chapter (of a hundred and fifty pages!) in which Weber presented his theoretical program for economic sociology. This is the famous chapter 2: "Sociological Categories of Economic Action." Weber's second great contribution to economic sociology has been translated into English as *General Economic History*. This work is actually a transcript of a course that Weber gave in 1919–1920. When the students complained that his theory of economic sociology (as reprinted in chapter 2 of *Economy and Society*) was much too abstract and difficult to grasp, Weber decided to add some "flesh and blood" to the theoretical skeleton; the result was a more historically oriented lecture series than his original chapter.

But as the twentieth century advanced, sociologists increasingly shied away from economic topics—which they perceived to be in the domain of professional economists. Still, some of Weber and Durkheim's students continued to produce studies in economic sociology. Some of these have lost their intellectual luster today. Others are still as fresh as the day when they were written; this is especially true for Joseph Schumpeter's writings in economic sociology. We especially recommend his essays on imperialism and the tax state as well as his true masterpiece *Capitalism, Socialism, and Democracy* (Schumpeter [1942] 1990b, 1990a, [1942] 1975).

Until now we have only mentioned the European sociologists when we have discussed economic sociology. But some of the early U.S. sociologists—

we especially think of Cooley (who received his doctorate in economics)—did excellent work in economic sociology (see, for example, Cooley 1930). Still, the American sociologists basically came to see themselves as dealing only with "social" problems, which by definition were different from "economic" problems. This development was due in part to the sharp division of labor recommended by Talcott Parsons in the 1930s. Parsons, whose earliest academic positions had been in departments of economics (at Amherst and Harvard), came to see sociology as focusing exclusively on the values, or "ends," in "means-ends" chains, with economics assigned the task of analyzing the most efficient ways to achieve ends taken as given. (See Granovetter 1990 for a more detailed account.) In the 1950s, however, Parsons, with his student Neil Smelser, partially reversed this view, making an effort to expand sociology and take on some economic problems. Their programmatic work was *Economy and Society* (Parsons and Smelser 1956).

By this time, scholars in other social sciences also felt that mainstream economists had gone too far in isolating themselves. In 1956, for example, a few young Harvard economists (spurred on by a young sociologist, Francis X. Sutton) published *The American Business Creed* (Sutton et al. 1956). In the 1950s Karl Polanyi also energized some of his colleagues in anthropology into taking on those anthropologists who felt that economic theory was applicable not only to industrial societies but also to pre-industrial societies. One book, *Trade and Market in the Early Empires* (1957), which Polanyi coedited with some colleagues, was especially important in this context. This work actually became the opening shot in a long and hard battle between the so-called formalists and substantivists in economic anthropology. This battle still flares up now and then, even if the intense hostility of the 1960s is gone (see, for example, Orlove 1986).

We are now getting close to the present revival of economic sociology, also known as New Economic Sociology, which started in the early 1980s. One possible reason for sociologists to become interested in economic topics at about this time was because scholars like Gary Becker had challenged the existing division of labor between economics and sociology, which meant that economists were now taking on sociological topics and beginning to step on the toes of the sociologists. Again, it was at Harvard that the revival began. This time around, however, it was not under the guidance of Talcott Parsons but of Harrison White. In the 1960s and 1970s White had a number of students and young colleagues—Robert Eccles, Mark Granovetter, Michael Schwartz, and others—who were interested in economic topics. Harrison White mainly wrote about production markets; Wayne Baker studied securities markets; Robert Eccles, economic organization; Mark Granovetter, labor markets; and Michael Schwartz, financial networks (see, for example, White 1981, Baker 1984, Eccles 1985, Granovetter 1974, Mintz and Schwartz 1985).

Independently of the Harvard group, several individual sociologists had begun to study economic topics on their own. Viviana Zelizer was writing about life insurance; Mitchel Abolafia about the Hunt brothers' attempt to corner the silver market in the 1970s; and Susan Shapiro about the attempt by the Securities and Exchange Commission to keep "wayward capitalists" in line (see, for example, Zelizer 1983, Abolafia 1984, Shapiro 1984). During the last few years the number of studies in economic sociology has increased very rapidly. Many of these works are referred to in the Editors' Notes on Further Reading, which accompany each article in this anthology.

KEY PROPOSITIONS IN ECONOMIC SOCIOLOGY

The central tradition in economic sociology is rich and draws on many different sources. For example, it contains works of Weber as well as of Marx and Durkheim. Still, there is a common core of central propositions. We suggest these three:

1. Economic action is a form of social action;
2. Economic action is socially situated; and
3. Economic institutions are social constructions.

We will say a few words about each of them.

Economic Action as Social Action

It is generally recognized in economic theory as well as in economic sociology that *economic action* should constitute the basic theoretical building block. Definitions of the economy that focus on the production of material objects—as, for example, in the analysis of wealth of the seventeenth century, which preceded "political economy"—are considered unsuitable today. Economic theory and economic sociology also agree in a general way that economic action is a type of behavior that has to do with choosing among scarce means that have alternative uses (see, for example, Robbins [1932] 1984:16; Weber [1922] 1978:65).

At this point, however, the agreement ends. From the viewpoint of economic sociology, the current concept of economic action in mainstream economic theory goes much too far in eliminating all noneconomic motives. This does not mean that the exercise of assuming that there only exist economic motives is without value. On the contrary, as any orthodox demand-supply analysis shows, this type of exercise can be extremely important. But to make this assumption in each and every situation, as in today's mainstream economics, is profoundly misleading.

How has economics come to its present, rather peculiar position that economic action is essentially maximizing, rational behavior, and everything else belongs to "noneconomic" action? This is difficult to say, but it is clear that the answer is to be found far back in time. According to Adam Smith, it was quite obvious that people have a "propensity . . . to truck, barter and exchange one thing for another" (Smith [1776] 1976:17). On the one hand, Smith presented this narrow concept of economic action as something given by human nature. Social influences, on the other hand, were seen as something that basically *disturbed* economic action. In another famous passage in *The Wealth of Nations,* Smith noted that "People of the same trade seldom meet together, even for merriment and diversion, but the conversation ends in a conspiracy against the public, or in some contrivance to raise prices" ([1776] 1976:144).

In *The Passions and the Interests,* Albert O. Hirschman (1977) pointed out that the idea of economic action as synonymous with rational and sensible behavior is a recent and somewhat accidental historical product in Western thought. "Trucking, bartering, and exchanging" was originally seen as a destructive passion in medieval Europe. With the coming of capitalism, it was hoped that industriousness and commerce would first counterbalance and gradually replace the destructive lust for power and glory of the feudal princes. Scholars including Montesquieu sang the praise of the civilizing effects of commerce *(doux commerce).* As we know, the process of industrialization was not "mild" in most societies but very disruptive. Still, the idea stuck that somehow economic action was different from all other types of human behavior and therefore could be understood apart from them.

In many respects, the study of economics has been advanced by the assumption that economic action is a one-dimensional and closed world. But this perspective has been exaggerated to an unhealthy extent, especially during the twentieth century when economics has had minimal contact with the other social sciences. How is one then to remedy the situation? On a general level, it is obvious that the discourse in mainstream economics needs to be opened up to a genuinely social perspective. There are several ways of doing this. One could, for example, keep the original perspective in economic theory and then try to add or incorporate the social perspective. One would then hope for results that would fit empirical reality better. This is, to some extent, the strategy that characterizes George Akerlof's work, which he calls "psycho-, socio-, anthropo-economics" (Akerlof 1984). In many cases, however, one would probably have to totally restructure the whole research question in order to do justice to the social dimension.

The task of economic sociologists in this situation is to try to engage the economists in a discussion about economic action by elaborating the sociological viewpoint as forcefully as possible. From a sociological perspective, it is clear that economic action cannot, in principle, be separated from the quest for approval, status, sociability, and power.

How these quests influence economic action is an old theme among economic sociologists and remains high on their agenda. Among the pioneers, Durkheim, for example, has especially emphasized how pure economic action fails to bind people together for more than a few moments. In *The Division of Labor in Society* he said that "even where society rests wholly upon the division of labour, it does not resolve itself into a myriad of atoms juxtaposed together, between which only external and transitory contact can be established." He stressed that "The members are linked by ties that extend well beyond the very brief moment when the act of exchange is being accomplished" (Durkheim [1893] 1984:173).

A similar viewpoint also underlies Marx's concept of the economy, which is centered on the necessity to cooperate in the labor process. However,

Weber first introduced a sophisticated sociological concept of economic action. Most of Weber's reflections on this topic can be found in the important chapter 2, "Sociological Categories of Economic Action," in *Economy and Society*. Weber begins the chapter by stressing that the concept of social action, as used in economic theory, is basically similar to that used in economic sociology. Both are actions oriented to economic means or, more precisely, to the satisfaction of desires for utilities. It is clear from Weber's discussion that he found economic theory a perfectly useful and legitimate enterprise.

On two points, however, Weber's sociological concept of economic action differs from economic action as used in economic theory. First of all, the action is always oriented toward people's behavior; it "takes account of the behavior of others," as Weber ([1922] 1978:4) phrased it. This taking account can be done in many ways—by seeing other people, by talking to them, by thinking of them, and so on. In all these cases, it should be emphasized, the actor always takes other people's behavior into account through *socially constructed* meanings. On this point Weber's thought comes close to Durkheim's. According to Durkheim, economic action—like all other forms of social action—is always oriented toward and inspired by certain "collective representations." The notion of monetary value would be an example of a collective representation (as well as a social construct of meaning in Weber's sense).

The second point of difference, according to Weber, is in relation to power. As Weber saw it, economic action makes little sense from a sociological viewpoint if it is divorced from the idea that the economy constitutes a major source of power in society. Weber insisted that the sociological concept of economic action, which he defined as the *"peaceful exercise of an actor's control over resources which is in its main impulse oriented to economic means"* (Weber [1922] 1978:63, 68; emphasis added), includes as an essential component the criterion of power. The word "peaceful" tells us that Weber had a special type of power in mind. The term he used is formally translated as "the legally sanctioned power of control and disposal" *(Verfügungsgewalt)*. In a looser sense it can simply be translated as "economic power."

Weber then went on to analyze a series of important economic facts from the viewpoint of this power-oriented concept of economic action. "Exchange," for example, should in his opinion essentially be understood as resolution of a conflict of interest by means of a compromise; markets that are formally free are nevertheless often influenced by the actual distribution of power ("substantive regulation" as opposed to the formal "market freedom"). Weber also extended the concept of economic power directly into his analyses of prices and money.

> Money prices are the product of conflicts of interest and of compromises; they thus result from power constellations. Money is not a mere "voucher for unspecified utilities," which could be altered at will without any fundamental effect on the character of the price system as a struggle of man against man. "Money" is, rather, primarily a weapon in this struggle; they are instruments

of calculation only as estimated quantifications of relative chances in this struggle of interests (Weber [1922] 1978:108).

It should finally be noted that throughout his academic career Weber was very concerned with improving communication between economic theorists and economic sociologists. He had grown up under the *Methodenstreit,* which in his opinion had been an absolute disaster and split economics into *"two* sciences" (Weber 1949:63). This division was unacceptable to Weber, and he spent a great deal of energy trying to reconcile the theoretically oriented economists with the more historically and sociologically oriented ones. Weber's own recipe for how to solve the impasse of the *Methodenstreit* was something he called "social economics" *(Sozial-ökonomik).* This kind of economic analysis was very broad and incorporated not only marginal utility theory but also historical economics and economic sociology. As Weber saw it, the point was not so much in trying to force all these different ideas into one coherent, logical system—he abhorred this type of system for various reasons—but to let all of them peacefully coexist under the big umbrella of "social economics."

Economic Action as Socially Situated

Economic action is socially situated and cannot be explained by reference to individual motives alone. It is embedded in ongoing networks of personal relationships rather than being carried out by atomized actors. By *network* we mean a regular set of contacts or similar social connections among individuals or groups. An action by a member of a network is *embedded,* because it is expressed in interaction with other people. The network approach helps avoid not only the conceptual trap of atomized actors but also theories that point to technology, the structure of ownership, or culture as the exclusive explanation of economic events.

The concept of *networks* is especially useful in the sociological analysis of the economy. Because it is very close to concrete, empirical reality, its use thereby prevents conceptual errors common in mainstream economic theory, New Institutional Economics, and some abstract sociological analyses. In the New Institutional Economics, the emergence and maintenance of social institutions is typically explained through their alleged efficiency. We will argue that such propositions, popular because of their apparently parsimonious solution of otherwise intractable problems, appear increasingly inadequate as soon as one starts to seriously map out the social structure involved.

For all its obvious virtues, Karl Polanyi's notion of embeddedness suffers from a similar limitation. Polanyi formulated his theory of embeddedness in direct opposition to the atomistic viewpoint of mainstream economics (see Chapter 1 in this anthology). In the 1930s and 1940s, some anthropologists had started to introduce concepts from conventional economics into their studies. Polanyi felt that this was totally wrong, and he spent a large part of his intellectual career formulating a "substantivist" alternative to these "formalistic" economic anthropologists. The economy in pre-industrial societies, he argued, was embedded in social, religious, and political institutions. This meant that such phenomena as trade, money, and markets were inspired by motives other than profit making. Economic life in these early societies was instead ruled either by reciprocity or by redistribution. The market mechanism was not allowed to dominate economic life: Demand and supply did not set the price but rather tradition or political authorities. In modern societies, however, it was exactly "the price-making market" that determined all of economic life. A new logic ruled these societies, a logic that dictated that economic action must *not* be embedded in society. The economy, as Polanyi phrased it, was in this type of society "directed by market prices and nothing but market prices" where "human beings behave in such a way as to achieve maximum money gains (Polanyi et al. 1957:43, 68)." In brief, the industrial revolution had created just the kind of society presupposed in conventional economic theory.

But if we apply a networks perspective to the kind of societies Polanyi discusses and take a careful look at their social structures, we quickly find out that the level of embeddedness varies considerably—*both in industrial and in pre-industrial societies.* There are some pre-industrial societies where people are as obsessed with making money as in the most capitalistic society—for example, some tribes in the Melanesian region north of Australia (see Pospisil 1963). And if we look at capitalist societies, we find that economic action is not "disembedded," as Polanyi thought. Rather, economic actions are embedded in a different way. In brief, network analysis can help to address many of the problems traditionally associated with Polanyi's substantivist theory.[1]

By using the term *network* we do not mean to impose an imperialist claim over other interpretations in economic sociology, such as Weberian theory, symbolic interaction, or Marxist sociology. Our claim is, rather, that regardless of the perspective one identifies with in sociology, it is absolutely essential to look at the actual, concrete interactions of individuals and groups. In, for example, Michael Burawoy's neo-Marxist *Manufacturing Consent* (1979) we find an excellent network analysis of the work situation in a manufacturing plant in Chicago—despite the fact that the author is no network analyst. Burawoy, who worked in the factory, found that in order to avoid monotony and boredom the workers in various ways tried to compete among themselves. This game of "making out" kept the workers going during the long hours of work, and they related to the other workers in terms of this game. In his later book, *The Politics of Production* (1985), Burawoy built a more general argument that relied in part on the idea that proper Marxist analysis of the workplace must have as an essential part an analysis of the informal relations and networks that constitute the everyday system of production.

Another case where network analysis helps illuminate the economy is in the role of ethnic networks. The burgeoning literature on "middleman minorities" illustrates this (see, for example, Bonacich 1973). It is also common in studies of international banking to point to the importance of ethnic and religious minorities and to note how easily members of the same ethnic background can form well-functioning networks over huge geographical areas (cf. Curtin 1984). David Landes, to cite just one example, has analyzed the success of the Huguenots in French banking from this perspective:

> No sooner were the French Calvinists, or Huguenots, settled in cities of refuge than they sent their children back to France, not as Frenchmen subject to discrimination and persecution, but as foreigners covered by Swiss or Dutch citizenship. By the beginning of the eighteenth century, there was in Paris an active colony of Calvinist bankers, whose close relations with relatives abroad were supplemented by invaluable ties with Protestants who had never left the country. . . . Solid, conservative, extremely conscious of their faith and their dignity as a religious minority, they formed a coherent financial bloc, anchored on Paris and Geneva, but reaching into every important market on the Continent. In discount transactions and foreign exchange, they had enormous respect for, and implicit confidence in, one another and received similar respect and confidence from outsiders; in loan flotations and industrial promotions, they were quick to consult and share among themselves. And though not particularly wealthy, their prudence, reliability, and co-operation as a group gave them power beyond their numbers and personal resources, so much so that in France, 'high finance,' *la haute banque,* and Protestant finance, *la banque protestante,* have been almost synonymous (Landes 1979:21–23).

Although it is true that the role of ethnic and religious minorities in banking provides a particularly striking example of the role of networks in the economy, the usefulness of network analysis extends well beyond this and similar obvious cases. Many students of finance in general have found that a network approach answers much more to empirical reality than the atomistic approach of mainstream economic theory. When George Katona decided to analyze the relationship between banks and their corporate clients in the early 1950s, he quickly found out there was a great deal of stability to these ties. Indeed, two-thirds of the corporations had not changed their primary banking partner during the previous ten years, and nearly half of them had had the same partner for more than twenty years (Katona 1957:112). A corporation that changed banks too often ran the risk of becoming known as a "bank changer." According to Katona (1957:115), "change in banking connections appears to constitute an unpleasant process which is sometimes avoided even if the relationships appear not quite satisfactory."

In their recent study, Robert Eccles and Dwight Crane (1988) see investment banking as a kind of network business, where the investment banker mediates the flow of assets between investors and those that need capital ("issuers"). The network approach, however, is not only applicable to the "external ties" of an investment bank. By the very nature of its work, an investment bank has to have a particularly flat and flexible structure ("internal ties"). Every deal is carried out under tremendous pressure, Eccles and Crane explain, and a rigid and sharply hierarchical structure would make it hard to quickly put together a complicated deal. The fact that corporations today often work with several investment banks also adds to the pressure to perform fast and efficiently.

It should be stressed that network analysis can be applied as well to a series of key problems in economic theory, such as the management of trust and malfeasance. For a discussion of these two particular cases, the reader is referred to the discussion in Mark Granovetter's "Economic Action and Social Structure" (Chapter 2 of this anthology). Moreover, in our opinion the whole question of price formation—so central to neoclassical theory—can be illuminated in a most useful manner by a network approach. Polanyi had claimed that prices in pre-industrial societies were primarily determined by *tradition* (where the main principle of economic life was reciprocity) or by *command* (where the guiding principle was redistribution). Marshall Sahlins later tried to bolster Polanyi's case, especially in *Stone Age Economics*. In this work Sahlins (1974:277–314) argued in great detail that rates of exchange in pre-industrial societies are not set through demand and supply. Instead a certain rate is set that is then maintained unless something of major importance occurs—which results in the setting of a new rate.

Sahlins's analysis, however, can be reinterpreted from a network perspective. At closer inspection, it becomes clear that Sahlins has not at all succeeded in showing that demand and supply have no impact on the rate of exchange. What he does show is that these rates are "sticky"—that is, they only respond to *major* shifts in demand and supply. And the reason for the "stickiness" is that the economic relations are embedded in networks that restrain the pure economic forces. Our main conclusion is that Sahlins demonstrated not the absence of demand-supply influence on prices but rather that prices in pre-industrial societies are essentially set through a *mixture* of social influence and demand-supply. Fernand Braudel came to a similar conclusion in his masterful analysis of markets in *Civilization and Capitalism* (1985). Polanyi, he said, was clearly wrong in arguing that in pre-industrial society demand and supply play no role, but in industrial society they alone account for the price. "It is too easy to call one form of exchange economic and another social. *In real life, all types are both economic and social*" (Braudel 1985:227; emphasis added).

Braudel's insight that also in contemporary, capitalist societies prices are set through economic as well as social forces is similar to that of macroeconomist Arthur Okun in *Prices and Quantities*. Okun here introduced and discussed two types of prices that are formed in product markets: "auction-market prices" and "customer-market prices." The former are characterized by the fact that they are exclusively shaped by demand and supply forces and thereby fit the classical paradigm of continuous market-clearing. This is typical, Okun said, of certain homogeneous products such as agricultural and mining products. More common, however, are "customer-market prices," or prices where the social relationship between the buyer and the seller influences the price in combination with the ordinary demand and supply forces. "Customers avoid shopping costs by sticking with their supplier much as workers avoid search costs by sticking with their employer," Okun

(1981:142) noted. When, and under which circumstances, social forces or the demand-supply forces predominate in the formation of a special price is something for concrete research to show.[2]

The Social Construction of Economic Institutions

We do not mean to give the impression that economic sociology is mainly concerned with microeconomic events. On the contrary, economic sociology has a long tradition of analyzing macroeconomic events, as in the monumental works on capitalism by Marx, Weber, and Schumpeter.

Macroeconomic issues such as business cycles and the intervention of the state in the economy can be illuminated by a sociological approach. Here, however, we concentrate on one specific issue, the role of institutions. A major reason for this choice is that economists have recently begun to look at institutions and try to integrate them into their analyses—as in the New Institutional Economics. From the viewpoint of economic sociology, it is of course welcome that mainstream economics now attempts to analyze institutions (after having been extremely hostile to earlier efforts); and this mutual interest provides one area where a dialogue between economists and sociologists is possible. But how successful have the economists actually been in integrating an analysis of institutions into mainstream economics? Especially, how "social" are the analyses by the economists of social institutions? And how do they compare to the equivalent efforts by economic sociologists to analyze institutions?

According to Oliver Williamson (1975:1–19; 1985:15–42), who has tried to sketch the history of the New Institutional Economics, the interest in institutions reached an absolute nadir among economists just after World War II. Things started to change in the early 1960s with works by scholars like Coase, Alchian, Arrow, and Chandler on property rights, social costs, costs of information, and business organization. By the mid-1970s New Institutional Economics had reached a critical mass, and after this date the growth was exponential. Articles in this genre can be found in journals like the *Journal of Economic Behavior and Organization* and the *Journal of Institutional and Theoretical Economics* (JITE). Key works include Arrow's *The Limits of Organization* (1974), Davis and North's *Institutional Change and American Economic Growth* (1974), Doeringer and Piore's *Internal Labor Markets and Manpower Analysis* (1971), and Nelson and Winter's *An Evolutionary Theory of Economic Change* (1982).

Common to the analyses in the New Institutional Economics is a belief that mainstream economics should deal with institutions but does not do so. "From the viewpoint of the economic historian this neoclassical formulation [in mainstream economics] appears to beg all of the interesting questions. The world with which it is concerned is a frictionless one in which institutions do not exist and all change occurs through perfectly operating markets" (North 1981:5).

The second element that the New Institutional Economists have in common is that they argue that the missing institutional analysis can be built directly on the basis of the principles of neoclassical economics. Note that North says neoclassical economics only "appears" to beg all the interesting questions. He actually continues, "In short, the costs of acquiring information, uncertainty, and transaction costs do not exist. But precisely because of this nonexistence, the neoclassical formula does lay bare the underlying assumptions that must be explored in order to develop a useful theory of structure and change" (North 1981:5). Williamson (1975:1) expresses essentially the same idea as North when he says that as opposed to the "old" institutionalists like Veblen et al. the "new" institutionalists "regard what they are doing as complementary to, rather than a substitute for, conventional [economic] analysis."

It is clear from Williamson's account that the New Institutionalists represent a somewhat heterogeneous collection of economists. In Williamson's own writings, "economizing on transaction costs" is the key to the existence of all economic institutions. It is on the basis of this criterion that he proceeds to investigate "the economic institutions of capitalism" (Williamson 1985:1, 17). In Andrew Schotter's work *The Economic Theory of Social Institutions*, however, the basic approach is game theoretic, and institutions are essentially ways of solving "social coordination games," that is, of preventing individual rational actions from having irrational collective results. Schotter's approach is also influenced by Darwinian ideas. "Economic and social systems evolve the way species do. To ensure their survival and growth, they must solve a whole set of problems that arise as the system evolves. Each problem creates the need for some adaptive features, that is, a social institution. . . . Every evolutionary economic problem requires a social institution to solve it" (Schotter 1981:1–2).

A third version of New Institutional Economics can be found in the popular work *The Rise of the Western World* by Douglass North and Robert Paul Thomas. The main idea in this work is that the rapid economic growth of Western Europe was due to its efficient economic institutions. "Efficient economic organization is the key to growth; the development of an efficient economic organization in Western Europe accounts for the rise of the West. Efficient organization entails the establishment of institutional arrangements and property rights that create an incentive to channel individual economic effort into activities that bring the private rate of return close to the social rate of return" (North and Thomas 1973:1).

Other versions of New Institutional Economics exist as well, but the central theme in all of these analyses is efficiency. An institution exists because it is efficient—that is often the core idea. But there are many difficult problems with this proposition. For one thing, the concept of efficiency in mainstream economics is confusing and contradictory (see, for example, Granovetter 1979; Oberschall and Leifer 1986) and lacks subtlety. Take, for example, the argument in Bernard Bailyn's *The New England Merchants*— that failures are often needed in economic life to show how things can be done right. This is an idea that has no place in the black-and-white world of some New Institutional Economists.

This is connected to the negative attitude toward history in the works by Williamson and some (though not all) other New Institutional Economists. Opening a book entitled *The Economic Institutions of Capitalism* (Williamson 1985) one would expect to find an account of these institutions and their history. Instead one finds an ahistorical and abstract argument, constructed on the basis of what Williamson described as "human nature as we know it" (a phrase he has borrowed from Frank Knight).[3]

History finds even less place in Schotter's work, because historians do not address the kind of issues that interest him. Indeed, "the problem facing social scientists is to infer the evolutionary problem that *must have existed* for the institution as we see it to have developed" (Schotter 1981:1–2; emphasis added). That is, Schotter prefers hypothetical to actual history: If something exists, it must be (or have been) beneficial for someone or some organization. This type of argument was once popular in sociology but would today be dismissed as crude functionalism (see, for example, Stinchcombe 1975; Elster 1979:28–35).

As a historian, North is naturally more sensitive to the difficulties involved in the argument that institutions only exist because they are efficient solutions to various problems in the economy. At a recent conference about New Institutional Economics he explicitly cautioned against using "efficiency" as the key to an institutional analysis: "Institutions . . . facilitate certain kinds of exchange, although it should be carefully noted that doing so implies nothing about their efficiency" (North 1989:239). He suggested instead that institutions provide the basic "rules" for how to behave by providing different "incentives." A few other participants at the conference echoed North's critique of centering the institutional analysis on the concept of efficiency. Instead they recommended that "one might . . . concentrate on discovering the linkages between institutional structure and economic behavior, while refraining from any judgments on the desirability or efficiency of the observed outcomes" (Furubotn and Richter 1989:4). This thoughtful idea could be developed in interesting directions.

The works by New Institutional Economists like Oliver Williamson and Alfred Chandler (formally a business historian, but close to the thinking of scholars like Williamson) have also inspired a number of sociologists to work on economic organizations, especially the business firm. Thus we now have quite a few interesting studies of this type by such scholars as Robert Eccles, Walter Powell, Neil Fligstein, and others. Some of these also draw on the tradition of industrial sociology and organization theory. Robert Eccles, for example, has developed the notion of "quasifirm" for certain stable relationships—typically in the construction industry—between a general contractor and its subcontractors (Eccles 1981). Walter Powell and Arthur Stinchcombe have challenged Oliver Williamson's sharp distinction between "markets" and "hierarchies." Powell has done this by drawing attention to what he calls *hybrid organizational arrangements,* a term by which he more or less means network organizations of a certain stability (Powell 1985). Stinchcombe has criticized Williamson for not realizing that some contractual relationships are in reality very similar to hierarchical arrangements (Stinch-combe 1985).

Sociologists have also been very critical of the idea in New Institutional Economics that the chosen organizational form is always the most efficient one. According to Charles Perrow, for example, many economic organizations look the way they do because some actors have power over others—and not because one type of organization is more "efficient" than another (Perrow 1986). Oberschall and Leifer are less critical of the New Institutional Economics than Perrow but agree with him that power considerations make the efficiency analysis problematic. Two other factors, they say, add further to this: goal ambiguity and the fact that choice is not only rational but also influenced by the existing norms (Oberschall and Leifer 1986).

There are also sociologists who have challenged Alfred Chandler's claim that the multidivisional form, which is so characteristic for big corporations, is the result of efficiency, rationality, and market forces. Neil Fligstein has shown that Chandler's theory cannot account for the spread of the multi-divisional form among American corporations in the twentieth century (Fligstein 1985). On the contrary, as Fligstein pointed out, other perspectives are needed for this. It is, for example, clear that some corporations have changed their organizational structure in a multidivisional direction mainly because this *appears* more rational (see also DiMaggio and Powell 1983). In Chapter 7 in this anthology—Gary Hamilton and Nicole Biggart's "Market, Culture, and Authority: A Comparative Analysis of Management and Or-ganization in the Far East"—it is also noted that Chandler's theory is not powerful enough to explain the differences in organizational structure among Taiwan, Japan, and South Korea. Finally, it should be mentioned that a series of interesting sociological studies exist of economic institutions other than the business corporation. Contemporary economic sociologists have taken on auctions, stock exchanges, sales organizations, merchant banks, money, various types of insurance, and socialist economic institutions (see Abolafia 1984; Baker 1987; Biggart 1989; Eccles and Crane 1988; Heimer 1985; Nee and Stark 1989; Smith 1989; Zelizer 1983, 1989).

Even if there exist a large number of fine sociological studies of economic institutions, relatively little attention has been paid to the theoretical side or the elaboration of the notion of the economic institution itself. Some sociologists, however, have argued that economic institutions can be under-stood as *"social constructions."* In France, for example, a theme issue of Pierre Bourdieu's journal *Actes de la Recherche en Sciences Sociales* was recently devoted to "the social construction of the economy." In one article especially, "The Social Construction of a Perfect Market" by Marie-France Garcia, this idea found an interesting expression: The author portrayed the way in which a local market in fresh strawberries operates. The market is organized in a very modern way with buyers and sellers of strawberries negotiating with each other via electronic screen in a building specially constructed for this purpose. In one part of the house the strawberries are displayed; in another the sellers sit and watch the screen; and in a third we find the buyers interacting with the sellers via the same screen. What could be a better illustration of the neoclassical view of the market than this, the author asks?

If we, however, look at the way this market has come into being, we find no "invisible hand" behind its creation. The computerized market is instead the result of a sharp interest struggle between certain strawberry producers and their distributors. A few years ago the producers mustered the force to overthrow the traditional, "inefficient" way of selling strawberries, which in their opinion favored the distributors. Together with a local administrator, who was trained in economic theory and who had his own reasons for backing the producers, the new computerized market was organized. And this market will last, the author adds, only as long as the present balance of interests between producers and distributors remains roughly the same.

An attempt to further elaborate the idea of "social construction" in the economy has been made by Mark Granovetter (1990 and forthcoming). This idea can be understood more easily with the help of three ideas: the concept of "the social construction of reality" from the sociology of knowledge; the idea of path-dependent sequences from economics; and the concept of social networks. Peter Berger and Thomas Luckmann, in *The Social Construction of Reality*, argue (inspired by Weber via Schutz) that institutions are not the kind of objective, "external" realities that they seem. Instead they are typically the result of a slow, social creation; a way of doing something "hardens" and "thickens" and finally becomes "the way things are done." When an institution is finally in existence, people orient their actions to a set of activities sanctioned by other social actors, treating the pattern as one that exists out of time and could not be otherwise. But this sense of institutions as external and objective is a sort of obfuscation that society works on its members, and Berger and Luckmann (1966:54–55) emphasize throughout their work that "it is impossible to understand an institution adequately without an understanding of the historical process in which it was produced."

Path-dependent development is a term associated with Paul David (1986) and Brian Arthur (1989). With reference to alternative technological developments and standards, David and Arthur show that the most efficient solution does not always win out; chance elements often interfere at an early stage of a process, altering its course. A striking example of this is the development of the keyboard in typewriters, as described by Paul David (1986). On a modern keyboard, the upper left line reads Q-W-E-R-T-Y. But it has been long known that this is not the most efficient way of ordering the letters—if they were arranged in another way, one could type much faster. Why then has the keyboard not been changed? Why doesn't an entrepreneur appear with a new keyboard where the letters are placed more efficiently? In fact, such keyboards exist and are well known but not well adopted. David also notes that in the 1860s it was efficient to place the letters in the order of QWERTY. The machines in those days would easily jam and then repeat the same letter. Because the typist could not see the typed sentence before it was completed and an early mistake would affect everything that came afterward, it was a good idea to place the letters in such a way that the typist would be slowed down, minimizing the chance of jams. Typewriter technology, however, quickly changed and made this problem irrelevant; but by this time corporations had already bought QWERTY-machines, and secretaries had learned to type with the QWERTY-keyboard. It had become, and apparently remains, inefficient (in the short run) to switch to a more efficient keyboard (in the long run). QWERTY had become "locked in."

Granovetter has generalized the idea of path-dependent development to organizational and institutional forms, arguing that economic institutions are constructed by mobilization of resources through social networks, conducted, of course, against a background of constraints given by the previous historical development of society, polity, market, and technology. In one case study, which they argue illustrates the "social construction of industry," McGuire, Granovetter, and Michael Schwartz (forthcoming) treat the origins of the American electrical utility industry. In the 1880s, it was by no means clear that the industry would take the present form of investor-owned utility companies generating power in central stations for large areas. Instead, there were two other possibilities: generation of power by each household and business with its own equipment ("isolated stations") and public ownership of utility firms.[4]

Why did one of these alternatives not occur? McGuire et al. (forthcoming) argue that given the state of technology and the political and economic situation, all three were originally possible. The networks of two central individuals were crucial in orienting the industry into its present form. In the 1880s, the efforts and resource mobilization of Thomas Edison overcame the preference of such powerful bankers and financiers as J. P. Morgan for isolated stations and tipped the balance to central generation of power. Then Samuel Insull, who had come to the United States from Britain in 1881 at the age of twenty-one to be Edison's private secretary, determined much of the remaining history of the industry. Arriving in 1892 in Chicago to take over the small, new Chicago Edison, Insull first mobilized resources through his own network to reshape Chicago Edison and eventually used this as a template for the entire industry. Central in this effort was his position as a bridge among networks of politicians, financiers, and inventors. Mobilization through social networks had helped to decide which of the three alternatives came to dominate.

McGuire et al. also emphasize that although Edison and Insull were brilliant manipulators and made strenuous efforts to shape and reshape their network resources, many of these resources arose prior to and/or independently of their efforts—such as the crucial links between industrialists and financiers in Chicago and London, central in Insull's successful evasion of the power of hostile New York bankers such as J. P. Morgan. It was thus neither the "great men" nor the social structure that determined the outcome but the interaction between the two.

To summarize, in the sociological analysis, institutions are social constructions of reality. This idea goes back to the early sociologists and seems worth emphasizing also today—especially to bring out the difference between the sociological and the economic perspective on institutions. For today's research agenda, we can add the idea that networks may play a crucial role especially at an early stage in the formation of an economic institution; once the development is "locked in," their strategic importance declines. We emphasize, thereby, that only a dynamic analysis can handle the problem of institution formation in the economy. In cases where there is in fact only one viable equilibrium, then a static type of analysis is sufficient. Otherwise, a dynamic analysis is needed, and in such cases network mobilization comes to center stage.[5]

THE MACROECONOMY

Several valuable attempts to deal with macroeconomics in economic sociology already exist. There are first of all the three great classics: Marx's *Capital* ([1867] 1967), Weber's *Economy and Society* ([1922] 1978), and Durkheim's *The Division of Labor in Society* ([1893] 1984). The reader should also consult a few other works, especially Weber's *General Economic History* ([1919] 1981), Schumpeter's *Capitalism, Socialism, and Democracy* ([1942] 1975), Wallerstein's *The Modern World System* (1974–1989), and Braudel's *Civilization and Capitalism* (1985). All of these presented their own version of what makes the world economy develop in one direction rather than another. At first it may seem that the giant economic processes discussed in these works have little in common with our three key propositions, namely: (1) that economic action is a form of social action; (2) that economic action is socially situated; and (3) that economic institutions are social constructions. But we would suggest that even giant economic formations—postwar capitalism in the OECD countries or the national economies in Latin America during the same time period—are distinct social constructions with distinct consequences for the economic actors.

Clearly, today's sociologists have a lot of work left to do on macroeconomic issues of this type. There exists, for example, a sophisticated debate about the role of the state in the economy that should be taken into account in economic sociology (see Evans, Rueschemeyer, and Skocpol 1985; Katzenstein 1978). There also exist some studies of postindustrial society, which are of much interest (see especially Piore and Sabel 1984). Among our selections, those by Randall Collins (Chapter 3) and Alexander Gerschenkron (Chapter 4) point the way toward some of these large macroeconomic issues.

Daunting as the vast agenda that we have sketched for the micro- and macrosociology of economic life may be, we believe that economic sociology has now built a sufficiently solid theoretical structure that it can approach these problems with a certain amount of confidence and anticipation of exciting new developments. It is our hope that this book, by providing some guide to the structure, will add to the gathering momentum.

A NOTE ON THE SELECTIONS IN THIS BOOK

We present in this book a selection of some of what we believe to be the most interesting work done in modern economic sociology and related disciplines, along with some classic works that have set the scene for current efforts. The economics of edited anthologies constricts our selection to a far greater extent than it would have thirty or forty years ago. Thus many very important articles and authors could not be included. We propose only to whet the appetite of readers who, we hope, will be drawn from a number of different disciplines. Because our selection is necessarily limited, we have composed extensive annotated references following each article or excerpt, which put the piece in intellectual context, follow up debates that stimulated or resulted from the work, and suggest what other sources would give the interested reader a fuller picture of the subject area. Each of our selections should thus be seen as a somewhat arbitrary entry point into a complex network of literature on a series of related subjects.

There is no "best" way to read the items in this anthology. We suggest beginning with the Introduction and paying particular attention to the section called "Key Propositions in Economic Sociology." The two articles by Karl Polanyi and Mark Granovetter in Part I ("Sociological Approaches to the Economy") further elaborate on these key propositions, especially that economic action is always social and that it is always "embedded." In "The Economy as Instituted Process" (Chapter 1) Polanyi asserts that economic life in pre-industrial societies was embedded in various noneconomic institutions and in "Economic Action and Social Structure" (Chapter 2) Granovetter extends parts of this argument to contemporary societies with their advanced economies. Granovetter also criticizes some contemporary economists' attempts to explain the emergence of economic institutions by way of efficiency arguments ("New Institutional Economics"). Existing economic institutions, Granovetter shows, need not have come into being simply because they were the most "efficient" way to solve some economic problem.

It is possible to read the remaining texts in different order, depending on one's degree of knowledge in economic sociology or one's particular purpose in using this anthology. But there may be some advantage in following the order in which we have placed the different texts. Part II ("Historical and Comparative Perspectives on the Economy") introduces the reader to a series of readings that show that economic sociology is not only interested in microevents in the economy but also in broad, macroeconomic phenomena. Being comparative is a way to counteract ethnocentrism and intellectual myopia; and being historical helps to avoid trendiness and hasty generalizations. Randall Collins's "Weber's Last Theory of Capitalism" (Chapter 3) exposits and extends some of the seminal ideas of Max Weber on the birth of capitalism. Alexander Gerschenkron's classic essay "Economic Backwardness in Historical Perspective" (Chapter 4) reminds us that there were many ways, not just one, in which the European countries (including Russia) industrialized during the nineteenth century.

In "The Emergence of Managerial Capitalism" (Chapter 5), Alfred D. Chandler, Jr., compares the role that the modern multidivisional firm has played in the United States, Great Britain, Japan, and Germany. Japan is also discussed in Ronald Dore's "Goodwill and the Spirit of Market Capitalism" (Chapter 6) and in Gary G. Hamilton and Nicole Woolsey Biggart's "Market, Culture, and Authority" (Chapter 7). Weber had been convinced that in order to properly grasp the nature of Western capitalism you also have to understand something about the way the economy works in other parts of the world. By contrasting the manner in which British industry operates with industry in Japan, Dore clearly follows in this tradition. And so do Hamilton and Biggart, who look at the economic systems of South Korea, Japan, and Taiwan.

Part III ("The Sociology of Economic Institutions") starts out with two articles that emphasize the need to draw *both* on an economic approach and a social approach when analyzing economic phenomena. Clifford Geertz, the well-known anthropologist, argues in "The Bazaar Economy" (Chapter 8) that one can get a better grasp of the way a traditional bazaar works if one uses the economists' theory of search for information. In the next article Mark Granovetter contrasts the way economists and sociologists have looked at labor markets in "The Sociological and Economic Approaches to Labor Market Analysis" (Chapter 9). He also argues that a perspective *purely* based on methodological individualism is unable to explain the existence of various institutional phenomena in the labor market. Stewart Macaulay's "Non-Contractual Relations in Business" (Chapter 10) contains further arguments against using a purely individualistic model of economic behavior centered on the idea of maximizing behavior. More precisely, Macaulay shows that in the manufacturing industry legal sanctions are rarely used and that businesspeople much prefer to solve their problems privately, through their contacts in other firms. The last reading in Part III—Viviana A. Zelizer's "Human Values and the Market" (Chapter 11)—is a study of the emergence of the life insurance industry in nineteenth-century America. Zelizer's main point is that there was initially great resistance to the idea that one can put a price on a human life and that it took quite some time before the institution of life insurance was generally accepted. Or to phrase it differently: There is nothing "natural" about the fact that something has a price; a price, like everything else in the economy, has to be socially constructed.

The fourth and last part of this anthology is "The Sociology of the Firm and Industrial Organization." Here we have included readings from the traditions of industrial and organizational sociology that are of great interest to economic sociology. George Strauss's "Group Dynamics and Intergroup Relations" (Chapter 12) is, for example, a highly interesting piece of analysis, based on participant observation, of what happened in a toy factory when the incentives were changed for one small group of workers. The general thrust of Strauss's analysis is that a firm or a factory constitutes a distinct social system of its own, in which each part affects all the other parts. The next reading—Melville Dalton's "Men Who Manage" (Chapter 13)—is also the result of participant observation; and the author's general contention is that strife and struggle within a firm are just part and parcel of the productive process. Conflict is not, in other words, something that either can or should be eliminated, as economic theory would have us believe with its insistence that the economy must be frictionless in order to function well. The article by Arthur L. Stinchcombe, "Bureaucratic and Craft Administration of Production" (Chapter 14), argues against the common notion that there only exists one rational way of organizing production. In the construction industry, as Stinchcombe shows, decentralization is much more rational than centralization. The latter, in Stinchcombe's terminology, may better suit "bureaucratic industries" than "craft industries." Paul M. Hirsch's analysis in the last reading, "Processing Fads and Fashions" (Chapter 15), makes a similar point but in reverse: Certain phenomena in the cultural industries (books, records, and movies) that may look quite irrational to the casual observer are in fact perfectly rational—once you understand the social structure of these industries. And on this last point we may also end because it contains the message of economic sociology in a nutshell: In order to grasp the way the economy works, it is necessary to investigate its social structure.

NOTES

1. But we oversimplify Polanyi's complex position. Although in many places he argued that the nineteenth century ushered in an utterly new type of society, dominated by the "self-regulating market," he also made the (incompatible) argument that such a situation was never really possible except as an ideological construct or rhetorical device because society had to immediately intervene to prevent such an awful outcome. Both positions can be found in his first major work, *The Great Transformation* (1944).

2. The general problem of how prices are affected by embeddedness is discussed in Granovetter, 1990; the Sahlins and Okun material is elaborated in Granovetter, forthcoming: chapter 3.

3. In Knight, [1921] 1971:270. On this point, see Swedberg's interview with Williamson (1990a:126).

4. This argument derives from work that originated in Patrick McGuire's "The Control of Power: The Political Economy of Electric Utility Development in the United States, 1870–1930," Ph.D. dissertation, Department of Sociology, SUNY–Stony Brook, 1986, and is elaborated in the forthcoming publication by McGuire, Granovetter, and Schwartz.

5. This assertion is similar in spirit to Brian Arthur's (1989) argument that (1) increasing returns to scale in the development of technologies generates the peculiarities of path-dependent development and (2) if the standard assumption of constant returns was met, comparative statics might well be adequate.

REFERENCES

Abolafia, Mitchel. 1984. "Structured Anarchy: Formal Organization in the Commodities Futures Market," pp. 129–150 in P. A. Adler and P. Adler, eds., *The Social Dynamics of Financial Markets*. Greenwood, Conn.: JAI Press.

Akerlof, George. 1984. *An Economic Theorist's Book of Tales: Essays That Entertain the Consequences of New Assumptions in Economic Theory.* New York: Cambridge University Press.

Arrow, Kenneth. 1974. *The Limits of Organization.* New York: W. W. Norton.

Arthur, W. Brian. 1989. "Competing Technologies, Increasing Returns, and Lock-In by Historical Events," *Economic Journal* 99, no. 394 (March):116–131.

Bailyn, Bernard. 1979. *The New England Merchants in the Seventeenth Century.* Cambridge: Harvard University Press.

Baker, Wayne E. 1984. "The Social Structure of a Securities Market," *American Journal of Sociology* 89:775–811.

———. 1987. "What Is Money? A Social Structural Interpretation," pp. 109–144 in M. S. Mizruchi and M. Schwartz, eds., *Intercorporate Relations.* Cambridge: Cambridge University Press.

Becker, Gary. 1976. *The Economic Approach to Human Behavior.* Chicago: University of Chicago Press.

Berger, Peter L., and Thomas Luckmann. 1966. *The Social Construction of Reality: A Treatise in the Sociology of Knowledge.* New York: Anchor Books.

Biggart, Nicole. 1989. *Charismatic Capitalism: Direct Selling Organizations in America.* Chicago: University of Chicago Press.

Bonacich, Edna. 1973. "A Theory of Middleman Minorities," *American Sociological Review* 38:583–594.

Braudel, Fernand. 1985. *Civilization and Capitalism, 15th–18th Century.* Vol. 2, *The Wheels of Commerce.* London: Fontana Press.

Burawoy, Michael. 1979. *Manufacturing Consent: Changes in the Labor Process Under Monopoly Capitalism.* Chicago: University of Chicago Press.

———. 1985. *The Politics of Production.* London: Verso.

Cooley, Charles Horton, 1930. "The Theory of Transportation," pp. 17–121 in *Sociological Theory and Research.* New York: Henry Holt and Company.

Curtin, Philip. 1984. *Cross-cultural Trade in World History.* New York: Cambridge University Press.

David, Paul A. 1986. "Understanding the Economics of QWERTY: The Necessity of History," pp. 30–49 in William N. Parker, ed., *Economic History and the Modern Economist.* Oxford: Basil Blackwell.

Davis, Lance E., and Douglass C. North. 1974. *Institutional Change and American Economic Growth.* Cambridge: Cambridge University Press.

DiMaggio, Paul, and Walter Powell. 1983. "The Iron Cage Revisited: Institutional Isomorphism and Collective Rationality in Organizational Fields," *American Sociological Review* 48:147–160.

Doeringer, P., and Michael Piore. 1971. *Internal Labor Markets and Manpower Analysis.* Lexington, Mass.: D. C. Heath.

Durkheim, Emile. 1897. "Préface." *l'Année Sociologique* 1:i–vii.

———. 1915. *The Rules of Sociological Method.* New York: Free Press.

———. 1983. "The Rule Prohibiting Attacks on Property," pp. 121–170 in *Professional Ethics and Civic Morals.* Westport, Conn.: Greenwood Press.

———. [1893] 1984. *The Division of Labor in Society.* New York: Free Press.

Durkheim, Emile, and Paul Fauconnet. 1903. "Sociologie et Sciences Sociales," *Revue Philosophique* 55: 465–497.

Eccles, Robert G. 1981. "The Quasifirm in the Construction Industry," *Journal of Economic Behavior and Organization* 2:335–357.

———. 1985. *The Transfer Pricing Problem: A Theory for Practice.* Lexington, Mass.: Lexington Books.

Eccles, Robert G., and Dwight B. Crane. 1988. *Doing Deals: Investment Banks at Work.* Boston: Harvard Business School.

Elster, Jon. 1979. *Ulysses and the Sirens: Studies in Rationality and Irrationality.* Cambridge: Cambridge University Press.

Etzioni, Amitai. 1988. *The Moral Dimension: Toward a New Economics.* New York: Free Press.

Evans, Peter B., Dietrich Rueschemeyer, and Theda Skocpol, eds. 1985. *Bringing the State Back In.* Cambridge: Cambridge University Press.

Fligstein, Neil. 1985. "The Spread of the Multidivisional Form Among Large Firms: 1919–1979," *American Sociological Review* 50:377–391.

Furubotn, Eirik G., and Rudolf Richter, eds., 1989. "The New Institutional Approach to Economics," *Journal of Institutional and Theoretical Economics* 145:1–5.

Garcia, Marie-France. 1986. "La Construction Sociale d'un Marché au Cadran de Fontaine-en-Sologne," *Actes de la Recherche en Sciences Sociales* 65:1–13.

Granovetter, Mark. 1974. *Getting A Job: A Study of Contact and Careers.* Cambridge: Harvard University Press.

———. 1979. "The Idea of 'Advancement' in Theories of Social Evolution and Development," *American Journal of Sociology* 85:489–515.

———. 1990. "The Old and the New Economic Sociology: A History and an Agenda," pp. 89–112 in A. F. Robertson and R. Friedland, eds., *Beyond the Marketplace: Rethinking Economy and Society.* New York: Aldine.

———. Forthcoming. *Society and Economy: The Social Construction of Economic Institutions.* Cambridge: Harvard University Press.

Heimer, Carol A. 1985. *Reactive Risk and Rational Action: Managing Moral Hazard in Insurance Contracts.* Berkeley: University of California Press.

Hirsch, Paul. 1986. "From Ambushes to Golden Parachutes: Corporate Takeovers as an Instance of Cultural Framing and Institutional Integration," *American Journal of Sociology* 91:800–837.

Hirschman, Albert O. 1977. *The Passions and the Interests: Political Arguments for Capitalism Before Its Triumph.* Princeton: Princeton University Press.

Katona, George. 1957. *Business Looks at Banks: A Study of Business Behavior.* Ann Arbor: University of Michigan Press.

Katzenstein, Peter J., ed. 1978. *Between Power and Plenty: Foreign Economic Policies of Advanced Industrial States.* Madison: University of Wisconsin Press.

Knight, Frank H. [1921] 1971. *Risk, Uncertainty, and Profit.* Chicago: University of Chicago Press.

Landes, David S. 1979. *Bankers and Pashas: International Finance and Economic Imperialism in Egypt.* Cambridge: Harvard University Press.

McGuire, Patrick. 1986. "The Control of Power: The Political Economy of Electric Utility Development in the United States, 1870–1930." Ph.D. diss., Department of Sociology, State University of New York at Stony Brook.

McGuire, Patrick, Mark Granovetter, and Michael Schwartz. Forthcoming. "The Social Construction of Industry: Human Agency in the Development, Diffusion, and Institutionalization of the Electric Utility Industry."

Marshall, Alfred. 1891. *Principles of Economics.* London: Macmillan.

Marx, Karl. [1867] 1967. *Capital: A Critique of Political Economy.* New York: International Publishers.

Mintz, Beth, and Michael Schwartz. 1985. *The Power Structure of American Business.* Chicago: University of Chicago Press.

Mizruchi, Mark S., and Michael Schwartz, eds. 1987. *Intercorporate Relations: The Structural Analysis of Business.* Cambridge: Cambridge University Press.

Nee, Victor, and David Stark, eds. 1989. *Remaking the Economic Institutions of Socialism: China and Eastern Europe.* Stanford: Stanford University Press.

Nelson, Richard, and S. G. Winter. 1982. *An Evolutionary Theory of Economic Change.* Cambridge: Harvard University Press.

North, Douglass C. 1981. *Structure and Change in Economic History.* New York: W. W. Norton.

————. 1989. "Final Remarks: Institutional Change and Economic History," *Journal of Institutional and Theoretical Economics* 145:238–245.

North, Douglass, and Robert Paul Thomas. 1973. *The Rise of the Western World: A New Economic History.* Cambridge: Cambridge University Press.

Oberschall, Anthony, and Eric M. Leifer. 1986. "Efficiency and Social Institutions: Uses and Misuses of Economic Reasoning in Sociology," *Annual Review of Sociology* 12:233–253.

Okun, Arthur. 1981. *Prices and Quantities: A Macroeconomic Analysis.* Washington, D.C.: Brookings Institution.

Orlove, B. 1986. "Barter and Cash Sale on Lake Titicaca: A Test of Competing Approaches." *Current Anthropology* 27:85–106.

Parsons, Talcott. 1947. "Introduction," pp. 1–86 in Max Weber, *The Theory of Social and Economic Organization.* New York: Oxford University Press.

Parsons, Talcott, and Neil J. Smelser. 1956. *Economy and Society: A Study in the Integration of Economic and Social Theory.* New York: Free Press.

Perrow, Charles. 1986. "Economic Theories of Organization," pp. 219–257 in *Complex Organizations.* 3d ed. New York: Random House.

Piore, Michael, and Charles Sabel. 1984. *The Second Industrial Divide.* New York: Basic Books.

Polanyi, Karl. 1944. *The Great Transformation.* Boston: Beacon Press.

Polanyi, Karl et al. 1957. *Trade and Market in the Early Empires.* Glencoe, Ill.: Free Press.

Pospisil, Leopold. 1963. *Kapauku Papuan Economy.* Yale: Yale University Publications in Anthropology, no. 67.

Powell, Walter. 1985. "Hybrid Organizational Arrangements: New Form or Transitional Development," *California Management Review* 30, no. 1:67–87.

Robbins, Lionel. [1932] 1984. *An Essay on the Nature and Significance of Economic Science.* London: Macmillan.

Sahlins, Marshall. 1974. *Stone Age Economics.* London: Tavistock Publications.

Schotter, Andrew. 1981. *The Economic Theory of Social Institutions.* Cambridge: Cambridge University Press.

Schumpeter, Joseph A. [1942] 1975. *Capitalism, Socialism, and Democracy.* New York: Harper and Row.

————. 1990a. "The Crisis of the Tax State," pp. 99–140 in Richard Swedberg, ed., *The Economics and Sociology of Capitalism.* Princeton: Princeton University Press.

————. 1990b. "The Sociology of Imperialism," pp. 141–219 in Richard Swedberg, ed., *The Economics and Sociology of Capitalism.* Princeton: Princeton University Press.

Shapiro, Susan P. 1984. *Wayward Capitalists: Target of the Securities and Exchange Commission.* New Haven: Yale University Press.

Smith, Adam. [1776] 1976. *An Inquiry into the Nature and Causes of the Wealth of Nations.* Edited by Edwin Canaan, with a preface by George Stigler. Chicago: University of Chicago Press.

Smith, Charles. 1989. *Auctions: The Social Construction of Value.* New York: Free Press.

Stigler, George J. 1968. "Competition," pp. 181–186 in vol. 3 of *International Encyclopaedia of the Social Sciences*. New York: Macmillan.

Stinchcombe, Arthur. 1975. "Merton's Theory of Social Structure," pp. 11–33 in L. A. Coser, ed., *The Idea of Social Structure*. New York: Harcourt Brace Jovanovich.

———. 1985. "Contracts as Hierarchical Documents," pp. 121–171 in Arthur Stinchcombe and Carol Heimer, eds., *Organization Theory and Project Management*. Oslo: Norwegian University Press.

———. 1990. "Interview," pp. 285–302 in Richard Swedberg, *Economics and Sociology: On Redefining Their Boundaries. Conversations with Economists and Sociologists*. Princeton: Princeton University Press.

Sutton, Francis X. et al. 1956. *The American Business Creed*. Cambridge: Harvard University Press.

Swedberg, Richard. 1987. "Economic Sociology: Past and Present," *Current Sociology* 35, no. 1:1–221.

———. 1990a. *Economics and Sociology: On Redefining Their Boundaries. Conversations with Economists and Sociologists*. Princeton: Princeton University Press.

———. 1990b. "Socioeconomics and the New 'Battle of the Methods'—Towards a Paradigm Shift?" *Journal of Behavioral Economics* 19:141–154.

Wallerstein, Immanuel. 1974–1989. *The Modern World System*. 3 vols. New York: Academic Press.

Weber, Max. 1949. *The Methodology of the Social Sciences*. New York: Free Press.

———. 1976a. "Economic Theory and Ancient Society," pp. 37–79 in *The Agrarian Sociology of Ancient Civilizations*. London: Verso.

———. 1976b. "The Agrarian History of the Major Centres of Ancient Civilizations," pp. 81–386 in *The Agrarian Sociology of Ancient Civilizations*. London: Verso.

———. [1922] 1978. *Economy and Society: An Outline of Interpretive Sociology*. Berkeley: University of California Press.

———. [1919] 1981. *General Economic History*. New York: Transaction Books.

———. 1988a. "Die Börse," pp. 256–322 in *Gesammelte Aufsätze zur Soziologie und Sozialpolitik*. Tübingen: J.C.B. Mohr.

———. 1988b. "Zur Psychophysik der industriellen Arbeit," pp. 61–255 in *Gesammelte Aufsätze zur Soziologie und Sozialpolitik*. Tübingen: J.C.B. Mohr.

———. 1988c. "Zur Geschichte der Handelsgesellschaften im Mittelalter," pp. 312–443 in *Gesammelste Aufsätze zur Sozial- und Wirtschaftsgeschichte*. Tübingen: J.C.B. Mohr.

White, Harrison. 1981. "Where Do Markets Come From?" *American Journal of Sociology* 87 (November):517–547.

Williamson, Oliver E. 1975. *Markets and Hierarchies: Analysis and Antitrust Implications*. New York: Free Press.

———. 1985. *The Economic Institutions of Capitalism*. New York: Free Press.

Zelizer, Viviana A. 1983. *Morals and Markets: The Development of Life Insurance in the United States*. New Brunswick: Transaction Press.

———. 1989. "The Social Meaning of Money: 'Special Monies,'" *American Journal of Sociology* 95:342–377.

PART I

Sociological Approaches to the Economy

1

The Economy
as Instituted Process

KARL POLANYI

Our main purpose in this chapter is to determine the meaning that can be attached with consistency to the term "economic" in all the social sciences.

The simple recognition from which all such attempts must start is the fact that in referring to human activities the term economic is a compound of two meanings that have independent roots. We will call them the substantive and the formal meaning.

The substantive meaning of economic derives from man's dependence for his living upon nature and his fellows. It refers to the interchange with his natural and social environment, in so far as this results in supplying him with the means of material want satisfaction.

The formal meaning of economic derives from the logical character of the means-ends relationship, as apparent in such words as "economical" or "economizing." It refers to a definite situation of choice, namely, that between the different uses of means induced by an insufficiency of those means. If we call the rules governing choice of means the logic of rational action, then we may denote this variant of logic, with an improvised term, as formal economics.

The two root meanings of "economic," the substantive and the formal, have nothing in common. The latter derives from logic, the former from fact. The formal meaning implies a set of rules referring to choice between the alternative uses of insufficient means. The substantive meaning implies neither choice nor insufficiency of means; man's livelihood may or may not involve the necessity of choice and, if choice there be, it need not be induced by the limiting effect of a "scarcity" of the means; indeed, some of the most important physical and social conditions of livelihood such as the availability of air and water or a loving mother's devotion to her infant are not, as a rule, so limiting. The cogency that is in play in the one case and in the other differs as the power of syllogism differs from the force of gravitation. The laws of the one are those of the mind; the laws of the other are those of nature. The two meanings could not be further apart; semantically they lie in opposite directions of the compass.

It is our proposition that only the substantive meaning of "economic" is capable of yielding the concepts that are required by the social sciences for an investigation of all the empirical economies of the past and present. The general frame of reference that we endeavor to construct requires, therefore, treatment of the subject matter in substantive terms. The immediate obstacle in our path lies, as indicated in that concept of "economic" in which the two meanings, the substantive and the formal, are naively compounded. Such a merger of meanings is, of course, unexceptionable as long as we remain conscious of its restrictive effects. But the current concept of economic fuses the "subsistence" and the "scarcity" meanings of economic without a sufficient awareness of the dangers to clear thinking inherent in that merger.

This combination of terms sprang from logically adventitious circumstances. The last two centuries produced in Western Europe and North America an organization of man's livelihood to which the rules of choice happened to be singularly applicable. This form of the economy consisted in a system of price-making markets. Since acts of exchange, as practiced under such a system, involve the participants in choices induced by an insufficiency of means, the system could be reduced to a pattern that lent itself to the application of methods based on the formal meaning of "economic." As long as the economy was controlled by such a system, the formal and the substantive meanings would in practice coincide. Laymen accepted this compound concept as a matter of course; a Marshall, Pareto or Durkheim equally adhered to it. Menger alone in his posthumous work criticized the term, but neither he nor Max Weber, nor Talcott Parsons after him, apprehended the significance of the distinction for sociological analysis. Indeed, there seemed to be no valid reason for distinguishing between two root meanings of a term which, as we said, were bound to coincide in practice.

While it would have been therefore sheer pedantry to differentiate in common parlance between the two meanings of "economic," their merging in one concept nevertheless proved a bane to a precise methodology in the social sciences. Economics naturally formed an exception, since under the market system its terms were bound to be fairly realistic. But the anthropologist, the sociologist or the historian, each in his study of the place occupied by the economy in human society, was faced with a great variety of institutions other than markets, in which man's livelihood was embedded. Its problems could not be attacked with the help of an analytical method devised for a special form of the economy, which was dependent upon the presence of specific market elements.[1]

This lays down the rough sequence of the argument.

We will begin with a closer examination of the concepts derived from the two meanings of "economic," starting with the formal and thence proceeding to the substantive meaning. It should then prove possible to describe the empirical economies—whether primitive or archaic—according to the manner in which the economic process is instituted. The three institutions of trade, money and market will provide a test case. They have previously been defined in formal terms only; thus any other than a marketing approach was barred. Their treatment in substantive terms should then bring us nearer to the desired universal frame of reference.

THE FORMAL AND THE SUBSTANTIVE
MEANINGS OF "ECONOMIC"

Let us examine the formal concepts starting from the manner in which the logic of rational action produces formal economics, and the latter, in turn, gives rise to economic analysis.

Rational action is here defined as choice of means in relation to ends. Means are anything appropriate to serve the end, whether by virtue of the laws of nature or by virtue of the laws of the game. Thus "rational" does not refer either to ends or to means, but rather to the relating of means to ends. It is not assumed, for instance, that it is more rational to wish to live than to wish to die, or that, in the first case, it is more rational to seek a long life through the means of science than through those of superstition. For whatever the end, it is rational to choose one's means accordingly; and as to the means, it would not be rational to act upon any other test than that which one happens to believe in. Thus it is rational for the suicide to select means that will accomplish his death; and if he be an adept of black magic, to pay a witch doctor to contrive that end.

The logic of rational action applies, then, to all conceivable means and ends covering an almost infinite variety of human interests. In chess or technology, in religious life or philosophy ends may range from commonplace issues to the most recondite and complex ones. Similarly, in the field of the economy, where ends may range from the momentary assuaging of thirst to the attaining of a sturdy old age, while the corresponding means comprise a glass of water and a combined reliance on filial solicitude and open air life, respectively.

Assuming that the choice is induced by an insufficiency of the means, the logic of rational action turns into that variant of the theory of choice which we have called formal economics. It is still logically unrelated to the concept of the human economy, but it is closer to it by one step. Formal economics refers, as we said, to a situation of choice that arises out of an insufficiency of means. This is the so-called scarcity postulate. It requires, first, insufficiency of means; second, that choice be induced by that insufficiency. Insufficiency of means in relation to ends is determined with the help of the simple operation of "earmarking," which demonstrates whether there is or is not enough to go round. For the insufficiency to induce choice there must be given more than one use to the means, as well as graded ends, i.e., at least two ends ordered in sequence of preference. Both conditions are factual. It is irrelevant whether the reason for which means can be used in one way only happens to be conventional or technological; the same is true of the grading of ends.

Having thus defined choice, insufficiency and scarcity in operational terms, it is easy to see that as there is choice of means without insufficiency, so there is insufficiency of means without choice. Choice may be induced by a preference for right against wrong (moral choice) or, at a crossroads, where two or more paths happen to lead to our destination, possessing identical advantages and disadvantages (operationally induced choice). In either case an abundance of means, far from diminishing the difficulties of choice, would rather increase them. Of course, scarcity may or may not be present in almost all fields of rational action. Not all philosophy is sheer imaginative creativity, it may also be a matter of economizing with assumptions. Or, to get back to the sphere of man's livelihood, in some civilizations scarcity situations seem to be almost exceptional, in others they appear to be painfully general. In either case the presence or absence of scarcity is a question of fact, whether the insufficiency is due to Nature or to Law.

Last but not least, economic analysis. This discipline results from the application of formal economics to an economy of a definite type, namely, a market system. The economy is here embodied in institutions that cause individual choices to give rise to interdependent movements that constitute the economic process. This is achieved by generalizing the use of price-making markets. All goods and services, including the use of labor, land and capital are available for purchase in markets and have, therefore, a price; all forms of income derive from the sale of goods and services— wages, rent and interest, respectively, appearing only as different instances of price according to the items sold. The general introduction of purchasing power as the means of acquisition converts the process of meeting requirements into an allocation of insufficient means with alternative uses, namely, money. It follows that both the conditions of choice and its consequences are quantifiable in the form of prices. It can be asserted that by concentrating on price as the economic fact *par excellence*, the formal method of approach offers a total description of the economy as determined by choices induced by an insufficiency of means. The conceptual tools by which this is performed make up the discipline of economic analysis.

From this follow the limits within which economic analysis can prove effective as a method. The use of the formal meaning denotes the economy as a sequence of acts of economizing, i.e., of choices induced by scarcity situations. While the rules governing such acts are universal, the extent to which the rules are applicable to a definite economy depends upon whether or not that economy is, in actual fact, a sequence of such acts. To produce quantitative results, the locational and appropriational movements, of which the economic process consists, must here present themselves as functions of social actions in regard to insufficient means and oriented on resulting prices. Such a situation obtains only under a market system.

The relation between formal economics and the human economy is, in effect, contingent. Outside of a system of price-making markets economic analysis loses most of its relevance as a method of inquiry into the working of the economy. A centrally planned economy, relying on nonmarket prices is a well-known instance.

The fount of the substantive concept is the empirical economy. It can be briefly (if not engagingly) defined as an instituted process of interaction between man and his environment, which results in a continuous supply of want satisfying material means. Want satisfaction is "material," if it involves the use of material means to satisfy ends; in the case of a definite type of physiological wants, such as food or shelter, this includes the use of so-called services only.

The economy, then, is an instituted process. Two concepts stand out, that of "process" and its "institutedness." Let us see what they contribute to our frame of reference.

Process suggests analysis in terms of motion. The movements refer either to changes in location, or in appropriation, or both. In other words, the material elements may alter their position either by changing place or by changing "hands"; again, these otherwise very different shifts of position may go together or not. Between them, these two kinds of movements may be said to exhaust the possibilities comprised in the economic process as a natural and social phenomenon.

Locational movements include production, alongside of transportation, to which the spatial shifting of objects is equally essential. Goods are of a lower order or of a higher order, according to the manner of their usefulness from the consumer's point of view. This famous "order of goods" sets consumer's goods against producers' goods, according to whether they satisfy wants directly, or only indirectly, through a combination with other goods. This type of movement of the elements represents an essential of the economy in the substantive sense of the term, namely, production.

The appropriative movement governs both what is usually referred to as the circulation of goods and their administration. In the first case, the appropriative movement results from transactions, in the second case, from dispositions. Accordingly, a transaction is an appropriative movement as between hands; a disposition is a one-sided act of the hand, to which by force of custom or of law definite appropriative effects are attached. The term "hand" here serves to denote public bodies and offices as well as private persons or firms, the difference between them being mainly a matter of internal organization. It should be noted, however, that in the nineteenth century private hands were commonly associated with transactions, while public hands were usually credited with dispositions.

In this choice of terms a number of further definitions are implied. Social activities, insofar as they form part of the process, may be called economic; institutions are so called to the extent to which they contain a concentration of such activities; any components of the process may be regarded as economic elements. These elements can be conveniently grouped as ecological, technological or societal according to whether they belong primarily to the natural environment, the mechanical equipment, or the human setting. Thus a series of concepts, old and new, accrue to our frame of reference by virtue of the process aspect of the economy.

Nevertheless, reduced to a mechanical, biological and psychological interaction of elements that economic process would possess no all-round reality. It contains no more than the bare bones of the processes of production and transportation, as well as of the appropriative changes. In the absence of any indication of societal conditions from which the motives of the individuals spring, there would be little, if anything, to sustain the interdependence of the movements and their recurrence on which the unity and the stability of the process depends. The interacting elements of nature and humanity would form no coherent unit, in effect, no structural entity that could be said to have a function in society or to possess a history. The process would lack the very qualities which cause everyday thought as well as scholarship to turn towards matters of human livelihood as a field of eminent practical interest as well as theoretical and moral dignity.

Hence the transcending importance of the institutional aspect of the economy. What occurs on the process level between man and soil in hoeing a plot or what on the conveyor belt in the constructing of an automobile is, *prima facie* a mere jig-sawing of human and nonhuman movements. From the institutional point of view it is a mere referent of terms like labor and capital, craft and union, slacking and speeding, the spreading of risks and the other semantic units of the social context. The choice between capitalism and socialism, for instance, refers to two different ways of instituting modern technology in the process of production. On the policy level, again, the industrialization of underdeveloped countries involves, on the one hand, alternative techniques; on the other, alternative methods of instituting them. Our conceptual distinction is vital for any understanding of the interdependence of technology and institutions as well as their relative independence.

The instituting of the economic process vests that process with unity and stability; it produces a structure with a definite function in society; it shifts the place of the process in society, thus adding significance to its history; it centers interest on values, motives and policy. Unity and stability, structure and function, history and policy spell out operationally the content of our assertion that the human economy is an instituted process.

The human economy, then, is embedded and enmeshed in institutions, economic and noneconomic. The inclusion of the noneconomic is vital. For religion or government may be as important for the structure and functioning of the economy as monetary institutions or the availability of tools and machines themselves that lighten the toil of labor.

The study of the shifting place occupied by the economy in society is therefore no other than the study of the manner in which the economic process is instituted at different times and places.

This requires a special tool box.

RECIPROCITY, REDISTRIBUTION, AND EXCHANGE

A study of how empirical economies are instituted should start from the way in which the economy acquires unity and stability, that is the inter-dependence and recurrence of its parts. This is achieved through a combination of a very few patterns which may be called forms of integration. Since they occur side by side on different levels and in different sectors of the economy it may often be impossible to select one of them as dominant so that they could be employed for a classification of empirical economies as a whole. Yet by differentiating between sectors and levels of the economy those forms offer a means of describing the economic process in comparatively simple terms, thereby introducing a measure of order into its endless variations.

Empirically, we find the main patterns to be reciprocity, redistribution and exchange. Reciprocity denotes movements between correlative points of symmetrical groupings; redistribution designates appropriational movements toward a center and out of it again; exchange refers here to vice-versa movements taking place as between "hands" under a market system. Reciprocity, then, assumes for a background symmetrically arranged group-ings; redistribution is dependent upon the presence of some measure of centricity in the group; exchange in order to produce integration requires a system of price-making markets. It is apparent that the different patterns of integration assume definite institutional supports.

At this point some clarification may be welcome. The terms reciprocity, redistribution and exchange, by which we refer to our forms of integration, are often employed to denote personal interrelations. Superficially then it might seem as if the forms of integration merely reflected aggregates of the respective forms of individual behavior: If mutuality between individuals were frequent, a reciprocative integration would emerge; where sharing among individuals were common, redistributive integration would be present; similarly, frequent acts of barter between individuals would result in exchange as a form of integration. If this were so, our patterns of integration would be indeed no more than simple aggregates of corresponding forms of behavior on the personal level. To be sure, we insisted that the integrative effect was conditioned by the presence of definite institutional arrangements, such as symmetrical organizations, central points and market systems, respectively. But such arrangements seem to represent a mere aggregate of the same personal patterns the eventual effects of which they are supposed to condition. The significant fact is that mere aggregates of the personal behaviors in question do not by themselves produce such structures. Reciprocity behavior between individuals integrates the economy only if symmetrically organized structures, such as a symmetrical system of kinship groups, are given. But a kinship system never arises as the result of mere reciprocating behavior on the personal level. Similarly, in regard to redistribution. It presupposes the presence of an allocative center in the community, yet the organization and validation of such a center does not come about merely as a consequence of frequent acts of sharing as between individuals. Finally, the same is true of the market system. Acts of exchange on the personal level produce prices only if they occur under a system of price-making markets, an institutional setup which is nowhere created by mere random acts of exchange. We do not wish to imply, of course, that those supporting patterns are the outcome of some mysterious forces acting outside the range of personal or individual behavior. We merely insist that if, in any given case, the societal effects of individual behavior depend on the presence of definite institutional conditions, these conditions do not for that reason result from the personal behavior in question. Superficially, the supporting pattern may seem to result from a cumulation of a corresponding kind of personal behavior, but the vital elements of organization and validation are necessarily contributed by an altogether different type of behavior.

The first writer to our knowledge to have hit upon the factual connection between reciprocative behavior on the interpersonal level, on the one hand, and given symmetrical groupings, on the other, was the anthropologist Richard Thurnwald, in 1915, in an empirical study on the marriage system of the Bánaro of New Guinea. Bronislaw Malinowski, some ten years later, referring to Thurnwald, predicted that socially relevant reciprocation would regularly be found to rest on symmetrical forms of basic social organization. His own description of the Trobriand kinship system as well as of the Kula trade bore out the point. This lead was followed up by this writer, in regarding symmetry as merely one of several supporting patterns. He then added redistribution and exchange to reciprocity, as further forms of integration; similarly, he added centricity and market to symmetry, as other instances of institutional support. Hence our forms of integration and supporting structure patterns.

This should help to explain why in the economic sphere interpersonal behavior so often fails to have the expected societal effects in the absence of definite institutional preconditions. Only in a symmetrically organized environment will reciprocative behavior result in economic institutions of any importance; only where allocative centers have been set up can individual acts of sharing produce a redistributive economy; and only in the presence of a system of price-making markets will exchange acts of individuals result in fluctuating prices that integrate the economy. Otherwise such acts of barter will remain ineffective and therefore tend not to occur. Should they nevertheless happen, in a random fashion, a violent emotional reaction would set in, as against acts of indecency or acts of treason, since trading behavior is never emotionally indifferent behavior and is not, therefore, tolerated by opinion outside of the approved channels.

Let us now return to our forms of integration.

A group which deliberately undertook to organize its economic relationships on a reciprocative footing would, to effect its purpose, have to split up into sub-groups the corresponding members of which could identify one another as such. Members of Group A would then be able to establish relationships of reciprocity with their counterparts in Group B and vice versa. But symmetry is not restricted to duality. Three, four, or more groups may be symmetrical in regard to two or more axes; also members of the groups need not reciprocate with one another but may do so with the corresponding members of third groups toward which they stand in analogous relations. A Trobriand man's responsibility is toward his sister's family. But he himself is not on that account assisted by his sister's husband, but, if he is married, by his own wife's brother—a member of a third, correspondingly placed family.

Aristotle taught that to every kind of community (*koinōnia*) there corresponded a kind of good-will (*philia*) amongst its members which expressed itself in reciprocity (*antipeponthos*). This was true both of the more permanent communities such as families, tribes or city states as of those less permanent ones that may be comprised in, and subordinate to, the former. In our terms this implies a tendency in the larger communities to develop a multiple symmetry in regard to which reciprocative behavior may develop in the subordinate communities. The closer the members of the encompassing community feel drawn to one another, the more general will be the tendency among them to develop reciprocative attitudes in regard to specific relationships limited in space, time or otherwise. Kinship, neighborhood, or totem belong to the more permanent and comprehensive groupings; within their compass voluntary and semi-voluntary associations of a military, vocational, religious or social character create situations in which, at least transitorily or in regard to a given locality or a typical situation, there would form symmetrical groupings the members of which practice some sort of mutuality.

Reciprocity as a form of integration gains greatly in power through its capacity of employing both redistribution and exchange as subordinate methods. Reciprocity may be attained through a sharing of the burden of labor according to definite rules of redistribution as when taking things "in turn." Similarly, reciprocity is sometimes attained through exchange at set equivalencies for the benefit of the partner who happens to be short of some kind of necessities—a fundamental institution in ancient Oriental societies. In nonmarket economies these two forms of integration—reciprocity and redistribution—occur in effect usually together.

Redistribution obtains within a group to the extent to which the allocation of goods is collected in one hand and takes place by virtue of custom, law or *ad hoc* central decision. Sometimes it amounts to a physical collecting accompanied by storage-cum-redistribution, at other times the "collecting" is not physical, but merely appropriational, i.e., rights of disposal in the physical location of the goods. Redistribution occurs for many reasons, on all civilizational levels, from the primitive hunting tribe to the vast storage systems of ancient Egypt, Sumeria, Babylonia or Peru. In large countries differences of soil and climate may make redistribution necessary; in other cases it is caused by discrepancy in point of time, as between harvest and consumption. With a hunt, any other method of distribution would lead to disintegration of the horde or band, since only "division of labor" can here ensure results; a redistribution of purchasing power may be valued for its own sake, i.e., for the purposes demanded by social ideals as in the modern welfare state. The principle remains the same—collecting into, and distributing from, a center. Redistribution may also apply to a group smaller than society, such as the household or manor irrespective of the way in which the economy as a whole is integrated. The best known instances are the Central African *kraal*, the Hebrew patriarchal household, the Greek estate of Aristotle's time, the Roman *familia*, the medieval manor, or the typical large peasant household before the general marketing of grain. However, only under a comparatively advanced form of agricultural society is householding practicable, and then, fairly general. Before that, the widely spread "small family" is not economically instituted, except for some cooking of food; the use of pasture, land, or cattle is still dominated by redistributive or reciprocative methods on a wider than family scale.

Redistribution, too, is apt to integrate groups at all levels and all degrees of permanence from the state itself to units of a transitory character. Here, again, as with reciprocity, the more closely knit the encompassing unit, the more varied will the subdivisions be in which redistribution can effectively operate. Plato taught that the number of citizens in the state should be 5040. This figure was divisible in 59 different ways, including division by the first ten numerals. For the assessment of taxes, the forming of groups for business transactions, the carrying of military and other burdens "in turn," etc., it would allow the widest scope, he explained.

Exchange in order to serve as a form of integration requires the support of a system of price-making markets. Three kinds of exchange should therefore be distinguished: The merely locational movement of a "changing of places" between the hands (operational exchange); the appropriational movements of exchange, either at a set rate (decisional exchange) or at a bargained rate (integrative exchange). In so far as exchange at a set rate is in question, the economy is integrated by the factors which fix that rate, not by the market mechanism. Even price-making markets are integrative only if they are linked up in a system which tends to spread the effect of prices to markets other than those directly affected.

Higgling-haggling has been rightly recognized as being of the essence of bargaining behavior. In order for exchange to be integrative the behavior of the partners must be oriented on producing a price that is as favorable to each partner as he can make it. Such a behavior contrasts sharply with that of exchange at a set price. The ambiguity of the term "gain" tends to cover up the difference. Exchange at set prices involves no more than the gain to either party implied in the decision of exchanging; exchange at fluctuating prices aims at a gain that can be attained only by an attitude involving a distinctive antagonistic relationship between the partners. The element of antagonism, however diluted, that accompanies this variant of exchange is ineradicable. No community intent on protecting the fount of solidarity between its members can allow latent hostility to develop around a matter as vital to animal existence and, therefore, capable of arousing as tense anxieties as food. Hence the universal banning of transactions of a gainful nature in regard to food and foodstuffs in primitive and archaic society. The very widely spread ban on higgling-haggling over victuals automatically removes price-making markets from the realm of early institutions.

Traditional groupings of economies which roughly approximate a classification according to the dominant forms of integration are illuminating. What historians are wont to call "economic systems" seem to fall fairly into this pattern. Dominance of a form of integration is here identified with the degree to which it comprises land and labor in society. So-called savage society, is characterized by the integration of land and labor into the economy by way of the ties of kinship. In feudal society the ties of fealty determine the fate of land and the labor that goes with it. In the floodwater empires land was largely distributed and sometimes redistributed by temple or palace, and so was labor, at least in its dependent form. The rise of the market to a ruling force in the economy can be traced by noting the extent to which land and food were mobilized through exchange, and labor was turned into a commodity free to be purchased in the market. This may help to explain the relevance of the historically untenable stages theory of slavery, serfdom and wage labor that is traditional with Marxism—a grouping which flowed from the conviction that the character of the economy was set by the status of labor. However, the integration of the soil into the economy should be regarded as hardly less vital.

In any case, forms of integration do not represent "stages" of development. No sequence in time is implied. Several subordinate forms may be present alongside of the dominant one, which may itself recur after a temporary eclipse. Tribal societies practice reciprocity and redistribution, while archaic societies are predominantly redistributive, though to some extent they may allow room for exchange. Reciprocity, which plays a dominant part in some Melanesian communities, occurs as a not unimportant although subordinate trait in the redistributive archaic empires, where foreign trade (carried on by gift and countergift) is still largely organized on the principle of reciprocity. Indeed, during a war emergency it was reintroduced on a large scale in the twentieth century, under the name of lend-lease, with societies where otherwise marketing and exchange were dominant. Redistribution, the ruling method in tribal and archaic society beside which exchange plays only a minor part, grew to great importance in the later Roman Empire and is actually gaining ground today in some modern industrial states. The Soviet Union is an extreme instance. Conversely, more than once before in the course of human history markets have played a part in the economy, although never on a territorial scale, or with an institutional comprehensiveness comparable to that of the nineteenth century. However, here again a change is noticeable. In our century, with the lapse of the gold standard, a recession of the world role of markets from their nineteenth century peak set in—a turn of the trend which, incidentally, takes us back to our starting point, namely, the increasing inadequacy of our limited marketing definitions for the purposes of the social scientist's study of the economic field.

FORMS OF TRADE, MONEY USES,
AND MARKET ELEMENTS

The restrictive influence of the marketing approach on the interpretation of trade and money institutions is incisive: inevitably, the market appears as the locus of exchange, trade as the actual exchange, and money as the means of exchange. Since trade is directed by prices and prices are a function of the market, all trade is market trade, just as all money is exchange money. The market is the generating institution of which trade and money are the functions.

Such notions are not true to the facts of anthropology and history. Trade, as well as some money uses, are as old as mankind; while markets, although meetings of an economic character may have existed as early as the neolithic, did not gain importance until comparatively late in history. Price-making markets, which alone are constitutive of a market system, were to all accounts non-existent before the first millennium of antiquity, and then only to be eclipsed by other forms of integration. Not even these main facts however could be uncovered as long as trade and money were thought to be limited to the exchange form of integration, as its specifically "economic" form. The long periods of history when reciprocity and redistribution integrated the economy and the considerable ranges within which, even in modern times, they continued to do so, were put out of bounds by a restrictive terminology.

Viewed as an exchange system, or, in brief, catallactically, trade, money and market form an indivisible whole. Their common conceptual framework is the market. Trade appears as a two-way movement of goods through the market, and money as quantifiable goods used for indirect exchange in order to facilitate that movement. Such an approach must induce a more or less tacit acceptance of the heuristic principle according to which, where trade is in evidence, markets should be assumed, and where money is in evidence trade, and therefore markets, should be assumed. Naturally, this leads to seeing markets where there are none and ignoring trade and money where they are present, because markets happen to be absent. The cumulative effect must be to create a stereotype of the economies of less familiar times and places, something in the way of an artificial landscape with only little or no resemblance to the original.

A separate analysis of trade, money and markets is therefore in order.

1. Forms of Trade

From the substantive point of view, trade is a relatively peaceful method of acquiring goods which are not available on the spot. It is external to the group, similar to activities which we are used to associating with hunts, slaving expeditions, or piratic raids. In either case the point is acquisition and carrying of goods from a distance. What distinguishes trade from the questing for game, booty, plunder, rare woods or exotic animals, is the two-sidedness of the movement, which also ensures its broadly peaceful and fairly regular character.

From the catallactic viewpoint, trade is the movement of goods on their way through the market. All commodities—goods produced for sale—are potential objects of trade; one commodity is moving in one direction, the other in the opposite direction; the movement is controlled by prices: trade and market are co-terminous. All trade is market trade.

Again, like hunt, raid or expedition under native conditions, trade is not so much an individual as rather a group activity, in this respect closely akin to the organization of wooing and mating, which is often concerned with the acquisition of wives from a distance by more or less peaceful means. Trade thus centers in the meeting of different communities, one of its purposes being the exchange of goods. Such meetings do not, like price-making markets, produce rates of exchange, but on the contrary they rather presuppose such rates. Neither the persons of individual traders nor motives of individual gain are involved. Whether a chief or king is acting for the community after having collected the "export" goods from its members, or whether the group meets bodily their counterparts on the beach for the purpose of exchange—in either case the proceedings are essentially collective. Exchange between "partners in trade" is frequent, but so is, of course, partnership in wooing and mating. Individual and collective activities are intertwined.

Emphasis on "acquisition of goods from a distance" as a constitutive element in trade should bring out the dominant role played by the import interest in the early history of trade. In the nineteenth century export interests loomed large—a typically catallactic phenomenon.

Since something must be carried over a distance and that in two opposite directions, trade, in the nature of things, has a number of constituents such as personnel, goods, carrying, and two-sidedness, each of which can be broken down according to sociologically or technologically significant criteria. In following up those four factors we may hope to learn something about the changing place of trade in society.

First, the persons engaged in trade.

"Acquisition of goods from a distance" may be practiced either from motives attaching to the trader's standing in society, and as a rule comprising elements of duty of public service (status motive); or it may be done for the sake of the material gain accruing to him personally from the buying and selling transaction in hand (profit motive).

In spite of many possible combinations of those incentives, honor and duty on the one hand, profit on the other, stand out as sharply distinct primary motivations. If the "status motive," as is quite often the case, is reinforced by material benefits, the latter do not as a rule take the form of gain made on exchange, but rather of treasure or endowment with landed revenue bestowed on the trader by king or temple or lord, by way of recompense. Things being what they are, gains made on exchange do not usually add up to more than paltry sums that bear no comparison with the wealth bestowed by his lord upon the resourceful and successfully venturing trader. Thus he who trades for the sake of duty and honor grows rich, while he who trades for filthy lucre remains poor—an added reason why gainful motives are under a shadow in archaic society.

Another way of approaching the question of personnel is from the angle of the standard of life deemed appropriate to their status by the community to which they belong.

Archaic society in general knows, as a rule, no other figure of a trader than that which belongs either to the top or to the bottom rung of the social ladder. The first is connected with rulership and government, as required by the political and military conditions of trading, the other depends for his livelihood on the coarse labor of carrying. This fact is of great importance for the understanding of the organization of trade in ancient times. There can be no middle-class trader, at least among the citizenry. Apart from the Far East which we must disregard here, only three significant instances of a broad commercial middle class in premodern times are on record: the Hellenistic merchant of largely metic ancestry in the Eastern Mediterranean city states; the ubiquitous Islamitic merchant who grafted Hellenistic maritime traditions on to the ways of the bazaar; lastly, the descendants of Pirenne's "floating scum" in Western Europe, a sort of continental metic of the second third of the Middle Ages. The classical Greek middle class preconized by Aristotle was a landed class, not a commercial class at all.

A third manner of approach is more closely historical. The trader types of antiquity were the *tamkarum*, the metic or resident alien, and the "foreigner."

The *tamkarum* dominated the Mesopotamian scene from the Sumerian beginnings to the rise of Islam, i.e., over some 3000 years. Egypt, China, India, Palestine, pre-conquest Mesoamerica, or native West Africa knew no other type of trader. The metic became first historically conspicuous in Athens and some other Greek cities as a lower-class merchant, and rose with Hellenism to become the prototype of a Greek-speaking or Levantine commercial middle class from the Indus Valley to the Pillars of Hercules. The *foreigner* is of course ubiquitous. He carries on trade with foreign crews and in foreign bottoms; he neither "belongs" to the community, nor enjoys the semi-status of resident alien, but is a member of an altogether different community.

A fourth distinction is anthropological. It provides the key to that peculiar figure, the trading foreigner. Although the number of "trading peoples" to which these "foreigners" belonged was comparatively small, they accounted for the widely spread institution of "passive trade." Amongst themselves, trading peoples differed again in an important respect: trading peoples proper, as we may call them, were exclusively dependent for their subsistence on trade in which, directly or indirectly, the whole population was engaged, as with the Phoenicians, the Rhodians, the inhabitants of Gades (the modern Cadix), or at some periods Armenians and Jews; in the case of others—a more numerous group—trade was only one of the occupations in which from time to time a considerable part of the population engaged, travelling abroad, sometimes with their families, over shorter or longer periods. The Haussa and the Mandingo in the Western Sudan are instances. The latter are also known as Duala, but, as recently turned out, only when trading abroad. Formerly they were taken to be a separate people by those whom they visited when trading.

Second, the organization of trade in early times must differ according to the goods carried, the distance to be travelled, the obstacles to be overcome by the carriers, the political and the ecological conditions of the venture. For this, if for no other reason, all trade is originally specific. The goods and their carriage make it so. There can be, under these conditions, no such things as trading "in general."

Unless full weight is given to this fact, no understanding of the early development of trading institutions is possible. The decision to acquire some kinds of goods from a definite distance and place of origin will be taken under circumstances different from those under which other kinds of goods would have to be acquired from somewhere else. Trading ventures are, for this reason, a discontinuous affair. They are restricted to concrete under-takings, which are liquidated one by one and do not tend to develop into a continuous enterprise. The Roman *societas*, like the later *commenda*, was a trade partnership limited to one undertaking. Only the *societas publicanorum*, for tax farming and contracting, was incorporated—it was the one great exception. Not before modern times were permanent trade associations known.

The specificity of trade is enhanced in the natural course of things by the necessity of acquiring the imported goods with exported ones. For under nonmarket conditions imports and exports tend to fall under different regimes. The process through which goods are collected for export is mostly separate from, and relatively independent of, that by which the imported goods are repartitioned. The first may be a matter of tribute or taxation or feudal gifts or under whatever other designation the goods flow to the center, while the repartitioned imports may cascade along different lines. Hammurabi's "Seisachtheia" appears to make an exception of *simu* goods, which may have sometimes been imports passed on by the king via the *tamkarum* to such tenants who wished to exchange them for their own produce. Some of the preconquest long-distance trading of the *pochteca* of the Aztec of Mesoamerica appears to carry similar features.

What nature made distinct, the market makes homogeneous. Even the difference between goods and their transportation may be obliterated, since in the market both can be bought and sold—the one in the commodity market, the other in the freight and insurance market. In either case there is supply and demand, and prices are formed in the same fashion. Carrying and goods, these constituents of trade, acquire a common denominator in terms of cost. Preoccupation with the market and its artificial homogeneity thus makes for good economic theory rather than for good economic history. Eventually, we will find that trade routes, too, as well as means of trans-

portation may be of no less incisive importance for the institutional forms
of trade than the types of goods carried. For in all these cases the geographical
and technological conditions interpenetrate with the social structure.

According to the rationale of two-sidedness we meet with three main
types of trade: gift trade, administered trade, and market trade.

Gift trade links the partners in relationships of reciprocity, such as: guest
friends; Kula partners; visiting parties. Over millennia trade between empires
was carried on as gift trade—no other rationale of two-sidedness would
have met quite as well the needs of the situation. The organization of
trading is here usually ceremonial, involving mutual presentation; embassies;
political dealings between chiefs or kings. The goods are treasure, objects
of élite circulation; in the border case of visiting parties they may be of a
more "democratic" character. But contacts are tenuous and exchanges few
and far between.

Administered trade has its firm foundation in treaty relationships that
are more or less formal. Since on both sides the import interest is as a rule
determinative, trading runs through government-controlled channels. The
export trade is usually organized in a similar way. Consequently, the whole
of trade is carried on by administrative methods. This extends to the manner
in which business is transacted, including arrangements concerning "rates"
or proportions of the units exchanged; port facilities; weighing; checking of
quality; the physical exchange of the goods; storage; safekeeping; the control
of the trading personnel; regulation of "payments"; credits; price differentials.
Some of these matters would naturally be linked with the collection of the
export goods and the repartition of the imported ones, both belonging to
the redistributive sphere of the domestic economy. The goods that are
mutually imported are standardized in regard to quality and package, weight,
and other easily ascertainable criteria. Only such "trade goods" can be
traded. Equivalencies are set out in simple unit relations; in principle, trade
is one-to-one.

Higgling and haggling is not part of the proceedings; equivalencies are
set once and for all. But since to meet changing circumstances adjustments
cannot be avoided, higgling-haggling is practiced only on *other items than
price*, such as measures, quality, or means of payment. Endless arguments
are possible about the quality of the foodstuffs, the capacity and weight of
the units employed, the proportions of the currencies if different ones are
jointly used. Even "profits" are often "bargained." The rationale of the
procedure is, of course, to keep prices unchanged; if they must adjust to
actual supply situations, as in an emergency, this is phrased as trading two-
to-one or two-and-a-half-to-one, or, as we would say, at 100 per cent or
150 per cent profit. This method of haggling on profits at stable prices,
which may have been fairly general in archaic society, is well authenticated
from the Central Sudan as late as the nineteenth century.

Administered trade presupposes relatively permanent trading bodies such
as governments or at least companies chartered by them. The understanding
with the natives may be tacit, as in the case of traditional or customary

relationships. Between sovereign bodies, however, trade assumes formal treaties even in the relatively early times of the second millennium B.C.

Once established in a region, under solemn protection of the gods, administrative forms of trade may be practiced without any previous treaty. The main institution, as we now begin to realize, is the port of trade, as we here call this site of all administered foreign trade. The port of trade offers military security to the inland power; civil protection to the foreign trader; facilities of anchorage, debarkation and storage; the benefit of judicial authorities; agreement on the goods to be traded; agreement concerning the "proportions" of the different trade goods in the mixed packages or "sortings."

Market trade is the third typical form of trading. Here exchange is the form of integration that relates the partners to each other. This comparatively modern variant of trade released a torrent of material wealth over Western Europe and North America. Though presently in recession, it is still by far the most important of all. The range of tradable goods—the commodities—is practically unlimited and the organization of market trade follows the lines traced out by the supply-demand-price mechanism. The market mechanism shows its immense range of application by being adaptable to the handling not only of goods, but of every element of trade itself—storage, transportation, risk, credit, payments, etc.—through the forming of special markets for freight, insurance, short-term credit, capital, warehouse space, banking facilities, and so on.

The main interest of the economic historian today turns towards the questions: When and how did trade become linked with markets? At what time and place do we meet the general result known as market trade?

Strictly speaking, such questions are precluded under the sway of catallactic logic, which tends to fuse trade and market inseparably.

2. Money Uses

The catallactic definition of money is that of means of indirect exchange. Modern money is used for payment and as a "standard" precisely because it is a means of exchange. Thus our money is "all-purpose" money. Other uses of money are merely unimportant variants of its exchange use, and all money uses are dependent upon the existence of markets.

The substantive definition of money, like that of trade, is independent of markets. It is derived from definite uses to which quantifiable objects are put. These uses are payment, standard and exchange. Money, therefore, is defined here as quantifiable objects employed in any one or several of these uses. The question is whether independent definitions of those uses are possible.

The definitions of the various money uses contain two criteria: the sociologically defined situation in which the use arises, and the operation performed with the money objects in that situation.

Payment is the discharge of obligations in which quantifiable objects change hands. The situation refers here not to one kind of obligation only, but to several of them, since only if an object is used to discharge more than one obligation can we speak of it as "means of payment" in the distinctive sense of the term (otherwise merely an obligation to be discharged in kind is so discharged).

The payment use of money belongs to its most common uses in early times. The obligations do not here commonly spring from transactions. In unstratified primitive society payments are regularly made in connection with the institutions of bride price, blood money, and fines. In archaic society such payments continue, but they are overshadowed by customary dues, taxes, rent and tribute that give rise to payments on the largest scale.

The standard, or accounting use of money is the equating of amounts of different kinds of goods for definite purposes. The "situation" is either barter or the storage and management of staples; the "operation" consists in the attaching of numerical tags to the various objects to facilitate the manipulation of those objects. Thus in the case of barter, the summation of objects on either side can eventually be equated; in the case of the management of staples a possibility of planning, balancing, budgeting, as well as general accounting is attained.

The standard use of money is essential to the elasticity of a redistributive system. The equating of such staples as barley, oil and wool in which taxes or rent have to be paid or alternatively rations or wages may be claimed is vital, since it ensures the possibility of choice between the different staples for payer and claimant alike. At the same time the precondition of large scale finance "in kind" is created, which presupposes the notion of funds and balances, in other words, the interchangeability of staples.

The exchange use of money arises out of a need for quantifiable objects for indirect exchange. The "operation" consists in acquiring units of such objects through direct exchange, in order to acquire the desired objects through a further act of exchange. Sometimes the money objects are available from the start, and the twofold exchange is merely designed to net an increased amount of the same objects. Such a use of quantifiable objects develops not from random acts of barter—a favored fancy of eighteenth century rationalism—but rather in connection with organized trade, especially in markets. In the absence of markets the exchange use of money is no more than a subordinate culture trait. The surprising reluctance of the great trading peoples of antiquity such as Tyre and Carthage to adopt coins, that new form of money eminently suited for exchange, may have been due to the fact that the trading ports of the commercial empires were not organized as markets, but as "ports of trade."

Two extensions of the meaning of money should be noted. The one extends the definition of money other than physical objects, namely, ideal units; the other comprises alongside of the three conventional money uses, also the use of money objects as operational devices.

Ideal units are mere verbalizations or written symbols employed as if they were quantifiable units, mainly for payment or as a standard. The "operation" consists in the manipulation of debt accounts according to the rules of the game. Such accounts are common facts of primitive life and not, as was often believed, peculiar to monetarized economies. The earliest temple economies of Mesopotamia as well as the early Assyrian traders practiced the clearing of accounts without the intervention of money objects.

At the other end it seemed advisable not to omit the mention of operational devices among money uses, exceptional though they be. Occasionally quantifiable objects are used in archaic society for arithmetical, statistical, taxational, administrative or other non-monetary purposes connected with economic life. In eighteenth-century Whydah cowrie money was used for statistical ends, and *damba* beans (never employed as money) served as a gold weight and, in that capacity, were cleverly used as a device for accountancy.

Early money is, as we saw, special-purpose money. Different kinds of objects are employed in the different money uses; moreover, the uses are instituted independently of one another. The implications are of the most far-reaching nature. There is, for instance, no contradiction involved in "paying" with a means with which one cannot buy, nor in employing objects as a "standard" which are not used as a means of exchange. In Hammurabi's Babylonia barley was the means of payment; silver was the universal standard; in exchange, of which there was very little, both were used alongside of oil, wool, and some other staples. It becomes apparent why money uses—like trade activities—can reach an almost unlimited level of development, not only outside of market-dominated economies, but in the very absence of markets.

3. Market Elements

Now, the market itself. Catallactically, the market is the *locus* of exchange; market and exchange are co-extensive. For under the catallactic postulate economic life is both reducible to acts of exchange effected through higgling-haggling and it is embodied in markets. Exchange is thus described as *the* economic relationship, with the market as *the* economic institution. The definition of the market derives logically from the catallactic premises.

Under the substantive range of terms, market and exchange have independent empirical characteristics. What then is here the meaning of exchange and market? And to what extent are they necessarily connected?

Exchange, substantively defined, is the mutual appropriative movement of goods between hands. Such a movement as we saw may occur either at set rates or at bargained rates. The latter only is the result of higgling-haggling between the partners.

Whenever, then, there is exchange, there is a rate. This remains true whether the rate be bargained or set. It will be noted that exchange at bargained prices is identical with catallactic exchange or "exchange as a form of integration." This kind of exchange alone is typically limited to a definite type of market institution, namely price-making markets.

Market institutions shall be defined as institutions comprising a supply crowd or a demand crowd or both. Supply crowds and demand crowds, again, shall be defined as a multiplicity of hands desirous to acquire, or alternatively, to dispose of, goods in exchange. Although market institutions, therefore, are exchange institutions, market and exchange are *not* coterminous. Exchange at set rates occurs under reciprocative or redistributive forms of integration; exchange at bargained rates, as we said, is limited to price-making markets. It may seem paradoxical that exchange at set rates should be compatible with any form of integration except that of exchange: yet this follows logically since only bargained exchange represents exchange in the catallactic sense of the term, in which it is a form of integration.

The best way of approaching the world of market institutions appears to be in terms of "market elements." Eventually, this will not only serve as a guide through the variety of configurations subsumed under the name of markets and market type institutions, but also as a tool with which to dissect some of the conventional concepts that obstruct our understanding of those institutions.

Two market elements should be regarded as specific, namely, supply crowds and demand crowds; if either is present, we shall speak of a market institution (if both are present, we call it a market, if one of them only, a market-type institution). Next in importance is the element of equivalency, i.e., the rate of the exchange; according to the character of the equivalency, markets are set-price markets or price-making markets.

Competition is another characteristic of some market institutions, such as price-making markets and auctions, but in contrast to equivalencies, economic competition is restricted to markets. Finally, there are elements that can be designated as functional. Regularly they occur apart from market institutions, but if they make their appearance alongside of supply crowds or demand crowds, they pattern out those institutions in a manner that may be of great practical relevance. Amongst these functional elements are physical site, goods present, custom and law.

This diversity of market institutions was in recent times obscured in the name of the formal concept of a supply-demand-price mechanism. No wonder that it is in regard to the pivotal terms of supply, demand and price that the substantive approach leads to a significant widening of our outlook.

Supply crowds and demand crowds were referred to above as separate and distinct market elements. In regard to the modern market this would be, of course, inadmissible; here there is a price level at which bears turn bulls, and another price level at which the miracle is reversed. This had induced many to overlook the fact that buyers and sellers are separate in any other than the modern type of market. This again gave support to a twofold misconception. Firstly, "supply and demand" appeared as combined elemental forces while actually each consisted of two very different components, namely, an amount of *goods*, on the one hand, and a number of *persons*, related as buyers and sellers to those goods, on the other. Secondly, "supply and demand" seemed inseparable like Siamese twins, while actually forming distinct groups of persons, according to whether they disposed of the goods as resources, or sought them as requirements. Supply crowds and demand crowds need not therefore be present together. When, for instance, booty is auctioned by the victorious general to the highest bidder only a demand crowd is in evidence; similarly, only a supply crowd is met with when contracts are assigned to the lowest submission. Yet auctions and submissions were widespread in archaic society, and in ancient Greece auctions ranked amongst the precursors of markets proper. This distinctness of "supply" and "demand" crowds shaped the organization of all premodern market institutions.

As to the market element commonly called "price," it was here subsumed under the category of equivalencies. The use of this general term should help avoid misunderstandings. Price suggests fluctuation, while equivalency lacks this association. The very phrase "set" or "fixed" price suggests that the price, before being fixed or set was apt to change. Thus language itself makes it difficult to convey the true state of affairs, namely, that "price" is originally a rigidly fixed quantity, in the absence of which trading cannot start. Changing or fluctuating prices of a competitive character are a comparatively recent development and their emergence forms one of the main interests of the economic history of antiquity. Traditionally, the sequence was supposed to be the reverse: price was conceived of as the result of trade and exchange, not as their precondition.

"Price" is the designation of quantitative ratios between goods of different kinds, effected through barter or higgling-haggling. It is that form of equivalency which is characteristic of economies that are integrated through exchange. But equivalencies are by no means restricted to exchange relations. Under a redistributive form of integration equivalencies are also common. They designate the quantitative relationship between goods of different kinds that are acceptable in payment of taxes, rents, dues, fines, or that denote qualifications for a civic status dependent on a property census. Also the equivalency may set the ratio at which wages or rations in kind can be claimed, at the beneficiary's choosing. The elasticity of a system of staple finance—the planning, balancing and accounting—hinges on this device. The equivalency here denotes not what should be given *for* another good, but what can be claimed *instead* of it. Under reciprocative forms of integration, again, equivalencies determine the amount that is "adequate" in relation to the symmetrically placed party. Clearly, this behavioral context is different from either exchange or redistribution.

Price systems, as they develop over time, may contain layers of equivalencies that historically originated under different forms of integration. Hellenistic market prices show ample evidence of having derived from redistributive equivalencies of the cuneiform civilization that preceded them. The thirty pieces of silver received by Judas as the price of a man for betraying Jesus was a close variant of the equivalency of a slave as set out in Hammurabi's Code some 1700 years earlier. Soviet redistributive equivalencies, on the other hand, for a long time echoed nineteenth century world market prices. These, too, in their turn, had their predecessors. Max Weber remarked that for lack of a costing basis Western capitalism would not have been possible but for the medieval network of statuated and regulated prices, customary rents, etc., a legacy of gild and manor. Thus price systems may have an institutional history of their own in terms of the types of equivalencies that entered into their making.

It is with the help of noncatallactic concepts of trade, money and markets of this kind that such fundamental problems of economic and social history as the origin of fluctuating prices and the development of market trading can best be tackled and, as we hope, eventually resolved.

To conclude: A critical survey of the catallactic definitions of trade, money and market should make available a number of concepts which form the raw material of the social sciences in their economic aspect. The bearing of this recognition on questions of theory, policy and outlook should be viewed in the light of the gradual institutional transformation that has been in progress since the first World War. Even in regard to the market system itself, the market as the sole frame of reference is somewhat out of date. Yet, as should be more clearly realized than it sometimes has been in the past, the market cannot be superseded as a general frame of reference unless the social sciences succeed in developing a wider frame of reference to which the market itself is referable. This indeed is our main intellectual task today in the field of economic studies. As we have attempted to show, such a conceptual structure will have to be grounded on the substantive meaning of economic.

NOTES

1. The uncritical employment of the compound concept fostered what may well be called the "economistic fallacy." It consisted in an artificial identification of the economy with its market form. From Hume and Spencer to Frank H. Knight and Northrop, social thought suffered from this limitation wherever it touched on the economy. Lionel Robbins' essay (1932), though useful to economists, fatefully distorted the problem. In the field of anthropology Melville Herskovits' recent work (1952) represents a relapse after his pioneering effort of 1940.

REFERENCES

Herskovits, Melville. 1940. *The Economic Life of Primitive Peoples.* New York: A. A. Knopf.
_____. 1952. *Economic Anthropology: A Study in Comparative Economics.* New York: A. A. Knopf.
Robbins, Lionel. 1932. *An Essay on the Nature and Significance of Economic Science.* London: Macmillan.

EDITORS' NOTES ON FURTHER READING: POLANYI

Economic historian Karl Polanyi, a Hungarian refugee, held no regular academic positions for most of his life (1886–1964), although he became one of the most influential scholars of the twentieth century. His first major work, *The Great Transformation* (1944), argued that markets dominated other aspects of society in the nineteenth century in a way they never had before, that the resulting "self-regulating market" was a grave threat to social order, and that the economists' assumption that self-interest was a major organizing motive in all societies was a distortion resulting from taking this unique development as the norm. In a companion piece published in 1947, "Our Obsolete Market Mentality," *Commentary* 3:109–117, he urged transcending the conception that it is reasonable for markets to dominate the social order.

The paper we have reprinted, and the book in which it appeared, followed up the earlier arguments by exploring the economic organization of ancient societies and setting out a typology of three ways to organize the economy—by reciprocity, redistribution, and exchange. Polanyi's paper became the rallying point for an entire school of anthropologists who, following his distinction between the "formal" and the "substantive" meanings of the term *economic*, identified themselves as "substantivists." Adherents to the argument that formal economics indeed sheds light on tribal economies became identified as "formalists." Some of the main formalist statements and studies are contained in Edward LeClair and Harold Schneider's edited collection *Economic Anthropology: Readings in Theory and Analysis* (1968). Notable among these is Scott Cook's manifesto, "The Obsolete 'Anti-Market' Mentality: A Critique of the Substantive Approach to Economic Anthropology," originally in *American Anthropologist* 68 (1966):323–345. A general treatment in the formalist vein is Harold Schneider's *Economic Man: The Anthropology of Economics* (1974). For anthropological monographs that attempt to demonstrate the value of formal economic reasoning for tribal economies, see Sol Tax, *Penny Capitalism* (1953); Richard Salisbury, *From Stone to Steel: Economic Consequences of a Technological Change in New Guinea* (1962); and Ralph Beals, *The Peasant Marketing System of Oaxaca, Mexico* (1975).

A series of studies in the substantivist tradition was reprinted in George Dalton, ed., *Tribal and Peasant Economies: Readings in Economic Anthropology* (1967), and an important new statement of the substantivist argument was made by anthropologist Marshall Sahlins in 1972, in *Stone Age Economics*. An incomplete manuscript of Polanyi's that was meant to be a systematic theoretical statement of his position was reconstructed posthumously by Harry Pearson, with valuable commentary, as *Karl Polanyi's The Livelihood of Man* (New York: Academic Press, 1977).

By the 1980s, most of the steam had gone out of the substantivist-formalist debate, though the arguments continued in modified forms between groups no longer wishing to be closely identified with the earlier polemics. A good review of recent trends is to be found in Benjamin Orlove's "Barter and Cash Sale on Lake Titicaca: A Test of Competing Approaches," *Current Anthropology* 27, no. 2 (1986):85–106. Fred Block and Margaret Somers argue that modern sociology can be revitalized by close attention to Polanyi's work in "Beyond the Economistic Fallacy: The Holistic Social Science of Karl Polanyi," in T. Skocpol, ed., *Vision and Method in Historical Sociology* (1984). Block elaborates this argument for economic sociology in his *Postindustrial Possibilities: A Critique of Economic Discourse* (1990). Especially active in urging a Polanyi revival has been the Karl Polanyi Institute of Political Economy, headquartered at Concordia University in Montreal. The institute's executive board includes Fred Block and Polanyi's daughter, Kari Polanyi-Levitt.

2

Economic Action and Social Structure: The Problem of Embeddedness[1]

MARK GRANOVETTER

INTRODUCTION: THE PROBLEM OF EMBEDDEDNESS

How behavior and institutions are affected by social relations is one of the classic questions of social theory. Since such relations are always present, the situation that would arise in their absence can be imagined only through a thought experiment like Thomas Hobbes's "state of nature" or John Rawls's "original position." Much of the utilitarian tradition, including classical and neoclassical economics, assumes rational, self-interested behavior affected minimally by social relations, thus invoking an idealized state not far from that of these thought experiments. At the other extreme lies what I call the argument of "embeddedness": the argument that the behavior and institutions to be analyzed are so constrained by ongoing social relations that to construe them as independent is a grievous misunderstanding.

This article concerns the embeddedness of economic behavior. It has long been the majority view among sociologists, anthropologists, political scientists, and historians that such behavior was heavily embedded in social relations in premarket societies but became much more autonomous with modernization. This view sees the economy as an increasingly separate, differentiated sphere in modern society, with economic transactions defined no longer by the social or kinship obligations of those transacting but by rational calculations of individual gain. It is sometimes further argued that the traditional situation is reversed: instead of economic life being submerged in social relations, these relations become an epiphenomenon of the market. The embeddedness position is associated with the "substantivist" school in anthropology, identified especially with Karl Polanyi (1944; Polanyi, Arensberg, and Pearson 1957) and with the idea of "moral economy" in history

From *American Journal of Sociology* 91 (November 1985):481–510. Copyright © 1985 by The University of Chicago. Reprinted by permission.

and political science (Thompson 1971; Scott 1976). It has also some obvious relation to Marxist thought.

Few economists, however, have accepted this conception of a break in embeddedness with modernization; most of them assert instead that embeddedness in earlier societies was not substantially greater than the low level found in modern markets. The tone was set by Adam Smith, who postulated a "certain propensity in human nature . . . to truck, barter and exchange one thing for another" ([1776] 1979, book 1, chap. 2) and assumed that since labor was the only factor of production in primitive society, goods must have exchanged in proportion to their labor costs—as in the general classical theory of exchange ([1776] 1979, book 1, chap. 6). From the 1920s on, certain anthropologists took a similar position, which came to be called the "formalist" one: even in tribal societies, economic behavior was sufficiently independent of social relations for standard neoclassical analysis to be useful (Schneider 1974). This position has recently received a new infusion as economists and fellow travelers in history and political science have developed a new interest in the economic analysis of social institutions—much of which falls into what is called the "new institutional economics"—and have argued that behavior and institutions previously interpreted as embedded in earlier societies, as well as in our own, can be better understood as resulting from the pursuit of self-interest by rational, more or less atomized individuals (e.g., North and Thomas 1973; Williamson 1975; Popkin 1979).

My own view diverges from both schools of thought. I assert that the level of embeddedness of economic behavior is lower in nonmarket societies than is claimed by substantivists and development theorists, and it has changed less with "modernization" than they believe; but I argue also that this level has always been and continues to be more substantial than is allowed for by formalists and economists. I do not attempt here to treat the issues posed by nonmarket societies. I proceed instead by a theoretical elaboration of the concept of embeddedness, whose value is then illustrated with a problem from modern society, currently important in the new institutional economics: which transactions in modern capitalist society are carried out in the market, and which subsumed within hierarchically organized firms? This question has been raised to prominence by the "markets and hierarchies" program of research initiated by Oliver Williamson (1975).

OVER- AND UNDERSOCIALIZED
CONCEPTIONS OF HUMAN ACTION
IN SOCIOLOGY AND ECONOMICS

I begin by recalling Dennis Wrong's 1961 complaint about an "oversocialized conception of man in modern sociology"—a conception of people as overwhelmingly sensitive to the opinions of others and hence obedient to the dictates of consensually developed systems of norms and values, internalized through socialization, so that obedience is not perceived as a burden. To the extent that such a conception was prominent in 1961, it resulted in large part from Talcott Parsons's recognition of the problem of order as posed by Hobbes and his own attempt to resolve it by transcending the atomized, *undersocialized* conception of man in the utilitarian tradition of which Hobbes was part (Parsons 1937, pp. 89–94). Wrong approved the break with atomized utilitarianism and the emphasis on actors' embeddedness in social context—the crucial factor absent from Hobbes's thinking—but warned of exaggerating the degree of this embeddedness and the extent to which it might eliminate conflict:

> It is frequently the task of the sociologist to call attention to the intensity with which men desire and strive for the good opinion of their immediate associates in a variety of situations, particularly those where received theories or ideologies have unduly emphasized other motives. . . . Thus sociologists have shown that factory workers are more sensitive to the attitudes of their fellow workers than to purely economic incentives. . . . It is certainly not my intention to criticize the findings of such studies. My objection is that . . . [a]lthough sociologists have criticized past efforts to single out one fundamental motive in human conduct, the desire to achieve a favorable self-image by winning approval from others frequently occupies such a position in their own thinking. [1961, pp. 188–89]

Classical and neoclassical economics operates, in contrast, with an atomized, *under*socialized conception of human action, continuing in the utilitarian tradition. The theoretical arguments disallow by hypothesis any impact of social structure and social relations on production, distribution, or consumption. In competitive markets, no producer or consumer noticeably influences aggregate supply or demand or, therefore, prices or other terms of trade. As Albert Hirschman has noted, such idealized markets, involving as they do "large numbers of price-taking anonymous buyers and sellers supplied with perfect information . . . function without any prolonged human or social contact between the parties. Under perfect competition there is no room for bargaining, negotiation, remonstration or mutual adjustment and the various operators that contract together need not enter into recurrent or continuing relationships as a result of which they would get to know each other well" (1982, p. 1473).

It has long been recognized that the idealized markets of perfect competition have survived intellectual attack in part because self-regulating economic structures are politically attractive to many. Another reason for this survival, less clearly understood, is that the elimination of social relations from economic analysis removes the problem of order from the intellectual agenda, at least in the economic sphere. In Hobbes's argument, disorder arises because conflict-free social and economic transactions depend on trust and the absence of malfeasance. But these are unlikely when individuals are conceived to have neither social relationships nor institutional context—as in the "state of nature." Hobbes contains the difficulty by superimposing a structure of autocratic authority. The solution of classical liberalism, and correspondingly of classical economics, is antithetical: repressive political structures are rendered unnecessary by competitive markets that make force or fraud unavailing. Competition determines the terms of trade in a way that individual traders cannot manipulate. If traders encounter complex or difficult relationships, characterized by mistrust or malfeasance, they can simply move on to the legion of other traders willing to do business on market terms; social relations and their details thus become frictional matters.

In classical and neoclassical economics, therefore, the fact that actors may have social relations with one another has been treated, if at all, as a frictional drag that impedes competitive markets. In a much-quoted line, Adam Smith complained that "people of the same trade seldom meet together, even for merriment and diversion, but the conversation ends in a conspiracy against the public, or in some contrivance to raise prices." His laissez-faire politics allowed few solutions to this problem, but he did suggest repeal of regulations requiring all those in the same trade to sign a public register; the public existence of such information "connects individuals who might never otherwise be known to one another and gives every man of the trade a direction where to find every other man of it." Noteworthy here is not the rather lame policy prescription but the recognition that *social atomization is prerequisite to perfect competition* (Smith [1776] 1979, pp. 232–33).

More recent comments by economists on "social influences" construe these as processes in which actors acquire customs, habits, or norms that are followed mechanically and automatically, irrespective of their bearing on rational choice. This view, close to Wrong's "oversocialized conception," is reflected in James Duesenberry's quip that "economics is all about how people make choices; sociology is all about how they don't have any choices to make" (1960, p. 233) and in E. H. Phelps Brown's description of the "sociologists' approach to pay determination" as deriving from the assumption that people act in "certain ways because to do so is customary, or an obligation, or the 'natural thing to do,' or right and proper, or just and fair" (1977, p. 17).

But despite the apparent contrast between under- and oversocialized views, we should note an irony of great theoretical importance: both have in common a conception of action and decision carried out by atomized actors. In the undersocialized account, atomization results from narrow utilitarian pursuit of self-interest; in the oversocialized one, from the fact that behavioral patterns have been internalized and ongoing social relations thus have only peripheral effects on behavior. That the internalized rules of behavior are social in origin does not differentiate this argument decisively from a utilitarian one, in which the source of utility functions is left open, leaving room for behavior guided entirely by consensually determined norms and values—as in the oversocialized view. Under- and oversocialized res-olutions of the problem of order thus merge in their atomization of actors from immediate social context. This ironic merger is already visible in Hobbes's *Leviathan*, in which the unfortunate denizens of the state of nature, overwhelmed by the disorder consequent to their atomization, cheerfully surrender all their rights to an authoritarian power and subsequently behave in a docile and honorable manner; by the artifice of a social contract, they lurch directly from an undersocialized to an oversocialized state.

When modern economists do attempt to take account of social influences, they typically represent them in the oversocialized manner represented in the quotations above. In so doing, they reverse the judgment that social influences are frictional but sustain the conception of how such influences operate. In the theory of segmented labor markets, for example, Michael Piore has argued that members of each labor market segment are characterized by different styles of decision making and that the making of decisions by rational choice, custom, or command in upper-primary, lower-primary, and secondary labor markets respectively corresponds to the origins of workers in middle-, working-, and lower-class subcultures (Piore 1975). Similarly, Samuel Bowles and Herbert Gintis, in their account of the consequences of American education, argue that different social classes display different cognitive processes because of differences in the education provided to each. Those destined for lower-level jobs are trained to be dependable followers of rules, while those who will be channeled into elite positions attend "elite four-year colleges" that "emphasize social relationships conformable with the higher levels in the production hierarchy. . . . As they 'master' one type of behavioral regulation they are either allowed to progress to the next or are channeled into the corresponding level in the hierarchy of production" (Bowles and Gintis 1975, p. 132).

But these oversocialized conceptions of how society influences individual behavior are rather mechanical: once we know the individual's social class or labor market sector, everything else in behavior is automatic, since they are so well socialized. Social influence here is an external force that, like the deists' God, sets things in motion and has no further effects—a force that insinuates itself into the minds and bodies of individuals (as in the movie *Invasion of the Body Snatchers*), altering their way of making decisions. Once we know in just what way an individual has been affected, ongoing social relations and structures are irrelevant. Social influences are all contained inside an individual's head, so, in actual decision situations, he or she can be atomized as any *Homo economicus*, though perhaps with different rules for decisions. More sophisticated (and thus less oversocialized) analyses of cultural influences (e.g., Fine and Kleinman 1979; Cole 1979, chap. 1) make it clear that culture is not a once-for-all influence but an ongoing process, continuously constructed and reconstructed during interaction. It not only shapes its members but also is shaped by them, in part for their own strategic reasons.

Even when economists do take social relationships seriously, as do such diverse figures as Harvey Leibenstein (1976) and Gary Becker (1976), they invariably abstract away from the history of relations and their position with respect to other relations—what might be called the historical and structural embeddedness of relations. The interpersonal ties described in their arguments are extremely stylized, average, "typical"—devoid of specific content, history, or structural location. Actors' behavior results from their named role positions and role sets; thus we have arguments on how workers and supervisors, husbands and wives, or criminals and law enforcers will interact with one another, but these relations are not assumed to have individualized content beyond that given by the named roles. This procedure is exactly what structural sociologists have criticized in Parsonian sociology—the relegation of the specifics of individual relations to a minor role in the overall conceptual scheme, epiphenomenal in comparison with enduring structures of normative role prescriptions deriving from ultimate value orientations. In economic models, this treatment of social relations has the paradoxical effect of preserving atomized decision making even when decisions are seen to involve more than one individual. Because the analyzed set of individuals—usually dyads, occasionally larger groups—is abstracted out of social context, it is atomized in its behavior from that of other groups and from the history of its own relations. Atomization has not been eliminated, merely transferred to the dyadic or higher level of analysis. Note the use of an oversocialized conception—that of actors behaving exclusively in accord with their prescribed roles—to implement an atomized, undersocialized view.

A fruitful analysis of human action requires us to avoid the atomization implicit in the theoretical extremes of under- and oversocialized conceptions. Actors do not behave or decide as atoms outside a social context, nor do they adhere slavishly to a script written for them by the particular intersection of social categories that they happen to occupy. Their attempts at purposive action are instead embedded in concrete, ongoing systems of social relations. In the remainder of this article I illustrate how this view of embeddedness alters our theoretical and empirical approach to the study of economic behavior. I first narrow the focus to the question of trust and malfeasance in economic life and then use the "markets and hierarchies" problem to illustrate the use of embeddedness ideas in analyzing this question.[2]

EMBEDDEDNESS, TRUST, AND
MALFEASANCE IN ECONOMIC LIFE

Since about 1970, there has been a flurry of interest among economists in the previously neglected issues of trust and malfeasance. Oliver Williamson has noted that real economic actors engage not merely in the pursuit of self-interest but also in "opportunism"—"self-interest seeking with guile; agents who are skilled as dissembling realize transactional advantages.[3] Economic man . . . is thus a more subtle and devious creature than the usual self-interest seeking assumption reveals" (1975, p. 255).

But this points out a peculiar assumption of modern economic theory, that one's economic interest is pursued only by comparatively gentlemanly means. The Hobbesian question—how it can be that those who pursue their own interest do not do so mainly by force and fraud—is finessed by this conception. Yet, as Hobbes saw so clearly, there is nothing in the intrinsic meaning of "self-interest" that excludes force or fraud.

In part, this assumption persisted because competitive forces, in a self-regulating market, could be imagined to suppress force and fraud. But the idea is also embedded in the intellectual history of the discipline. In *The Passions and the Interests*, Albert Hirschman (1977) shows that an important strand of intellectual history from the time of *Leviathan* to that of *The Wealth of Nations* consisted of the watering down of Hobbes's problem of order by arguing that certain human motivations kept others under control and that, in particular, the pursuit of economic self-interest was typically not an uncontrollable "passion" but a civilized, gentle activity. The wide though implicit acceptance of such an idea is a powerful example of how under- and oversocialized conceptions complement one another: atomized actors in competitive markets so thoroughly internalize these normative standards of behavior as to guarantee orderly transactions.[4]

What has eroded this confidence in recent years has been increased attention to the micro-level details of imperfectly competitive markets, characterized by small numbers of participants with sunk costs and "specific human capital" investments. In such situations, the alleged discipline of competitive markets cannot be called on to mitigate deceit, so the classical problem of how it can be that daily economic life is not riddled with mistrust and malfeasance has resurfaced.

In the economic literature, I see two fundamental answers to this problem and argue that one is linked to an undersocialized, and the other to an oversocialized, conception of human action. The undersocialized account is found mainly in the new institutional economics—a loosely defined confederation of economists with an interest in explaining social institutions from a neoclassical viewpoint. (See, e.g., Furubotn and Pejovich 1972; Alchian and Demsetz 1973; Lazear 1979; Rosen 1982; Williamson 1975, 1979, 1981; Williamson and Ouchi 1981.) The general story told by members of this school is that social institutions and arrangements previously thought to be the adventitious result of legal, historical, social, or political forces are better viewed as the efficient solution to certain economic problems. The tone is similar to that of structural-functional sociology of the 1940s to the 1960s, and much of the argumentation fails the elementary tests of a sound functional explanation laid down by Robert Merton in 1947. Consider, for example, Schotter's view that to understand any observed economic institution requires only that we "infer the evolutionary problem that must have existed for the institution as we see it to have developed. Every evolutionary economic problem requires a social institution to solve it" (1981, p. 2).

Malfeasance is here seen to be averted because clever institutional arrangements make it too costly to engage in, and these arrangements— many previously interpreted as serving no economic function—are now seen as having evolved to discourage malfeasance. Note, however, that they do not produce trust but instead are a functional substitute for it. The main such arrangements are elaborate explicit and implicit contracts (Okun 1981), including deferred compensation plans and mandatory retirement—seen to reduce the incentives for "shirking" on the job or absconding with proprietary secrets (Lazear 1979; Pakes and Nitzan 1982)—and authority structures that deflect opportunism by making potentially divisive decisions by fiat (Williamson 1975). These conceptions are undersocialized in that they do not allow for the extent to which concrete personal relations and the obligations inherent in them discourage malfeasance, quite apart from institutional arrangements. *Substituting* these arrangements for trust results actually in a Hobbesian situation, in which any rational individual would be motivated to develop clever ways to evade them; it is then hard to imagine that everyday economic life would not be poisoned by ever more ingenious attempts at deceit.

Other economists have recognized that some degree of trust *must* be assumed to operate, since institutional arrangements alone could not entirely stem force or fraud. But it remains to explain the source of this trust, and appeal is sometimes made to the existence of a "generalized morality." Kenneth Arrow, for example, suggests that societies, "in their evolution have developed implicit agreements to certain kinds of regard for others, agreements which are essential to the survival of the society or at least contribute greatly to the efficiency of its working" (1974, p. 26; see also Akerlof [1983] on the origins of "honesty").

Now one can hardly doubt the existence of some such generalized morality; without it, you would be afraid to give the gas station attendant a 20-dollar bill when you had bought only five dollars' worth of gas. But this conception has the oversocialized characteristic of calling on a generalized and automatic response, even though moral action in economic life is hardly automatic or universal (as is well known at gas stations that demand exact change after dark).

Consider a case where generalized morality does indeed seem to be at work: the legendary (I hesitate to say apocryphal) economist who, against all economic rationality, leaves a tip in a roadside restaurant far from home. Note that this transaction has three characteristics that make it somewhat unusual: (1) the transactors are previously unacquainted, (2) they are unlikely to transact again, and (3) information about the activities of either is unlikely to reach others with whom they might transact in the future. I argue that it is only in situations of this kind that the absence of force and fraud can mainly be explained by generalized morality. Even there, one might wonder how effective this morality would be if large costs were incurred.

The embeddedness argument stresses instead the role of concrete personal relations and structures (or "networks") of such relations in generating trust and discouraging malfeasance. The widespread preference for transacting with individuals of known reputation implies that few are actually content to rely on either generalized morality *or* institutional arrangements to guard against trouble. Economists *have* pointed out that one incentive not to cheat is the cost of damage to one's reputation; but this is an undersocialized conception of reputation as a generalized commodity, a ratio of cheating to opportunities for doing so. In practice, we settle for such generalized information when nothing better is available, but ordinarily we seek better information. Better than the statement that someone is known to be reliable is information from a trusted informant that he has dealt with that individual and found him so. Even better is information from one's own past dealings with that person. This is better information for four reasons: (1) it is cheap; (2) one trusts one's own information best—it is richer, more detailed, and known to be accurate; (3) individuals with whom one has a continuing relation have an economic motivation to be trustworthy, so as not to discourage future transactions; and (4) departing from pure economic motives, continuing economic relations often become overlaid with social content that carries strong expectations of trust and abstention from opportunism.

It would never occur to us to doubt this last point in more intimate relations, which make behavior more predictable and thus close off some of the fears that create difficulties among strangers. Consider, for example, why individuals in a burning theater panic and stampede to the door, leading to desperate results. Analysts of collective behavior long considered this to be prototypically irrational behavior, but Roger Brown (1965, chap. 14) points out that the situation is essentially an *n*-person Prisoner's Dilemma: each stampeder is actually being quite rational given the absence of a guarantee that anyone else will walk out calmly, even though all would be better off if everyone did so. Note, however, that in the case of the burning houses featured on the 11:00 P.M. news, we never hear that everyone stampeded out and that family members trampled one another. In the family, there is no Prisoner's Dilemma because each is confident that the others can be counted on.

In business relations the degree of confidence must be more variable, but Prisoner's Dilemmas are nevertheless often obviated by the strength of personal relations, and this strength is a property not of the transactors but of their concrete relations. Standard economic analysis neglects the identity and past relations of individual transactors, but rational individuals know better, relying on their knowledge of these relations. They are less interested in *general* reputations than in whether a particular other may be expected to deal honestly with *them*—mainly a function of whether they or their own contacts have had satisfactory past dealings with the other. One sees this pattern even in situations that appear, at first glance, to approximate the classic higgling of a competitive market, as in the Moroccan bazaar analyzed by Geertz (1979).

Up to this point, I have argued that social relations, rather than institutional arrangements or generalized morality, are mainly responsible for the production of trust in economic life. But I then risk rejecting one kind of optimistic functionalism for another, in which networks of relations, rather than morality or arrangements, are the structure that fulfills the function of sustaining order. There are two ways to reduce this risk. One is to recognize that as a solution to the problem of order, the embeddedness position is less sweeping than either alternative argument, since networks of social relations penetrate irregularly and in differing degrees in different

sectors of economic life, thus allowing for what we already know: distrust, opportunism, and disorder are by no means absent.

The second is to insist that while social relations may indeed often be a necessary condition for trust and trustworthy behavior, they are not sufficient to guarantee these and may even provide occasion and means for malfeasance and conflict on a scale larger than in their absence. There are three reasons for this.

1. The trust engendered by personal relations presents, by its very existence, enhanced opportunity for malfeasance. In personal relations it is common knowledge that "you always hurt the one you love"; that person's trust in you results in a position far more vulnerable than that of a stranger. (In the Prisoner's Dilemma, knowledge that one's coconspirator is certain to deny the crime is all the more rational motive to confess, and personal relations that abrogate this dilemma may be less symmetrical than is believed by the party to be deceived.) This elementary fact of social life is the bread and butter of "confidence" rackets that simulate certain relationships, sometimes for long periods, for concealed purposes. In the business world, certain crimes, such as embezzling, are simply impossible for those who have not built up relationships of trust that permit the opportunity to manipulate accounts. The more complete the trust, the greater the potential gain from malfeasance. That such instances are statistically infrequent is a tribute to the force of personal relations and reputation; that they do occur with regularity, however infrequently, shows the limits of this force.

2. Force and fraud are most efficiently pursued by teams, and the structure of these teams requires a level of internal trust—"honor among thieves"— that usually follows preexisting lines of relationship. Elaborate schemes for kickbacks and bid rigging, for example, can hardly be executed by individuals working alone, and when such activity is exposed it is often remarkable that it could have been kept secret given the large numbers involved. Law-enforcement efforts consist of finding an entry point to the network of malfeasance—an individual whose confession implicates others who will, in snowball-sample fashion, "finger" still others until the entire picture is fitted together.

Both enormous trust and enormous malfeasance, then, may follow from personal relations. Yoram Ben-Porath, in the functionalist style of the new institutional economics, emphasizes the positive side, noting that "continuity of relationships can generate behavior on the part of shrewd, self-seeking, or even unscrupulous individuals that could otherwise be interpreted as foolish or purely altruistic. Valuable diamonds change hands on the diamond exchange, and the deals are sealed by a handshake" (1980, p. 6). I might add, continuing in this positive vein, that this transaction is possible in part because it is not atomized from other transactions but embedded in a close-knit community of diamond merchants who monitor one another's behavior closely. Like other densely knit networks of actors, they generate clearly defined standards of behavior easily policed by the quick spread of information about instances of malfeasance. But the temptations posed by this level of trust are considerable, and the diamond trade has also been the scene of numerous well-publicized "insider job" thefts and of the notorious "CBS murders" of April 1982. In this case, the owner of a diamond company was defrauding a factoring concern by submitting invoices from fictitious sales. The scheme required cooperation from his accounting personnel, one of whom was approached by investigators and turned state's evidence. The owner then contracted for the murder of the disloyal employee and her assistant; three CBS technicians who came to their aid were also gunned down (Shenon 1984).

3. The extent of disorder resulting from force and fraud depends very much on how the network of social relations is structured. Hobbes exaggerated the extent of disorder likely in his atomized state of nature where, in the absence of sustained social relations, one could expect only desultory dyadic conflicts. More extended and large-scale disorder results from coalitions of combatants, impossible without prior relations. We do not generally speak of "war" unless actors have arranged themselves into two sides, as the end result of various coalitions. This occurs only if there are insufficient cross-cutting ties, held by actors with enough links to both main potential combatants to have a strong interest in forestalling conflict. The same is true in the business world, where conflicts are relatively tame unless each side can escalate by calling on substantial numbers of allies in other firms, as sometimes happens in attempts to implement or forestall takeovers.

Disorder and malfeasance do of course occur also when social relations are absent. This possibility is already entailed in my earlier claim that the presence of such relations inhibits malfeasance. But the *level* of malfeasance available in a truly atomized social situation is fairly low; instances can only be episodic, unconnected, small scale. The Hobbesian problem is truly a problem, but in transcending it by the smoothing effect of social structure, we also introduce the possibility of disruptions on a larger scale than those available in the "state of nature."

The embeddedness approach to the problem of trust and order in economic life, then, threads its way between the oversocialized approach of generalized morality and the undersocialized one of impersonal, institutional arrangements by following and analyzing concrete patterns of social relations. Unlike either alternative, or the Hobbesian position, it makes no sweeping (and thus unlikely) predictions of universal order or disorder but rather assumes that the details of social structure will determine which is found.

THE PROBLEM OF MARKETS AND HIERARCHIES

As a concrete application of the embeddedness approach to economic life, I offer a critique of the influential argument of Oliver Williamson in *Markets and Hierarchies* (1975) and later articles (1979, 1981; Williamson and Ouchi 1981). Williamson asked under what circumstances economic functions are performed within the boundaries of hierarchical firms rather than by market processes that cross these boundaries. His answer, consistent with the general emphasis of the new institutional economics, is that the organizational form observed in any situation is that which deals most efficiently with the cost of economic transactions. Those that are uncertain in outcome, recur frequently, and require substantial "transaction-specific investments"—for example, money, time, or energy that cannot be easily transferred to interaction with others on different matters—are more likely to take place within hierarchically organized firms. Those that are straightforward, nonrepetitive, and require no transaction-specific investment—such as the one-time purchase of standard equipment—will more likely take place between firms, that is, across a market interface.

In this account, the former set of transactions is internalized within hierarchies for two reasons. The first is "bounded rationality," the inability of economic actors to anticipate properly the complex chain of contingencies that might be relevant to long-term contracts. When transactions are internalized, it is unnecessary to anticipate all such contingencies; they can be handled within the firm's "governance structure" instead of leading to complex negotiations. The second reason is "opportunism," the rational pursuit by economic actors of their own advantage, with all means at their command, including guile and deceit. Opportunism is mitigated and constrained by authority relations and by the greater identification with transaction partners that one allegedly has when both are contained within one corporate entity than when they face one another across the chasm of a market boundary.

The appeal to authority relations in order to tame opportunism constitutes a rediscovery of Hobbesian analysis, though confined here to the economic sphere. The Hobbesian flavor of Williamson's argument is suggested by such statements as the following: "Internal organization is not beset with the same kinds of difficulties that autonomous contracting [among independent firms] experiences when disputes arise between the parties. Although interfirm disputes are often settled out of court . . . this resolution is sometimes difficult and interfirm relations are often strained. Costly litigation is sometimes unavoidable. Internal organization, by contrast . . . is able to settle many such disputes by appeal to fiat—an enormously efficient way to settle instrumental differences" (1975, p. 30). He notes that complex, recurring transactions require long-term relations between identified individuals but that opportunism jeopardizes these relations. The adaptations to changing market circumstances required over the course of a relationship are too complex and unpredictable to be encompassed in some initial contact, and promises of good faith are unenforceable in the absence of an overarching authority:

> A general clause . . . that "I will behave responsibly rather than seek individual advantage when an occasion to adapt arises," would, in the absence of opportunism, suffice. Given, however, the unenforceability of general clauses and the proclivity of human agents to make false and misleading (self-disbelieved) statements, . . . both buyer and seller are strategically situated to bargain over the disposition of any incremental gain whenever a proposal to

adapt is made by the other party. . . . Efficient adaptations which would otherwise be made thus result in costly haggling or even go unmentioned, lest the gains be dissipated by costly subgoal pursuit. *Governance structures which attenuate opportunism and otherwise infuse confidence are evidently needed.* [1979, pp. 241–42, emphasis mine]

This analysis entails the same mixture of under- and oversocialized assumptions found in *Leviathan*. The efficacy of hierarchical power within the firm is overplayed, as with Hobbes's oversocialized sovereign state.[5] The "market" resembles Hobbes's state of nature. It is the atomized and anonymous market of classical political economy, minus the discipline brought by fully competitive conditions—an undersocialized conception that neglects the role of social relations among individuals in different firms in bringing order to economic life. Williamson does acknowledge that this picture of the market is not always appropriate: "Norms of trustworthy behavior sometimes extend to markets and are enforced, in some degree, by group pressures. . . . Repeated personal contacts across organizational boundaries support some minimum level of courtesy and consideration between the parties. . . . In addition, expectations of repeat business discourage efforts to seek a narrow advantage in any particular transaction. . . . Individual aggressiveness is curbed by the prospect of ostracism among peers, in both trade and social circumstances. The reputation of a firm for fairness is also a business asset not to be dissipated" (1975, pp. 106–8).

A wedge is opened here for analysis of social structural influences on market behavior. But Williamson treats these examples as exceptions and also fails to appreciate the extent to which the dyadic relations he describes are themselves embedded in broader systems of social relations. I argue that the anonymous market of neoclassical models is virtually nonexistent in economic life and that transactions of all kinds are rife with the social connections described. This is not necessarily more the case in transactions between firms than within—it seems plausible, on the contrary, that the network of social relations within the firm might be more dense and long-lasting on the average than that existing between—but all I need show here is that there is sufficient social overlay in economic transactions across firms (in the "market," to use the term as in Williamson's dichotomy) to render dubious the assertion that complex market transactions approximate a Hobbesian state of nature that can only be resolved by internalization within a hierarchical structure.

In a general way, there is evidence all around us of the extent to which business relations are mixed up with social ones. The trade associations deplored by Adam Smith remain of great importance. It is well known that many firms, small and large, are linked by interlocking directorates so that relationships among directors of firms are many and densely knit. That business relations spill over into sociability and vice versa, especially among business elites, is one of the best-documented facts in the sociological study of business (e.g., Domhoff 1971; Useem 1979). In his study of the extent to which litigation was used to settle disputes between firms, Macaulay notes that disputes are "frequently settled without reference to the contract or potential or actual legal sanctions. There is a hesitancy to speak of legal rights or to threaten to sue in these negotiations. . . . Or as one businessman put it, 'You can settle any dispute if you keep the lawyers and accountants out of it. They just do not understand the give-and-take needed in business.' . . . Law suits for breach of contract appear to be rare" (1963, p. 61). He goes on to explain that the

> top executives of the two firms may know each other. They may sit together on government or trade committees. They may know each other socially and even belong to the same country club. . . . Even where agreement can be reached at the negotiation stage, carefully planned arrangements may create undesirable exchange relationships between business units. Some businessmen object that in such a carefully worked out relationship one gets performance only to the letter of the contract. Such planning indicates a lack of trust and blunts the demands of friendship, turning a cooperative venture into an antagonistic horse trade. . . . Threatening to turn matters over to an attorney may cost no more money than postage or a telephone call; yet few are so skilled in making such a threat that it will not cost some deterioration of the relationship between the firms. [Pp. 63–64]

It is not only at top levels that firms are connected by networks of personal relations, but at all levels where transactions must take place. It is, for example, a commonplace in the literature on industrial purchasing that buying and selling relationships rarely approximate the spot-market model of classical theory. One source indicates that the "evidence consistently suggests that it takes some kind of 'shock' to jolt the organizational buying out of a pattern of placing repeat orders with a favored supplier or to extend the constrained set of feasible suppliers. A moment's reflection will suggest several reasons for this behavior, including the costs associated with searching for new suppliers and establishing new relationships, the fact that users are likely to prefer sources, the relatively low risk involved in dealing with known vendors, and the likelihood that the buyer has established personal relationships that he values with representatives of the supplying firm" (Webster and Wind 1972, p. 15).

In a similar vein, Macaulay notes that salesmen "often know purchasing agents well. The same two individuals may have dealt with each other from five to 25 years. Each has something to give the other. Salesmen have gossip about competitors, shortages and price increases to give purchasing agents who treat them well" (1963, p. 63). Sellers who do not satisfy their customers "become the subject of discussion in the gossip exchanged by purchasing agents and salesmen, at meetings of purchasing agents' associations and trade associations or even at country clubs or social gatherings . . ." (p. 64). Settlement of disputes is eased by this embeddedness of business in social relations: "Even where the parties have a detailed and carefully planned agreement which indicates what is to happen if, say, the seller fails to deliver on time, often they will never refer to the agreement but will negotiate a solution when the problem arises as if there never had been any original contract. One purchasing agent expressed a common business attitude when he said, 'If something comes, you get the other man on the telephone and deal with the problem. You don't read legalistic contract clauses at each other if you ever want to do business again. One doesn't run to lawyers if he wants to stay in business because one must behave decently'" (Macaulay 1963, p. 61).

Such patterns may be more easily noted in other countries, where they are supposedly explained by "cultural" peculiarities. Thus, one journalist recently asserted,

> Friendships and longstanding personal connections affect business connections everywhere. But that seems to be especially true in Japan. . . . The after-hours sessions in the bars and nightclubs are where the vital personal contacts are established and nurtured slowly. Once these ties are set, they are not easily undone. . . . The resulting tight-knit nature of Japanese business society has long been a source of frustration to foreign companies trying to sell products in Japan. . . . Chalmers Johnson, a professor at . . . Berkeley, believes that . . . the exclusive dealing within the Japanese industrial groups, buying and selling to and from each other based on decades-old relationships rather than economic competitiveness . . . is . . . a real nontariff barrier [to trade between the United States and Japan]. [Lohr 1982]

The extensive use of subcontracting in many industries also presents opportunities for sustained relationships among firms that are not organized hierarchically within one corporate unit. For example, Eccles cites evidence from many countries that in construction, when projects "are not subject to institutional regulations which require competitive bidding . . . relations between the general contractor and his subcontractors are stable and continuous over fairly long periods of time and only infrequently established through competitive bidding. This type of 'quasi-integration' results in what I call the 'quasifirm.' It is a preferred mode to either pure market transactions or formal vertical integration" (1981, pp. 339–40). Eccles describes this "quasifirm" arrangement of extensive and long-term relationships among contractors and subcontractors as an organizational form logically intermediate between the pure market and the vertically integrated firm. I would argue, however, that it is not *empirically* intermediate, since the former situation is so rare. The case of construction is closer to vertical integration than some other situations where firms interact, such as buying and selling relations, since subcontractors are physically located on the same site as the contractor and are under his general supervision. Furthermore, under the usual fixed-price contracts, there are "obvious incentives for shirking performance requirements" (Eccles 1981, p. 340).

Yet a hierarchical structure associated with the vertically integrated firm does not arise to meet this "problem." I argue this is because the long-term relations of contractors and subcontractors, as well as the embeddedness of those relations in a community of construction personnel, generate standards of expected behavior that not only obviate the need for but are superior to pure authority relations in discouraging malfeasance. Eccles's own empirical study of residential construction in Massachusetts shows not only that subcontracting relationships are long term in nature but also that it is very rare for a general contractor to employ more than two or three subcontractors in a given trade, whatever number of projects is handled in the course of a year (1981, pp. 349–51). This is true despite the availability of large numbers of alternative subcontractors. This phenomenon can be explained in part in investment terms—through a "continuing association both parties can benefit from the somewhat idiosyncratic investment of learning to work together" (Eccles 1981, p. 340)—but also must be related to the desire of individuals to derive pleasure from the social interaction that accompanies their daily work, a pleasure that would be considerably blunted by spot-market procedures requiring entirely new and strange work partners each day. As in other parts of economic life, the overlay of social relations on what may begin in purely economic transactions plays a crucial role.

Some comments on labor markets are also relevant here. One advantage that Williamson asserts for hierarchically structured firms over market transactions is the ability to transmit accurate information about employees. "The principal impediment to effective interfirm experience-rating," he argues, "is one of communications. By comparison with the firm, markets lack a rich and common rating language. The language problem is particularly severe where the judgments to be made are highly subjective. The advantages of hierarchy in these circumstances are especially great if those persons who are most familiar with a worker's characteristics, usually his immediate supervisor, also do the experience-rating" (1975, p. 78). But the notion that good information about the characteristics of an employee can be transmitted only within firms and not between can be sustained only by neglecting the widely variegated social network of interaction that spans firms. Information about employees travels among firms not only because personal relations exist between those in each firm who do business with each other but also, as I have shown in detail (Granovetter 1974), because the relatively high levels of interfirm mobility in the United States guarantee that many workers will be reasonably well known to employees of numerous other firms that might require and solicit their services. Furthermore, the idea that internal information is necessarily accurate and acted on dispassionately by promotion procedures keyed to it seems naive. To say, as Williamson does, that reliance "on internal promotion has affirmative incentive properties because workers can anticipate that differential talent and degrees of cooperativeness will be rewarded" (1975, p. 78) invokes an ideal type of promotion as reward-for-achievement that can readily be shown to have only limited correspondence to existing internal labor markets (see Granovetter 1983, pp. 40–51, for an extended analysis).

The other side of my critique is to argue that Williamson vastly overestimates the efficacy of hierarchical power ("fiat," in his terminology) within organizations. He asserts, for example, that internal organizations have a great auditing advantage: "An external auditor is typically constrained to review written records. . . . An internal auditor, by contrast has greater freedom of action. . . . Whereas an internal auditor is not a partisan but regards himself and is regarded by others in mainly instrumental terms, the external auditor is associated with the 'other side' and his motives are regarded suspiciously. The degree of cooperation received by the auditor from the audited party varies accordingly. The external auditor can expect to receive only perfunctory cooperation" (1975, pp. 29–30). The literature on intrafirm audits is sparse, but one thorough account is that of Dalton, in *Men Who Manage*, for a large chemical plant. Audits of parts by the central office were supposed to be conducted on a surprise basis, but warning was typically surreptitiously given. The high level of cooperation shown in these internal audits is suggested by the following account: "Notice that a count of parts was to begin provoked a flurry among the executives to hide certain parts and equipment . . . materials *not* to be counted were moved to: 1) little-known and inaccessible spots; 2) basements and pits that were dirty and therefore unlikely to be examined; 3) departments that had already been inspected and that could be approached circuitously while the counters were en route between official storage areas and 4) places where materials and supplies might be used as a camouflage for parts. . . . As the practice developed, cooperation among the [department] chiefs to use each other's storage areas and available pits became well organized and smoothly functioning" (Dalton 1959, pp. 48–49).

Dalton's work shows brilliantly that cost accounting of all kinds is a highly arbitrary and therefore easily politicized process rather than a technical procedure decided on grounds of efficiency. He details this especially for the relationship between the maintenance department and various production departments in the chemical plant; the department to which maintenance work was charged had less to do with any strict time accounting than with the relative political and social standing of department executives in their relation to maintenance personnel. Furthermore, the more aggressive department heads expedited their maintenance work "by the use of friendships, by bullying and implied threats. As all the heads had the same formal rank, one could say that an inverse relation existed between a given officer's personal influence and his volume of uncompleted repairs" (1959, p. 34). Questioned about how such practices could escape the attention of auditors, one informant told Dalton, "If Auditing got to snooping around, what the hell could they find out? And if they did find anything, they'd know a damn sight better than to say anything about it. . . . All those guys [department heads] have got lines through Cost Accounting. That's a lot of bunk about Auditing being independent" (p. 32).

Accounts as detailed and perceptive as Dalton's are sadly lacking for a representative sample of firms and so are open to the argument that they are exceptional. But similar points can be made for the problem of transfer pricing—the determination of prices for products traded between divisions of a single firm. Here Williamson argues that though the trading divisions "may have profit-center standing, this is apt to be exercised in a restrained way. . . . Cost-plus pricing rules, and variants thereof, preclude supplier divisions from seeking the monopolistic prices [to] which their sole source supply position might otherwise entitle them. In addition, the managements of the trading divisions are more susceptible to appeals for cooperation" (1975, p. 29). But in an intensive empirical study of transfer-pricing practices, Eccles, having interviewed nearly 150 managers in 13 companies, concluded that no cost-based methods could be carried out in a technically neutral way, since there is "no universal criterion for what is cost. . . . Problems often exist with cost-based methods when the buying division does not have access to the information by which the costs are generated. . . . Market prices are especially difficult to determine when internal purchasing is mandated and no external purchases are made of the intermediate good. . . . There is no obvious answer to what is a markup for profit . . ." (1982, p. 21). The political element in transfer-pricing conflicts strongly affects whose definition of "cost" is accepted: "In general, when transfer pricing practices are seen to enhance one's power and status they will be viewed favorably. When they do not, a countless number of strategic and other sound business reasons will be found to argue for their inadequacy" (1982, p. 21; see also Eccles 1983, esp. pp. 26–32). Eccles notes the "somewhat ironic fact that many managers consider internal transactions to be more difficult than external ones, even though vertical integration is pursued for presumed advantages" (1983, p. 28).

Thus, the oversocialized view that orders within a hierarchy elicit easy obedience and that employees internalize the interests of the firm, suppressing any conflict with their own, cannot stand scrutiny against these empirical studies (or, for that matter, against the experience of many of us in actual organizations). Note further that, as shown especially well in Dalton's detailed ethnographic study, resistance to the encroachment of organizational interests on personal or divisional ones requires an extensive network of coalitions. From the viewpoint of management, these coalitions represent malfeasance generated by teams; it could not be managed at all by atomized individuals. Indeed, Dalton asserted that the level of cooperation achieved by divisional chiefs in evading central audits involved joint action "of a kind rarely, if ever, shown in carrying on official activities . . ." (1959, p. 49).

In addition, the generally lower turnover of personnel characteristic of large hierarchical firms, with their well-defined internal labor markets and elaborate promotion ladders, may make such cooperative evasion more likely. When many employees have long tenures, the conditions are met for a dense and stable network of relations, shared understandings, and political coalitions to be constructed. (See Homans 1950, 1974, for the relevant social psychological discussions; and Pfeffer 1983, for a treatment of the "demography of organizations.") James Lincoln notes, in this connection, that in the ideal-typical Weberian bureaucracy, organizations are "designed to function independently of the collective actions which can be mobilized through [internal] interpersonal networks. Bureaucracy prescribes fixed relationships among positions through which incumbents flow, without, in theory, affecting organizational operations" (1982, p. 26). He goes on to summarize studies showing, however, that "when turnover is low, relations take on additional contents of an expressive and personal sort which may ultimately transform the network and change the directions of the organization" (p. 26).

To this point I have argued that social relations between firms are more important, and authority within firms less so, in bringing order to economic life than is supposed in the markets and hierarchies line of thought. A balanced and symmetrical argument requires attention to power in "market" relations and social connections within firms. Attention to power relations is needed lest my emphasis on the smoothing role of social relations in the market lead me to neglect the role of these relations in the conduct of conflict. Conflict is an obvious reality, ranging from well-publicized litigation between firms to the occasional cases of "cutthroat competition" gleefully reported by the business press. Since the effective exercise of power between firms will prevent bloody public battles, we can assume that such battles represent only a small proportion of actual conflicts of interest. Conflicts probably become public only when the two sides are fairly equally matched; recall that this rough equality was precisely one of Hobbes's arguments for a probably "war of all against all" in the "state of nature." But when the power position of one firm is obviously dominant, the other is apt to capitulate early so as to cut its losses. Such capitulation may require not even explicit confrontation but only a clear understanding of what the other side requires (as in the recent Marxist literature on "hegemony" in business life; see, e.g., Mintz and Schwartz 1985).

Though the exact extent to which firms dominate other firms can be debated, the voluminous literature on interlocking directorates, on the role of financial institutions vis-á-vis industrial corporations, and on dual economy surely provides enough evidence to conclude that power relations cannot be neglected. This provides still another reason to doubt that the complexities that arise when formally equal agents negotiate with one another can be resolved only by the subsumption of all parties under a single hierarchy; in fact, many of these complexities are resolved by implicit or explicit power relations *among* firms.

Finally, a brief comment is in order on the webs of social relations that are well known from industrial and organizational sociology to be important within firms. The distinction between the "formal" and the "informal" organization of the firm is one of the oldest in the literature, and it hardly needs repeating that observers who assume firms to be structured in fact by the official organization chart are sociological babes in the woods. The connection of this to the present discussion is that insofar as internalization within firms does result in a better handling of complex and idiosyncratic transactions, it is by no means apparent that hierarchical organization is the best explanation. It may be, instead, that the effect of internalization is to provide a focus (see Feld 1981) for an even denser web of social relations than had occurred between previously independent market entities. Perhaps this web of interaction is mainly what explains the level of efficiency, be it high or low, of the new organizational form.

It is now useful to summarize the differences in explanation and prediction between Williamson's markets and hierarchies approach and the embeddedness view offered here. Williamson explains the inhibition of "opportunism" or malfeasance in economic life and the general existence of cooperation and order by the subsumption of complex economic activity in hierarchically integrated firms. The empirical evidence that I cite shows, rather, that even with complex transactions, a high level of order can often be found in the "market"—that is, across firm boundaries—and a correspondingly high level of disorder within the firm. Whether these occur, instead of what Williamson expects, depends on the nature of personal relations and networks of relations between and within firms. I claim that both order *and* disorder, honesty *and* malfeasance have more to do with structures of such relations than they do with organizational form.

Certain implications follow for the conditions under which one may expect to see vertical integration rather than transactions between firms in a market. Other things being equal, for example, we should expect pressures toward vertical integration in a market where transacting firms lack a network of personal relations that connects them or where such a network eventuates in conflict, disorder, opportunism, or malfeasance. On the other hand, where a stable network of relations mediates complex transactions and generates standards of behavior between firms, such pressures should be absent.

I use the word "pressures" rather than predict that vertical integration will always follow the pattern described in order to avoid the functionalism implicit in Williamson's assumption that whatever organizational form is most efficient will be the one observed. Before we can make this assumption, two further conditions must be satisfied: (i) well-defined and powerful selection pressures toward efficiency must be operating, and (ii) some actors must have the ability and resources to "solve" the efficiency problem by constructing a vertically integrated firm.

The selection pressures that guarantee efficient organization of transactions are nowhere clearly described by Williamson. As in much of the new institutional economics, the need to make such matters explicit is obviated by an implicit Darwinian argument that efficient solutions, however they may originate, have a staying power akin to that enforced by natural selection in the biological world. Thus it is granted that not all business executives "accurately perceive their business opportunities and faultlessly respond. Over time, however, those [vertical] integration moves that have better rationality properties (in transaction cost and scale-economy terms) tend to have better survival properties" (Williamson and Ouchi 1981, p. 389); see also Williamson 1981, pp. 573–74). But Darwinian arguments, invoked in this cavalier fashion, career toward a Panglossian view of whatever institution is analyzed. The operation of alleged selection pressures is here neither an object of study nor even a falsifiable proposition but rather an article of faith.

Even if one could document selection pressures that made survival of certain organizational forms more likely, it would remain to show how such forms could be implemented. To treat them implicitly as mutations, by analogy to biological evolution, merely evades the issue. As in other functionalist explanations, it cannot be automatically assumed that the solution to some problem is feasible. Among the resources required to implement vertical integration might be some measure of market power, access to capital through retained earnings or capital markets, and appropriate connections to legal or regulatory authorities.

Where selection pressures are weak (especially likely in the imperfect markets claimed by Williamson to produce vertical integration) and resources problematic, the social-structural configurations that I have outlined are still related to the efficiency of transaction costs, but no guarantee can be given that an efficient solution will occur. Motives for integration unrelated to efficiency, such as personal aggrandizement of CEOs in acquiring firms, may in such settings become important.

What the viewpoint proposed here requires is that future research on the markets-hierarchies question pay careful and systematic attention to the actual patterns of personal relations by which economic transactions are carried out. Such attention will not only better sort out the motives for vertical integration but also make it easier to comprehend the various complex intermediate forms between idealized atomized markets and completely integrated firms, such as the quasi firm discussed above for the construction industry. Intermediate forms of this kind are so intimately bound up with networks or personal relations that any perspective that considers these relations peripheral will fail to see clearly what "organizational form" has been effected. Existing empirical studies of industrial organization pay little attention to patterns of relations, in part because relevant data are harder to find than those on technology and market structure but also because the dominant economic framework remains one of atomized actors, so personal relations are perceived as frictional in effect.

DISCUSSION

In this article, I have argued that most behavior is closely embedded in networks of interpersonal relations and that such an argument avoids the extremes of under- and oversocialized views of human action. Though I believe this to be so for all behavior, I concentrate here on economic behavior for two reasons: (i) it is the type-case of behavior inadequately interpreted because those who study it professionally are so strongly committed to atomized theories of action; and (ii) with few exceptions, sociologists have refrained from serious study of any subject already claimed by neoclassical economics. They have implicitly accepted the presumption of economists that "market processes" are not suitable objects of sociological study because social relations play only a frictional and disruptive role, not a central one, in modern societies. (Recent exceptions are Baker 1983; Burt 1983; and White 1981.) In those instances in which sociologists study processes where markets are central, they usually still manage to avoid their analysis. Until recently, for example, the large sociological literature on wages was cast in term of "income attainment," obscuring the labor market context in which wages are set and focusing instead on the background and attainment of individuals (see Granovetter 1981 for an extended critique). Or, as Stearns has pointed out, the literature on who controls corporations has implicitly assumed that analysis must be at the level of political relations and broad assumptions about the nature of capitalism. Even though it is widely admitted that how corporations acquire capital is a major determinant of control, most relevant research "since the turn of the century has eliminated that [capital] market as an objective of investigation" (1982, pp. 5–6). Even in organization theory, where considerable literature implements the limits placed on economic decisions by social structural complexity, little attempt has been made to demonstrate the implications of this for the neoclassical theory of the firm or for a general understanding of production or such macroeconomic outcomes as growth, inflation, and unemployment.

In trying to demonstrate that all market processes are amenable to sociological analysis and that such analysis reveals central, not peripheral, features of these processes, I have narrowed by focus to problems of trust and malfeasance. I have also used the "market and hierarchies" argument of Oliver Williamson as an illustration of how the embeddedness perspective generates different understandings and predictions from that implemented by economists. Williamson's perspective is itself "revisionist" within economics, diverging from the neglect of institutional and transactional considerations typical of neoclassical work. In this sense, it may appear to have more kinship to a sociological perspective than the usual economic arguments. But the main thrust of the "new institutional economists" is to deflect the analysis of institutions from sociological, historical, and legal argumentation and show instead that they arise as the efficient solution to economic problems. This mission and the pervasive functionalism it implies discourage the detailed analysis of social structure that I argue here is the key to understanding how existing institutions arrived at their present state.

Insofar as rational choice arguments are narrowly construed as referring to atomized individuals and economic goals, they are inconsistent with the embeddedness position presented here. In a broader formulation of rational choice, however, the two views have much in common. Much of the revisionist work by economists that I criticize above in my discussion of over- and undersocialized conceptions of action relies on a strategy that might be called "psychological revisionism"—an attempt to reform economic theory by abandoning an absolute assumption of rational decision making. This strategy has led to Leibenstein's "selective rationality" in his arguments on "X-inefficiency" (1976), for example, and to the claims of segmented labor-market theorists that workers in different market segments have different kinds of decision-making rules, rational choice being only for upper-primary (i.e., professional, managerial, technical) workers (Piore 1979).

I suggest, in contrast, that while the assumption of rational action must always be problematic, it is a good working hypothesis that should not easily be abandoned. What looks to the analyst like nonrational behavior may be quite sensible when situational constraints, especially those of embeddedness, are fully appreciated. When the social situation of those in nonprofessional labor markets is fully analyzed, their behavior looks less like the automatic application of "cultural" rules and more like a reasonable response to their present situation (as, e.g., in the discussion of Liebow 1966). Managers who evade audits and fight over transfer pricing are acting nonrationally in some strict economic sense, in terms of a firm's profit maximization; but when their position and ambitions in intrafirm networks and political coalitions are analyzed, the behavior is easily interpreted.

That such behavior is rational or instrumental is more readily seen, moreover, if we note that it aims not only at economic goals but also at sociability, approval, status, and power. Economists rarely see such goals as rational, in part on account of the arbitrary separation that arose historically, as Albert Hirschman (1977) points out, in the 17th and 18th centuries, between the "passions" and the "interests," the latter connoting economic motives only. This way of putting the matter has led economists to specialize in analysis of behavior motivated only by "interest" and to assume that other motives occur in separate and nonrationally organized spheres; hence Samuelson's much-quoted comment that "many economists would separate economics from sociology upon the basis of rational or irrational behavior" (1947, p. 90). The notion that rational choice is derailed by social influences had long discouraged detailed sociological analysis of economic life and led revisionist economists to reform economic theory by focusing on its naive psychology. My claim here is that however naive that psychology may be, this is not where the main difficulty lies—it is rather in the neglect of social structure.

Finally, I should add that the level of causal analysis adopted in the embeddedness argument is a rather proximate one. I have had little to say about what broad historical or macrostructural circumstances have led systems to display the social-structural characteristics they have, so I make no claims for this analysis to answer large-scale questions about the nature of modern society or the sources of economic and political change. But the focus on proximate causes is intentional, for these broader questions cannot be satisfactorily addressed without more detailed understanding of the mechanisms by which sweeping change has its effects. My claim is that one of the most important and least analyzed of such mechanisms is the impact of such change on the social relations in which economic life is embedded. If this is so, no adequate link between macro- and micro-level theories can be established without a much fuller understanding of these relations.

The use of embeddedness analysis in explicating proximate causes of patterns of macro-level interest is well illustrated by the markets and hierarchies question. The extent of vertical integration and the reasons for the persistence of small firms operating through the market are not only narrow concerns of industrial organization; they are of interest to all students of the institutions of advanced capitalism. Similar issues arise in the analysis of "dual economy," dependent development, and the nature of modern corporate elites. But whether small firms are indeed eclipsed by giant corporations is usually analyzed in broad and sweeping macropolitical or macroeconomic terms, with little appreciation of proximate social structural causes.

Analysts of dual economy have often suggested, for example, that the persistence of large numbers of small firms in the "periphery" is explained by large corporations' need to shift the risks of cyclical fluctuations in demand or of uncertain R & D activities; failures of these small units will not adversely affect the larger firms' earnings. I suggest here that small firms in a market setting may persist instead because a dense network of social relations is overlaid on the business relations connecting such firms and reduces pressures for integration. This does not rule out risk shifting as an explanation with a certain face validity. But the embeddedness account may be more useful in explaining the large number of small establishments not characterized by satellite or peripheral status. (For a discussion of the surprising extent of employment in small establishments, see Granovetter 1984.) This account is restricted to proximate causes: it logically leads to but does not answer the questions why, when, and in what sectors does the market display various types of social structure. But those questions, which link to a more macro level of analysis, would themselves not arise without a prior appreciation of the importance of social structure in the market.

The markets and hierarchies analysis, important as it may be, is presented here mainly as an illustration. I believe the embeddedness argument to have very general applicability and to demonstrate not only that there is a place for sociologists in the study of economic life but that their perspective is urgently required there. In avoiding the analysis of phenomena at the center of standard economic theory, sociologists have unnecessarily cut themselves off from a large and important aspect of social life and from the European tradition—stemming especially from Max Weber—in which economic action is seen only as a special, if important, category of social action. I hope to have shown here that this Weberian program is consistent with and furthered by some of the insights of modern structural sociology.

NOTES

1. Earlier drafts of this paper were written in sabbatical facilities kindly provided by the Institute for Advanced Study and Harvard University. Financial support was provided in part by the institute, by a John Simon Guggenheim Memorial Foundation fellowship, and by NSF Science Faculty Professional Development grant SPI 81-65055. Among those who have helped clarify the arguments are Wayne Baker, Michael

Bernstein, Albert Hirschman, Ron Jepperson, Eric Leifer, Don McCloskey, Charles Perrow, James Rule, Michael Schwartz, Theda Skocpol, and Harrison White.

2. There are many parallels between what are referred to here as the "under-socialized" and "oversocialized" views of action and what Burt (1982, chap. 9) calls the "atomistic" and "normative" approaches. Similarly, the embeddedness approach proposed here as a middle ground between under- and oversocialized views has an obvious family resemblance to Burt's "structural" approach to action. My distinctions and approach also differ from Burt's in many ways that cannot be quickly summarized; these can be best appreciated by comparison of this article with his useful summary (1982, chap. 9) and with the formal models that implement his conception (1982, 1983). Another approach that resembles mine in its emphasis on how social connections affect purposive action is Marsden's extension of James Coleman's theories of collective action and decision to situations where such connections modify results that would occur in a purely atomistic situation (Marsden 1981, 1983).

3. Students of the sociology of sport will note that this proposition had been put forward previously, in slightly different form, by Leo Durocher.

4. I am indebted to an anonymous referee for pointing this out.

5. Williamson's confidence in the efficacy of hierarchy leads him, in discussing Chester Barnard's "zone of indifference"—that realm within which employees obey orders simply because they are indifferent about whether or not they do what is ordered—to speak instead of a "zone of acceptance" (1975, p. 77), thus undercutting Barnard's emphasis on the problematic nature of obedience. This transformation of Barnard's usage appears to have originated with Herbert Simon, who does not justify it, noting only that he "prefer[s] the term 'acceptance'"(Simon 1957, p. 12)

REFERENCES

Akerlof, George. 1983. "Loyalty Filters." *American Economic Review* 73 (1): 54–63.

Alchian, Armen, and Harold Demsetz. 1973. "The Property Rights Paradigm." *Journal of Economic History* 33 (March): 16–27.

Arrow, Kenneth. 1974. *The Limits of Organization*. New York: Norton.

Baker, Wayne. 1983. "Floor Trading and Crowd Dynamics." in *Social Dynamics of Financial Markets*, edited by Patricia Adler and Peter Adler. Greenwich, Conn.: JAI.

Becker, Gary. 1976. *The Economic Approach to Human Behavior*. Chicago: University of Chicago Press.

Ben-Porath, Yoram. 1980. "The F-Connection: Families, Friends and Firms in the Organization of Exchange." *Population and Development Review* 6 (1): 1–30.

Bowles, Samuel, and Herbert Gintis. 1975. *Schooling in Capitalist America*. New York: Basic.

Brown, Roger. 1965. *Social Psychology*. New York: Free Press.

Burt, Ronald. 1982. *Toward a Structural Theory of Action*. New York: Academic Press.

———. 1983. *Corporate Profits and Cooptation*. New York: Academic Press.

Cole, Robert. 1979. *Work, Mobility and Participation: A Comparative Study of American and Japanese Industry*. Berkeley and Los Angeles: University of California Press.

Dalton, Melville. 1959. *Men Who Manage*. New York: Wiley.

Doeringer, Peter, and Michael Piore. 1971. *Internal Labor Markets and Manpower Analysis*. Lexington, Mass.: Heath.

Domhoff, G. William. 1971. *The Higher Circles*. New York: Random House.

Duesenberry, James. 1960. Comment on "An Economic Analysis of Fertility." In *Demographic and Economic Change in Developed Countries*, edited by the Universities–

National Bureau Committee for Economic Research. Princeton, N.J.: Princeton University Press.

Eccles, Robert. 1981. "The Quasifirm in the Construction Industry." *Journal of Economic Behavior and Organization* 2 (December): 335–57.

————. 1982. "A Synopsis of *Transfer Pricing: An Analysis and Action Plan.*" Mimeographed. Cambridge, Mass.: Harvard Business School.

————. 1983. "Transfer Pricing, Fairness and Control." Working Paper no. HBS 83-167. Cambridge, Mass.: Harvard Business School. Reprinted in *Harvard Business Review* (in press).

Feld, Scott. 1981. "The Focused Organization of Social Ties." *American Journal of Sociology* 86 (5): 1015–35.

Fine, Gary, and Sherryl Kleinman. 1979. "Rethinking Subculture: An Interactionist Analysis." *American Journal of Sociology* 85 (July): 1–20.

Furubotn, E., and S. Pejovich. 1972. "Property Rights and Economic Theory: A Survey of Recent Literature." *Journal of Economic Literature* 10 (3): 1137–62.

Geertz, Clifford. 1979. "Suq: The Bazaar Economy in Sefrou." Pp. 123–225 in *Meaning and Order in Moroccan Society*, edited by C. Geertz, H. Geertz, and L. Rosen. New York: Cambridge University Press.

Granovetter, Mark. 1974. *Getting a Job: A Study of Contacts and Careers*. Cambridge, Mass.: Harvard University Press.

————. 1981. "Toward a Sociological Theory of Income Differences." Pp. 11–47 in *Sociological Perspectives on Labor Markets*, edited by Ivar Berg. New York: Academic Press.

————. 1983. "Labor Mobility, Internal Markets and Job-Matching: A Comparison of the Sociological and Economic Approaches." Mimeographed.

————. 1984. "Small Is Bountiful: Labor Markets and Establishment Size." *American Sociological Review* 49 (3): 323–34.

Hirschman, Albert. 1977. *The Passions and the Interests*. Princeton, N.J.: Princeton University Press.

————. 1982. "Rival Interpretations of Market Society: Civilizing, Destructive or Feeble?" *Journal of Economic Literature* 20 (4): 1463–84.

Homans, George. 1950. *The Human Group*. New York: Harcourt Brace & Co.

————. 1974. *Social Behavior*. New York: Harcourt Brace Jovanovich.

Lazear, Edward. 1979. "Why Is There Mandatory Retirement?" *Journal of Political Economy* 87 (6): 1261–84.

Leibenstein, Harvey. 1976. *Beyond Economic Man*. Cambridge, Mass.: Harvard University Press.

Liebow, Elliot. 1966. *Tally's Corner*. Boston: Little, Brown.

Lincoln, James. 1982. "Intra- (and Inter-) Organizational Networks." Pp. 1–38 in *Research in the Sociology of Organizations*, vol. 1. Edited by S. Bacharach. Greenwich, Conn.: JAI.

Lohr, Steve. 1982. "When Money Doesn't Matter in Japan." *New York Times* (December 30).

Macaulay, Stewart. 1963. "Non-Contractual Relations in Business: A Preliminary Study." *American Sociological Review* 28 (1): 55–67.

Marsden, Peter. 1981. "Introducing Influence Processes into a System of Collective Decisions." *American Journal of Sociology* 86 (May): 1203–35.

————. 1983. "Restricted Access in Networks and Models of Power." *American Journal of Sociology* 88 (January): 686–17.

Merton, Robert. 1947. "Manifest and Latent Functions." Pp. 19–84 in *Social Theory and Social Structure*. New York: Free Press.

Mintz, Beth, and Michael Schwartz. 1985. *The Power Structure of American Business.* Chicago: University of Chicago Press.

North, D., and R. Thomas. 1973. *The Rise of the Western World.* Cambridge: Cambridge University Press.

Okun, Arthur. 1981. *Prices and Quantities.* Washington, D.C.: Brookings.

Pakes, Ariel, and S. Nitzan. 1982. "Optimum Contracts for Research Personnel, Research Employment and the Establishment of 'Rival' Enterprises." NBER Working Paper no. 871. Cambridge, Mass.: National Bureau of Economic Research.

Parsons, Talcott. 1937. *The Structure of Social Action.* New York: Macmillan.

Pfeffer, Jeffrey. 1983. "Organizational Demography." In *Research in Organizational Behavior,* vol. 5. Edited by L. L. Cummings and B. Staw. Greenwich, Conn.: JAI.

Phelps Brown, Ernst Henry. 1977. *The Inequality of Pay.* Berkeley: University of California Press.

Piore, Michael. 1975. "Notes for a Theory of Labor Market Stratification." Pp. 125–50 in *Labor Market Segmentation,* edited by R. Edwards, M. Reich, and D. Gordon. Lexington, Mass.: Heath.

———, ed. 1979. *Unemployment and Inflation.* White Plains, N.Y.: Sharpe.

Polanyi, Karl. 1944. *The Great Transformation.* New York: Holt, Rinehart.

Polanyi, Karl, C. Arensberg, and H. Pearson. 1957. *Trade and Market in the Early Empires.* New York: Free Press.

Popkin, Samuel. 1979. *The Rational Peasant.* Berkeley and Los Angeles: University of California Press.

Rosen, Sherwin. 1982. "Authority, Control and the Distribution of Earnings." *Bell Journal of Economics* 13 (2): 311–23.

Samuelson, Paul. 1947. *Foundations of Economic Analysis.* Cambridge, Mass.: Harvard University Press.

Schneider, Harold. 1974. *Economic Man: The Anthropology of Economics.* New York: Free Press.

Schotter, Andrew. 1981. *The Economic Theory of Social Institutions.* New York: Cambridge University Press.

Scott, James. 1976. *The Moral Economy of the Peasant.* New Haven, Conn.: Yale University Press.

Shenon, Philip. 1984. "Margolies Is Found Guilty of Murdering Two Women." *New York Times* (June 1).

Simon, Herbert. 1957. *Administrative Behavior.* Glencoe, Ill.: Free Press.

Smith, Adam. (1776) 1979. *The Wealth of Nations.* Edited by Andrew Skinner. Baltimore: Penguin.

Stearns, Linda. 1982. "Corporate Dependency and the Structure of the Capital Market: 1880–1980." Ph.D. dissertation, State University of New York at Stony Brook.

Thompson, E. P. 1971. "The Moral Economy of the English Crowd in the Eighteenth Century." *Past and Present* 50 (February): 76–136.

Useem, Michael. 1979. "The Social Organization of the American Business Elite and Participation of Corporation Directors in the Governance of American Institutions." *American Sociological Review* 44:553–72.

Webster, Frederick, and Yoram Wind. 1972. *Organizational Buying Behavior.* Englewood Cliffs, N.J.: Prentice-Hall.

White, Harrison C. 1981. "Where Do Markets Come From?" *American Journal of Sociology* 87 (November): 517–47.

Williamson, Oliver. 1975. *Markets and Hierarchies.* New York: Free Press.

———. 1979. "Transaction-Cost Economics: The Governance of Contractual Relations." *Journal of Law and Economics* 22 (2): 233–61.

————. 1981. "The Economics of Organization: The Transaction Cost Approach."
American Journal of Sociology 87 (November): 548–77.
Williamson, Oliver, and William Ouchi. 1981. "The Markets and Hierarchies and
Visible Hand Perspectives." Pp. 347–70 in *Perspectives on Organizational Design
and Behavior*, edited by Andrew Van de Ven and William Joyce. New York: Wiley.
Wrong, Dennis. 1961. "The Oversocialized Conception of Man in Modern Sociology."
American Sociological Review 26 (2): 183–93.

EDITORS' NOTES ON FURTHER READING: GRANOVETTER

For other broad programmatic statements of the agenda for economic sociology,
see Paul Hirsch, Stuart Michaels, and Ray Friedman, " 'Dirty Hands' Versus 'Clean
Models': Is Sociology in Danger of Being Seduced by Economics?" *Theory and Society*
16 (1987):317–336; Richard Swedberg, Göran Brulin, and Ulf Himmelstrand, "The
Paradigm of Economic Sociology: Premises and Promises," *Theory and Society* 16
(1987):169–213 (both reprinted in Sharon Zukin and Paul DiMaggio, eds., *Structures
of Capital: The Social Organization of the Economy* [1990]); and Fred Block, "Economic
Sociology," pp. 21–45 in *Postindustrial Possibilities: A Critique of Economic Discourse*
(1990). For an overview of old and new economic sociology, see Richard Swedberg,
"Major Traditions of Economic Sociology," *Annual Review of Sociology* 17 (1991):251–
276.

Empirical studies of the role of social networks in the economy include two
studies of banking—Beth Mintz and Michael Schwartz, *The Power Structure of American
Business* (1985) and Robert Eccles and Dwight Crane, *Doing Deals: Investment Banks
at Work* (1988)—and Mark Granovetter's earlier study of the labor market, *Getting
A Job: A Study of Contacts and Careers* (1974). Network studies of economic topics
such as money, markets, and corporations can also be found in Mark Mizruchi and
Michael Schwartz, eds., *Intercorporate Relations: The Structural Analysis of Business*
(1987) and Barry Wellman and S. D. Berkowitz, eds., *Social Structures: A Network
Approach* (1988). An attempt to spell out the meaning of "network forms of organization" can be found in Walter Powell's "Neither Market Nor Hierarchy," pp. 295–
336 in L. L. Cummings and B. Staw, eds., *Research in Organizational Behavior* (1990).

On the importance of trust in the economy, see Susan Shapiro, *Wayward Capitalists:
Target of the Securities and Exchange Commission* (1984) and "The Social Control of
Impersonal Trust," *American Journal of Sociology* 93 (1987):623–658; and Lynne G.
Zucker, "Production of Trust: Institutional Sources of Economic Structure, 1840–
1920," *Research in Organizational Behavior* 8 (1986):53–111. The idea that trust is
essential to economic life also informs the sociological classic: Georg Simmel, *The
Philosophy of Money* (Eng. tr. 1978). An unorthodox economist's view of the matter
can be found in Kenneth Arrow's *The Limits of Organization* (1974).

An important part of Granovetter's argument is his critique of New Institutional
Economics. Other sociological critiques include Charles Perrow's biting "Economic
Theories of Organization," chapter 7 in *Complex Organizations: A Critical Essay*, 3d
ed. (1987); Amitai Etzioni's *The Moral Dimension: Toward a New Economics* (1988);
and Richard Swedberg's "The New 'Battle of the Methods,'" *Challenge* (January–
February 1990):33–38. Less critical toward this literature are Mayer Zald, "Review
Essay (of Oliver Williamson's *The Economic Institutions of Capitalism*): The New
Institutional Economics," *American Journal of Sociology* 93 (1987):701–708; Anthony
Oberschall and Eric M. Leifer, "Efficiency and Social Institutions: Uses and Misuses
of Economic Reasoning in Sociology," *Annual Review of Sociology* 12 (1986):233–253;
Robert Bates, "Contra Contractarianism: Some Reflections on the New Institution-

alism," *Politics and Society* 16 (1988):387–401; and Christopher Winship and Sherwin Rosen, "Introduction: Sociological and Economic Approaches to the Analysis of Social Structure," *American Journal of Sociology (Supplement)* 94 (1988):S1–S16. Economists' views of sociological critiques can be found in the interviews with Gary Becker and Oliver Williamson in Richard Swedberg's *Economics and Sociology: On Redefining Their Boundaries. Conversations with Economists and Sociologists* (1990). This book also contains an interview with Granovetter in which, among other things, he extends the structural approach to account for the emergence of such economic institutions as firms and industries.

PART II

Historical and Comparative Perspectives on the Economy

3

Weber's Last Theory of Capitalism: A Systematization

RANDALL COLLINS

Max Weber had many intellectual interests, and there has been considerable debate over the question of what constitutes the central theme of his life work. Besides treating the origins of capitalism, Weber dealt extensively with the nature of modernity and of rationality (Tenbruck, 1975; Kalberg, 1979; 1980; Seidman, 1980), and with politics, methodology, and various substantive areas of sociology. Amid all the attention which has been paid to these concerns, one of Weber's most significant contributions has been largely ignored. This is his mature theory of the development of capitalism, found in his last work (1961), *General Economic History.*

This is ironic because Weber's (1930) first major work, *The Protestant Ethic and the Spirit of Capitalism,* has long been the most famous of all. The argument that the Calvinist doctrine of predestination gave the psychological impetus for rationalized, entrepreneurial capitalism is only a fragment of Weber's full theory. But many scholars have treated it as Weber's distinctive contribution, or Weber's distinctive fallacy, on the origins of capitalism (e.g., Tawney, 1938; McClelland, 1961; Samuelsson, 1961; Cohen, 1980). Debate about the validity of this part of Weber's theory has tended to obscure the more fundamental historical and institutional theory which he presented in his later works.

The so-called "Weber thesis," as thus isolated, has been taken to be essentially idealist. Weber (1930:90) defines his purpose in *The Protestant Ethic* as "a contribution to the manner in which ideas become effective forces in history." He (1930:183) polemically remarks against the Marxists

I am indebted to Vatro Murvar and other participants at the Max Weber Symposium at the University of Wisconsin at Milwaukee, March, 1978, and to Samuel W. Kaplan, Stephen Kalberg, Guenther Roth, Walter Goldfrank, Norbert Wiley, and Whitney Pope, for their suggestions on an earlier version of this argument.

From *American Sociological Review* 45 (December 1980):925–942. Reprinted by permission.

that he does not intend to replace a one-sided materialism with its opposite, but his correcting of the balance sheet in this work concentrates largely on ideal factors. The germ of Weber's institutional theory of capitalism can also be found in *The Protestant Ethic* (1930:58, 76).[1] But it remained an undeveloped backdrop for his main focus on the role of religious ideas. The same may be said about his (1951; 1952; 1958b) comparative studies of the world religions. These broadened considerably the amount of material on social, economic, and political conditions, but the main theme still stressed that divergent ideas made an autonomous contribution to the emergence of world-transforming capitalism in the Christian West rather than elsewhere in the world.[2] Thus, Parsons (1963; 1967) treats these works as extending the early Weber thesis from Protestantism to Christianity in general, describing an evolution of religious ideas and their accompanying motivational propensities from ancient Judaism up through the secularized achievement culture of the modern United States.

From these works, and from (1968) Part II of *Economy and Society*, it is possible to pull out an extensive picture of institutional factors which Weber includes in his overall theory of capitalism. But *Economy and Society* is organized encyclopedically, by analytically defined topics, and does not pull together the theory as a whole. There is only one place in Weber's works where he brings together the full theory of capitalism as a historical dynamic. This is in the *General Economic History*, and, especially, in the 70-page section comprising Part IV of that work. These lectures, delivered in the winter and spring of 1919–20, before Weber's death that summer, are Weber's last word on the subject of capitalism. They are also the most neglected of his works; *General Economic History* is the only one of Weber's major works that remains out of print today, both in English and in German.

One important change in the *General Economic History* is that Weber pays a good deal more attention to Marxian themes than previously. This is a significant difference from the anti-Marxist comments scattered through *The Protestant Ethic* (e.g., pp. 55–56, 61, 90–91, 183). In the *General Economic History*, Weber reduces the ideal factor to a relatively small place in his overall scheme. During this same period, to be sure, Weber was preparing a new introduction and footnotes for the reissue of *The Protestant Ethic* among his collected religious writings, in which he defended his original thesis about Calvinism. But his claims for its importance in the overall scheme of things were not large, and the well-rounded model which he presents in *General Economic History* does not even mention the doctrine of predestination. Instead, what we find is a predominantly institutional theory, in which religious *organization* plays a key role in the rise of modern capitalism but especially in conjunction with particular forms of political organization.

In what follows, I will attempt to state systematically Weber's mature theory of capitalism, as it appears in the *General Economic History*, bolstered where appropriate by the building blocks presented in *Economy and Society*. This argument involves a series of causes, which we will trace backward, from the most recent to the most remote. This model, I would suggest, is the most comprehensive general theory of the origins of capitalism that is yet available. It continues to stand up well in comparison with recent theories, including Wallerstein's (1974) historical theory of the capitalist world-system.

Weber himself was primarily concerned with the sensitizing concepts necessary for an interpretation of the unique pattern of history and, in his methodological writings, he disavowed statements in the form of general causal principles (cf. Burger, 1976). Nevertheless, Weber's typologies contain implicit generalizations about the effects of institutional arrangements upon each other, and statements of cause-and-effect abound in his substantive writings. There is nothing to prevent us from stating his historical picture of changing institutional forms in a more abstract and generalized manner than Weber did himself.

Weber's model continues to offer a more sophisticated basis for a theory of capitalism than any of the rival theories of today. I put forward this formalization of Weber's mature theory, not merely as an appreciation of one of the classic works of the past, but to make clear the high-water mark of sociological theory about capitalism. Weber's last theory is not the last word on the subject of the rise of capitalism, but if we are to surpass it, it is the high point from which we ought to build.

THE COMPONENTS OF RATIONALIZED CAPITALISM

Capitalism, says Weber (1961:207–8, 260) is the provision of human needs by the method of enterprise, which is to say, by private businesses seeking profit. It is exchange carried out for positive gain, rather than forced contributions or traditionally fixed gifts or trades. Like all of Weber's categories, capitalism is an analytical concept; capitalism can be found as part of many historical economies, as far back as ancient Babylon. It became the indispensable form for the provision of everyday wants only in Western Europe around the middle of the nineteenth century. For this large-scale and economically predominant capitalism, the key is the "rational permanent enterprise" characterized by "rational capital accounting."

The concept of "rationality" which appears so often in Weber's works has been the subject of much debate. Marxist critics of capitalism, as well as critics of bureaucracy, have attacked Weber's alleged glorification of these social forms (e.g., Hirst, 1976). On the other hand, Parsons (1947), in his long introduction to the definitional section of *Economy and Society*, gives "rationalization" both an idealist and an evolutionary bent, as the master trend of world history, involving an inevitable upgrading of human cognitive and organizational capacities. Tenbruck (1975) claims the key to Weber's works is an inner logic of rational development found within the realm of religious solutions to the problem of suffering.

It is clear that Weber himself used the term "rationalism" in a number of different senses.[3] But for his *institutional* theory of capitalist development, there is only one sense that need concern us. The "rational capitalistic establishment," says Weber (1961:207), "is one with capital accounting, that is, an establishment which determines its income yielding power by calculation according to the methods of modern bookkeeping and the striking of a balance." The key term is *calculability;* it occurs over and over again in those pages. What is distinctive about modern, large-scale, "rational" capitalism—in contrast to earlier, partial forms—is that it is methodical and predictable, reducing all areas of production and distribution as much as possible to a routine. This is also Weber's criterion for calling bureaucracy the most "rational" form of organization.[4]

For a capitalist economy to have a high degree of predictability, it must have certain characteristics. The logic of Weber's argument is first to describe these characteristics; then to show the obstacles to them that were prevalent in virtually all societies of world history until recent centuries in the West; and, finally, by the method of comparative analysis, to show the social conditions responsible for their emergence.

According to his argument, the components of "rationalized" capitalism are as follows:

There must be *private appropriation of all the means of production,* and their concentration under the control of entrepreneurs. Land, buildings, machinery, and materials must all be assembled under a common management, so that decisions about their acquisition and use can be calculated with maximal efficiency. All these factors must be subject to sale as private goods on an open market. This development reaches its maximal scope when all such property rights are represented by commercial instruments, especially shares in ownership which are themselves negotiable in a stock market.

Within this enterprise, capital accounting is optimized by a *technology which is "reduced to calculation to the largest possible degree"* (1961:208). It is in this sense that mechanization is most significant for the organization of large-scale capitalism.

Labor must be free to move about to any work in response to conditions of demand. Weber notes that this is a formal and legal freedom, and that it goes along with the economic compulsion of workers to sell their labor on the market. Capitalism is impossible without a propertyless stratum selling its services "under the compulsion of the whip of hunger" (1961:209), for only this completes a mass market system for the factors of production which makes it possible to clearly calculate the costs of products in advance.

Trading in the market must not be limited by irrational restrictions. That is to say, noneconomic restrictions on the movement of goods or of any of the factors of production must be minimized. Such restrictions include class monopolies upon particular items of consumption (such as sumptuary laws regulating dress), or upon ownership or work (such as prohibitions on townspeople owning land, or on knights or peasants carrying on trade; more extensively, caste systems in general). Other obstacles under this heading include transportation difficulties, warfare, and robbery—which make long-distance trading hazardous and unreliable.

Finally, there must be *calculable law, both in adjudication and in public administration.* Laws must be couched in general terms applicable to all persons, and administered in such a way as to make the enforcement of economic contracts and rights highly predictable. Such a legal system is implicated in most of the above characteristics of rational capitalism: the extension of private property rights over the factors of production; the subdivision and easy transferability of such rights through financial instruments and banking operations; formal freedom for laborers; and legally protected markets.

The picture that Weber gives us, then, is of the institutional foundations of the market as viewed by neoclassical economics. He sees the market as providing the maximal amount of calculability for the individual entrepreneur. Goods, labor, and capital flow continuously to the areas of maximal return; at the same time, competition in all markets reduces costs to their minimum. Thus, prices serve to summarize all the necessary information about the optimal allocation of resources for maximizing profit; on this basis, entrepreneurs can most reliably make calculations for long-term production of large amounts of goods. "To sum up," says Weber (1961:209), "it must be possible to conduct the provision for needs exclusively on the basis of market opportunities and the calculation of net income."

It is, of course, the model of the laissez-faire capitalist economy that Weber wishes to ground. At the extreme, this is an unrealistic view of any economy that has ever existed. Weber treats it as an ideal type and, hence, in a fuller exposition would doubtless have been prepared to see it as only partially realized even in the great capitalist takeoff period of the nineteenth century. But it is worth noting that a critique of Weber along these lines could certainly not be a classical Marxian one. The central dynamic of capitalism in Marx's theory, in fact, depends even more immediately than Weber's on the unrestricted competitiveness of the open market for all factors of production (cf. Sweezy, 1942). And Weber and Marx agree in claiming that the initial breakthrough to an industrial society had to occur in the form of capitalism. Thus, although Weber may have a personal bias toward the neoclassical market economy, both as analytical model and as political preference, this would give no grounds for a critique of the adequacy of his explanation of this phase of world history. Even for a later period, Weber is hardly dogmatic. As we shall see, he recognizes the possibility of socialism emerging, once capitalism has matured—although he does not admire the prospect—and he even gives some indications of the forces that might produce it. Like German and Austrian non-Marxist economists of his generation, Weber includes socialism within his analytical scheme.

Weber's model of the modern economy is particularly striking with regard to the concept of the "industrial revolution." For it is not mechanization per se that is the key to the economic transformation, despite the far-reaching consequences of shifts from agrarian to inanimate-energy-based technologies (cf. Lenski, 1966). In Weber's scheme, technology is essentially a dependent variable. The key *economic* characteristic of mechanization is that it is feasible only with mass production (Weber, 1961:129, 247). The costs of even simpler machines such as steam-powered looms would make them worthless without a large-scale consumers' market for cloth, as well as a large-scale producers' market in wool or cotton. Similar considerations apply a fortiori to machinery on the scale of a steel rolling mill. But large-scale production is impossible without a high degree of predictability that markets will exist for the products, and that all the factors of production will be forthcoming at a reasonable cost. Thus, mechanization depends on the prior emergence of all the institutional factors described above.

Weber does not elaborate a systematic theory of technological innovation, but it would be possible to construct one along these lines. He does note that all the crucial inventions of the period of industrial takeoff were the result of deliberate efforts to cheapen the costs of production (1961:225–6, 231). These efforts took place because previous conditions had intensified the capitalist pursuit of profits. The same argument could be made, although Weber did not make it, in regard to the search for methods to improve agricultural production that took place in the seventeenth and eighteenth centuries. The "green revolution" which preceded (and made possible) the industrial revolution was not a process of mechanization (agricultural mechanization took place only in the late nineteenth century) but was, more simply, the application of capitalist methods of cost accounting to hitherto traditional agriculture. Thus, it is the shift to the calculating practices of the capitalist market economy which makes technological innovation itself predictable, rather than, as previously, an accidental factor in economic life (1961:231).[5]

THE CAUSAL CHAIN

What are the social preconditions for the emergence of capitalism as thus described?

Note, first of all, that economic life, even in the most prosperous of agrarian societies, generally lacked most of these traits. Property systems frequently tied land ownership to aristocratic status, while commercial occupations were often prohibited to certain groups and monopolized by others. The labor force was generally unfree—being either slaves or tied to the land as serfs. Technologies of mass production hardly existed. The market was generally limited either to local areas or to long-distance trade in luxuries, due to numerous near-confiscatory tax barriers, unreliable and varying coinage, warfare, robbery, and poor transportation. And legal systems, even in literate states, tended to be characterized by patrimonial or magical-religious procedures, by differential application to different social groups and by different localities, and by the practices of officials seeking private gain. Reliable financial transactions, including the operation of a banking system relatively free from political interference and plundering, were particularly handicapped by these conditions.

The social preconditions for large-scale capitalism, then, involved the destruction of the obstacles to the free movement or economic transfer of labor, land, and goods. Other preconditions were the creation of the institutional supports for large-scale markets, especially the appropriate systems of property, law, and finance.

These are not the only preconditions of capitalism, but, specifically, Weber is seeking the organizational forms that made capitalism a world-transforming force in the West but not elsewhere. By a series of comparisons, Weber shows that a number of other factors that have been advanced to account for the Western takeoff cannot have been crucial. Against Sombart, he points out that standardized mass production for war cannot have been decisive for, although a good deal of this existed in Europe in the seventeenth century, and thereafter, it also existed in the Mogul Empire and in China without giving an impetus to capitalism (1961:229). Similarly, the enormous expenditures for court luxury found in both Orient and Occident were incapable of generating a mass market (1961:229–30). Against the simpler arguments of Adam Smith, which attribute the industrial division of labor to the extension of trade, Weber points out that trade can be found everywhere, even in the Stone Age. In ancient Babylon, for example, trade was such as to disintegrate "primitive economic fixity" to a considerable degree (1961:232). On the other hand, politically determined agrarian economies show how "specialization takes place without exchange" (1961:103). Nor is the pursuit of profit per se the crucial motive for mass capitalism; the "ruthlessness" and "unscrupulousness" of the traditional foreign trader was incapable of transforming the economy at large (1961:232). Nor can population growth have been the cause of Western capitalism, for the same trend occurred in China without the same result (1961:258–9). Neither, finally, can the price revolution of the sixteenth century, due to the influx of precious metals from the Americas, have been decisive (see the later discussion on Wallerstein).[6]

The features that Weber finds unique to the West constitute a causal chain.[7] I have represented this schematically in Figure [3.]1. The characteristics of rational capitalism itself are the entrepreneurial organization of capital, rational technology, free labor, unrestricted markets, and calculable law. These make up a complex: the markets for goods, labor, and capital all mesh around entrepreneurial property using mass production technology; the operation of all of these factors together creates further pressures to both rationalize technology and expand each factor market—while yet distributing wealth in such a way as to further the demand. The legal system is both an ongoing prop for all of these features and a causal link backward to their social preconditions. At this intermediate causal level there is a second crucial factor which, like the law, is essentially cultural, although not in the sense of disembodied ideas, but, rather, in the sense of beliefs expressed in institutionalized behavior. This is the "lifting of the barrier . . . between internal and external ethics" (1961:232).

In virtually all premodern societies there are two sharply divergent sets of ethical beliefs and practices. Within a social group, economic transactions are strictly controlled by rules of fairness, status, and tradition: in tribal

FIGURE [3.]1 The Weberian causal chain

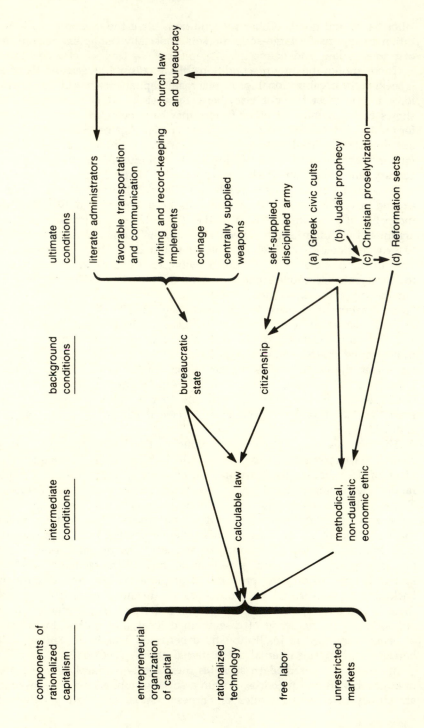

societies, by ritualized exchanges with prescribed kin; in India, by rules of caste; in medieval Europe, by required contributions on the manor or to the great church properties. The prohibition on usury reflected this internal ethic, requiring an ethic of charity and the avoidance of calculation of gain from loans within the community (cf. Nelson, 1949).[8] In regard to outsiders, however, economic ethics were at the opposite extreme: cheating, price gouging, and loans at exorbitant interest were the rule. Both forms of ethic were obstacles to rational, large-scale capitalism: the internal ethic because it prevented the commercialization of economic life, the external ethic because it made trading relations too episodic and distrustful. The lifting of this barrier and the overcoming of this ethical dualism were crucial for the development of any extensive capitalism. Only this could make loans available regularly and promote the buying and selling of all services and commodities for moderate gain. Through innumerable daily repetitions, such small (but regular) profits could add up to much more massive economic transactions than could either the custom-bound or the predatory economic ethics of traditional societies.

What, then, produced the calculable legal system of saleable private property and free labor and the universal ethic of the pursuit of moderate economic profit? The next links in the causal chain are political and religious. The bureaucratic state is a crucial background determinant for all legal and institutional underpinnings of capitalism. Moreover, its legal system must be based on a concept of universal citizenship, which requires yet further political preconditions. The religious factor operates both as a direct influence on the creation of an economic ethic and as a final level of causality implicated in the rise of the rational-legal state and of legal citizenship.

The state is the factor most often overlooked in Weber's theory of capitalism. Yet it is the factor to which he gave the most attention; in *Economy and Society*, he devoted eight chapters of 519 pages to it, as opposed to one chapter of 236 pages to religion, with yet another chapter—the neglected but very important chap. XIV of Part II—to the relations between politics and religion. In the *General Economic History*, he gives the state the two penultimate chapters, religion the final chapter. For Weber, this political material was not an extraneous interest but, instead, the key to all of the *institutional* structures of rational capitalism. Only the West developed the highly bureaucratized state, based on specialized professional administrators and on a law made and applied by full-time professional jurists for a populace characterized by rights of citizenship. It is this bureaucratic-legal state that broke down feudalism and patrimonialism, freeing land and labor for the capitalist market. It is this state that pacified large territories, eliminated internal market barriers, standardized taxation and currencies. It is this state that provided the basis for a reliable system of banking, investment, property, and contracts, through a rationally calculable and universally applied system of law courts. One may even argue that the bureaucratic state was the proximate cause of the impulse to rationalization, generally—above all, via the late seventeenth- and eighteenth-century spirit of enlightened absolutism, which set the stage for the industrial revolution.

There are three causal questions about the rational/legal state. Why did it rise to predominance? Where did its structural characteristics come from? How did its legal system take the special form of conceiving of its subjects as holding the rights of citizenship?

The first question is easily answered. The bureaucratic state rose to predominance because it is the most efficient means of pacifying a large territory. It is effective externally in that it can supply a larger military, with better weapons, than can nonbureaucratic states; and it is effective, internally, as it tends to be relatively safe against disintegration by civil war or political *coup*.[9]

The sources of the bureaucratic state are, to a degree, quite familiar. In the widely reprinted section on bureaucracy from *Economy and Society* (1968:956–1005), Weber outlines the prerequisites: literate administrators, a technology of long-distance transportation and communication, writing and record-keeping materials, monetary coinage. The extent to which these could be put into effect, however, depended on a number of other factors. Geographical conditions such as easy transportation in river valleys, or favorable situations for state-controlled irrigation (1961:237), fostered bureaucratic centralization, as did intense military competition among adjacent heartlands. Types of weapons which are centrally (rather than individually supplied) also favor bureaucratization. If such conditions make central control easy, however, bureaucratization need not proceed very deeply, and the society may be ruled by a thin stratum of officials above a local structure which remains patrimonial. In China, for example, this superficial bureaucratization constituted a long-term obstacle to capitalism, as it froze the economy under the patrimonial control of local clans.

The most thorough bureaucratization, as well as that uniquely favorable to capitalism, is that which incorporates a formalistic legal code based on citizenship. Citizenship meant, first of all, membership in a city; by extension, membership in a state and hence holder of political rights within it. This was an alien concept throughout most of history. In the patrimonial state, political office was a form of private property or personal delegation, and even in most premodern quasi-bureaucratic states the populace at large was only subject to the state, not holders of rights within it. The latter condition arose only in the West. In both Mediterranean antiquity and the European Middle Ages, cities came under the control of brotherhoods of warriors banded together for mutual protection. Such cities had their own laws and courts, administered by the citizens themselves, all of whom stood under it in relation of formal equality. Such citizenship rights remained historically significant after the original civic forms changed or disappeared. The formal rights and legal procedures originally applied only to a local elite, but when cities were incorporated into large-scale bureaucratic states, they provided the basis for a much more widely inclusive system of adjudication. This was the case when Rome, originally one of these military-fraternity cities, became an empire and, again, in the Middle Ages, when cities in alliance with kings lost their independence but contributed their legal structures to the larger states.[10]

Nearing the end of our chain of causality, we ask: What factors enabled this distinctive type of city to arise in the West? Weber gives two conditions: one military, the other religious.

The military condition is that in the West the city consisted of "an organization of those economically competent to bear arms, to equip and train themselves" (1961:237). This was the case in the formative period of the ancient Greek and Italian cities and, again, in the medieval cities with their disciplined infantries fielded by the guilds. In both cases, the money power of the cities bolstered their military power and, hence, democratization and concomitant legal citizenship. In the Orient and in ancient Egypt, on the contrary, the military princes with their armies were older than the cities and, hence, legally independent cities did not arise; Weber attributed this pattern to the impetus to early centralization given by irrigation.

The second condition is that in the East, magical taboos prevented the organization of military alliances among strangers and, hence, did not allow formation of independent cities. In India, for example, the ritual exclusion of castes had this effect. More generally, in Asia and the Middle East, the traditional priests held monopolies over communion with the gods, whereas in Western antiquity it was the officials of the city who themselves performed the rites (1961:238). In the one case, the boundaries of religious communion reinforced preexisting group divisions; in the other, religious boundaries were an explicit political tool by which civic alliances could be established and enlarged. It is at this point that the two main lines of Weber's chain of causality converge.

We have been tracing the causal links behind the emergence of the rational/legal state, which is one of the two great intermediate conditions of the emergence of an open market economy. The other great intermediate condition (noted earlier) is an economic ethic which breaks the barrier between internal and external economies. Now we see that the religious factors that produced the citizenship revolution and those that produced the economic ethic are essentially the same.

Our last question, then, is: What brought about this religious transformation? Weber gives a series of reasons, each intensifying the effects of the last (1961:238). Ethical prophecy within ancient Judaism was important, even though it did not break down ritual barriers between Jews and Gentiles, because it established a tradition of hostility to magic, the main ethos within which barriers flourished. The transformation of Christianity from a Jewish sect into a proselytizing universal religion gave this tradition widespread currency, while the pentacostal spirit of Christian proselytization set aside the ritual barriers among clans and tribes, which still characterized the ancient Hellenistic cities to some degree. The Judeo-Christian innovations are not the whole story, however; the earlier development of Greek religion into the civic cults had already done much to make universalistic legal membership possible.

The religious factors, as we have seen, entwine with political ones, and their influence in the direction of legal citizenship and upon an economic ethic have fluctuated historically. There is no steady nor inevitable trend toward increasing rationalization of these spheres, but Western history does contain a series of episodes which happen to have built up these effects at particular points in time so that, eventually, a whole new economic dynamic was unleashed. On the political side, the Christian cities of the Middle Ages, drawing upon the institutional legacies of the ancient world, were able to establish religiously sworn confraternities which reestablished a legal system based on citizenship. A second political factor was fostered by religion: the Christian church provided the literate administrators, the educational system, and the example of its own bureaucratic organization as bases upon which the bureaucratic states of the West could emerge. And, on the strictly motivational side, the development of European Christianity gave a decisive ethical push toward rationalized capitalism.

Here, at last, we seem to touch base with Weber's original Protestant Ethic thesis. But in the mature Weber, the thesis is greatly transformed. Protestantism is only the last intensification of one of the chains of factors leading to rational capitalism. Moreover, its effect now is conceived to be largely negative, in the sense that it removes one of the last institutional obstacles diverting the motivational impetus of Christianity away from economic rationalization. For, in medieval Christianity, the methodical, disciplined organization of life was epitomized by the monastic communities.[11] Although the monasteries contributed to economic development by rationalizing agriculture and promoting their own industries, Weber generally saw them as obstacles to the full capitalist development of the secular economy. As long as the strongest religious motivation was siphoned off for essentially otherworldly ends, capitalism in general could not take off (1961:267–9). Hence, the Reformation was most significant because it abolished the monasteries. The most advanced section of the economy would, henceforth, be secular. Moreover, the highest ethics of a religious life could no longer be confined to monks but had to apply to ordinary citizens living in the world. Calvinism and the other voluntary sects were the most intense version of this motivation, not because of the idea of Predestination (which no longer receives any mention in Weber's last text) but only because they required a specific religious calling for admission into their ranks, rather than automatic and compulsory membership in the politically more conservative churches. Weber's (1961:269–70) last word on the subject of Protestantism was simply this:

> The development of the concept of the calling quickly gave to the modern entrepreneur a fabulously clear conscience—and also industrious workers; he gave to his employees as the wages of their ascetic devotion to the calling and of co-operation in his ruthless exploitation of them through capitalism the prospect of eternal salvation, which in an age when ecclesiastical discipline took control of the whole of life to an extent inconceivable to us now, represented a reality quite different from any it has today. The Catholic and Lutheran churches also recognized and practiced ecclesiastical discipline. But in the Protestant ascetic communities admission to the Lord's Supper was conditioned

on ethical fitness, which again was identified with business honor, while into the content of one's faith no one inquired. Such a powerful, unconsciously refined organization for the production of capitalistic individuals has never existed in any other church or religion.

WEBER'S GENERAL THEORY OF HISTORY

Is there an overall pattern in Weber's argument? It is not a picture of a linear trend toward ever-increasing rationality. Nor is it an evolutionary model of natural selection, in the sense of random selection of the more advanced forms, accumulating through a series of stages. For Weber's constant theme is that the *pattern of relations among the various factors* is crucial in determining their effect upon economic rationalization. Any one factor occurring by itself tends to have opposite effects, overall, to those which it has in combination with the other factors.

For example, self-supplied military coalitions produce civic organizations and legal systems which are favorable to capitalism. But if the self-armed civic groups are too strong, the result is a series of guild monopolies which stifle capitalism by overcontrolling markets. Cities, on the other hand, have to be balanced by the bureaucratic state. But when the state is too strong by itself, it, too, tends to stifle capitalism. This can happen by bolstering the immobility of labor (as in the case of "the second serfdom" produced in Russia and eastern Europe as absolutist states developed in the seventeenth and eighteenth centuries); or by directly controlling the division of labor by forced contributions instead of allowing a market to develop. In the areas of the world where bureaucratization was relatively easy, as in ancient Egypt or China, or the Byzantine Empire, the unrestrained power of the state stereotyped economic life and did not allow the dynamics of capitalism to unfold.

The same is true of the religious variables. The creation of the great world religions, with their universalism and their specialized priesthoods, was crucial for the possibility of breaking the ritual barriers among localized groups, with all the consequences this might have for subsequent developments. But, in the absence of other factors, this could actually bolster the obstacles to capitalism. This happened in India, where the development of Hinduism fostered the caste system; the universalistic religion set an external seal upon the lineup of particularistic groups that happened to exist at the time. Even in Christianity, where moral prophecy had a much more barrier-breaking and world-transforming effect, the Church (in the period when it was predominant) created another obstacle against its capitalist implications. This was the period of the High Middle Ages in Europe, when monasticism proliferated and, thus, channeled all the energy of religious motivation into a specialized role and away from the economic concerns of ordinary life.[12]

Weber saw the rise of large-scale capitalism, then, as the result of a series of combinations of conditions which had to occur together. This makes world history look like the result of configurations of events so rare as to appear accidental. Weber's position might well be characterized as historicist, in the sense of seeing history as a concatenation of unique events and unrepeatable complexities. Once a crucial conjuncture occurs, its results transform everything else—and not just locally but also in the larger world of competing states. This was true of the great charismatic revelations of the world religions, which shut off China, India, or the West from alternative lines of development as well as determined the ways that states upon these territories would interact with the rest of the world. Similarly, the full-scale capitalist breakthrough itself was a once-only event, radiating outward to transform all other institutions and societies. Hence, the original conditions necessary for the emergence of capitalism were not necessary for its continuation. The original religious ethic could fade, once the calculability of massive economic transactions had become a matter of routine. Hence, late-industrializing states need not follow the route of classic capitalism. In the advanced societies, the skeleton of the economic structure might even be taken over by socialism.

Weber's account of the rise of capitalism, then, is in a sense not a theory at all, in that it is not a set of universal generalizations about economic change. Nevertheless, on a more abstract level, Weber is at least implicitly proposing such a theory. On one level, he may be read as a collection of separate hypotheses about specific processes and their effects.[13] The foregoing caveat about the necessary balance among factors may be incorporated by specifying that the causal variables must operate at a given strength—that is, by turning them into quantitative generalizations specified to a given range of variation.

On a second level, one may say that the fundamental generalizations in Weber's theory of capitalism concern the crucial role of balances and tensions between opposing elements. "All in all," says Weber in a little-known passage (1968:1192–3), "the specific roots of Occidental culture must be sought in the tension and peculiar balance, on the one hand, between office charisma and monasticism, and on the other between the contractual character of the feudal state and the autonomous bureaucratic hierarchy."[14] No one element must predominate if rationalization is to increase. More concretely, since each "element" is composed of real people struggling for precedence, the creation of a calculable, open-market economy depends upon a continuous balance of power among differently organized groups. The formal egalitarianism of the law depends upon balances among competing citizens and among competing jurisdictions. The nondualistic economic ethic of moderated avarice depends upon a compromise between the claims of in-group charity and the vicious circle of out-group rapaciousness.

The capitalist economy depends on this balance. The open-market system is a situation of institionalized strife. Its essence is struggle, in an expanded version of the Marxian sense, but with the qualification that this could go on continuously, and indeed must, if the system is to survive.[15] Hence, if there is any generalization implicit in Weber's theory applicable to economic history after the initial rise of capitalism, it is this: The possibility for the follower-societies of the non-Western world to acquire the dynamism of industrial capitalism depends on there being a balance among class forces, and among competing political forces and cultural forces as well. In the highly industrialized societies also, the continuation of capitalism depends on continuation of the same conflicts. The victory of any one side would spell the doom of the system. In this respect, as in others, Weber's theory is a conflict theory indeed.

AN ASSESSMENT: WEBER'S CONFRONTATION WITH MARXISM

How valid is Weber's theory? To fully answer this question would require extensive comparative analyses and a good deal of explication of principles on different levels of abstraction. These tasks are beyond the scope of any one paper. What I can present is a confrontation between Weber's theory and the one rival theory of capitalism which claims a comparable degree of historical and theoretical comprehensiveness, Marxism. This is especially appropriate because Weber himself devoted a great deal of attention in the *General Economic History* to the points at which his analysis impinges on Marxist theories.

The book begins and ends on Marxian themes. The first chapter deals with the question of primitive agrarian communism. Characteristically, Weber finds it to be only one variant of primitive agriculture; where it does exist, it is usually the result of fiscal organization imposed from above (1961:21–36). The closing words of the book speak of the threat of working class revolution which appears once capitalism matures and work discipline loses its religious legitimation (1961:270). In between, there are numerous references to Marxism, far more than in any other of Weber's works. His attitude is critically respectful, as in his comment on the Engels-Bebel theory of the origins of the family: "although it is untenable in detail it forms, taken as a whole, a valuable contribution to the solution of the problem. Here again is the old truth exemplified that an ingenious error is more fruitful for science than stupid accuracy." (1961:40)[16]

Weber's intellectual maturity coincides with a period of high-level debate in Germany and Austria between Marxian and non-Marxian economists. In the years between 1885 and 1920 appeared Engels's editions of the later volumes of *Capital*, as well as the principal works of Kautsky, Hilferding, and Luxemburg. On the other side, Sombart, Bortkiewitz, and Tugan-Baranowski provided what they considered to be revisions in the spirit of Marxian economics, while Böhm-Bawerk (1898) and Schumpeter (1954) launched explicit efforts to shore up the weaknesses of neoclassical economics vis-à-vis Marxism, and attacked the technical weaknesses of Marxian theory.[17] This period was in many ways the high-water mark in political economy for an atmosphere of balanced debate is beneficial for intellectual advance. Weber in particular was concerned to meet the Marxian challenge on its own grounds, leaving out nothing that must be conceded, but also turning up whatever factors the Marxists left out. Moreover, the German Marxists had suddenly become stronger with the end of the World War and the downfall of the German monarchy. Weber delivered his lectures in Munich just after the short-lived Communist commune of 1919, and his lecture room contained many radical students. It is not surprising that Weber was so much more explicitly concerned with Marxism in his last work than in the religious studies he published while the war was going on.

Weber had one great advantage over the Marxists. The discipline of historical scholarship reached its maturity around the end of the nineteenth century. Not only had political and military history reached a high degree of comprehensiveness and accuracy, but so had the history of law, religion, and economic institutions not only for Europe and the ancient Mediterranean but for the Orient as well. The historical researches of the twentieth century have not brought to light any great body of facts about the past that has radically changed our view of world history since Weber's day. Weber was perhaps the first great master of the major institutional facts of world history. By contrast, Marx, pursuing his assiduous researches in the 1840s and 50s, had much narrower materials at his disposal (Hobsbawm 1964:20–7). The histories of India, China, Japan, or Islam had scarcely begun to be available; the permeation of the ancient Greco-Roman world by religious institutions was only beginning to be analyzed; and the complex civilization of the European High Middle Ages was hidden beneath what Marx considered the "feudal rubbish" of the *Ancien Regime* of the eighteenth century. Marx wrote before the great coming-of-age of historical scholarship; Weber, just as it reached its peak. Weber thus represents for us the first and in many ways still the only effort to make a truly informed comparative analysis of major historical developments.

It should be borne in mind that Marx and most of his followers have devoted their attention primarily to showing the dynamics of capitalism, not to the preconditions for its emergence. Weber's concerns were almost entirely the reverse. Hence, it is possible that the two analyses could be complementary, Marx's taking up where Weber's leaves off. Only in the 1970s have there been efforts comparable to Weber's from within the Marxian tradition, notably that of Wallerstein (1974). Interestingly enough, Weber anticipated Wallerstein's major points in the *General Economic History*. On the other side, Wallerstein's revision of Marxism is in many ways a movement toward a more Weberian mode of analysis, stressing the importance of external relations among states.

The classical Marxian model of the preconditions for capitalism covers only a few points (Marx, 1967: I, 336–70, 713–64; II, 323–37, 593–613; 1973: 459–514). Some of these are a subset of Weber's model, while two of them are distinctive to Marx. Weber and Marx both stressed that capitalism requires a pool of formally free but economically propertyless labor; the sale of all factors of production on the market; and the concentration of all factors in the hands of capitalist entrepreneurs. Marx did not see the importance of the *calculable* aspect of technology; at times, he seemed to make the sheer productive power of technology the central moving force in economic changes, while at others, he downplayed this as part of a larger economic system—much in the way Weber did. Unlike Weber, Marx gave no causal importance at all to calculable law, nor did he see the earlier links in Weber's causal chain: economic ethics, citizenship, bureaucratization, and their antecedents.[18]

The uniqueness of Marx's discussion is in two factors: primitive accumulation, and revolution. About the latter, Marx had surprisingly little to say beyond the dramatic imagery of revolution breaking the bonds imposed by the property system upon the growing engines of production (Marx, 1959: 43–4). Primitive accumulation takes up nearly the whole of his historical discussion. It means the accumulation of enough raw materials, tools, and food for laborers to live on before subsequent production was completed; hence, it is the quantitative prerequisite for any takeoff into expanded economic production. Such accumulation took place historically in two ways. One was by the expropriation of peasants from their land, which simultaneously concentrated wealth in the hands of the capitalists who received the lands and required the expropriated masses to sell their labor on the market. The other means of primitive accumulation was by usury and merchants' capital. Marx downplayed the importance of monetary factors by themselves, as they operated only in the realm of circulation and did nothing to productive relations; but he did assert that the growth of money capital furthered the dissolution of the feudal economy once it was already under way (1967:III, 596–7).

Of these two factors, Weber says almost nothing explicitly about primitive accumulation. However, the entire earlier sections of the *General Economic History* (1961:21–203) deal with the various forms of appropriation of material and financial means, which have made up, among other things, the capitalism that has been omnipresent throughout history, although not in a rationalized form. The idea that there must be a specific accumulation of surplus for the purpose of a capitalist takeoff, I suspect, is one that Weber would reject. The assumption ought to be subjected to proof. After all, agrarian societies already have the most exreme concentration of wealth at the top of the social hierarchy of any type of society in world history (Lenski, 1966); the industrial takeoff need only have been fueled by a shift in the use of this wealth, not by a further extraction process. As Weber understood, and as subsequent research has shown, capitalists do not have to rise "from below," having amassed their own wealth; it has been far more typical for the aristocracy themselves to go into capitalist production (Stone, 1965; Moore, 1966).[19]

Weber is somewhat more sympathetic to the importance of revolutions. Perhaps the final conditions for the capitalist takeoff in England were the revolutions of 1640 and 1688. These put the state under the control of political groups favorable to capitalism, thus fulfilling the condition of keeping markets and finances free of "irrational" and predatory state policies. Of more fundamental institutional consequence were the revolutions within the cities of ancient Greece and of medieval Italy. The latter, Weber lists among "the five great revolutions that decided the destiny of the occident" (1951:62).[20] For it was the uprising of the plebeians which replaced the charismatic law of the older patrician class with the universalistic and "rationally instituted" law upon which so much of the institutional development of capitalism was to depend (Weber, 1968:1312–3, 1325). In effect, this was a revolution in a system of property, but not in the gross sense of a replacement of one form of appropriation with another. For Weber, a system of property is a complex of daily actions—above all, the making of transfers and contracts and the adjudication of disputes. Hence, political revolutions are most crucial where they set the pattern for ongoing legal actions in a highly calculable form, with all the consequences noted above.

Wallerstein's (1974) theory, as developed in volume I, emphasizes two conditions in the origins of capitalism. One is the influx of bullion from the European colonies, which caused the price inflation of the 16th century. During this period, wages remained approximately constant. The gap between prices and wages constituted a vast extraction of surplus which could be invested in expanding capitalist enterprises (Wallerstein, 1974:77–84).[21] This is Wallerstein's version of the primitive accumulation factor.

Wallerstein's (1974:348) second condition also emerges from the international situation. "[C]apitalism as an economic system is based on the fact that economic factors operate within an arena larger than that which any political entity can totally control. This gives capitalists a freedom of maneuver that is structurally based." He (1974:355) goes on to say that the different states must be of different strengths, so that not all states "would be in the position of blocking the effective operation of transnational economic entities whose locus were in another state." Capitalists in effect must have opportunities to shift their grounds among varied political climates to wherever the situation is most favorable.

Weber (1961:259) was generally aware of both conditions. Regarding the effects of gold and silver influx, however, he was largely unfavorable.

> It is certainly true that in a given situation an increase in the supply of precious metals may give rise to price revolutions, such as that which took place after 1530 in Europe, and when other favorable conditions are present, as when a certain form of labor organization is in the process of development, the progress may be stimulated by the fact that large stocks of cash come into the hands of certain groups. But the case of India proves that such an importation of metal will not alone bring about capitalism. In India in the period of the Roman power, an enormous mass of precious metal—some twenty-five million *sestertii* annually—came in exchange for domestic goods, but this inflow gave rise to commercial capitalism only to a slight extent. The greater part of this precious metal disappeared into the hoards of the rajahs instead of being converted into cash and applied in the establishment of enterprises of a rational capitalistic character. This fact proves that it depends entirely upon the nature of the labor system what tendency will result from an inflow of precious metal.

In another passage, Weber (1961:231) does say that the price revolution of the sixteenth and seventeenth centuries "provided a powerful lever for the specifically capitalistic tendencies of seeking profit through cheapening production and lowering the price." This came about for industrial (but not agricultural) products, because the quickened economic tempo put on pressures toward further rationalizing economic relations and inventing cheaper technologies of production. Weber thus gives the influx of precious metals a place as a contributory factor, though apparently not an indispensable one, *within* the framework of economic institutions which had already appeared in Europe at the time.[22]

Weber (1961:249) largely agrees, however, with Wallerstein's argument about the international character of capitalism. Modern cities, he points out,

> came under the power of competing national states in a condition of perpetual struggle for power in peace or war. This competitive struggle created the largest opportunities for modern Western capitalism. The separate states had to compete for mobile capital, which dictated to them the conditions under which it would assist them to power. Out of this alliance of the state with capital, dictated by necessity, arose the national citizen class, the bourgeoisie in the modern sense of the word. Hence it is the closed national state which afforded to capitalism its chance for development—and as long as the national state does not give place to a world empire capitalism will also endure.

Here the coincidence with Wallerstein is remarkable. Weber does not emphasize the contours of Wallerstein's world system, with its tiers of core, semiperiphery, and periphery, but Weber does show the central importance of mobile capital among militarily competing states, and he gives a more specific analysis than Wallerstein of the mechanism by which this is transformed into an advantage for capitalism.

In general, there is considerable convergence, as well as complementarity, between Weber's last theory of the origins of capitalism, and the mature Marxian theory which is only now emerging. Weber largely rejects Marxian theories of primitive accumulation, or at least relegates them to minor factors. On the other side, Wallerstein, as well as modern Marxism in general, has moved the state into the center of the analysis. Weber had already gone much further in that direction, so that the main Weberian criticism of the Marxian tradition, even in its present form, is that it does not yet recognize the set of institutional forms, especially as grounded in the legal system, upon which capitalism has rested.

For Weber, the state and the legal system are by no means a superstructure of ideas determining the material organization of society. Rather, his theory of the development of the state is to a considerable extent an analogy to the Marxian theory of the economy. The key factor is the form of appropriation of the material conditions of domination. We have seen the significance of the organization of weapons for Weber's chain of causes of capitalism. In this connection, Weber (1961:237) remarks:

Whether the military organization is based on the principle of self-equipment or on that of military equipment by an overlord who furnishes horses, arms and provisions, is a distinction quite as fundamental for social history as the question whether the means of economic production are the property of the worker or of a capitalistic entrepreneur . . . [T]he army equipped by the war lord, and the separation of the soldier from the paraphernalia of war, [is] in a way analogous to the separation of the worker from the means of production. . . ."

Similarly, state bureaucracy depends upon a set of material conditions, and upon the separation of the administrator from treating the office and its incomes as private property (1968:980–3). Weber diverges from the Marxian analogy by being a more thoroughgoing conflict theorist. As we have seen, and as the quotation given above on the international basis of capitalism bears out, for Weber the conditions of rationalized organization, in political and economic spheres alike, depend upon a continuous open struggle.[23]

The main disagreements between Marx and Weber have less to do with the origins of capitalism than with its future. Weber thought that capitalism could endure indefinitely as an economic system, although political factors could bring it down. As we have seen, he thought that the disappearance of religious legitimation in mature capitalism opened the way for workers to express their discontents in the form of a political movement for socialism. Ironically, it is the rationalized world view promoted by the underlying conditions of capitalism that gave birth to rational socialism, a doctrine that proclaims that the social order itself, rather than the gods, is to blame for economic distress; and that having been deliberately instituted, that order is capable of being consciously changed (1961:217–8). For Weber, however, economic crises may be endemic to modern capitalism, but they are not caused by a fundamental contradiction in it, nor is there any necessary tendency for them to worsen toward an ultimate breakdown. He attributes crises to overspeculation and the resulting overproduction of producers' (but not consumers') goods (1961:217). To decide who is right on these points requires further consideration than can be given here.

CONCLUSION

Weber's last theory is still today the only comprehensive theory of the origins of capitalism. It is virtually alone in accounting for the emergence of the full range of institutional and motivational conditions for large-scale, world-transforming capitalism. Even so, it is incomplete. It needs to be supplemented by a theory of the operation of mature capitalism, and of its possible demise. And even on the home territory of Weber's theory, there remain to be carried out the comprehensive tests that would provide adequate proof. But sociological science, like any other, advances by successive approximations. The theory expressed in Weber's *General Economic History* constitutes a base line from which subsequent investigations should depart.

NOTES

1. The list of institutional characteristics given on pp. 21–25 of the English-language edition of *The Protestant Ethic* (1930), however, are not in the 1904–5 original, but are from an introduction written in 1920 (1930:ix–x).

2. Cf. the closing words of *The Religion of China*: "To be sure the basic characteristics of the 'mentality,' in this case practical attitudes towards the world, were deeply co-determined by political and economic destinies. Yet, in view of their autonomous laws, one can hardly fail to ascribe to these attitudes effects strongly counteractive to capitalist development" (1951:249), and of *The Religion of India*: "However, for the plebeian strata no ethic of everyday life derived from its rationality formed missionary prophecy. The appearance of such in the Occident, however—above all, in the Near East—with the extensive consequences borne with it, was conditioned by highly particular historical constellations without which, despite differences of natural conditions, development there could easily have taken the course typical of Asia, particularly of India" (1958b:343).

3. In Part I of *Economy and Society* (written 1918–20), Weber distinguishes formal and substantive rationality of economic action (1968:85–6). In "The Social Psychology of the World Religions" (written 1913), Weber (1946:293–4) defines three different types of rationalism: (1) a systematic world view based on precise, abstract concepts; (2) practical means-ends calculations; (3) a systematic method, including that of magic or prayer. In *The Protestant Ethic* (1904–5), Weber (1930:76–78) attacks the notion that the spirit of capitalism is "part of the development of rationalism as a whole," and says he is interested in "the origin of precisely the irrational element which lies in this, as in every conception of a calling." Kalberg (1980) points out that under one or another of Weber's types of rationality, *every* action, even the most superstitious, might be called "rational." Kalberg argues that only one type of rationality is relevant for the methodical conduct of affairs.

4. It is plain that Weber (1968:85–6) is referring to what in *Economy and Society* he calls "formal" rationality, efficiency based on quantitative calculation of means, rather than "substantive" rationality, the adequacy of actions for meeting ultimate values. Such values could be criteria of economic welfare, whether maximal production, quality of life, or a socialist economic distribution, or they could be ethical or religious values. Weber makes it clear that formal and substantive rationality can diverge widely, especially in his late political writings about the dangers of bureaucracy (1946:77–128; 1968:1393–1415). Weber himself tended to defend the formal rationality of modern capitalism as coinciding to a fair degree with substantive rationality in meeting the value of maximizing the economic welfare of the population at large (1968:108–9). It goes without saying that this is an empirical, not an analytical judgment.

5. Weber does not mention "rational science and in connection with it a rational technology" (1961:232) as one of the features of the West important for modern capitalism. On the other hand he says: "It is true that most of the inventions of the 18th century were not made in a scientific manner. . . . The connection of industry with modern science, especially the systematic work of the laboratories, beginning with Justus von Liebig [i.e., *Circa* 1830], enabled industry to become what it is today and so brought capitalism to its full development." On the balance, I think science comes out as a secondary factor in the model.

6. Weber (1961:260) also mentions geographical conditions as more favorable to capitalism in Europe than in China or India, due to transportation advantages in the former via the Mediterranean sea and the interconnecting rivers. But he goes

on (p. 261) to discount this, in that no capitalism arose in Mediterranean antiquity, when civilization was predominantly coastal, whereas early modern capitalism in Europe was born in the cities of the interior.

7. Weber does not clearly describe a chain, and sometimes he lumps characteristics of rational capitalism with its preconditions. Although some of these preconditions continue into the operation of modern capitalism, a logical chain of explanation, I believe, requires something like the separation I have given. It should be understood that Weber gives a highly condensed summary in these lectures.

8. Hence the role of "guest peoples" such as the Jews and the Caursines in Christian Europe, or the Christians in Islamic societies, or the Parsees in India, as groups of tolerated outsiders who were available for making loans, which otherwise would not be forthcoming within the controlled internal economy (1961:267).

9. The main exception is that revolutions can occur after the military breakdown of the state itself due to foreign wars. But historical instances of these have occurred mainly in states which have been only partially bureaucratized. (See Skocpol, 1979.)

10. Contractual forms of feudalism also contributed somewhat to legal citizenship. Weber neglected this in the *General Economic History*, but considered it in *Economy and Society* (1968:1101). The earlier preconditions (military and religious) for contractual feudalism and for independent cities, however, are essentially the same.

11. Weber did not live to write his planned volume on medieval Christianity. If he had, I believe he would have found that the High Middle Ages were the most significant institutional turning point of all on the road to the capitalist takeoff. His commitment to the vestiges of his Protestantism argument may have kept him from recognizing this earlier. I will deal with this point in a subsequent article, "The Weberian Revolution of the High Middle Ages."

12. This was also the time when the church took the offensive against incipient capitalism, in the form of pronouncements against usury (Weber, 1968:584–6).

13. One clearly formulated proposition, for example, is that armies based on coalitions of self-supplied individuals produce citizenship rights. (For a series of such propositions, see Collins, 1975:356–64.)

14. In other words, the main features of the West depend on a tension between the routinization of religious charisma in the church and the participatory communities of monks, and on a tension between the democratizing tendencies of self-supplied armies and the centralized bureaucratic state. These give us Weber's two great intermediate factors, a nondualistic religious ethic and calculable law, respectively.

15. ". . . . the formal rationality of money calculation is dependent on certain quite specific substantive conditions. Those which are of a particular sociological importance for present purposes are the following: (1) Market struggle of economic units which are at least relatively autonomous. Money prices are the product of conflicts of interest and of compromises; they thus result from power constellations. Money is not a mere 'voucher for unspecified utilities,' which could be altered at will without any fundamental effect on the character of the price system as a struggle of man against man. 'Money' is, rather, primarily a weapon in this struggle, and prices are expressions of the struggle; they are instruments of calculation only as estimated quantifications of relative chances in this struggle of interests" (Weber, 1968:107–8).

16. Weber goes on to say, "A criticism of the theory leads to consideration first of the evolution of prostitution, in which connection, it goes without saying, no ethical evaluation is involved." There follows (1961:40–53) a brilliant outline of a theory of the organization of the family as one set of variants on sexual property relations, in which material transactions and appropriations are fundamentally in-

volved. Later versions of this line of theory are found in Levi-Strauss (1968), and in Collins (1975:228–59).

17. Thus, Böhm-Bawerk (1898) and Schumpeter (1954) developed a previously missing link in classical and neoclassical economics, a theory of capitalist profits. This they based on time-lags in the competitive process and resulting time-preference among investment returns, displacing the Marxian theory of profit based on the exploitation of labor. Böhm-Bawerk also made an analysis of socialist economies. He regarded these as possible *politically* (as did Schumpeter and Weber), but denied that production would be organized differently than in capitalism. Socialism could affect only the distribution of capitalist profits among the populace. For the economic thought of this period, see Schumpeter (1954:800–20, 843–55, 877–85) and Sweezy (1942:190–213).

18. Marx (1973:459–514) gave a very general outline of early forms of property as based on family and tribal membership, and he recognized that the ancient cities were military coalitions. He missed the central organizing role of religion in these developments, and failed to see the crucial effect of the revolutions within the ancient cities upon the uniquely Western legal tradition. For Marx, the rise of cities simply meant the growing separation of town and country, an instance of dialectical antithesis, and of the progress of the division of labor (1967:I, 352). For the period immediately preceding the capitalist takeoff, Marx noted that the state had hastened the transition from feudalism to capitalism by creating public finance and conquering foreign markets. These effects Marx subsumed under his concept of "primitive accumulation."

19. Weber also anticipated Barrington Moore's (1966) theory of the political consequences of different property modes in the commercialization of agriculture (1961:81–94).

20. The others were "the Netherland revolution of the sixteenth century, the English revolution of the seventeenth century, and the American and French revolutions of the eighteenth century."

21. To this, Wallerstein adds the argument that surplus is further extracted by coerced labor on the periphery, to be consumed in the core, where however (somewhat contrary to the point about the price revolution) labor is well enough paid to constitute a potential consumers' market for capitalist production.

22. Weber's (1961:223) comment on the economic benefits of the colonies is even more negative. "This accumulation of wealth brought about through colonial trade has been of little significance for the development of modern capitalism—a fact which must be emphasized in opposition to Werner Sombart. It is true that the colonial trade made possible the accumulation of wealth to an enormous extent, but this did not further the specifically occidental form of the organization of labor, since colonial trade itself rested on the principle of exploitation and not that of securing an income through market operations. Furthermore, we know that in Bengal for example, the English garrison cost five times as much as the money value of all goods carried thither. It follows that the markets for domestic industry furnished by the colonies under the conditions of the time were relatively unimportant, and that the main profit was derived from the transport business."

23. It is true that Weber continues to leave more room for religious conditions than any of the Marxians. Yet even here, military conditions play a key role in the ultimate determinants of religions. The earliest Greek civic cults were war coalitions; and the this-worldly, antimagical character of Judaism derives from the cult of Jahweh, the war god of the coalition of Jewish tribes.

REFERENCES

Böhm-Bawerk, Eugen von
1898   Karl Marx and the Close of his System. London: T.F. Unwin.
Burger, Thomas
1976   Max Weber's Theory of Concept Formation. Durham, North Carolina: Duke University Press.
Cohen, Jere
1980   "Rational capitalism in Renaissance Italy." American Journal of Sociology 85:1340–55.
Cohen, Jere, Lawrence E. Hazelrigg, and Whitney Pope
1975   "De-Parsonizing Weber: a critique of Parsons' interpretation of Weber's sociology." American Sociological Review 40:229–41.
Collins, Randall
1975   Conflict Sociology: Toward an Explanatory Science. New York: Academic.
Hirst, Paul Q.
1976   Evolution and Social Categories. London: Allen and Unwin.
Hobsbawn, E. J.
1964   "Introduction." Pp. 9–65 in Karl Marx, Pre-Capitalist Economic Formations. New York: International Publishers.
Kalberg, Stephen
1979   "The Search for thematic orientations in a fragmented oeuvre: the discussion of Max Weber in recent German sociological literature." Sociology 13:127–39.
1980   "Max Weber's types of rationality: cornerstones for the analysis of rationalization processes in his history." American Journal of Sociology 85:1145–79.
Lenski, Gerhard E.
1966   Power and Privilege. New York: McGraw-Hill.
Levi-Strauss, Claude
1968   The Elementary Forms of Kinship. Boston: Beacon Press.
(1949)
Marx, Karl
1959   Preface to A Contribution to the Critique of Political Economy. In L.
(1856)   Feuer (ed.), Marx and Engels: Basic Writings on Politics and Philosophy. New York: Doubleday.
1967   (1867, 1885, 1894) Capital. New York: International Publishers.
1973   (1857–1858) Grundrisse. New York: Random House.
McClelland, David C.
1961   The Achieving Society. Princeton: Van Nostrand.
Moore, Barrington
1966   Social Origins of Dictatorship and Democracy. Boston: Beacon Press.
Nelson, Benjamin
1949   The Idea of Usury. Princeton: Princeton University Press.
Parsons, Talcott
1947   "Introduction." In Max Weber, The Theory of Social and Economic Organization. New York: Oxford University Press.
1963   "Introduction." In Max Weber, The Sociology of Religion. Boston: Beacon Press.
1967   Societies: Comparative and Evolutionary Perspectives. Englewood Cliffs: Prentice-Hall.

Samuelsson, Kurt
  1961   Religion and Economic Action. New York: Basic Books.
Schumpeter, Joseph A.
  1954   A History of Economic Analysis. New York: Oxford University Press.
Seidman, Steven
  1980   Enlightenment and Reaction: Aspects of the Enlightenment Origins of
           Marxism and Sociology. Unpublished Ph.D. dissertation, University of
           Virginia.
Skocpol, Theda
  1979   States and Social Revolutions. New York: Cambridge University Press.
Stone, Lawrence
  1965   The Crisis of the Aristocracy. New York: Oxford University Press.
Sweezy, Paul M.
  1942   The Theory of Capitalist Development. New York: Oxford University
           Press.
Tawney, R. H.
  1938   Religion and the Rise of Capitalism. Harmondsworth: Penguin.
Tenbruck, F. H.
  1975   "Das Werk Max Webers." Koelner Zeitschrift fuer Soziologie und So-
           zialpsychologie 27:663–702.
Wallerstein, Immanuel
  1974   The Modern World System. New York: Academic.
Weber, Max
  1930   (1904–1905) The Protestant Ethic and the Spirit of Capitalism. Translated
           by Talcott Parsons. New York: Scribner's.
  1946   (1922) From Max Weber: Essays in Sociology. Translated by Hans H.
           Gerth and C. Wright Mills. New York: Oxford University Press.
  1947   (1922) The Theory of Social and Economic Organization. Translated by
           A. M. Henderson and Talcott Parsons. New York: Oxford University Press.
  1949   (1904, 1906, 1917–1918) The Methodology of the Social Sciences. Translated
           by Edward A. Shils and Henry A. Finch. Glencoe, Ill.: Free Press.
  1951   (1916) The Religion of China. Translated by Hans H. Gerth. Glencoe, Ill.:
           Free Press.
  1952   (1917–1919) Ancient Judaism. Translated by Hans H. Gerth and Don
           Martindale. Glencoe, Ill.: Free Press.
  1954   (1922) Max Weber on Law in Economy and Society. Translated by Edward
           Shils and Max Rheinstein. Cambridge, Mass.: Harvard University Press.
  1958a   (1922) The City. Translated by Don Martindale and Gertrud Neuworth.
           Glencoe, Ill.: The Free Press.
  1958b   (1916–1917) The Religion of India. Translated by Hans H. Gerth and Don
           Martindale. Glencoe, Ill.: Free Press.
  1961   (1923) General Economic History. Translated by Frank H. Knight. New
           York: Collier Books.
  1963   (1922) The Sociology of Religion. Translated by Ephraim Fischoff. Boston:
           Beacon Press.
  1968   (1922) Economy and Society. Edited by Guenther Roth and Claus Wittich.
           New York: Bedminster Press.

EDITORS' NOTES ON FURTHER READING: COLLINS

This article about Max Weber's "last theory of capitalism" has been published together with some other relevant texts by Randall Collins in his *Weberian Sociological*

Theory (1986). In a recent paper, Collins further develops the Weberian model of markets: "Market Dynamics as the Engine of Historical Change," in *Sociological Theory*, pp. 111–135 (1990). Collins has also written a short and easily read introduction to Weber's life and work, *Max Weber: A Skeleton Key* (1986).

Weber's theory about the emergence of capitalism—especially his idea that Protestantism played a key role in this process—is much debated. For an overview of this famous controversy, see, for example, Gordon Marshall, *In Search of the Spirit of Capitalism: An Essay on Max Weber's Protestant Ethic Thesis* (1982). Some of the key texts in the debate can be found in Robert W. Green, ed., *Protestantism and Capitalism: The Weber Thesis and Its Critics* (1959). An introduction to Weber's study of Protestantism and capitalism can be found in Gianfranco Poggi's short book *Calvinism and the Capitalist Spirit: Max Weber's Protestant Ethic* (1983).

Because there does not exist a consensus about what Weber "really" meant, the reader is strongly encouraged to consult Weber's study of the Protestant ethic and also to complement this reading with Weber's *General Economic History* (Eng. tr. 1927) and related writings (such as chapter 2 in *Economy and Society* and the excellent selection of texts that can be found in Hans Gerth and C. Wright Mills, eds., *From Max Weber* [1946]). "The Social Psychology of the World Religions" (included in the Gerth and Mills anthology) contains a succinct statement of Weber's thesis about the rise of rationalism in the West. This topic also forms the focus of Wolfgang Schluchter's *The Rise of Western Rationalism: Max Weber's Developmental History* (Engl. tr. 1981). A general bibliography that indicates which works by Weber are available in English translation and where to find the critical literature is Peter Kivisto and William H. Swatos, eds., *Max Weber: A Bio-Bibliography* (1988).

There are several theories of why capitalism emerged in the West as opposed to somewhere else. For a quick overview, see, for example, Daniel Chirot, "The Rise of the West," *American Sociological Review* 50 (1985):181–195; Immanuel Wallerstein, *The Modern World-System* (three of the projected four volumes have appeared between 1974 and 1989); Douglass North and Robert Thomas, *The Rise of the Western World: A New Economic History* (1973)—a view akin to that of the New Institutional Economics; and historian Fernand Braudel's remarkable three-volume work, *Civilization and Capitalism, 15th–18th Century* (Eng. tr. 1981). The difference between Marx's and Weber's ideas is outlined with great clarity in Karl Löwith's *Max Weber and Karl Marx* (Eng. tr. 1982). An account of the considerable debate about Wallerstein's work is found in Daniel Chirot and T. D. Hall's review article "World-System Theory," *Annual Review in Sociology* 8 (1982):385–405. For those interested in Weber's relationship to economics, several of the essays in Wolfgang Mommsen and Jürgen Osterhammel's anthology *Max Weber and His Contemporaries* (Engl. tr. 1987) are of interest.

4

Economic Backwardness in Historical Perspective

ALEXANDER GERSCHENKRON

A historical approach to current problems calls perhaps for a word of explanation. Unlike so many of their predecessors, modern historians no longer announce to the world what inevitably will, or at least what ideally should, happen. We have grown modest. The prophetic fervor was bound to vanish together with the childlike faith in a perfectly comprehensible past whose flow was determined by some exceedingly simple and general historical law. Between Seneca's assertion of the absolute certainty of our knowledge of the past and Goethe's description of history as a book eternally kept under seven seals, between the *omnia certa sunt* of the one and the *ignorabimus* of the other, modern historical relativism moves gingerly. Modern historians realize full well that comprehension of the past—and that perforce means the past itself—changes perpetually with the historian's emphasis, interest, and point of view. The search is no longer for a determination of the course of human events as ubiquitous and invariant as that of the course of the planets. The iron necessity of historical processes has been discarded. But along with what John Stuart Mill once called "the slavery of antecedent circumstances" have been demolished the great bridges between the past and the future upon which the nineteenth-century mind used to travel so safely and so confidently.

Does this mean that history cannot contribute anything to the understanding of current problems? Historical research consists essentially in application to empirical material of various sets of empirically derived hypothetical generalizations and in testing the closeness of the resulting fit, in the hope that in this way certain uniformities, certain typical situations, and certain typical relationships among individual factors in these situations can be ascertained. None of these lends itself to easy extrapolations. All that can be achieved is an extraction from the vast storehouse of the past

From Alexander Gerschenkron in Burt Hoselitz, ed., *The Progress of Underdeveloped Countries* (Chicago: University of Chicago Press, 1952). Reprinted by permission.

of sets of intelligent questions that may be addressed to current materials. The importance of this contribution should not be exaggerated. But it should not be underrated either. For the quality of our understanding of current problems depends largely on the broadness of our frame of reference. Insularity is a limitation on comprehension. But insularity in thinking is not peculiar to any special geographic area. Furthermore, it is not only a spatial but also a temporal problem. All decisions in the field of economic policies are essentially decisions with regard to combinations of a number of relevant factors. And the historian's contribution consists in pointing at *potentially* relevant factors and at *potentially* significant combinations among them which could not be easily perceived within a more limited sphere of experience. These are the questions. The answers themselves, however, are a different matter. No past experience, however rich, and no historical research, however thorough, can save the living generation the creative task of finding their own answers and shaping their own future. The following remarks, therefore, purport to do no more than point at some relationships which existed in the past and the consideration of which in current discussions might prove useful.

THE ELEMENTS OF BACKWARDNESS

A good deal of our thinking about industrialization of backward countries is dominated—consciously or unconsciously—by the grand Marxian generalization according to which it is the history of advanced or established industrial countries which traces out the road of development for the more backward countries. "The industrially more developed country presents to the less developed country a picture of the latter's future."[1] There is little doubt that in some broad sense this generalization has validity. It is meaningful to say that Germany, between the middle and the end of the last century, followed the road which England began to tread at an earlier time. But one should beware of accepting such a generalization too wholeheartedly. For the half-truth that it contains is likely to conceal the existence of the other half—that is to say, in several very important respects the development of a backward country may, by the very virtue of its backwardness, tend to differ fundamentally from that of an advanced country.

It is the main proposition of this essay that in a number of important historical instances industrialization processes, when launched at length in a backward country, showed considerable differences, as compared with more advanced countries, not only with regard to the speed of the development (the rate of industrial growth) but also with regard to the productive and organizational structures of industry which emerged from those processes. Furthermore, these differences in the speed and character of industrial development were to a considerable extent the result of application of institutional instruments for which there was little or no counterpart in an established industrial country. In addition, the intellectual climate within which industrialization proceeded, its "spirit" or "ideology," differed considerably among advanced and backward countries. Finally, the extent to which these attributes of backwardness occurred in individual instances appears to have varied directly with the degree of backwardness and the natural industrial potentialities of the countries concerned.

Let us first describe in general terms a few basic elements in the industrialization processes of backward countries as synthesized from the available historical information on economic development of European countries[2] in the nineteenth century and up until the beginning of the First World War. Thereupon, on the basis of concrete examples, more will be said on the effects of what may be called "relative backwardness" upon the course of industrial development in individual countries.

The typical situation in a backward country prior to the initiation of considerable industrialization processes may be described as characterized by the tension between the actual state of economic activities in the country and the existing obstacles to industrial development, on the one hand, and the great promise inherent in such a development, on the other. The extent of opportunities that industrialization presents varied, of course, with the individual country's endowment of natural resources. Furthermore, no industrialization seemed possible, and hence no "tension" existed, as long as certain formidable institutional obstacles (such as the serfdom of the peasantry or the far-reaching absence of political unification) remained. Assuming an adequate endowment of usable resources, and assuming that the great blocks to industrialization had been removed, the opportunities inherent in industrialization may be said to vary directly with the backwardness of the country. Industrialization always seemed the more promising the greater the backlog of technological innovations which the backward country could take over from the more advanced country. Borrowed technology, so much and so rightly stressed by Veblen, was one of the primary factors assuring a high speed of development in a backward country entering the stage of industrialization. There always has been the inevitable tendency to deride the backward country because of its lack of originality. German mining engineers of the sixteenth century accused the English of being but slavish imitators of German methods, and the English fully reciprocated these charges in the fifties and sixties of the past century. In our own day, Soviet Russia has been said to have been altogether imitative in its industrial development, and the Russians have retorted by making extraordinary and extravagant claims. But all these superficialities tend to blur the basic fact that the contingency of large imports of foreign machinery and of foreign know-how, and the concomitant opportunities for rapid industrialization with the passage of time, increasingly widened the gulf between economic potentialities and economic actualities in backward countries.

The industrialization prospects of an underdeveloped country are frequently judged, and judged adversely, in terms of cheapness of labor as against capital goods and of the resulting difficulty in substituting scarce capital for abundant labor. Sometimes, on the contrary, the cheapness of labor in a backward country is said to aid greatly in the processes of industrialization. The actual situation, however, is more complex than would appear on the basis of simple models. In reality, conditions will vary from industry to industry and from country to country. But the overriding fact to consider is that industrial labor, in the sense of a stable, reliable, and disciplined group that has cut the umbilical cord connecting it with the land and has become suitable for utilization in factories, is not abundant but extremely scarce in a backward country. Creation of an industrial labor force that really deserves its name is a most difficult and protracted process. The history of Russian industry provides some striking illustrations in this respect. Many a German industrial laborer of the nineteenth century had been raised in the strict discipline of a Junker estate which presumably made him more amenable to accept the rigors of factory rules. And yet the difficulties were great, and one may recall the admiring and envious glances which, toward the very end of the century, German writers like Schulze-Gaevernitz kept casting across the Channel at the English industrial worker, "the man of the future . . . born and educated for the machine . . . [who] does not find his equal in the past." In our time, reports from industries in India repeat in a still more exaggerated form the past predicaments of European industrializations in the field of labor supply.

Under these conditions the statement may be hazarded that, to the extent that industrialization took place, it was largely by application of the most modern and efficient techniques that backward countries could hope to achieve success, particularly if their industrialization proceeded in the face of competition from the advanced country. The advantages inherent in the use of technologically superior equipment were not counteracted but reinforced by its labor-saving effect. This seems to explain the tendency on the part of backward countries to concentrate at a relatively early point of their industrialization on promotion of those branches of industrial activities in which recent technological progress had been particularly rapid; while the more advanced countries, either from inertia or from unwillingness to require or impose sacrifices implicit in a large investment program, were more hesitant to carry out continual modernizations of their plant. Clearly, there are limits to such a policy, one of them being the inability of a backward country to extend it to lines of output where very special technological skills are required. Backward countries (although not the United States) were slow to assimilate production of modern machine tools. But a branch like iron and steel production does provide a good example of the tendency to introduce most modern innovations, and it is instructive to see, for example, how German blast furnaces so very soon became superior to the English ones, while in the early years of this century blast furnaces in still more backward southern Russia were in the process of outstripping in equipment their German counterparts. Conversely, in the nineteenth century, England's superiority in cotton textile output was challenged neither by Germany nor by any other country.

To a considerable extent (as in the case of blast furnaces just cited), utilization of modern techniques required, in nineteenth-century conditions, increases in the average size of plant. Stress on bigness in this sense can be found in the history of most countries on the European continent. But industrialization of backward countries in Europe reveals a tendency toward bigness in another sense. The use of the term "industrial revolution" has been exposed to a good many justifiable strictures. But, if industrial revolution is conceived as denoting no more than cases of sudden considerable increases in the rate of industrial growth, there is little doubt that in several important instances industrial development began in such a sudden, eruptive, that is, "revolutionary," way.

The discontinuity was not accidental. As likely as not the period of stagnation (in the "physiocratic" sense of a period of low rate of growth) can be terminated and industrialization processes begun only if the industrialization movement can proceed, as it were, along a broad front, starting simultaneously along many lines of economic activities. This is partly the result of the existence of complementarity and indivisibilities in economic processes. Railroads cannot be built unless coal mines are opened up at the same time; building half a railroad will not do if an inland center is to be connected with a port city. Fruits of industrial progress in certain lines are received as external economies by other branches of industry whose progress in turn accords benefits to the former. In viewing the economic history of Europe in the nineteenth century, the impression is very strong that only when industrial development could commence on a large scale did the tension between the preindustrialization conditions and the benefits expected from industrialization become sufficiently strong to overcome the existing obstacles and to liberate the forces that made for industrial progress.

This aspect of the development may be conceived in terms of Toynbee's relation between challenge and response. His general observation that very frequently small challenges do not produce any responses and that the volume of response begins to grow very rapidly (at least up to a point) as the volume of the challenge increases seems to be quite applicable here. The challenge, that is to say, the "tension," must be considerable before a response in terms of industrial development will materialize.

The foregoing sketch purported to list a number of basic factors which historically were peculiar to economic situations in backward countries and made for higher speed of growth and different productive structure of industries. The effect of these basic factors was, however, greatly reinforced by the use in backward countries of certain institutional instruments and the acceptance of specific industrialization ideologies. Some of these specific factors and their mode of operation on various levels of backwardness are discussed in the following sections.

THE BANKS

The history of the Second Empire in France provides rather striking illustrations of these processes. The advent of Napoleon III terminated a long period of relative economic stagnation which had begun with the restoration of the Bourbons and which in some sense and to some extent was the result of the industrial policies pursued by Napoleon I. Through a policy of reduction of tariff duties and elimination of import prohibitions, culminating in the Cobden-Chevalier treaty of 1860, the French government destroyed the hothouse in which French industry had been kept for decades and exposed it to the stimulating atmosphere of international competition. By abolishing monopoly profits in the stagnating coal and iron production, French industry at length received profitable access to basic industrial raw materials.

To a not inconsiderable extent, the industrial development of France under Napoleon III must be attributed to that determined effort to untie the strait jacket in which weak governments and strong vested interests had inclosed the French economy. But along with these essentially, though not exclusively, negative policies of the government, French industry received a powerful positive impetus from a different quarter. The reference is to the development of industrial banking under Napoleon III.

The importance of that development has seldom been fully appreciated. Nor has it been properly understood as emanating from the specific conditions of a relatively backward economy. In particular, the story of the Crédit Mobilier of the brothers Pereire is often regarded as a dramatic but, on the whole, rather insignificant episode. All too often, as, for instance, in the powerful novels of Émile Zola, the actual significance of the developments is almost completely submerged in the description of speculative fever, corruption, and immorality which accompanied them. It seems to be much better in accord with the facts to speak of a truly momentous role of investment banking of the period for the economic history of France and of large portions of the Continent.

In saying that, one has in mind, of course, the immediate effects of creating financial organizations designed to build thousands of miles of railroads, drill mines, erect factories, pierce canals, construct ports, and modernize cities. The ventures of the Pereires and of a few others did all that in France and beyond the boundaries of France over vast areas stretching from Spain to Russia. This tremendous change in economic scenery took place only a few years after a great statesman and a great historian of the July monarchy assured the country that there was no need to reduce the duties on iron because the sheltered French iron production was quite able to cope with the iron needs of the railroads on the basis of his estimate of a prospective annual increase in construction by some fifteen to twenty miles.

But no less important than the actual economic accomplishments of a few men of great entrepreneurial vigor was their effect on their environment. The Crédit Mobilier was from the beginning engaged in a most violent conflict with the representatives of "old wealth" in French banking, most notably with the Rothschilds. It was this conflict that had sapped the force of the institution and was primarily responsible for its eventual collapse in 1867. But what is so seldom realized is that in the course of this conflict the "new wealth" succeeded in forcing the old wealth to adopt the policies of its opponents. The limitation of old wealth in banking policies to flotations of government loans and foreign-exchange transactions could not be maintained in the face of the new competition. When the Rothschilds prevented the Pereires from establishing the Austrian Credit-Anstalt, they succeeded only because they became willing to establish the bank themselves and to conduct it not as an old-fashioned banking enterprise but as a crédit mobilier, that is, as a bank devoted to railroadization and industrialization of the country.

This conversion of the old wealth to the creed of the new wealth points out the direction of the most far-reaching effects of the Crédit Mobilier. Occasional ventures of that sort had been in existence in Belgium, Germany, and France herself. But it was the great eruptive effect of the Pereires that profoundly influenced the history of Continental banking in Europe from the second half of the past century onward. The number of banks in various countries shaped upon the image of the Pereire bank was considerable. But more important than their slavish imitations was the creative adaption of the basic idea of the Pereires and its incorporation in the new type of bank, the universal bank, which in Germany, along with most other countries on the Continent, became the dominant form of banking. The difference between banks of the crédit-mobilier type and commercial banks in the advanced industrial country of the time (England) was absolute. Between the English bank essentially designed to serve as a source of short-term capital and a bank designed to finance the long-run investment needs of the economy there was a complete gulf. The German banks, which may be taken as a paragon of the type of the universal bank, successfully combined the basic idea of the crédit mobilier with the short-term activities of commercial banks.

They were as a result infinitely sounder financial institutions than the Crédit Mobilier, with its enormously swollen industrial portfolio, which greatly exceeded its capital, and its dependence on favorable developments on the stock exchange for continuation of its activities. But the German banks, and with them the Austrian and Italian banks, established the closest possible relations with industrial enterprises. A German bank, as the saying went, accompanied an industrial enterprise from the cradle to the grave, from establishment to liquidation throughout all the vicissitudes of its existence. Through the device of formally short-term but in reality long-term current account credits and through development of the institution of the supervisory boards to the position of the most powerful organs within corporate organizations, the banks acquired a formidable degree of ascendancy over industrial enterprises, which extended far beyond the sphere of financial control into that of entrepreneurial and managerial decisions.

It cannot be the purpose of this presentation to go into the details of this development. All that is necessary is to relate its origins and effects to the subject under discussion. The industrialization of England had proceeded without any substantial utilization of banking for long-term investment purposes. The more gradual character of the industrialization process and the more considerable accumulation of capital, first from earnings in trade and modernized agriculture and later from industry itself, obviated the pressure for developing any special institutional devices for provision of long-term capital to industry. By contrast, in a relatively backward country capital is scarce and diffused, the distrust of industrial activities is considerable, and, finally, there is greater pressure for bigness because of the scope of the industrialization movement, the larger average size of plant, and the concentration of industrialization processes on branches of relatively high ratios of capital to output. To these should be added the scarcity of entrepreneurial talent in the backward country.

It is the pressure of these circumstances which essentially gave rise to the divergent development in banking over large portions of the Continent as against England. The continental practices in the field of industrial investment banking must be conceived as specific instruments of industrialization in a backward country. It is here essentially that lies the historical and geographic locus of theories of economic development that assign a central role to processes of forced saving by the money-creating activities of banks. As will be shown presently, however, use of such instruments must be regarded as specific, not to backward countries in general, but rather to countries whose backwardness does not exceed certain limits. And even within the latter for a rather long time it was mere collection and distribution of available funds in which the banks were primarily engaged. This circumstance, of course, did not detract from the paramount importance of such activities on the part of the banks during the earlier industrialization periods with their desperate shortages of capital for industrial ventures.

The effects of these policies were far-reaching. All the basic tendencies inherent in industrial development in backward countries were greatly emphasized and magnified by deliberate attitudes on the part of the banks. From the outset of this evolution the banks were primarily attracted to certain lines of production to the neglect, if not virtual exclusion, of others. To consider Germany until the outbreak of World War I, it was essentially coal mining, iron- and steelmaking, electrical and general engineering, and heavy chemical output which became the primary sphere of activities of German banks. The textile industry, the leather industry, and the foodstuff-producing industries remained on the fringes of the banks' interest. To use modern terminology, it was heavy rather than light industry to which the attention was devoted.

Furthermore, the effects were not confined to the productive structure of industry. They extended to its organizational structure. The last three decades of the nineteenth century were marked by a rapid concentration movement in banking. This process indeed went on in very much the same way on the other side of the English Channel. But in Britain, because of the different nature of relations between banks and industry, the process was not paralleled by a similar development in industry.

It was different in Germany. The momentum shown by the cartelization movement of German industry cannot be fully explained, except as the natural result of the amalgamation of German banks. It was the mergers in the field of banking that kept placing banks in the positions of controlling competing enterprises. The banks refused to tolerate fratricidal struggles among their children. From the vantage point of centralized control, they were at all times quick to perceive profitable opportunities of cartelization and amalgamation of industrial enterprises. In the process, the average size of plant kept growing, and at the same time the interests of the banks and their assistance were even more than before devoted to those branches of industry where cartelization opportunities were rife.

Germany thus had derived full advantages from being a relatively late arrival in the field of industrial development, that is to say, from having been preceded by England. But, as a result, German industrial economy, because of specific methods used in the catching-up process, developed along lines not insignificantly different from those in England.

THE STATE

The German experience can be generalized. Similar developments took place in Austria, or rather in the western sections of the Austrian-Hungarian Empire, in Italy, in Switzerland, in France, in Belgium, and in other countries, even though there were differences among the individual countries. But it certainly cannot be generalized for the European continent as a whole, and this for two reasons: (1) because of the existence of certain backward countries where no comparable features of industrial development can be discovered and (2) because of the existence of countries where the basic elements of backwardness appear in such an accentuated form as to lead to the use of essentially different institutional instruments of industrialization.

Little need be said with reference to the first type of country. The industrial development of Denmark may serve as an appropriate illustration. Surely, that country was still very backward as the nineteenth century entered upon its second half. Yet no comparable sudden spurts of industrialization and no peculiar emphasis on heavy industries could be observed. The reasons must be sought, on the one hand, in the paucity of the country's natural resources and, on the other hand, in the great opportunities for agricultural improvement that were inherent in the proximity of the English market. The peculiar response did not materialize because of the absence of the challenge.

Russia may be considered as the clearest instance of the second type of country. The characteristic feature of economic conditions in Russia was not only that the great spurt of modern industrialization came in the middle of the 1880s, that is to say, more than three decades after the beginning of rapid industrialization in Germany; even more important was the fact that at the starting point the level of economic development in Russia had been incomparably lower than that of countries such as Germany and Austria.

The main reason for the abysmal economic backwardness of Russia was the preservation of serfdom until the emancipation of 1861. In a certain sense, this very fact may be attributed to the play of a curious mechanism of economic backwardness, and a few words of explanation may be in order. In the course of its process of territorial expansion, which over a few centuries transferred the small duchy of Moscow into the huge land mass of modern Russia, the country became increasingly involved in military conflicts with the West. This involvement revealed a curious internal conflict between the tasks of the Russian government that were "modern" in the contemporaneous sense of the word and the hopelessly backward economy of the country on which the military policies had to be based. As a result, the economic development in Russia at several important junctures assumed the form of a peculiar series of sequences: (1) Basic was the fact that the state, moved by its military interest, assumed the role of the primary agent propelling the economic progress in the country. (2) The fact that economic development thus became a function of military exigencies imparted a peculiarly jerky character to the course of that development; it proceeded fast whenever military necessities were pressing and subsided as the military pressures relaxed. (3) The mode of economic progress by fits and starts implied that, whenever a considerable upsurge of economic activities was required, a very formidable burden was placed on the shoulders of the generations whose lifespan happened to coincide with the period of intensified development. (4) In order to exact effectively the great sacrifices it required, the government had to subject the reluctant population to a number of severe measures of oppression lest the burdens imposed be evaded by escape to the frontier regions in the southeast and east. (5) Precisely because of the magnitude of the governmental exactions, a period of rapid development was very likely to give way to prolonged stagnation, because the great effort had been pushed beyond the limits of physical endurance of the population and long periods of economic stagnation were the inevitable consequences. The sequences just mentioned present in a schematic way a pattern of Russian economic development in past centuries which fits best the period of the reforms under Peter the Great, but its applicability is by no means confined to that period.

What must strike the observer of this development is its curiously paradoxical course. While trying, as Russia did under Peter the Great, to adopt Western techniques, to raise output and the skills of the population to levels more closely approaching those of the West, Russia by virtue of this very effort was in some other respects thrown further away from the West. Broadly speaking, placing the trammels of serfdom upon the Russian peasantry must be understood as the obverse side of the processes of Westernization. Peter the Great did not institute serfdom in Russia, but perhaps more than anyone else he did succeed in making it effective. When in subsequent periods, partly because of point 2 and partly because of point 5 above, the state withdrew from active promotion of economic development and the nobility emancipated itself from its service obligations to the government, peasant serfdom was divested of its connection with economic development. What was once an indirect obligation to the state became a pure obligation toward the nobility and as such became by far the most important retarding factor in Russia's economic development.

Readers of Toynbee's may wish to regard this process, ending as it did with the emancipation of the peasantry, as an expression of the "withdrawal and return" sequence. Alternatively, they may justifiably prefer to place it under the heading of "arrested civilizations." At any rate, the challenge-response mechanism is certainly useful in thinking about sequences of that nature. It should be noted, however, that the problem is not simply one of quantitative relationship between the volume of the challenge and that of the response. The crucial point is that the magnitude of the challenge changes the *quality* of the response and, by so doing, not only injects powerful retarding factors into the economic process but also more likely leads to a number of undesirable noneconomic consequences. To this aspect, which is most relevant to the current problem of industrialization of backward countries, we shall advert again in the concluding remarks of this essay.

To return to Russian industrialization in the eighties and the nineties of the past century, it may be said that in one sense it can be viewed as a recurrence of a previous pattern of economic development in the country. The role of the state distinguishes rather clearly the type of Russian industrialization from its German or Austrian counterpart.

Emancipation of the peasants, despite its manifold deficiencies, was an absolute prerequisite for industrialization. As such it was a negative action of the state designed to remove obstacles that had been earlier created by the state itself and in this sense was fully comparable to acts such as the agrarian reforms in Germany or the policies of Napoleon III which have been mentioned earlier. Similarly, the great judicial and administrative reforms of the sixties were in the nature of creating a suitable framework for industrial development rather than promoting it directly.

The main point of interest here is that, unlike the case of Western Europe, actions of this sort did not per se lead to an upsurge of individual activities in the country; and for almost a quarter of a century after the emancipation the rate of industrial growth remained relatively low. The great industrial upswing came when, from the middle of the eighties on, the railroad building of the state assumed unprecedented proportions and became the main lever of a rapid industrialization policy. Through multifarious devices such as preferential orders to domestic producers of railroad materials, high prices, subsidies, credits, and profit guaranties to new industrial enterprises, the government succeeded in maintaining a high and, in fact, increasing rate of growth until the end of the century. Concomitantly, the Russian taxation system was reorganized, and the financing of industrialization policies was thus provided for, while the stabilization of the ruble and the introduction of the gold standard assured foreign participation in the development of Russian industry.

The basic elements of a backward economy were, on the whole, the same in Russia of the nineties and in Germany of the fifties. But quantitatively the differences were formidable. The scarcity of capital in Russia was such that no banking system could conceivably succeed in attracting sufficient funds to finance a large-scale industrialization; the standards of honesty in business were so disastrously low, the general distrust of the public so great, that no bank could have hoped to attract even such small capital funds as were available, and no bank could have successfully engaged in long-term credit policies in an economy where fraudulent bankruptcy had been almost elevated to the rank of a general business practice. Supply of capital for the needs of industrialization required the compulsory machinery of the government, which, through its taxation policies, succeeded in directing incomes from consumption to investment. There is no doubt that the government as an *agens movens* of industrialization discharged its role in a far less than perfectly efficient manner. Incompetence and corruption of bureaucracy were great. The amount of waste that accompanied the process was formidable. But, when all is said and done, the great success of the policies pursued under Vyshnegradski and Witte is undeniable. Not only in their origins but also in their effects, the policies pursued by the Russian government in the nineties resembled closely those of the banks in Central Europe. The Russian state did not evince any interest in "light industry." Its whole attention was centered on output of basic industrial materials and on machinery production; like the banks in Germany, the Russian bureaucracy was primarily interested in large-scale enterprises and in amalgamations and coordinated policies among the industrial enterprises which it favored or had helped to create. Clearly, a good deal of the government's interest in industrialization was predicated upon its military polices. But these policies only reinforced and accentuated the basic tendencies of industrialization in conditions of economic backwardness.

Perhaps nothing serves to emphasize more these basic uniformities in the situation and the dependence of actual institutional instruments used on the degree of backwardness of the country than a comparison of policies pursued within the two halves of the Austrian-Hungarian monarchy, that is to say, within one and the same political body. The Austrian part of the monarchy was backward in relation to, say, Germany, but it was at all times much more advanced than its Hungarian counterpart. Accordingly, in Austria proper the banks could successfully devote themselves to the promotion of industrial activities. But across the Leitha Mountains, in Hungary, the activities of the banks proved altogether inadequate, and around the turn of the century the Hungarian government embarked upon vigorous policies of industrialization. Originally, the government showed a considerable interest in developing the textile industry of the region. And it is instructive to watch how, under the pressure of what the French like to call the "logic of things," the basic uniformities asserted themselves and how the generous government subsidies were more and more deflected from textile industries to promotion of heavy industries.

THE GRADATIONS OF BACKWARDNESS

To return to the basic German-Russian paradigm: what has been said in the foregoing does not exhaust the pattern of parallels. The question remains as to the effects of successful industrializations, that is to say, of the gradual diminution of backwardness.

At the turn of the century, if not somewhat earlier, changes became apparent in the relationship between German banks and German industry. As the former industrial infants had grown to strong manhood, the original undisputed ascendancy of the banks over industrial enterprises could no longer be maintained. This process of liberation of industry from the decades of tutelage expressed itself in a variety of ways. Increasingly, industrial enterprises transformed connection with a single bank into cooperation with several banks. As the former industrial protectorates became economically sovereign, they embarked upon the policy of changing alliances with regard to the banks. Many an industrial giant, such as the electrical engineering industry, which could not have developed without the aid and entrepreneurial daring of the banks, began to establish its own banks. The conditions of capital scarcity to which the German banks owed their historical position were no longer present. Germany had become a developed industrial country. But the specific features engendered by a process of industrialization in conditions of backwardness were to remain, and so was the close relation between banks and industry, even though the master-servant relation gave way to cooperation among equals and sometimes was even reversed.

In Russia the magnificent period of industrial development of the nineties was cut short by the 1900 depression and the following years of war and civil strife. But, when Russia emerged from the revolutionary years 1905–1906 and again achieved a high rate of industrial growth in the years 1907–1914, the character of the industrialization processes had changed greatly. Railroad construction by the government continued but on a much smaller scale both absolutely and even more so relatively to the increased industrial output. Certain increases in military expenditures that took place could not begin to compensate for the reduced significance of railroad-building. The conclusion is inescapable that, in that last period of industrialization under a prerevolutionary government, the significance of the state was very greatly reduced.

At the same time, the traditional pattern of Russian economic development happily failed to work itself out. The retrenchment of government activities led not to stagnation but to a continuation of industrial growth. Russian industry had reached a stage where it could throw away the crutches of government support and begin to walk independently—and, yet, very much less independently than industry in contemporaneous Germany, for at least to some extent the role of the retreating government was taken over by the banks.

A great transformation had taken place with regard to the banks during the fifty years that had elapsed since the emancipation. Commercial banks had been founded. Since it was the government that had fulfilled the function of industrial banks, the Russian banks, precisely because of the backwardness of the country, were organized as "deposit banks," thus resembling very much the type of banking in England. But, as industrial development proceeded apace and as capital accumulation increased, the standards of business behavior were growingly Westernized. The paralyzing atmosphere of distrust began to vanish, and the foundation was laid for the emergence of a different type of bank. Gradually, the Moscow deposit banks were overshadowed by the development of the St. Petersburg banks that were conducted upon principles that were characteristic not of English but of German banking. In short, after the economic backwardness of Russia had been reduced by state-sponsored industrialization processes, use of a different instrument of industrialization, suitable to the new "stage of backwardness," became applicable.

IDEOLOGIES OF DELAYED INDUSTRIALIZATIONS

Before drawing some general conclusions, a last differential aspect of industrialization in circumstances of economic backwardness should be mentioned. So far, important differences with regard to the character of industrial developments and its institutional vehicles were related to conditions and degrees of backwardness. A few words remain to be said on the ideological climate within which such industrialization proceeded.

Again we may revert to the instructive story of French industrialization under Napoleon III. A large proportion of the men who reached positions of economic and financial influence upon Napoleon's advent to power were not isolated individuals. They belonged to a rather well-defined group. They were not Bonapartists but Saint-Simonian socialists. The fact that a man like Isaac Pereire, who contributed so much, perhaps more than any other single person, to the spread of the modern capitalist system in France should have been—and should have remained to the end of his days—an ardent admirer of Saint-Simonian doctrines is on the face of it surprising. It becomes much less so if a few pertinent relationships are considered.

It could be argued that Saint-Simon was in reality far removed from being a socialist; that in his vision of an industrial society he hardly distinguished between laborers and employers; and that he considered the appropriate political form for his society of the future some kind of corporate state in which the "leaders of industry" would exercise major political functions. Yet arguments of that sort would hardly explain much. Saint-Simon had a profound interest in what he used to call the "most numerous and most suffering classes"; more importantly, Saint-Simonian doctrines, as expanded and redefined by the followers of the master (particularly by Bazard), incorporated into the system a good many socialist ideas, including abolition of inheritance and establishment of a system of planned economy designed to direct and to develop the economy of the country. And it was this interpretation of the doctrines which the Pereires accepted.

It is more relevant to point to the stress laid by Saint-Simon and his followers upon industrialization and the great task they had assigned to banks as an instrument of organization and development of the economy. This, no doubt, greatly appealed to the creators of Crédit Mobilier, who liked to think of their institution as of a "bank to a higher power" and of themselves as "missionaries" rather than bankers. That Saint-Simon's stress upon the role to be played by banks in economic development revealed a truly amazing—and altogether "unutopian"—insight into the problems of that development is as true as the fact that Saint-Simonian ideas most decisively influenced the course of economic events inside and outside France. But the question remains: why was the socialist garment draped around an essentially capitalist idea? And why was it the socialist form that was so readily accepted by the greatest capitalist entrepreneurs France ever possessed?

It would seem that the answer must again be given in terms of basic conditions of backwardness. Saint-Simon, the friend of J. B. Say, was never averse to ideas of laissez-faire policies. Chevalier, the coauthor of the Franco-English treaty of commerce of 1860 that ushered in the great period of European free trade, had been an ardent Saint-Simonian. And yet under French conditions a laissez-faire ideology was altogether inadequate as a spiritual vehicle of an industrialization program.

To break through the barriers of stagnation in a backward country, to ignite the imaginations of men, and to place their energies in the service of economic development, a stronger medicine is needed than the promise of better allocation of resources or even of the lower price of bread. Under such conditions even the businessman, even the classical daring and innovating entrepreneur, needs a more powerful stimulus than the prospect of high profits. What is needed to remove the mountains of routine and prejudice is faith—faith, in the words of Saint-Simon, that the golden age lies not behind but ahead of mankind. It was not for nothing that Saint-Simon devoted his last years to the formulation of a new creed, the New Christianity, and suffered Auguste Comte to break with him over this "betrayal of true science." What sufficed in England did not suffice in France.

Shortly before his death, Saint-Simon urged Rouget de Lisle, the aged author of the "Marseillaise," to compose a new anthem, an "Industrial Marseillaise." Rouget de Lisle complied. In the new hymn the man who once had called upon "enfants de la patrie" to wage ruthless war upon the tyrants and their mercenary cohorts addresses himself to "enfants de l'industrie"—the "true nobles"—who would assure the "happiness of all" by spreading industrial arts and by submitting the world to the peaceful "laws of industry."

Ricardo is not known to have inspired anyone to change "God Save the King" into "God Save Industry." No one would want to detract from the force of John Bright's passionate eloquence, but in an advanced country rational arguments in favor of industrialization policies need not be supplemented by a quasi-religious fervor. Buckle was not far wrong when in a famous passage of his *History* he presented the conversion of public opinion in England to free trade as achieved by the force of incontrovertible logic. In a backward country the great and sudden industrialization effort calls for a New Deal in emotions. Those carrying out the great transformation as well as those on whom it imposes burdens must feel, in the words of Matthew Arnold, that

> . . . Clearing a stage
> Scattering the past about
> Comes the new age.

Capitalist industrialization under the auspices of socialist ideologies may be, after all, less surprising a phenomenon than would appear at first sight.

Similarly, Friedrich List's industrialization theories may be largely conceived as an attempt, by a man whose personal ties to Saint-Simonians had been very strong, to translate the inspirational message of Saint-Simonism into a language that would be accepted in the German environment, where the lack of both a preceding political revolution and an early national unification rendered nationalist sentiment a much more suitable ideology of industrialization.

After what has been just said it will perhaps not seem astonishing that, in the Russian industrialization of the 1890s, orthodox Marxism can be said to have performed a very similar function. Nothing reconciled the Russian intelligentsia more to the advent of capitalism in the country and to the destruction of its old faith in the mir and the artel than a system of ideas which presented the capitalist industrialization of the country as the result of an iron law of historical development. It is this connection which largely explains the power wielded by Marxist thought in Russia when extended to men like Struve and in some sense even Milyukov, whose Weltanschauung was altogether alien to the ideas of Marxian socialism. In conditions of Russian "absolute" backwardness, again, a much more powerful ideology was required to grease the intellectual and emotional wheels of industrialization than either in France or in Germany. The institutional gradations of backwardness seem to find their counterpart in men's thinking about backwardness and the way in which it can be abolished.

CONCLUSIONS

The story of European industrialization in the nineteenth century would seem to yield a few points of view which may be helpful for appreciation of present-day problems.

1. If the spurtlike character of the past century's industrialization on the European continent is conceived of as the result of the specific preindustrial situations in backward countries and if it is understood that pressures for high-speed industrializations are inherent in those situations, it should become easier to appreciate the oft-expressed desires in this direction by the governments of those countries. Slogans like "Factories quick!" which played such a large part in the discussions of the pertinent portions of the International Trade Organization charter, may then appear less unreasonable.

2. Similarly, the tendencies in backward countries to concentrate much of their efforts on introduction of the most modern and expensive technology,

their stress on large-scale plant, and their interest in developing investment-goods industries need not necessarily be regarded as flowing mainly from a quest for prestige and from economic megalomania.

3. What makes it so difficult for an advanced country to appraise properly the industrialization policies of its less fortunate brethren is the fact that, in every instance of industrialization, imitation of the evolution in advanced countries appears in combination with different, indigenously determined elements. If it is not always easy for advanced countries to accept the former, it is even more difficult for them to acquiesce in the latter. This is particularly true of the institutional instruments used in carrying out industrial developments and even more so of ideologies which accompany it. What can be derived from a historical review is a strong sense for the significance of the native elements in the industrialization of backward countries.

A journey through the last century may, by destroying what Bertrand Russell once called the "dogmatism of the untravelled," help in formulating a broader and more enlightened view of the pertinent problems and in replacing the absolute notions of what is "right" and what is "wrong" by a more flexible and relativistic approach.

It is, of course, not suggested here that current policies vis-à-vis backward areas should be formulated on the basis of the general experience of the past century without taking into account, in each individual instance, the degree of endowment with natural resources, the climatic disabilities, the strength of institutional obstacles to industrialization, the pattern of foreign trade, and other pertinent factors. But what is even more important is the fact that, useful as the "lessons" of the nineteenth century may be, they cannot properly be applied without understanding the climate of the present century, which in so many ways has added new and momentous aspects to the problems concerned.

Since the present problem of industrialization of backward areas largely concerns non-European countries, there is the question of the effects of their specific preindustrial cultural development upon their industrialization potentialities. Anthropological research of such cultural patterns has tended to come to rather pessimistic conclusions in this respect. But perhaps such conclusions are unduly lacking in dynamic perspective. At any rate, they do not deal with the individual factors involved in terms of the specific changeabilities. At the same time, past Russian experience does show how quickly in the last decades of the past century a pattern of life that had been so strongly opposed to industrial values, that tended to consider any nonagricultural economic activity as unnatural and sinful, began to give way to very different attitudes. In particular, the rapid emergence of native entrepreneurs with peasant-serf backgrounds should give pause to those who stress so greatly the disabling lack of entrepreneurial qualities in backward civilizations. Yet there are other problems.

In certain extensive backward areas the very fact that industrial development has been so long delayed has created, along with unprecedented opportunities for technological progress, great obstacles to industrialization.

Industrial progress is arduous and expensive; medical progress is cheaper and easier of accomplishment. To the extent that the latter has preceded the former by a considerable span of time and has resulted in formidable overpopulation, industrial revolutions may be defeated by Malthusian counterrevolutions.

Closely related to the preceding but enormously more momentous in its effect is the fact that great delays in industrialization tend to allow time for social tensions to develop and to assume sinister proportions. As a mild example, the case of Mexico may be cited, where the established banks have been reluctant to cooperate in industrialization activities that are sponsored by a government whose radical hue they distrust. But the real case in point overshadowing everything else in scope and importance is, of course, that of Soviet Russia.

If what has been said in the preceding pages has validity, Soviet industrialization undoubtedly contains all the basic elements that were common to the industrializations of backward countries in the nineteenth century. The stress on heavy industry and oversized plant is, as such, by no means peculiar to Soviet Russia. But what is true is that in Soviet Russia those common features of industrialization processes have been magnified and distorted out of all proportion.

The problem is as much a political as it is an economic one. The Soviet government can be properly described as a product of the country's economic backwardness. Had serfdom been abolished by Catherine the Great or at the time of the Decembrist uprising in 1825, the peasant discontent, the driving force and the earnest of success of the Russian Revolution, would never have assumed disastrous proportions, while the economic development of the country would have proceeded in a much more gradual fashion. If anything is a "grounded historical assumption," this would seem to be one: the delayed industrial revolution was responsible for a political revolution in the course of which the power fell into the hands of a dictatorial government to which in the long run the vast majority of the population was opposed. It is one thing for such a government to gain power in a moment of great crisis; it is another to maintain this power for a long period. Whatever the strength of the army and the ubiquitousness of the secret police which such a government may have at its disposal, it would be naive to believe that those instruments of physical oppression can suffice. Such a government can maintain itself in power only if it succeeds in making people believe that it performs an important social function which could not be discharged in its absence.

Industrialization provided such a function for the Soviet government. All the basic factors in the situation of the country pressed in that direction. By reverting to a pattern of economic development that should have remained confined to a long-bygone age, by substituting collectivization for serfdom, and by pushing up the rate of investment to the maximum point within the limits of endurance of the population, the Soviet government did what no government relying on the consent of the governed could have done.

That these policies, after having led through a period of violent struggles, have resulted in permanent day-to-day friction between the government and the population is undeniable. But, paradoxical as it may sound, these policies at the same time have secured some broad acquiescence on the part of the people. If all the forces of the population can be kept engaged in the processes of industrialization and if this industrialization can be justified by the promise of happiness and abundance for future generations and—much more importantly—by the menace of military aggression from beyond the borders, the dictatorial government will find its power broadly unchallenged. And the vindication of a threatening war is easily produced, as is shown by the history of the cold-war years. Economic backwardness, rapid industrialization, ruthless exercise of dictatorial power, and the danger of war have become inextricably intertwined in Soviet Russia.

This is not the place to elaborate this point further with regard to Soviet Russia. The problem at hand is not Soviet Russia but the problem of attitudes toward industrialization of backward countries. If the Soviet experience teaches anything, it is that it demonstrates *ad oculos* the formidable dangers inherent in our time in the existence of economic backwardness. There are no four-lane highways through the parks of industrial progress. The road may lead from backwardness to dictatorship and from dictatorship to war. In conditions of a "bipolar world" this sinister sequence is modified and aggrandized by deliberate imitation of Soviet policies by other backward countries and by their voluntary or involuntary incorporation in the Soviet orbit.

Thus, conclusions can be drawn from the historical experience of both centuries. The paramount lesson of the twentieth century is that the problems of backward nations are not exclusively their own. They are just as much problems of the advanced countries. It is not only Russia but the whole world that pays the price for the failure to emancipate the Russian peasants and to embark upon industrialization policies at an early time. Advanced countries cannot afford to ignore economic backwardness. But the lesson of the nineteenth century is that the policies toward the backward countries are unlikely to be successful if they ignore the basic peculiarities of economic backwardness. Only by frankly recognizing their existence and strength, and by attempting to develop fully rather than to stifle what Keynes once called the "possibilities of things," can the experience of the nineteenth century be used to avert the threat presented by its successor.

NOTES

1. Karl Marx, *Das Kapital* (1st ed.), preface.

2. It would have been extremely desirable to transcend the European experience at least by including some references to the industrialization of Japan. Unfortunately, the writer's ignorance of Japanese economic history has effectively barred him from thus broadening the scope of his observations. The reader must be referred, however, to the excellent study by Henry Rosovsky, *Capital Formation in Japan, 1868–1940*

(Glencoe, 1961), in which the validity of this writer's approach for Japanese industrial history is explicitly discussed.

EDITORS' NOTES ON FURTHER READING: GERSCHENKRON

Alexander Gerschenkron was one of the foremost economic historians of the twentieth century; for an introduction to his life and work, see Albert Fishlow, "Alexander Gerschenkron (1904–1978)," pp. 518–519 in volume 2 of *The New Palgrave Dictionary of Economics* (1987) and Lewis Coser, *Refugee Scholars in America*, pp. 157–163 (1984). There is a vast literature on how to overcome economic "backwardness." Walter Rostow's *The Stages of Economic Growth* (1960) was one of the first and most influential works to assert that certain conditions are necessary for an economic "takeoff," implying that there is only one way that a country can industrialize. Thorstein Veblen, however, had argued (in *Imperial Germany and the Industrial Revolution*, 1915), long before Rostow or Gerschenkron, that being a latecomer can have its advantages. A contemporary version of Veblen's argument can be found in Mancur Olson's *The Rise and Decline of Nations: Economic Growth, Stagflation, and Social Rigidities* (1982), where the author points out that certain events—for example, the devastation of a country in a war—may clear the road for economic growth by eliminating various interest organizations. That the different ways in which a country industrializes also will affect its political system is emphasized especially by Barrington Moore in *Social Origins of Dictatorship and Democracy: Lord and Peasant in the Making of the Modern World* (1966). A critical appraisal of this argument can be found in Jonathan M. Wiener's "The Barrington Moore Thesis and Its Critics," *Theory and Society* 2 (1975):301–330.

Though Gerschenkron only dealt with nineteenth-century Europe (including Tzarist Russia) in his article, his argument about economic backwardness has been generalized. See Marion Levy, *Modernization: Latecomers and Survivors* (1972). There is a great deal of related literature on economic development in the Third World; an excellent introduction that assesses trends in the literature on socioeconomic development over the last thirty years, by arguing against simple "convergence" models in favor of historically informed theory, can be found in Peter B. Evans and John D. Stephens's "Development and the World Economy," pp. 739–773 in Neil Smelser, ed., *Handbook of Sociology* (1988). One influential perspective discussed in this article is Immanuel Wallerstein's, as developed in *The Modern World-System* (1974, 1979, 1989). For work along Wallerstein's lines, see the series *Political Economy of the World-System Annuals* (1978–); and for critical appraisal of Wallerstein's ideas, see, for example, Charles Ragin and Daniel Chirot, "The World-System of Immanuel Wallerstein," pp. 276–312 in Theda Skocpol, ed., *Vision and Method in Historical Sociology* (1984). Dependency theory provides another influential perspective on Third World development. The classic study in the genre is F. H. Cardoso and Enzo Faletto's *Dependency and Development in Latin America* (Eng. tr. 1979). The intellectual history of dependency theory and its unfolding is described well in Magnus Blomström and Björn Hettne's *Development Theory in Transition: The Dependency Debate and Beyond* (Eng. tr. 1984). A good general account is Ian Roxborough's *Theories of Development* (1977).

5

The Emergence
of Managerial Capitalism

ALFRED D. CHANDLER, JR.

In the late nineteenth and early twentieth centuries, a new type of capitalism emerged. It differed from traditional personal capitalism in that basic decisions concerning the production and distribution of goods and services were made by teams, or hierarchies, of salaried managers who had little or no equity ownership in the enterprises they operated. Such managerial hierarchies currently govern the major sectors of market economies in which the means of production are still owned privately, rather than by the state.

Managerial hierarchies of this kind are entirely modern. As late as the 1840s, with very few exceptions owners managed and managers owned. There were salaried managers before the nineteenth century, primarily on plantations and estates, but they worked directly with owners. There were no hierarchies of managers comparable to that depicted in Figure [5.]1. By the 1840s personally managed enterprises—those that carried out the processes of production and distribution in market economies—had become specialized, usually handling a single function and a single product. They operated a factory, mine, bank, or trading office. Where the volume of activity was not yet large enough to bring such specialization, merchants often remained involved in manufacturing and banking, as they had in the early years of capitalism. Some had partnerships in distant lands. But even the largest and most powerful of early capitalist enterprises were tiny by modern standards.

For example, the Medici Bank of the fifteenth century and that of the Fuggers in the sixteenth were far more powerful financial institutions in

Financial support for this article was provided by the Harvard Business School's Division of Research and the German Marshall Fund.

Alfred D. Chandler, Jr., "The Emergence of Managerial Capitalism," *Business History Review* 58 (Winter 1984):473–503. Copyright © 1984 by the President and Fellows of Harvard College. Reprinted by permission of Harvard Business School.

132

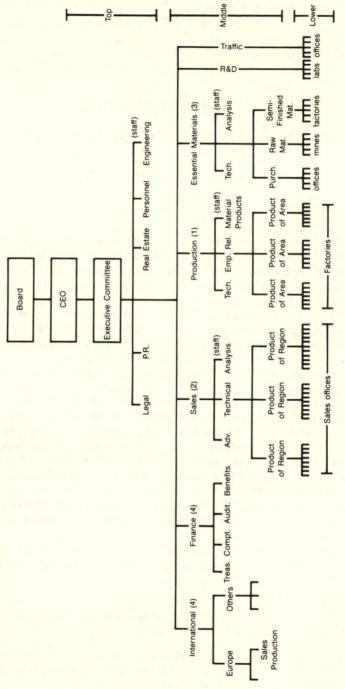

FIGURE [5.]1 The multifunctional structure

their day than the giant nonstate banks in America, Europe, and Japan are today. Yet the Medici Bank in 1470 operated only seven branches. The total number of individuals working in the branches and the home office in Florence was fifty-seven. Of these a dozen were considered managers. They were not salaried employees, however, but partners, albeit junior ones, who shared in the profits and who had "joint and unlimited liability" for losses.[1] Today's middling-size state banks each have as many as 200 branches, 5,000 employees, 300 salaried managers (who have no liability at all), and handle over a million transactions a day. They handle more transactions in a week than the Medici Bank processed in the century of its existence. Today, too, small industrial enterprises handle a far greater volume of transactions than did those giants of an earlier capitalism—the Hudson's Bay, the Royal African, or even the East India Company.

What made the difference was, of course, the technological revolution of modern times—an even more profound discontinuity in the history of civilized man than the urban revolution of the eleventh to thirteenth centuries that created the first modern market economies and with them modern capitalism. The enormous increase in the volume of output and transactions was not an inevitable consequence of the First Industrial Revolution, which began in Britain at the end of the eighteenth century. That is, it was not the result of the initial application of the new sources of energy—fossil fuel, coal—to the processes of production. A much more important cause was the coming of modern transportation and communication. The railroad, telegraph, steamship, and cable made possible the modern mass production and distribution that were the hallmarks of the Second Industrial Revolution of the late nineteenth and early twentieth centuries. These new high-volume technologies could not be effectively exploited unless the massive flows of materials were guided through the process of both production and distribution by teams of salaried managers.

The first such managerial hierarchies appeared during the 1850s and 1860s to coordinate the movements of trains and flow of goods over the new railroad networks, and messages over the new telegraph system.[2] They then quickly came into use to manage the new mass retailing establishments— the department stores, mail order houses, and chains or multiple shops— whose existence the railroad and the telegraph made possible. For example, by 1905 such an organization permitted Sears, Roebuck in Chicago to fill 100,000 mail orders in a single day—more than the average earlier American merchant filled in a lifetime. These administrative hierarchies grew to a still much greater size in industrial enterprises that, again on the basis of modern transportation and communication, integrated mass production and mass distribution within a single business enterprise.

One way to review the emergence of managerial capitalism is thus to focus on the evolution of this largest and most complex of managerial institutions, the integrated industrial enterprise. Whether American, European, or Japanese, these integrated enterprises have had much in common. They appeared at almost exactly the same moment in history in the United

States and Europe and a little later in Japan, only because Japan was later to industrialize. They clustered in much the same types of industries, and they grew in much the same manner. In nearly all cases they became large, first, by integrating forward (that is, investing in marketing and distribution facilities and personnel); then, by moving backward into purchasing and control of raw and semifinished material; and sometimes, though much less often, by investing in research and development. In this way they created the multifunctional organization depicted in Figure [5.]1. They soon became multinational by investing abroad, first in marketing and then in production. Finally they continued to expand their activities by investing in product lines related to their existing businesses, thus creating the organization depicted in Figure [5.]2.

THE SIMILARITIES

Tables [5.]1 through 5 document the similarities among the large integrated industrial enterprises of the United States, Europe, and Japan. Almost all are clustered in a limited number of industries. Table [5.]1 identifies the country and industry of all industrial corporations in the world that in 1973 employed more than 20,000 workers. (The industries are those defined as two-digit industrial groups by the U.S. Census Standard Industrial Classi-fication [SIC]). Of these 401 companies, 263 (65 percent) were in food, chemicals, oil, machinery, and primary metals. Just under 30 percent more, although in other two-digit groups, were in three-digit subcategories that had the same characteristics as those in which the 65 percent clustered—for example, cigarettes within the tobacco category; tires in rubber; newsprint in paper; plate glass in stone, glass, and clay; cans and razor blades in fabricated metals, and mass-produced cameras in instruments. Only twenty-one companies (5.2 percent) were in remaining two-digit categories—apparel, lumber, furniture, leather, publishing and printing, instruments, and mis-cellaneous.

American firms predominate among the world's largest industrial cor-porations—an observation central to an understanding of the evolution of this institution. Of the 401 companies shown in Table [5.]1, more than half (211 or 52.6 percent) were American. The United Kingdom followed with 50 (12.5 percent), Germany with 29 (7.2 percent), Japan with 28 (7.0 percent) and France with 24 (6.0 percent). Only in chemicals, metals, and electrical machinery were there as many as four or five more firms outside the United States than there were within it.

Throughout the twentieth century, Table [5.]2 shows, large U.S. industrial corporations clustered in the same industries in which they were concentrated in 1973. Much the same pattern is observed for Britain, Germany, and Japan (Tables [5.]3, [5.]4, and [5.]5). The American firms were larger, as well as more numerous, than those in other countries. For example, in 1948, only 50 to 55 of the British firms had assets comparable to those of the top 200 in the United States. In 1930, the number was about the same. For Germany

FIGURE [5.]2 The multidivisional structure

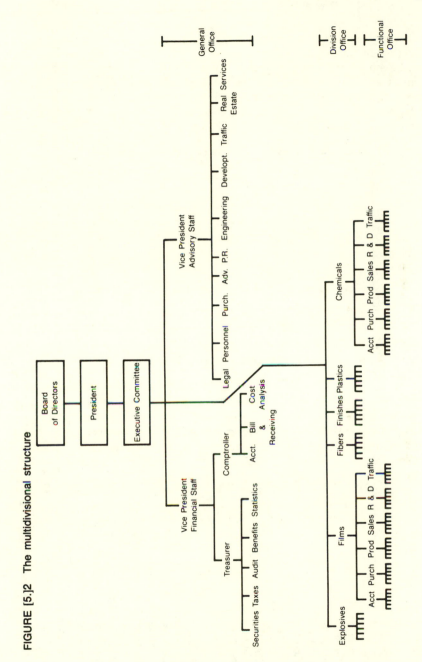

TABLE [5.]1 The Distribution of the Largest Manufacturing Enterprises (more than 20,000 employees), by Industry and Nationality, 1973

SIC Group	U.S.	U.K.	Germany	Japan	France	Others	Total Non-U.S.	Grand Total
20 Food	22	13	0	1	1	2	17	39
21 Tobacco	3	3	1	0	0	0	4	7
22 Textiles	7	3	0	2	1	0	6	13
23 Apparel	6	0	0	0	0	0	0	6
24 Lumber	4	0	0	0	0	2	2	6
25 Furniture	0	0	0	0	0	0	0	0
26 Paper	7	3	0	0	0	0	3	10
27 Printing	0	0	0	0	0	0	0	0
28 Chemical	24	4	5	3	6	10	28	52
29 Petroleum	14	2	0	0	2	8	12	26
30 Rubber	5	1	1	1	1	1	5	10
31 Leather	2	0	0	0	0	0	0	2
32 Stone, clay, and glass	7	3	0	0	3	2	8	15
33 Primary metal	13	2	9	5	4	15	35	48
34 Fabricated metal	8	5	1	0	0	0	6	14
35 Machinery	22	2	3	2	0	5	12	34
36 Electrical machinery	20	4	5	7	2	7	25	45
37 Transportation equipment	22	3	3	7	4	6	23	45
38 Measuring instruments	4	0	0	0	0	0	1	5
39 Miscellaneous	2	0	0	0	0	0	0	2
Diversified/conglomerate	19	2	1	0	0	0	3	22
TOTAL	211	50	29	28	24	59	190	401

Note: In 1970 the 100 largest industrials accounted for more than a third of net manufacturing output in the United States and over 45 percent in the United Kingdom. In 1930 they accounted for about 25 percent of total net output in both countries.

Source: Fortune, May 1974 and August 1974.

TABLE [5.]2   The Distribution of the 200 Largest Manufacturing Firms
in the United States, by Industry[a]

SIC Group	1917	1930	1948	1973
20 Food	30	32	26	22
21 Tobacco	6	5	5	3
22 Textiles	5	3	6	3
23 Apparel	3	0	0	0
24 Lumber	3	4	1	4
25 Furniture	0	1	1	0
26 Paper	5	7	6	9
27 Printing and publishing	2	3	2	1
28 Chemical	20	18	24	27
29 Petroleum	22	26	24	22
30 Rubber	5	5	5	5
31 Leather	4	2	2	0
32 Stone, clay, and glass	5	9	5	7
33 Primary metal	29	25	24	19
34 Fabricated metal	8	10	7	5
35 Machinery	20	22	24	17
36 Electrical machinery	5	5	8	13
37 Transportation equipment	26	21	26	19
38 Instruments	1	2	3	4
39 Miscellaneous	1	1	1	1
Diversified/conglomerate	0	0	0	19
TOTAL	200	200	200	200

[a]Ranked by assets.

and Japan it was smaller. Well before World War II the United States had many more and many larger managerial hierarchies than did other nations—underlining the fact that managerial capitalism first emerged in the new world.

These tables also suggest (though only barely so) basic differences within the broad pattern of evolution. For example, large enterprises in the United States were active throughout the twentieth century in the production of both consumer and industrial goods. Britain had proportionately more large firms in consumer goods than the United States, while the largest industrials in Germany and Japan concentrated much more on producers' goods. Even as late as 1973 (as Table [5.]1 shows), 13 of the 50 U.K. firms employing more than 20,000 persons were involved in the production and distribution of food and tobacco products; whereas Germany, France, and Japan each had only one such firm. Before World War II, Germany had many more firms in chemicals and heavy machinery than did the British; Japan, the late industrializer, still had a greater number of textile firms than did the other nations in its top 200. As Japan's economy grew, the number of chemical and machinery enterprises on that list increased substantially.

TABLE [5.]3   The Distribution of the 200 Largest Manufacturing Firms in the United Kingdom, by Industry[a]

SIC Group	1919	1930	1948	1973
20 Food	63	64	52	33
21 Tobacco	3	4	8	4
22 Textiles	26	24	18	10
23 Apparel	1	3	3	0
24 Lumber	0	0	0	2
25 Furniture	0	0	0	0
26 Paper	4	5	6	7
27 Printing and publishing	5	10	7	7
28 Chemical	11	9	15	21
29 Petroleum	3	3	3	8
30 Rubber	3	3	2	6
31 Leather	0	0	0	3
32 Stone, clay, and glass	2	6	5	16
33 Primary metal	35	18	28	14
34 Fabricated metal	2	7	8	7
35 Machinery	8	7	7	26
36 Electrical machinery	11	18	13	14
37 Transportation equipment	20	14	22	16
38 Instruments	0	1	4	3
39 Miscellaneous	3	4	3	1
Diversified/conglomerate	0	0	0	2
TOTAL	200	200	204	200

[a]Ranked by sales for 1973 and by market value of quoted capital for the other years.

EXPLANATION OF THE EVOLUTIONARY PROCESS

Why have these large integrated hierarchical enterprises appeared in some industries but rarely in others? And why did they appear at almost the same historical moment in the United States and Europe? Why did they grow in the same manner, first integrating forward into volume distribution, next taking on other functions, and then becoming multinational and finally multiproduct?

Because these enterprises initially grew by integrating mass production with volume distribution, answers to these critical questions require a careful look at both these processes. Mass production is an attribute of specific technologies. In some industries the primary way to increase output was to add more workers and machines; in others it was to improve and rearrange the inputs, by improving the machinery, furnaces, stills, and other equipment, by reorienting the process of production within the plant, by placing the several intermediate processes of production required for a finished product within a single works, and by increasing the application of energy (particularly fossil fuel energy). The first set of industries remained "labor intensive"; the second set became "capital intensive." In the latter category, the technology of production permitted much greater economies of scale than were

TABLE [5.]4   The Distribution of the 200 Largest Manufacturing Firms
in Germany, by Industry[a]

SIC Group	1913	1928	1953	1973
20 Food	23	28	23	24
21 Tobacco	1	0	0	6
22 Textiles	13	15	19	4
23 Apparel	0	0	0	0
24 Lumber	1	1	2	0
25 Furniture	0	0	0	0
26 Paper	1	2	3	2
27 Printing and publishing	0	1	0	6
28 Chemical	26	27	32	30
29 Petroleum	5	5	3	8
30 Rubber	1	1	3	3
31 Leather	2	3	2	1
32 Stone, clay, and glass	10	9	9	15
33 Primary metal	49	47	45	19
34 Fabricated metal	8	7	8	14
35 Machinery	21	19	19	29
36 Electrical machinery	18	16	13	21
37 Transportation equipment	19	16	14	14
38 Instruments	1	2	4	2
39 Miscellaneous	1	1	1	1
Diversified/conglomerate	0	0	0	1
TOTAL	200	200	200	200

[a]Ranked by sales for 1973 and by assets for the other three years.

possible in the former. That is, the cost per unit of output declined much more as volume increased. So in these capital-intensive industries with large batch or continuous process technologies, large works operating at minimum efficient scale (the scale of operation that brought the lowest unit costs) had a much greater cost advantage over small works than was true with labor-intensive technologies. Conversely, in comparison with labor-intensive industries, cost per unit rose much more rapidly when volume of production fell below minimum efficient scale (perhaps 80 to 90 percent of rated capacity).

The cost advantage of scale cannot be fully realized unless a constant flow of materials through the plant or factory is maintained to assure effective capacity utilization. The decisive figure in determining costs and profits is thus not rated capacity but throughput—the amount actually processed in a specified time period. Throughput is the proper economic measure of capacity utilization. In the capital-intensive industries the throughput needed to maintain minimum efficient scale requires careful coordination of not only the flow through the processes of production but also the flows of inputs from the suppliers and the flow of outputs to the retailers and final consumers. Such coordination cannot happen automatically. It demands the constant attention of a managerial team, or hierarchy. Scale is only a

TABLE [5.]5   The Distribution of the 200 Largest Manufacturing Firms
in Japan, by Industry[a]

SIC Group	1918	1930	1954	1973
20 Food	31	30	26	18
21 Tobacco	1	1	0	0
22 Textiles	54	62	23	11
23 Apparel	2	2	1	0
24 Lumber	3	1	0	1
25 Furniture	0	0	0	0
26 Paper	12	6	12	10
27 Printing and publishing	1	1	0	2
28 Chemical	23	22	38	34
29 Petroleum	6	5	11	13
30 Rubber	0	1	1	5
31 Leather	4	1	0	0
32 Stone, clay, and glass	16	14	8	14
33 Primary metal	21	22	28	27
34 Fabricated metal	4	3	6	5
35 Machinery	4	4	10	16
36 Electrical machinery	7	12	15	18
37 Transportation equipment	9	11	18	20
38 Instruments	1	1	3	5
39 Miscellaneous	1	1	0	1
Diversified/conglomerate	0	0	0	0
TOTAL	200	200	200	200

[a]Ranked by assets.

technological characteristic; the economies of scale, measured by throughput, are organizational. Such economies depend on knowledge, skills, and team-work—on the human organization essential to exploit the potential of technological processes.

A well-known example illustrates these generalizations. In 1882 the Standard Oil "alliance"—a loose federation of forty companies, each with its own legal and administrative identity but tied to John D. Rockefeller's Standard Oil Company through interchange of stock and other financial devices—formed the Standard Oil Trust.[3] The purpose was not to obtain control over the industry's output, for the alliance already controlled close to 90 percent of the American output of kerosene. Instead the trust was formed to provide a legal instrument to rationalize the industry and to exploit economies of scale more fully. The trust provided the essential legal means to create a corporate or central office that could, first, reorganize the processes of production by shutting down some refineries, reshaping others, and building new ones; and, second, coordinate the flow of materials, not only through the several refineries, but from the oil fields to the refineries and from the refineries to the consumers. The resulting rationalization made it possible to concentrate close to a quarter of the world's production of kerosene in three refineries, each within average daily charging capacity of

6,500 barrels, with two-thirds of their product going to overseas markets. (At this time the refined petroleum products were by far the nation's largest nonagricultural export.) Imagine the diseconomies of scale—the great increase in unit costs—that would result from placing close to one-fourth of the world's production of shoes, or textiles, or lumber in three factories or mills!

This reorganization of the trust's refining facilities brought a sharp reduction in the average cost of producing a gallon of kerosene. It dropped from 1.5 cents a gallon before reorganization to 0.54 cents in 1884 and 0.45 cents in 1885 (while profits rose from 0.53 to 1.003 cents per gallon), with costs at the giant refineries being still lower—far below those of any competitor. Maintaining this cost advantage, however, required that these large refineries have a continuing daily throughput of from 5,000 to 6,500 barrels—a three- to fourfold increase over their earlier daily flow of 1,500 to 2,000 barrels, with concomitant increases in the number of transactions handled and in the complexity of coordinating the flow of materials through the process of production and distribution.

The Standard Oil story was by no means unique. In the 1880s and 1890s new mass production technologies—those of the Second Industrial Revolution—brought sharp reduction in costs as plants reached minimum efficient scale. In many industries the level of output was so high at that scale that a few plants could meet existing national and even global demand. The structure of these industries quickly became oligopolistic. Their few large enterprises competed worldwide. In many instances the first enterprise to build a plant with a high minimum efficient scale and to recruit the essential management team has remained the leader in its industry until this day. A brief review of Tables [5.]1 through [5.]5 illustrates this close relationship between scale economies, the size of the enterprise, and industrial concentration in the industries in which large enterprises cluster.

In SIC groups 20 and 21—food, drink, and tobacco—brand new production processes in the refining of sugar and vegetable oils, in the milling of wheat and oats, and in the making of cigarettes brought rapid reductions in costs. In cigarettes, for example, the invention of the Bonsack machine in the early 1880s permitted the first entrepreneurs who adopted the machine—James B. Duke in the United States and the Wills brothers in Britain—to reduce labor costs sharply, in the Wills' case from 4 shillings per 1,000 to 0.3 pence per thousand.[4] Understandably Duke and the Wills soon dominated and then divided the world market. In addition, most companies in group 20, and also those producing consumer chemicals, such as soap, cosmetics, paints, and pills, pioneered in the use of new high-volume techniques for packaging their products in small units that could be placed directly on retailers' shelves. The most important of these was the "automatic-line" canning process invented in the mid 1880s, which permitted the filling of 4,000 cans per hour. The names of these pioneers—Campbell Soup, Heinz, Borden's, Carnation, Nestlé, Cadbury, Cross and Blackwell, Lever, Procter & Gamble, Colgate, and others—are still well known today.

In chemicals (group 29) the new technologies brought even sharper cost reductions in industrial than in packaged consumer products. The mass production of synthetic dyes and synthetic alkalis began in the 1880s. It came a little later in synthetic nitrates, synthetic fibers, plastics, and film. The first three firms to produce the new synthetic blue dye, alizarine, reduced their production costs from 200 marks per kilogram in the 1870s to 9 marks by 1886; and today, a century later, those three firms—Bayer, BASF, and Hochest—are still the three largest German chemical companies.[5]

Rubber production (group 30), like oil, benefited from scale economies, even more in the production of tires than in rubber footwear and clothing. Of the ten rubber companies listed in Table [5.]1, nine built their first large factory between 1900 and 1908.[6] Since then the Japanese company, Bridgestone, has been the only major new entrant into the global oligopoly.

In metals (group 34) the scale economies made possible by maintaining a high volume throughput were also striking. Andrew Carnegie was able to reduce the cost of making steel rails by the new Bessemer steel process from close to $100 a ton in the early 1870s to $12 by the late 1890s.[7] In nonferrous metals, the electrolytic refining process invented in the 1880s brought even more impressive cost reductions, permitting the price of a kilogram of aluminum to fall from 87.5 francs in 1888 to 47.5 francs in 1889, 19 francs at the end of 1890, and 3.75 francs in 1895.[8]

In the machinery-making industries (group 35–37) the new technologies based on the fabricating and assembling of interchangeable metal parts were perfected in the 1880s. By 1886, for example, Singer Sewing Machine had two plants, one in New Jersey and the other in Glasgow, each producing 8,000 machines a week.[9] To maintain their output, which satisfied three-fourths of the world demand, required an even more tightly scheduled coordination of flows of materials into, through, and out of the plant than did the mass production of packaged goods, chemicals, and metals. By the 1890s a tiny number of enterprises using comparable plants supplied the world demand for typewriters, cash registers, adding machines, and other office equipment; for harvesters, reapers, and other agricultural machinery; and for the newly invented electrical and other volume-produced industrial machinery. The culmination of these processes came with the mass production of the automobile. By installing the moving assembly line in his Highland Park plant in 1913, Henry Ford reduced the labor time used in putting together a Model T chassis from 12 hours 28 minutes to one hour 33 minutes.[10] This dramatic increase in throughput permitted Ford to drop the price of the touring car from more than $600 in 1913 to $490 in 1914 to $290 in the 1920s; to pay the highest wages; and to acquire one of the world's largest fortunes in an astonishingly short time.

In the older, technologically simple, labor-intensive industries such as apparel, textiles, leather, lumber, and publishing and printing, neither technological nor organizational innovation substantially increased minimum efficient scale. As the tables show, few large firms appeared in these SIC groups. In these industries the opportunities for cost reduction through material coordination of high volume throughput by managerial teams remained limited. Large plants could not achieve significant cost advantages over small ones.

The differentials in potential scale economies of different production technologies indicate not only why the large hierarchical firms appeared in some industries and not in others, but also why they appeared suddenly in the last decades of the nineteenth century. Only with the completion of the modern transportation and communication networks—those of the railroad, telegraph, steamship, and cable—could materials flow into a factory or processing plant and the finished goods move out at the speed and volume required to achieve substantial economies of throughput. Transportation that depended on the power of animals, wind, and current was too slow, too irregular, and too uncertain to maintain a level of throughput necessary to achieve modern economies of scale.

However, such scale and throughput economies do not in themselves explain why the new mass producers elected to integrate forward into mass distribution. Coordination might have been achieved through contractual agreement with intermediaries, both buyers and sellers. Such an explanation requires a more precise understanding of the process of volume distribution, particularly why the wholesaler, retailer, or other commercial intermediaries lost their cost advantage vis-à-vis the volume producer.

The intermediaries' cost advantage lay in exploiting both economies of scale and what have been termed "economies of scope." Because they handled the products of many manufacturers, they achieved a greater volume and lower unit cost (i.e. scale) than any one manufacturer in the marketing and distribution of a *single* line of products. Moreover, they increased this advantage by the broader *scope* of their operation, that is, by handling a number of *related* product lines through a single set of facilities. This was true of the new volume wholesalers in apparel, dry goods, groceries, hardware, and the like, and even more true of the new mass retailers—the department store, the mail order house, and the chain or multiple-shop enterprise.

The commercial intermediaries lost their cost advantages when manufacturers' output reached a comparable scale. As one economist has pointed out, "The intermediary will have a cost advantage over its customers and suppliers only as long as the volume of transactions in which he engages comes closer to that [minimum efficient] scale than do the transactions volumes of his customers or suppliers."[11] This rarely happened in retailing, except in heavily concentrated urban markets, but it often occurred in wholesaling. In addition, the advantages of scope were sharply reduced when marketing and distribution required specialized, costly, product-specific facilities and skills that could not be used to handle other product lines. By investing in such product-specific personnel and facilities, the intermediary not only lost the advantages of scope but became dependent on what were usually a small number of producers.

All these new high-volume enterprises created their own sales organizations to advertise and market their products nationally and often internationally. From the start they preferred to have their own sales forces to advertise and market their goods. Salesmen of wholesalers and other intermediaries who sold the products of many manufacturers, including those of their competitors, could not be relied upon to concentrate on the single product of a single manufacturer with the intensity needed to attain and maintain the market share necessary to keep throughput at minimum efficient scale.

Equally important, mass distribution of these products—many of them quite new—often required extensive investment in specialized, product-specific facilities and personnel. Because the existing wholesalers and mass retailers made their profits from handling related products of many manufacturers, they had little incentive to make large investments in facilities and personnel that could only be useful for a handful of specialized products processed by a handful of producers on whom they would become dependent for the supplies essential to make this investment pay.

Of all the new mass producers, those making packaged food products and consumer chemical products required the least in the way of product-specific distribution facilities and personnel. The new canning and packaging techniques, however, immediately eliminated one of the major functions of the wholesaler, that of converting large bulk shipments into small packages. Because the manufacturers now packaged, they, not the wholesalers, began to brand and to advertise on a national and global scale. Their sales forces now canvassed the retailers. But because mass sales of these branded packaged products demanded little in the way of specialized facilities and personnel, the processor typically continued to use the wholesaler to physically distribute the foods (for a fixed markup or commission) until the manufacturer's output became large enough to cancel out the wholesaler's scale advantages.

All other industrial groupings in which large firms clustered required major investments in either specialized distribution facilities or specialized personnel, and often both. The producers of perishables—meat, beer, and dairy products—particularly those in the United States, made the massive investment required in refrigerated or temperature cars, ships, and warehouses.[12] Gustavus Swift, an inventor of the refrigerated car, realized that effective distribution of fresh meat required the building of a national network of refrigerated storage facilities. When he began to build his branch house network in the mid 1880s, other leading meat packers quickly followed suit, racing Swift for the best sites. Those packers who had made the investment in refrigerated cars and storage facilities before the end of the decade continued as the "Big Five" to dominate the industry for a half-century. In the 1880s neither the railroad nor the wholesale butchers had an incentive to invest in this equipment. Indeed, they had a positive disincentive. The railroads already had a major investment in cattle cars to move live animals; this business was, next to wheat, their largest traffic generator. The wholesale butchers were organized specifically to handle the cattle delivered to them by the railroad. Both fought the packers and their new product vigorously, but with relatively little success. In this and the next decade, the producers of bananas—primarily United Fruit—and the makers of beer for the national market, including Pabst, Schlitz, and Anheuser-Busch, made comparable investment in refrigerated distribution facilities.

Refined petroleum as well as vegetable or animal oil could be shipped more cheaply in specialized tank cars and ships, stored in local tank farms, and then packaged close to the final markets. Wholesalers hesitated to make such extensive investments as they would be wholly dependent for their continued use and profitability on a small number of high-volume suppliers.[13] When the coming of the automobile required still another new and costly distribution investment in pumps and service stations to provide roadside supplies to motorists, wholesalers were even less enthusiastic about making the necessary investment. On the other hand, the refiners, by making the investment, were able not only to control the scheduling of throughput necessary to maintain their high minimum efficient scale but also to guard against adulteration, a danger if packaging were done by independent wholesalers. In the case of gasoline, in order to avoid the costs of operating the pumps and service stations, most oil companies preferred to lease the equipment they purchased or produced to franchised dealers. In tires, similarly, mass production benefited from the economies of throughput and mass sales required a specialized product-specific distribution network. Although tire companies occasionally owned their retail outlets, they preferred to rely on franchised retail dealers.

The mass marketing of new machines that were mass produced through the fabricating and assembling of interchangeable parts required a greater investment in personnel to provide the specialized marketing services than in product-specific plant and equipment.[14] The mass distribution of sewing machines for households and for the production of apparel; typewriters, cash registers, adding machines, mimeograph machines, and other office equipment; harvesters, reapers, and other agricultural machines; and, after 1900, automobiles and the more complex electrical appliances all called for demonstration, after-sales service, and consumer credit. As these machines had been only recently invented, few existing distributors had the necessary training and experience to provide the services, or the financial resources to provide extensive consumer credit.

On the other hand, the manufacturer had every incentive to do both. By providing repair and service, it could help ensure that the product performed as advertised; control of the wholesale organization assured inventory as well as quality control. However, as a great many retailers were needed to cover the national and international markets, the manufacturers preferred to rely, as did the oil and tire companies, on franchised dealers. These retail dealers, who sold their products exclusively, were supported by a branch office network that assured the provision of services, credit, and supplies on schedule. Only the makers of sewing machines, typewriters, and cash registers went so far as to invest in retail stores. They did so primarily in concentrated urban areas where, before the coming of the automobile, such stores were the only means to provide the necessary services and credit on a neighborhood basis.

The makers of heavier but still standardized machinery for industrial users had to offer their customers much the same market services and even more extensive credit. This was true of manufacturers of shoe machinery, pumps, boilers, elevators, printing presses, telephone equipment, and machinery that generated electric power and light. Manufacturers' agents and other intermediaries had neither the training nor the capital to provide the essential services and credit. For the makers of industrial chemicals, volume distribution demanded investment in product-specific capital equipment as well as salesmen with specialized skills. Dynamite, far more powerful than black powder, required careful education of customers, as well as specialized storage and transportation facilities. So too did the new synthetic dyes and synthetic fibers,whose use had to be explained to manufacturers and whose application often required new specialized machinery. On the other hand, metals produced by processes with a high minimum efficient scale required less investment in distribution. Even so, to obtain and fill volume orders to precise specifications on precise delivery schedules required a trained sales force and close coordination between production and sales managers.

In these ways and for these reasons, the large industrial firm that integrated mass production and mass distribution appeared in industries with two characteristics. The first and most essential was a technology of production in which the realization of potential scale economies and maintenance of quality control demanded close and constant coordination and supervision of materials flows by trained managerial teams. The second was that volume marketing and distribution of their products required investment in specialized, product-specific human and physical capital.

Where this was *not* the case—that is, in industries where technology did *not* have a potentially high minimum efficient scale, where coordination was *not* technically complex, and where mass distribution did *not* require specialized skills and facilities—there was little incentive for the manufacturer to integrate forward into distribution. In such industries as publishing and printing, lumber, furniture, leather, and apparel and textiles, and specialized instruments and machines, the large integrated firm had few competitive advantages. In these industries, the small, single-function firm continued to prosper and to compete vigorously.

Significantly, however, it was in just these industries that the new mass retailers—the department stores, the mail order houses, and the chain or multiple stores—began to coordinate the flow of goods from the manufacturer to the consumer. In industries that lacked substantial scale economies in production, economies of both scale and scope gave the mass retailers their economic advantage. In coordinating these flows the mass retailers, like the mass producers, reduced unit costs of distribution by increasing the daily flow or throughput within the distribution network. Such efficiency, in turn, further reduced the economic need for the wholesaler as a middleman between the retailer and manufacturer.

In industries that integrated mass production and mass distribution—those with significant scale economies in production and specialized requirements in distribution—the most important entrepreneurial act of the founders of an enterprise was the creation of an administrative organization.

It was essential first to recruit a team to supervise the process of production, then to build a national and very often international sales network, and finally to set up a corporate office of middle and top managers to integrate and coordinate the two. Only then did the enterprise become multinational. Investment in production abroad followed, almost never preceded, the building of an overseas marketing network. So too in the technologically advanced industries, the investment in research and development followed the creation of a marketing network. In these firms, this linkage between trained sales engineers, production engineers, product designers, and the research laboratory became a major impetus to continuing innovation in the industries in which they operated. The result of such growth was an enterprise whose characteristic organization is depicted in Figure [5.]1. The continuing growth of the firm rested on the ability of its managers to transfer resources in marketing, research and development, and production (usually those that were not fully utilized) into new and more profitable related product lines, a move that carried the organization shown in Figure [5.]1 to that illustrated by Figure [5.]2. If the first step—the integration production and distribution—was not taken, the rest did not follow. The firms remained small, personally managed producing enterprises that bought their materials and sold their products through intermediaries.

Thus, in major modern economies, the large managerial enterprise evolved in much the same way in industries with much the same characteristics. However, there were striking differences among these economies in the pace, the timing, and the specific industries in which the new institution appeared and continued to grow. These differences reflected differences in technologies and markers available to the industrialists of the different nations, in their entrepreneurial organizational skills, in laws, and in cultural attitudes and values. These dissimilarities can be pinpointed by very briefly reviewing the historical experiences of the 200 largest industrial enterprises in the United States, the United Kingdom, Germany, and Japan.[15]

THE UNITED STATES

In the United States the completion of the nation's basic railroad and telegraph network and the perfection of its operating methods in the 1870s and 1880s opened up the largest and fastest-growing market in the world. Its population, which already enjoyed the highest per capita income in the world, was equal to that of Britain in 1850, twice that in 1900, and three times that in 1920.[16] American entrepreneurs quickly recruited the managerial teams in production necessary to exploit scale economies and made the investment in distribution necessary to market their volume-produced goods at home and abroad, and did so in all the industries in which large industrial firms would cluster for the following century. Most of these firms quickly extended their marketing organizations overseas and then became multinational by investing in production facilities abroad, playing an influential role in a global oligopoly (see Table [5.]6). Indeed, in some cases, particularly

TABLE [5.]6   American Multinationals in 1914[a]

SIC Groups 20 and 21: Food and Tobacco	SIC Groups 35, 36, and 37: Machinery and Transportation Equipment
American Chicle	American Bicycle
American Cotton Oil	American Gramophone
Armour	American Radiator
Coca-Cola	Crown Cork & Seal
H. J. Heinz	Chicago Pneumatic Tool
Quaker Oats	Ford
Swift	General Electric
American Tobacco	International Harvester
British American Tobacco	International Steam Pump (Worthington)
SIC Groups 28, 29, and 30: Chemicals, Pharmaceuticals, Oil, and Rubber	Mergenthaler Linotype
	National Cash Register
Carborundum	Norton
Parke Davis (drug)	Otis Elevator
Sherwin-Williams	Singer
Sterns & Co. (drug)	Torrington
United Drug (drug)	United Shoe Machinery
Virginia-Carolina Chemical	Western Electric
Du Pont	Westinghouse Air Brake
Standard Oil of N.J.	Westinghouse Electric
U.S. Rubber	
	Other SIC Groups
	Alcoa (33)
	Gillette (34)
	Eastman Kodak (38)
	Diamond Match (39)

[a]American companies with two or more plants abroad or one plant and raw material producing facilities.
Source: Mira Wilkins, *The Emergence of Multinational Enterprise* (Cambridge, 1970), 212–13, 216.

in mass-produced light machinery, the Americans enjoyed close to global monopoly well before the outbreak of World War I. By that time those in the more technologically advanced industries had also begun to invest personnel and facilities in research and development.

These large manufacturing enterprises grew by direct investment in nonmanufacturing personnel and facilities. They also expanded by merger and acquisition.[17] Here they began by making the standard response of manufacturers, both European and American, to excess capacity—to which, because of the high minimum efficient scale of their capital-intensive production processes, they were particularly sensitive. American manufacturers first attempted to control competition by forming trade associations to control output and prices and to allocate marketing territories. However, because of the existing common-law prohibition against combinations in restraint of trade, these associations were unable to enforce their rulings in courts of law. So manufacturers turned to the holding company device. Members of their association exchanged their stock for that of a holding company, thus giving a central office legal power to determine output, prices, and marketing areas for the subsidiary firms.

For most American enterprises the motivation for the initial incorporation as a holding company was to control competition. For some, like John D. Rockefeller, however, this move became the first step toward rationalizing the resources of an enterprise or even an industry in order to exploit the potential of scale economies fully. Even before the enforcement of the Sherman Antitrust Law in the early twentieth century made contractual cooperation by means of a holding company legally suspect, a number of American enterprises had been transformed from holding companies to operating ones by consolidating the many factories of their subsidiaries into a single production department, unifying the several sales forces into a single sales department (including an international division) and then, though less often, investing in research and development. In a word, these enterprises were transformed from a loose federation of small operating concerns into a single centralized enterprise as depicted in Figure [5.]1. These firms competed for market share and profits, rarely on price—the largest (and usually the oldest) remained the price leader—but on productive efficiency, on advertising, on the proficiency of their marketing and distribution services, and on product performance and product improvement.

In such large, complex organizations, decisions as to both current production and distribution and the allocation of resources for future production and distribution came to be made by full-time salaried managers. At the time of World War I owners who still worked on a full-time basis with their hierarchies continued to have an influence on such decisions. By World War II growth by diversification into new product lines not only greatly increased the size and complexity of the enterprise but still further scattered stock ownership. By then owners rarely participated in managerial decisions. At best they or their representatives were "outside" directors who met with the inside directors (the full-time salaried managers) monthly at most and usually only four times a year. For these meetings the inside directors set the agenda, provided the information on which decisions were made, and of course were responsible for implementing the decisions. The outside directors still had the veto power, but they had neither the time, the information, nor the experience, and rarely even the motivation, to propose alternate courses of action. By World War I, managerial capitalism had become firmly entrenched in the major sectors of the American economy.

THE UNITED KINGDOM

The situation in the United Kingdom was very different. As late as World War II, the large integrated industrial enterprise administered through an extensive managerial hierarchy was still the exception. Nearly all of the 200 leading industrials in Britain had integrated production with distribution, but in a great number of these firms owners remained full-time executives.

They managed their enterprises with the assistance of a small number of "company servants," who only began to be asked to join boards of directors in the 1930s. In Britain, at the time of World War II, most of the top 200 consisted of two types of enterprises, neither of which existed among the American top 200 at the time of World War I. They were either personally managed enterprises or federations of such enterprises. The exceptions were, of course, Britain's largest and best-known industrial corporations—those that represented Britain in their global oligopolies. However, as late as 1948 these numbered less than 20 percent of the top 200 enterprises.

Large hierarchical enterprise did come when British entrepreneurs responded to the potential of new high-volume technologies by creating management teams for production and invested in distribution and research personnel and facilities. Between the 1880s and World War I such firms appeared in branded packaged products like soap, starch, biscuits, and chocolate, and in rayon, tires, plate and flat glass, explosives, and synthetic alkalis. For example, Courtaulds, the first to build a plant with a high minimum efficient scale in rayon, became and remained the largest producer of the first synthetic fiber, not only in Britain but also in the United States.

But where British industrialists failed to grasp the opportunity to make the investment and build the hierarchies, they lost not only the world market but the British home market itself. This was particularly striking in machinery, both light and heavy, and in industrial chemicals. The American firms quickly overpowered the British competitors in the production and distribution of light mass-produced machinery, including sewing, office, and agricultural machinery, automobiles, household appliances, and the like. The Germans as quickly dominated the synthetic dye business so critical to Britain's huge textile industry while the Germans and Americans shared the electrical machinery industry, the new producers of light and of the energy so critical to increased productivity in manufacturing. In 1912, for example, two-thirds of the output of the electrical manufacturing industry in Britain was produced by three companies, the subsidiaries of the American General Electric and Westinghouse and the German Siemens.[18] Even those few British firms that achieved and maintained their position in the domestic market and the global oligopoly created smaller hierarchies and had more direct owner management than did their American counterparts.

After World War I a few British firms in such volume producing industries began to challenge their American and German competition, but they did so only by making the necessary investment in nonmanufacturing personnel and facilities and by recruiting managerial staffs. This was the case for Anglo-Persian Oil Company, for British General Electric, and Imperial Chemical Industries (ICI) in each of their industries, for Metal Box in cans, and for Austin and Morris in automobiles. Nevertheless, the transformation from personal or family management to one of salaried managers came slowly and grudgingly. In even the largest enterprises—those with sizable hierarchies, such as Courtaulds, British Celanese, Pilkington, Metal Box, Reckitts, Cadbury's, Ranks, and others—the owners continued to have a much greater say in top management decisions than did their American counterparts.

Why was this the case? The answer is, of course, complex. It lies in Britain's industrial geography and history, in its educational system, in the lack of antitrust legislation, and in a continuing commitment to personal family management. Because the domestic market was smaller and was growing more slowly than the American, British industrialists had less incentive than their American counterparts to exploit scale economies. Moreover, Britain was the only nation to industrialize before the coming of modern transportation and communication. So its industrialists had become attuned to a slower, smaller-scale process of industrial production and distribution.

Nevertheless, precisely because it was the first industrial nation, Great Britain also became the world's first consumer society. The quadrangle bounded by London, Cardiff, Glasgow, and Edinburgh remained for almost a century after 1850 the richest and most concentrated consumer market in the world. British entrepreneurs quickly began to mass-produce branded packaged consumer goods (of all the new industries these required the least in the way of specialized skills in production and specialized services and facilities in distribution). But in other new industries, it was the foreign, not the British, entrepreneur who responded to the new opportunities. Even though that golden quadrangle remained the world's most concentrated market for mass-produced sewing machines, shoe machinery, office equipment, phonographs, batteries, automobiles, appliances, and other consumer durables, as well as electrical and other new heavy machinery and industrial chemicals, Germans and Americans were the first to set up *within Britain* the production teams and to make the investment in the product-specific distribution services and facilities essential to compete in these industries. Apparently British industrialists wanted to manage their own enterprises rather than turn over operating control to nonfamily, salaried managers. They seemed to regard their companies as family estates to be nurtured and passed down to their heirs rather than mere money-making machines. As a result they and the British economy as a whole failed to harvest many of the fruits of the Second Industrial Revolution.

The commitment to family control was reflected in the nature of British mergers. As in the United States, many British firms grew large by merger and acquisition. As in America, holding companies were formed to control legally the output, price, and marketing arrangements of hitherto small competing enterprises; but British holding companies, unlike their U.S. counterparts, remained federations of family firms. Until World War I British industrialists rarely viewed merger as a forerunner to the rationalization, consolidation, and centralized administration necessary to exploit the potential of scale economies. Indeed, the very first merger to centralize and rationalize in Britain came in 1920 at Nobel Explosives, the forerunner to ICI, which borrowed the necessary organizational techniques directly from its overseas ally, the Du Pont company of Wilmington, Delaware.[19] As late as 1928,

Lever Brothers, one of Britain's largest enterprises, had forty-one operating subsidiaries and thirty-nine different sales forces. For these reasons, then, the founders of most large British enterprises continued to manage their enterprises directly. Hierarchies remained small and controllable. Sons and grandsons and grandsons-in-law continued to move into the top offices.

Thus Britain continued until World War II to be the bastion of family capitalism. Thereafter the large industrial enterprise was transformed by several factors: the rapid decline of the old industries; the end of the cartel system at home and abroad, and therefore the increasing need to compete through efficiency; a new emphasis on engineering and business education for managers; and even changes in attitudes about family position and control. Ownership increasingly became separated from management. By the 1970s the size of the hierarchies, their composition, the organizational structure of the enterprise, the ways of competition, and growth were comparable to those of the large American firm thirty years earlier, except that family participation in top management was probably still greater.

GERMANY

In Germany, unlike Britain, integrated industrial firms as large as those in the United States existed well before the coming of World War I. They were fewer in number, however, and were concentrated in metals and the technologically advanced machinery and chemical industries. Among the top 200 German firms during the interwar years, very few produced branded packaged products, except for the regional breweries. One can only locate two chocolate and confectionery and two drug companies. The remaining few were subsidiaries of Nestlé, Lever Brothers, and the two Dutch margarine makers that joined Lever in 1929 to become Unilever. Nor did the large German firms manufacture light mass-produced machinery in the American manner. Singer Sewing Machine long remained the largest sewing machine maker in Germany. Well before World War I the factories of National Cash Register and American Radiator and the sales offices of International Harvester and Remington Typewriter dominated the German market for their products. In automobiles in 1929, a year when General Motors produced 1.6 million and Ford 1.5 million cars, only one German car company made more than 10,000. That firm, Adam Opel, which produced 25,000, was a General Motors subsidiary. Even in standardized industrial machines, American firms such as Mergenthaler Linotype (in printing presses) and Norton (in abrasives and grinding machines) dominated German markets.

The Germans did, like the British, have their one large representative in the rayon, rubber, and oil oligopolies. (The last, EPU, was dismembered during World War I.) It was in complex machinery and chemicals, however, that the Germans made their global mark. In giant production works German machinery and chemical enterprises produced in quantity a variety of complex machines and chemicals made from the same basic ingredients and processes. Managerial hierarchies even larger than those of the production departments of American firms guided the complicated flow of materials from one intermediate process to the next. In the 1880s and 1890s these enterprises built extended networks of branch offices throughout the world to market products, most of which were technologically new machinery and chemicals, to demonstrate their use, to install them where necessary, to provide continuing after-sales service, and to give customers the financial credit they often needed to make such purchases. Once established abroad they built and acquired branch factories. Finally, they invested, usually more heavily than the Americans, in research and development.

At home these large integrated enterprises reduced competition by making contractual arrangements for setting price and output and allocating markets. Because such arrangements were in Germany legally enforceable in courts of law, the arrangements became quite formal and elaborate. The IG, or the community of interest, became the closest legal form to the British and the American holding company. The difference between the British holding company and the German community of interest was that the latter involved large hierarchial firms rather than small family enterprises. Their extensive investment in marketing and distribution and in research and development permitted the large German enterprises to dominate the negotiations setting up cartels, associations, or communities of interest, and provided them the power essential to implement and enforce the contractual arrangements.

Finally, the capital requirements of these capital-intensive producers of industrial products were far greater than those of the American and British makers of branded packaged products or the American mass producers of light machinery. Because there were no highly developed capital markets in Germany comparable to those of London and New York, German banks became much more involved in the financing of large hierarchical enterprises than was true in Britain and the United States. Although the representatives of banks never sat at the *Vorstand*, the central administrative body of top managers, as did the founder and often full-time family executives, they did become important members of the *Aufsichtsrat* or supervisory board. Because the numbers of large enterprises were small, much smaller than in the United States, and because the major banks were even fewer, the full-time salaried bank managers were probably few enough in number to exchange information. Such outside sources of knowledge about the businesses may have made them less captive to the inside management than were the part-time outside directors on American boards. Thus, those sectors in which the supervisory board included managers of the leading banks can be said to have been administered through a system of finance capitalism.

Why were the large German industrial enterprises concentrated in metals and complex industrial products rather than branded packaged goods or light mass-produced machinery? Why did the Germans build large hierarchial organizations when the British did not? In the 1870s, when the transportation and communication revolution was being completed, manufacturers in the new German empire enjoyed neither the rapidly growing continental market of America nor the concentrated consumer market of Britain. Because per capita income was lower than in the United States or Britain and because Germany was neither a large importer of foodstuffs like the United Kingdom nor an exporter like the United States, there was relatively little entrepreneurial challenge to create large enterprises in packaged and perishable foodstuffs or other consumer products. The challenge to the German entrepreneurs came instead from the demand of industrializing and industrial countries, including Britain and Germany itself, for the new specialized industrial machinery, including electrical equipment, and new industrial chemicals, including synthetic dyes. In building their technical sales and research organizations—their basic weapons in international competition— the Germans had the advantage of what had become the world's best technical and scientific educational institutions. Therefore, despite the defeat in two wars the German strength in international competition still rests on the performance of their science-based industries.

Since World War II, convergence has occurred, as it has in Britain. German industrials successfully moved into the mass production of automobiles, appliances, and other consumer durables as well as into the high-volume production of light machinery. The number of producers of branded packaged products in foods and consumer chemicals increased. As the number of firms among the top 200 in industries other than machinery and chemicals grew larger, and as the firms in those older industries diversified into new product lines, the ability of representatives of banks to bypass the inside managers and therefore to participate in top management decisions lessened. Even so, banks still play a more significant role in German enterprises than they do in American, just as British family members are still more important in top management decisions than those in the United States.

JAPAN

Large industrial enterprises in Japan evolved very differently from those in the West. For Japan was just taking the first steps toward modern industrialization in the same decades that the new transportation and communication revolution was spawning the Second Industrial Revolution in Europe and the United States. Indeed, Japan's first steel mill only went into operation in 1902. Only in the years after World War II was the economy large and strong enough to support modern mass production and mass distribution. Yet even before that war, managerial hierarchies had appeared to exploit new technologies and to reach new markets.

In the early years of this century, Japan's domestic and foreign markets were of a totally different nature. At the time of the Meiji Restoration, Japanese manufacturers enjoyed a highly concentrated domestic market, comparable to Britain's during its early industrialization, with long-established channels for distribution of traditional consumer goods. As a result, only a few Japanese firms (and no foreign companies) began to create marketing networks to distribute branded packaged products within the country. By World War II a small number of makers of branded packaged products such as confectionery, soy sauce, canned sea food, beer, and soap, who advertised nationally and had their own extensive sales forces, were listed among the largest 200 Japanese industrial enterprises.

On the other hand, overseas, even in nearby East Asia, the Japanese had had no commercial contact at all for the more than 250 years of the Tokugawa period. Manufacturers using imported processes to produce textiles, fertilizers, and ceramic and metal products sought overseas as well as domestic markets, particularly in nonindustrialized East and Southeast Asia. Overseas they rarely set up their own branch offices. They had neither the volume nor the distribution needs to require large product-specific investments in distribution. They relied instead on allied trading companies to assure coordination of flow of goods from factories in Japan to customers abroad and at home, and the flow of essential materials and equipment from overseas to the producing facilities. These trading companies set up branch offices in Japan and in all parts of the world, and built large central offices in Tokyo or Osaka. That is, they invested in an extensive marketing and distribution organization that coordinated flows, provided marketing services, and generated information, thus lowering marketing and distribution costs. They became the linchpins of groups of firms consisting of single product manufacturing enterprises—each group having its own banks and trust companies as well as its own trading and warehouse concerns.

The close relationship between the managers of the manufacturing companies and those of the trading firms, either within the giant *zaibatsu* or between cooperating manufacturers in less formal groups, permitted the Japanese to capture an increased share of world trade, particularly in the relatively low-technology industries. However, where marketing and distribution did require product-specific skills, services, and facilities, enterprises set up their own distributing network and operated outside the *zaibatsu* and other group enterprises. Before World War II, only a few such enterprises had appeared, primarily in industrial machinery and particularly in electrical machinery. The latter was especially important, for until the 1950s Japan relied heavily on hydroelectric power for its energy. Only after the war, with the rapid growth of the domestic market, did the makers of automobiles, electric appliances, radio, and television build comparable organizations. In the postwar years these enterprises have been increasingly investing in distribution abroad and have come to operate through extensive managerial hierarchies comparable to those of the West. Like their western counterparts, they began in the 1960s to grow through diversification, particularly into appliances, radio, television, and other consumer durables. So by 1970 there were two types of industrial groups in Japan. One was the descendant of the old *zaibatsu*, whose central office had been abolished by the Allied occupational authorities after the war. The other was the maker of machinery, vehicles, and electrical equipment who, after diversifying in the manner of the western companies, often spun off their different product divisions. They remained part of the group, but operated as financially independent enterprises, unlike the divisions or subsidiaries of diversified western firms.

CONCLUSION

As the Japanese experience illustrates, the vast increase in the number and complexity of decisions required to coordinate the activities of a multitude of offices, plants, distribution facilities, research laboratories, and the like in different geographical areas, often for several product lines, brought a convergence in the type of enterprise and system of capitalism used by all advanced industrial economies for the production and distribution of goods. In Japan the rapid post–World War II growth of a concentrated domestic, urban, industrial market with a sharply increasing per capita income provided a base for a large integrated, hierarchical enterprise to exploit the potentials of scale economies. Such enterprises quickly took their place in the existing global oligopolies.

In this respect the Japanese challenge to the American and European industrial leadership differs markedly from the earlier challenges of the Americans and Germans to British leadership. The Americans and Germans took over world markets by creating international hierarchical enterprises producing and distributing new products because the British failed to create the organizations required for the development and exploitation of these products. The Japanese, on the other hand, have successfully moved into the international markets by using technological and organizational techniques very similar to those of the Americans and Europeans, indeed often borrowed directly from them—but using them more effectively and efficiently than the first comers.

Thus by the 1970s, in these advanced industrial economies, managers with little or no equity in the enterprises administered made the decisions about present production and distribution and the allocation of resources for future production and distribution. And they did so through much the same basic organizational forms. The type of structure depicted in Figure [5.]2 defines in broad outline the organization of Imperial Chemical Industries, Bayer, Mitsubishi Chemical, and Du Pont. Only in rare cases are any of the top 200 in these four leading industrial economies personally managed by their owners. In fact it is exceptional for owners to participate on a full-time basis in the top management decisions of an extensive hierarchy.

Nevertheless, variations within this new brand of capitalism are still significant. Enterprises of the four countries differ in terms of size, number, industry, and systems and styles of management, reflecting the different routes by which the leading sectors of each economy reached managerial capitalism—the United States by almost revolutionary changes at the turn of the century; Britain in a much more evolutionary manner that prolonged family capitalism; Germany by way of finance capitalism; and Japan by the development of group enterprise capitalism.

NOTES

1. Raymond de Roover, *The Rise and Decline of the Medici Bank, 1397–1494* (Cambridge, 1963), 87, 91. The earlier Peruzzi bank had branches managed by

employees (*fattore*). "However, all branches of major importance were managed by partners" (80).

2. Alfred D. Chandler, Jr., *The Visible Hand* (Cambridge, 1977), chaps. 3–6 for the coming of such hierarchies to manage railroad and telegraph systems, and chap. 7 for their use in the management of mass distribution. Pages 231–32 describe the organization of Sears Roebuck.

3. Details and documentation are given in a case by Alfred D. Chandler, Jr., "The Standard Oil Company—Combination, Consolidation and Integration," in *The Coming of Managerial Capitalism: A Casebook on the History of American Economic Institutions*, eds. Alfred D. Chandler, Jr., and Richard S. Tedlow (Homewood, Ill., 1985).

4. B. W. E. Alford, *W.D. & H.O. Wills and the Development of the U.K. Tobacco Industry* (London, 1973), 143–49. Also Chandler, *Visible Hand*, 249–58.

5. Sachio Kahu, "The Development and Structure of the German Coal-Tar Dyestuffs Firms," in *Development and Diffusion of Technology*, ed. Akio Okochi and Hoshimi Uchida (Tokyo, 1979), 78.

6. This statement is based on a review of histories of and internal reports and pamphlets by the leading rubber companies.

7. Harold Livesay, *Andrew Carnegie and the Rise of Big Business* (Boston, 1975), 102–6, 155. When in 1873 Carnegie opened the first works directed entirely to producing rails by the Bessemer process, he reduced cost to $56.64 a ton. By 1895, with increase in sales, the costs fell to $25 a ton.

8. L. F. Haber, *The Chemical Industry during the Nineteenth Century* (Oxford, 1958), 92.

9. Chandler, *Visible Hand*, 302–14.

10. Allan Nevins, *Ford: The Times, the Man, the Company* (New York, 1954), chaps. 18–20 (esp. 473, 489, 511); Alfred D. Chandler, Jr., *Giant Enterprise: Ford, General Motors and the Automobile Industry* (New York, 1980), 26.

11. Scott J. Moss, *An Economic Theory of Business Strategy* (New York, 1981), 110–11.

12. Chandler, *Visible Hand*, 299–302, 391–402.

13. Standard Oil only began to make an extensive investment in distribution after the formation of the Trust and the resulting rationalization of production and with it the great increase in throughput. Harold F. Williamson and Arnold R. Daum, *The American Petroleum Industry, The Age of Illumination, 1859–1899* (Evanston, Ill., 1959), 687–96. For investment in gasoline pumps and service stations see Harold F. Williamson et al., *The American Petroleum Industry: The Age of Energy, 1899–1959* (Evanston, Ill., 1963), 217–30, 466–87, 675–86.

14. Chandler, *Visible Hand*, 402–11.

15. The analysis of these differences is based on detail research by the author of available histories, company and government reports, business journals, and internal company documents dealing with these many enterprises.

16. W. S. and E. S. Woytinsky, *World Population and Production* (New York, 1953), 383–85.

17. Chandler, *Visible Hand*, Chap. 10.

18. I. C. R. Byatt, *The British Electrical Industry, 1875–1914* (Oxford, 1979), 150.

19. For Nobel, see W. J. Reader, *Imperial Chemical Industries: A History* (London, 1970), 1:388–94; for Lever Brothers, see Charles H. Wilson, *History of Unilever* (London, 1954), 2:302, 345.

EDITORS' NOTES ON FURTHER READING: CHANDLER

Alfred D. Chandler, Jr., is a distinguished business historian, and virtually all of his scholarship has been devoted to describing and analyzing the rise of large corporations. His first major work, *Strategy and Structure: Chapters in the History of the American Industrial Enterprise* (1962), treats the adoption of the multidivisional form of organization with case studies of Du Pont, General Motors, Standard Oil Company, and Sears, Roebuck. He elaborated the argument in *The Visible Hand: The Managerial Revolution in American Business* (1977), which treats the ascent of professional managers and growth of a "science" of management. His most recent book, *Scale and Scope: The Dynamics of Industrial Capitalism* (1990), extends the cross-national argument of the article we have reprinted, by analyzing the strategies of the 200 leading industrial companies in the United States, Great Britain, and Germany in the twentieth century and by trying to describe and account for differences among the countries in their "style" of industrial capitalism.

A list of Chandler's articles as well as a sketch of his life and an attempt to place his research within the tradition of business history can be found in Thomas K. McCraw, ed., *The Essential Alfred Chandler: Essays Toward a Historical Theory of Big Business* (1988). This volume also contains a critical interchange about Chandler's work between economist Oliver E. Williamson and sociologist Charles Perrow, in which Perrow argues that changes in industrial form are driven not by the efficiency considerations favored by Chandler but by a large corporation's drive for market power and dominance. Also critical of Chandler's work are Richard B. Duboff and Edward S. Herman, "Alfred Chandler's New Business History: A Review," *Politics and Society* 10 (1980):87–110 and Arthur Stinchcombe, in chapter 4 of *Information and Organizations* (1990). For an appraisal of Chandler from the viewpoint of industrial organization, see Richard Caves, "Industrial Organization, Corporate Strategy, and Structure," *Journal of Economic Literature* 18 (March 1980):64–92. An attempt to challenge Chandler's account of the rise of the multidivisional firm—with the help of organization theory and new historical data—has been made by Neil Fligstein in "The Spread of the Multidivisional Form Among Large Corporations, 1919–1979," *American Sociological Review* 50 (1985):377–391 and in his book *The Transformation of Corporate Control* (1990).

The paper by Chandler reprinted here is informed by a comparative perspective, which also constitutes the focus of *Managerial Hierarchies: Comparative Perspectives on the Rise of the Modern Industrial Enterprise* (1980), edited by Chandler and Herman Daems. Chandler's account of the rise of big business in other countries has been challenged by Gary Hamilton and Nicole Biggart in their article "Market, Culture, and Authority: A Comparative Analysis of Management and Organization in the Far East," reprinted in this anthology as Chapter 7. Chandler's paper also raises the issue of the role of the multinational corporation; for the basic literature on this topic see a review article by Peter Evans, "Recent Research on Multinational Corporations," *Annual Review of Sociology* 7 (1981):199–223. For an introduction to economists' research on U.S. corporations and their organizational structure, see F. M. Scherer and David Ross's well-known industrial organization textbook, *Industrial Market Structure and Economic Performance*, 3d ed. (1990).

6

Goodwill and the Spirit of Market Capitalism

RONALD DORE

One of economists' favourite Adam Smith quotations is the passage in the *Wealth of Nations* in which he sets out one of his basic premises.

> It is not from the benevolence of the butcher, the brewer and the baker, that we expect our dinner, but from their regard to their own interest. We address ourselves, not to their humanity, but to their self-love, and never talk to them of our necessities but of their advantages.[1]

I wish to question that sharp opposition between benevolence and self-interest. Perhaps, so that he should be alert for signs of possible bias, the reader should be warned that a prolonged soaking in the writings of Japanese eighteenth- and nineteenth-century Confucianists at an early age has left me with a soft spot for the virtue of benevolence, even a tendency to bristle when anyone too much disparages it. At any rate I wish to argue, apropos of benevolence, or goodwill, that there is rather more of it about than we sometimes allow, further that to recognize the fact might help in the impossible task of trying to run an efficient economy and a decent society—an endeavour which animated Hobhouse's life, and about which, as Ginsburg makes clear in his 1950s preface to *Morals in Evolution*, even the pains of old age and the rise of fascism in the 1920s did not destroy his eventual optimism.

My title refers to goodwill rather than benevolence because benevolence, in my Confucian book, though not I think in Adam Smith's, is something shown in relations between unequals, by superior to inferior, the reciprocal of which is usually called loyalty. Goodwill is more status-neutral, more an expression of Hobhouse's 'principle of mutuality'. And it is that broader

Hobhouse Memorial Lecture

From *British Journal of Sociology* 34 (1983):459–482. Copyright © R.K.P. Reprinted by permission of Routledge.

meaning which I intend. A formal definition of my subject might be: the sentiments of friendship and the sense of diffuse personal obligation which accrue between individuals engaged in recurring contractual economic exchange. (By 'economic', I mean only that the goods and services exchanged should be commonly subject to market valuation.)

Goodwill, of course, is a term of art in the commercial world. In the world of petty proprietorships, familiar to most of us, if you are selling a corner store you set a price on the premises, a price on the stock and a price on the goodwill. Back in the old Marshallian days when economists took their concepts from everyday life rather than trying to take everyday life from their concepts, goodwill meant the same thing to economists too. Palgrave's 1923 dictionary of economics defines goodwill as:

> The expectancy of a continuance, to the advantage of a successor in an established business, of the personal confidence, or of the habit of recurring to the place or premises or to the known business house or firm, on the part of a circle or connection of clients or customers.[2]

The next economics dictionary I find, McGraw-Hill's exactly half a century later, has a very different definition of goodwill:

> An accounting term used to explain the difference between what a company pays when it buys another company and what it gets in the form of tangible assets.[3]

Samuelson, to his credit one of the very few textbook writers in whose index one will find the word goodwill, illustrates the concept with J. P. Morgan taking over Carnegie's steel interests, making it clear that Morgan paid a premium well over the market value of the fixed assets primarily because he thereby advanced significantly towards a monopoly position.[4] In other words the goodwill concept is extended to cover not just the benefits accruing to the purchaser of a business from the affectionate or inertial habits of its customers, but also those accruing out of his consequent shift from the position of price-taker to that of price-maker—his enhanced ability to hold those customers up to ransom. To be fair to the economists who have adopted this use of the term, and partially to retract my earlier gibe, one could say that the standard definition of the term has changed because everyday life has changed. A world in which the terms appropriate to the small owner-managed business formed the dominant norm, has given way to a world dominated by the large corporations and their accountants' terms. Certainly, if anyone wanted to write an Old Testament Prophet-style denunciation of modern capitalism *à la* Marx, he could hardly ask for a better illustration than the corruption of the concept of 'goodwill', that primordial embodiment of basic social bonds, into a term for some of the more ugly anti-social forms of profit-seeking.

THE DISAGGREGATION OF FACTORY PRODUCTION

I have been caused to ponder the role of goodwill in economic life by the recent experience of studying the organization of the textile industry, or to be more precise, the weaving segment of it, in Britain and Japan. One place I visited in the course of that research was the small town of Nishiwaki in western Japan whose industry is almost wholly devoted to the weaving of ginghams chiefly for export to Hong Kong to be made up into garments for Americans to wear when square-dancing in the Middle West. This is an area where hand-loom weaving goes back some centuries. Power-looms came in in the late nineteenth century and they brought with them the factory system as they did everywhere else. And 25 years ago, although many small weaving establishments had survived, the bulk of the output was accounted for by larger mills, many of which were part of vertically integrated enterprises with their own cotton-importing, spinning and finishing establishments.

By 1980, however, the picture had changed. The larger mills had closed. The integrated firms had retreated, as far as direct production was concerned, to their original base in spinning. Most of them were still, either alone or in collaboration with a trading company, producing their own brand cloth, dyed and finished. But they were doing so through the coordination of the activities of a large number of family enterprises. The key family business was that of the merchant-converter who contracted with the spinning company to turn its yarn into a certain type of cloth at a given contract price. The converter would send the yarn to another small family concern specializing in yarn dyeing, then it would go on to a specialist beamer who would wind it on to the warp beams in the desired pattern and also put the warp through the sizing process. Then it would be delivered to the weaver who might do his own weft preparation and the drawing-in (putting the harness on the beams ready for the looms) or might use other family businesses— contract winders or drawers in—for the process. And so on to the finishers who did the bleaching or texturizing or over-printing.

What is the reason for this fragmentation? What changes in Japanese society and the Japanese economy account for what most orthodox notions of the direction of the evolution of modern economies would count as a regression—the replacement of a system of production coordination within a vertically integrated firm by a system of production coordination between a large number of fragmented small firms; the replacement, to use Williamson's terms, of coordination through hierarchy by coordination through the market?[5]

I can think of four possible long-term secular trends which might help to explain the change.

1. The first is the rise in wages and the shorter working week of employees in union-organized firms. Wages are commonly lower in small firms— especially in Japan where the privileged position of the large enterprise elite has become firmly conventionalized, and inter-scale wage differentials are very great. But that is not all. Family enterprisers

themselves are often willing to work much longer than 40 hours a week for what may or may not be a larger *total* income than wage workers get, for an *average* return per hour of labour—hence wage cost per metre of cloth—which is below the employee's wage. If you like, family enterprisers are now willing to exploit themselves more than the unions or the law permit employees to be exploited—a condition which did not hold when *employees* were already working close to the human maximum—a 70 hour week for a subsistence level wage. The clear superiority of the factory system at that time may have been lost since.

2. Second, the secular trend to a high taxation and higher levels of taxation-allergy make the family enterpriser's advantage in both tax avoidance and tax evasion more attractive—*vide* the growth of the secondary 'black' and quasi-black economy in many other countries.

3. Third, there is a technical factor: the capital lumpiness of some of the new technology. For example expensive, large and fast sizing machines can hardly get the through-put necessary to make them profitable within a single firm. Inter-firm specialization becomes the best way of realizing economies of scale.

4. Fourth, much higher levels of numeracy and literacy mean a much wider diffusion of the accounting and managerial skills necessary to run a small business, the prudent ability to calculate the rentability of investments, etc.

These are all features common to societies other than Japan and may well be part of the explanation why the woollen industry of Prato has also moved to a fragmented structure in recent years. But there is another factor which applies especially in Japan. The reason why the dominant trend in the west seems to be in the reverse direction—away from coordination through the market towards coordination through the hierarchy of a vertically integrated firm—is, as Oliver Williamson is never tired of telling us, because of the transaction costs entailed, the costs arising from the imperfections of markets with small numbers of buyers and sellers in which the bargaining transactions are made difficult by what the jargon calls 'impacted information'. These features so enhance the bargaining power of each party that, when there are no significant economies of scale to be gained by their mutual independence one party (usually the stronger one) buys out the other to put a stop to his 'opportunism' (rapid response not only to price signals—which of course is always admirable—but also to information about vulnerable weaknesses of the other party.)

RELATIONAL CONTRACTING

Here is another of those timeless generalizations about 'capitalist economies' about which Japan gives pause. Transaction costs for large Japanese firms may well be lower than elsewhere. 'Opportunism' may be a lesser danger in Japan because of the explicit encouragement, and actual prevalence, in the Japanese economy of what one might call moralized trading relationships of mutual goodwill.

The stability of the relationship is the key. Both sides recognize an obligation to try to maintain it. If a finisher re-equips with a new and more efficient dyeing process which gives him a cost advantage and the opportunity of offering discounts on the going contract price he does not immediately get all the business. He may win business from one or two converts if they had some *other* reason for being dissatisfied with their own finisher. But the more common consequence is that the other merchant-converters go to their finishers and say: 'Look how X has got his price down. We hope you can do the same because we really would have to reconsider our position if the price difference goes on for months. If you need bank finance to get the new type of vat we can probably help by guaranteeing the loan.'

It is a system, to use a distinction common in the Williamson school, of relational contracting rather than spot-contracting[6]—or to use Williamson's more recent phrase[7] 'obligational contracting'. More like a marriage than a one-night stand as Robert Solow has said about the modern employment relation.[8] The rules of chastity vary. As is commonly the case, for those at the lower end of the scale, monogamy is the rule. A weaver with a couple of dozen automatic looms in a back garden shed will usually weave for only one converter, so that there should be no dispute about prior rights to the fruits of his looms—no clash of loyalties. Specialists with faster, larger volume, through-puts, like beamers—scarcer, more attractive, more in demand, therefore—may have a relation *à trois* or *à quatre*. For the converters themselves, at the top of the local hierarchy, there have grown up curious conventions rather like polyandrous concubinage. The Japan Spinners Association is dominated by the so-called Big Nine firms. None of the Big Nine will tolerate one of its converters taking cotton yarn from *another* of the Big Nine. However, one rank below the Big Nine are the so-called New Spinners, and below them the postwar upstarts, the New New Spinners. A Big Nine spinner will tolerate its converters having relations with them, though, of course a New Spinner will not tolerate a relation with another New Spinner. So the converter can end up with one of each— a first husband and a number two and a number three husband as it were.

As in nearly all systems of marriage, divorce also happens. That is why I said that a finisher with a cost advantage could attract other converters who happen for other reasons to be dissatisfied with their finisher. When I use the analogy of divorce, I mean traditional divorce in obligation-conscious societies, rather than the 'sorry I like someone else better: let's be friends' divorce of modern California. That is to say, the break usually involves recrimination and some bitterness, because it usually has to be justified by accusing the partner of some failure of goodwill, some lack of benevolence—or, as the Japanese phrase is more often translated, 'lack of sincerity'. It is not enough that some external circumstances keep his prices high.

I have made these relations sound like the kinship system of a Himalayan village, but of course the specific patterns of who may trade with whom are of very recent origin. What are entirely traditional, however, are, first, the basic pattern of treating trading relations as particularistic personal relations; second, the values and sentiments which sustain the obligations involved, and third such things as the pattern of mid-summer and year-end gift exchange which symbolizes recognition of those obligations.

But how on earth, the economist will want to know, do the prices and ordered quantities get fixed? The answer seems to be that, once established, prices can be renegotiated at the initiative of either party on the grounds either of cost changes affecting either party, or else of changes in the competitive conditions in the final market in which the brand cloth is sold. There are also fringe spot-markets for cotton yarn and grey cloth, and the prices ruling in these markets and reported in the daily textile press provide guides. To further complicate the issue there is some collective bargaining. Both the weavers and the converters in Nishiwaki have their own cooperative union and guide prices may be agreed between them; alternatively, in some other textile areas, the weavers co-op sets a minimum contract price which its members are not supposed to undercut, though there is general scepticism about the effectiveness of such an agreement.

RELATIONAL CONTRACTING BETWEEN UNEQUALS

The basic principles on which these price and quantity negotiations rest appear to be three-fold. First that the losses of the bad times and the gains of the good times should be shared. Second, that in recognition of the hierarchical nature of the relationship—of the fact that weavers are more dependent on converters than converters are on weavers—a fair sharing of a fall in the market may well involve the weaker weaver suffering more than the converter—having his profits squeezed harder. But, third, the stronger converter should not use his bargaining superiority in recession times, and the competition between his weavers to have their orders cut as little as possible, to drive them over, or even to, the edge of bankruptcy.

It is in the interpretation of these principles, of course, that ambiguity enters. Benevolence all too easily shades into exploitation when the divorce option—the option of breaking off the relationship—is more costlessly available to one party than to the other. There is, even, an officially-sponsored Association for the Promotion of the Modernization of Trading Relations in the Textile Industry in Japan which urges the use of written rather than verbal contracts in these relationships and is devoted to strengthening moral constraints on what it calls the abuse—but our economic textbooks would presumably call the legitimate full use—of market power. As for the nature of such abuse, surveys conducted by the Association show that suppliers with verbal contracts are more likely to have goods returned for quality deficiencies than those with proper written contracts.[9] Weavers will wryly remark that returns become strangely more common when the price is falling (and a rejected lot contracted at a higher price can be replaced by a newly contracted cheaper lot).

The work of the Association is an interesting illustration of the formal institutionalization of the ethics of relational contracting—doing, perhaps, for contracting what the postwar labour reform did to transform the employment system of large firms from manipulative paternalism into something less exploitative and better described as welfare corporatism.[10] All one can say about the contemporary trading reality is that those ethics appear to be sufficiently institutionalized, to be sufficiently constraining on a sufficient number of the firms and families in Nishiwaku textiles, for the pattern of trading I have described to be a stable and viable one.

That pattern is repeated in many other areas of the Japanese economy—between, for example, an automobile firm like Toyota and its subcontractors. Here again, the obligations of the relationship are unequal; the subcontractor has to show more earnest goodwill, more 'sincerity', to keep its orders than the parent company to keep its supplies. But equally the obligatedness is not entirely one-sided, and it does limit the extent to which the parent company can, for example, end its contracts with a subcontractor in a recession in order to bring the work into its own factory and keep its own workforce employed.

I have been taken to task by Okumura, the Japanese economist who has written most interestingly about these relationships, for speaking of the 'obligatedness' of a firm like Toyota as if a corporation was, or behaved like, a natural person.[11] But I still think the term is apt. The mechanisms are easy to intuit, if ponderous to spell out. First of all, there are *real* personal relations between the purchasing manager of Toyota and the manager or owner-manager of a subcontracting firm. But, of course, managers change frequently, particularly in firms with a bureaucratic career-promotion structure like Toyota. It is part of the commitment of such managers, however, that they identify with their firm and their department. If it were said, therefore, in the world outside, that Toyota, or its purchasing department in particular, had behaved badly by playing fast and loose with its subcontractors, the manager responsible would feel that he had let his firm down. If the accountants in the costing department urge a tough line with subcontractors, he may well tell them that they are shortsighted and even disloyal to the firm in underestimating the importance of its reputation. These seem to me readily understandable mechanisms by which the patterns of obligation between individual owner-managing converters and weavers in Nishiwaki can be duplicated between corporations.

I have discussed two cases of obligated trading relationships which are explicitly hierarchical. If there is any doubt as to who pecks whom in the pecking order look at the mid-summer and year-end gifts. Although it may vary depending on the precise nature of the concessions sought or granted in the previous six months or anticipated in the next, the weaver's gift to the converter will usually cost more than vice versa—unless, that is, either of them miscalculates the gift inflation rate, the point of transition, say, from Black Label against Suntory Old to Napoleon brandy against Dimple Haig.

RELATIONAL CONTRACTING BETWEEN EQUALS

But these relations are not confined to the hierarchical case. Even between firms of relatively equal strength the same forms of obligated relational contracting exist. Competition between Japanese firms is intense, but only in markets which are (a) consumer markets and (b) expanding. In consumer markets which are not expanding cartelization sets in rather rapidly, but that is a rather different story which does not concern us here. What does concern us here are markets in producers' goods, in intermediates. And for many such commodities markets can hardly be said to exist. Take steel, for instance, and one of its major uses for automobiles. The seven car firms buy their steel through trading companies, each from two or three of the major steel companies, in proportions which vary little from year to year. Prices, in this market, are set by the annual contract between the champions— Toyota on the one side, New Japan Steel on the other.

It is the concentration of such relationships which is the dominant characteristic of the famous large enterprise groups, known to Japanese as *grūpu*, and to foreigners, usually, as *zaibatsu* or *keiretsu*. There are six main ones of which the two best known are Mitsui and Mitsubishi. These groups are quite distinct from the hierarchical groupings of affiliates and subsidiaries around some of the giant individual firms like Hitachi or Matsushita or MHI. The Mitsubishi group, for example, has no clear hierarchical structure. In its core membership of 28 firms, there is a certain amount of intra-group share ownership—on average about 26 percent of total equity widely dispersed throughout the group in three or four percent shares. There is a tiny amount of interlocking directorships—about three percent of all directors' seats. And most of the firms have the group bank as their lead bank, and bank of last pleading resort, but that bank provides on average less than 20 percent of all loan finance to group firms. The only thing which formally defines the identity of the group is the lunch on the last Friday of the month when the Presidents of every company in the group get together, often to listen to a lecture on, say, the oil market in the 1990s, to discuss matters like political party contributions, sometimes to hear news of, or give blessings to, some new joint venture started up by two or more member firms, or a rescue operation for a member firm in trouble.[12]

But the main *raison d'etre* of these groups is as networks of preferential, stable, obligated *bilateral* trading relationships, networks of relational contracting. They are not conglomerates because they have no central board or holding company. They are not cartels because they are all in diverse lines of business. Each group has a bank and a trading company, a steel firm, an automobile firm, a major chemical firm, a shipbuilding and plant engineering firm and so on—and, except by awkward accident, not more than one of each. (The 'one set' principle, as the Japanese say.) Hence, trade in producer goods within the group can be brisk. To extend earlier analogies: it is a bit like an extended family grouping, where business is kept as much as possible within the family, and a certain degree of give and take is expected to modify the adversarial pursuit of market advantage—a willingness, say, to pay above the market price for a while to help one's trading partner out of deep trouble.

THE PREFERENCE FOR RELATIONAL CONTRACTING: CULTURAL SOURCES?

The starting point of this discussion of relational contracting was the search for reasons to explain why it made sense for the spinning firms producing brand cloth to coordinate production neither through hierarchy in the usual Williamson sense of full vertical integration, nor through the market in the normal sense of continuously pursuing the best buy, but through 'relational contracting'. It was, I said, because such arrangements could be *relied on* in Japan more than in most other economies. There is one striking statistic which illustrates the extent to which it is in fact relied on. The volume of wholesale transactions in Japan is no less than four times as great as the volume of retail transactions. For France the multiple is not four but 1.2; for Britain, West Germany and the USA the figure is between 1.6 and 1.9.[13]

How does one explain the difference between Japan and other capitalist economies? Williamson has 'theorized' these 'obligational relationships' and explained the circumstances in which they will occur—when the extent to which the commodities traded are idiosyncratically specific (such that the economies of scale can be as easily appropriated by buyer or by seller), and the extent to which either party has invested in equipment or specialized knowledge for the trading relationship, are not quite such that vertical integration makes sense, but almost so. He also asserts that in such relationships quantity adjustments will be preferred to price adjustments and price adjustments will be pegged to objective exogenous indicators (though he allows, in passing, for the not very 'relevant' or 'interesting' possibility that 'ad hoc price relief' might be given as an act of kindness by one party to the other.)[14]

Perhaps Williamson has evidence that that is the way it is in America and the fact that his argument is couched in the terms of a timeless generalization merely reflects the tendency of American economists to write micro-economics as if all the world were America, and macro-economics as if all the world were Britain.) Or perhaps he does not have much evidence about America either, and just assumes that 'Man' is a hard-nosed short-run profit-maximizer suspicious of everyone he deals with, and allows everything else to follow from that. At any rate Williamson's account does not provide the tools for explaining the difference between the Japanese and the British or American economies. There is nothing particularly idiosyncratic about the steel or cloth traded in many of the obligated relationships, little specialized assets involved (though there are in automobile subcontracting). Nor is there clear avoidance of price adjustments—weaving contract prices, in fact, look like graphs of nineteenth century business cycles.

Clearly we have to look elsewhere for an explanation. Try as one might to avoid terms like 'national character' which came naturally to Hobhouse, in favour of the scientific pretensions of, say, 'modal behavioural dispositions', it is clearly national differences in value preferences, or dispositions to action, with which we are concerned. And, as Macfarlane showed when he looked into the origins of English individualism,[15] to attempt to explain *those* takes one on a long speculative journey—at least into distant ill-recorded history, even if, for ideological reasons, one wishes to rule out genes. But it is legitimate and useful to ask: what are the concomitants of these dispositions? What do they correlate with? Are they an expression of more general traits?

One candidate explanation is that the Japanese are generally very long-term-future-oriented. At this moment, for example, the Japanese Industry Ministry's Industrial Structure Council is already composing what it calls a 'vision' of the shape of the world economy in the mid-1990s. The economist is likely to seize on this explanation with relief, because it will allow him to ignore all dangerous thoughts about benevolence, and accommodate the relational contracting phenomenon in the conventional micro-economics of risk aversion and low time-discounts. Any sacrifice of short-run market advantage is just an insurance premium for more long-term gains.

And he would find some good evidence. Nakatani has recently done an interesting calculation comparing 42 large firms inside one of the large kinship groupings like Mitsui and Mitsubishi which I have just described and a matched sample of 42 loners. The loners had higher average profit levels and higher growth rates in the 1970s. *But* they also had a considerably higher dispersal around the means. The group firms were much more homogeneous in growth and profit levels. What went on in the groups, he concluded, was an overall sacrifice of efficiency in the interests of risk-sharing and greater equality.[16]

Relational contracts, in this interpretation, are just a way of trading off the short term loss involved in sacrificing a price advantage, against the insurance that one day you can 'call off' the same type of help from your trading partner if you are in trouble yourself. It is a calculation, perhaps, which comes naturally to a population which until recently was predominantly living in tightly nucleated hamlet communities in a land ravished by earthquake and typhoon. Traditionally, you set to, to help your neighbour rebuild his house after a fire, even though it might be two or three generations before yours was burnt down and your grandson needed the help returned.

But you could be *sure* that the help *would* be returned. And this is where we come back to Adam Smith. The Japanese, in spite of what their political leaders say at summit conferences about the glories of free enterprise in the Free World, and in spite of the fact that a British publisher with a new book about Adam Smith can expect to sell half the edition in Japan, have never really caught up with Adam Smith. They have never managed actually to bring themselves to *believe* in the invisible hand. They have always insisted—and teach in their schools and their 'how to get on' books of popular morality—that the butcher and the baker and the brewer *need* to be benevolent as well as self-interested. They need to be able to take some personal pleasure in the satisfaction of the diners quite over and above any expectation of future orders. It is not just that benevolence is the best policy—much as we say, rather more minimally, that honesty is the best policy. They do not doubt that it is—that it is not a matter of being played for a sucker, but actually the best way to material success. But that is not what they most commonly say. They most commonly say: benevolence is a duty. Full stop. It is that sense of duty—a duty over and above the terms of written contract—which gives the assurance of the payoff which makes relational contracting viable.

Note that this is a little different from what Durkheim had in mind when he was talking about the noncontractual elements in contract and refuting Spencer's claim that modern societies were held together solely by an organic web of individualistic contracts.[17] Durkheim was talking about the intervention of *society* both in enforcing the basic principles of honesty and the keeping of promises, and in regulating the content of contracts, deciding what was admissible and what offended social decency or basic human rights. And in Durkheim's book it is the consciousness of an obligation imposed by society as a whole—or, on its members, by an occupational group of professional practitioners—which enforces those rules. Hobhouse, likewise, in his brisker and more historically rooted discussion of the way freedom of contract and the rights or private property come to be curtailed by, for example, redistributive welfare measures, stressed the benefits the individual receives from society and the corresponding obligations to society.[18] In Japanese relational contracting, by contrast, it is a particular sense of diffuse obligation to the individual trading partner, not to society, which is at issue. To put the matter in Parson's terms, relational contracting is to be understood in the universalism/particularism dimension, whereas the Durkheim point relates to the fifth dichotomy that Parsons later lost from sight: collective-orientation versus individual-orientation. To put it another way, the Japanese share with Durkheim the perception that contract, far from being fundamentally integrative, is basically a marker for conflict. Every harmonization of interest in a contract simply conceals a conflict either latent or adjourned, as Durkheim said.[19] The Durkheim solution is to have universalistic social institutions contain the conflict—an engine-cooling system to take away the heat. The Japanese prefer particularistically to reduce the friction in all the moving parts with the emollient lubrication of mutual consideration.

Perhaps one should not overdraw the contrast, however, in view of the empirical fact that the Japanese, who stand out among other capitalist societies for their addiction to relational contracts, also stand out as the nation whose businessmen and trade unionists seem to have a more lively sense of their obligated membership in the national community than those of other nations. Japan has fewer free-rider problems in the management of the national economy; patriotism seems to supplement profit-seeking more substantially in, say, the search for export markets, and so on. Perhaps the common syndrome is a generalized dutifulness, or to put it in negative form, a relatively low level of individualistic, self-assertion. I am reminded of the Japanese scholar and publicist, Nitobe. In his lectures in the USA in the 1930s he used to tell the national character story about the international prize competition for an essay about the elephant. In his version the Japanese entry was entitled 'The duties and domestication of the elephant'.

But there is, it seems to me, a third element in the Japanese preference for relational contracting besides risk sharing and long-term advantage on the one hand and dutifulness on the other. That is the element, to go back to Parsons' variables again, best analysed in his affectivity/affective-neutrality dimension. People born and brought up in Japanese society do not much *like* openly adversarial bargaining relationships—which are inevitably low-trust relationships because information is hoarded for bargaining advantage and each tries to manipulate the responses of the other in his own interest. Poker is not a favourite Japanese game. Most Japanese feel more comfortable in high-trust relations of friendly give-and-take in which each side recognizes that he also has some stake in the satisfaction of the other.

All of which, of course, is not necessarily to say that the affect is genuine. Pecksniffs can do rather well in exploiting these relationships when they are in a stronger bargaining position—the point made earlier about the ambiguities of these relationships.

EMPLOYMENT PRACTICES
AND RELATIONAL CONTRACTS

The discussion so far has centred on markets in intermediates and capital goods, and about relational contracting between enterprises. I have not so far mentioned labour markets, though the predominance of relational contracting in Japanese labour markets is, of course, much more widely known than its predominance in inter-firm trading. By now every television viewer has heard of the life-time commitment pattern—the transformation of the employment contract from a short-term spot contract agreement to provide specific services for a specific wage (termination by one week or one month's notice on either side), into a long-term commitment to serve as needs may from time-to-time dictate, with wages negotiated according to criteria of fairness which have precious little to do with any notion of a market rate-for-the-job. The contract is seen, in fact, less as any kind of bilateral bargain, than as an act of admission to an enterprise community wherein benevolence, goodwill and sincerity are explicitly expected to temper the pursuit of self-interest. The parallel between relational contracting in the intermediates market and in the labour market is obvious. There can be little doubt that the same cultural values explain the preferred patterns in both fields.

RELATIONAL CONTRACTING AND EFFICIENCY

But anyone looking at the competitive strength of the Japanese economy today must also wonder whether this institutionalization of relational contracting, as well as serving the values of risk-sharing security, dutifulness and friendliness *also* conduces to a fourth valued end—namely economic efficiency. Any economist, at least any economist worth his neo-classical salt, would be likely to scoff at the idea. Just think, he would say, of the market imperfections, of the misallocation and loss of efficiency involved. Think how many inefficient producers are kept out of the bankruptcy courts by all this give-and-take at the expense of the consuming public. Think of the additional barriers to entry against new, more efficient, producers. Gary Becker, in a lecture at the LSE a couple of years ago, claimed that give-and-take trading was even an inefficient way of being altruistic. In the end, he said, through greater survival power, you get more dollars-worth of altruism by playing the market game and then using the profits to endow a charitable foundation like Rockefeller—which I suppose is true and would even be significant if 'altruism' were a homogeneous commodity indifferently produced either by being friendly to your suppliers or by posthumously endowing scholarship.[20]

But that apart, the main point about sub-optimality is well-taken. The Japanese economy is riddled with misallocation. A lot of the international dispute about non-tariff barriers, for example, has its origin in relational contracting. Take the market for steel which I mentioned earlier. Brazil and Korea can now land some kinds of steel in Japan more cheaply than Japanese producers can supply it. But very little of it is sold. Japan can remain as pure as the driven snow in GATT terms—no trigger prices, minimal tariffs, no quotas—and still have a kind of natural immunity to steel imports which Mr. MacGregor would envy. None of the major trading companies would touch Brazilian or Korean steel, especially now that things are going so badly for their customers, the Japanese steel companies. Small importers are willing to handle modest lots. But they will insist on their being landed at backwater warehouses away from where any domestic steel is going out, so that the incoming steel is not seen by a steel company employee. If that happens, the lorries taking the steel out might be followed to their destination. And the purchaser, if he turned out to be a disloyal customer, would be marked down for less than friendly treatment next time a boom brings a seller's market. What distortions, an economist would say. What a conspiracy against the consumer! What a welfare loss involved in sacrificing the benefits of comparative advantage! If the Japanese economy has a good growth record, that can only be *in spite of* relational contracting and the consequent loss of efficiency.

And yet there are some good reasons for thinking that it might be *because of*, and not *in spite of* relational contracting that Japan has a better growth performance than the rest of us. There is undoubtedly a loss of allocative efficiency. But the countervailing forces which more than outweigh that loss can *also* be traced to relational contracting. Those countervailing forces are those which conduce to, not allocative efficiency, but what Harvey Leibenstein calls X-efficiency—those abilities to plan and programme, to cooperate without bitchiness in production, to avoid waste of time or of materials, capacities which Leibenstein tries systematically to resolve into the constituent elements of selective degrees of rationality and of effort.[21] We have recently been told by a solemn defender of the neo-classical paradigm that we need not bother about Leibenstein and X-efficiency because he is only reformulating the utility-maximizing paradigm of the generalized equilibrium theory as developed by the Williamson school (i.e. that which incorporates transaction costs, property-right constraints, etc.).[22] To argue thus is not only to destroy the usefulness of 'utility-maximization' for any precise calculations, it is also to ignore the achievement of Leibenstein in actually noticing (a) that individuals, firms and nations differ greatly in degrees of generalized *sloppiness*, and (b) that other kinds of sloppiness are far more important for output growth and welfare than that involved in failing to fine-tune economic behaviour in response to changes in price signals—or *even* in failing to calculate the relative transaction costs of internal and external procurement.

In his book Leibenstein tries a rough comparison between the estimated welfare loss from tariffs and price distortions in a number of empirical cases, and that implied by the 'inefficiency' of business firms inferrable from the range in outputs with similar inputs as between 'best practice' and 'worst practice' firms. His evidence that for most economies for most of the time the latter vastly exceeds the former is of crucial policy importance, and any theory which succeeds in assimilating both phenomena within the same umbrella framework is, like unisex fashions, less an achievement than a distraction. The distinction between allocative efficiency which has to do with rational responses to price signals and all those other kinds of efficiency which raise the productivity of inputs in a business organization is an extremely useful one, and X-efficiency is as good a catch-all term for the second bundle of qualities as any other.

It is in the second dimension, in its effect in making 'best practice' better and more widely diffused, that the Japanese system of relational contracting has merits which, I suggest, more than compensate for its price-distorting consequences. To take the case of employment and the life-time commitment first, the compensatory advantages which go with the disadvantage of inflexible wage costs, are reasonably well known. In a career employment system people accept that they have continually to be learning new jobs; there can be great flexibility, it makes more sense for firms to invest in training, the organization generally is more likely to be a learning environment open to new ideas. If a firm's market is declining, it is less likely to respond simply by cutting costs to keep profits up, more likely to search desperately for new product lines to keep busy the workers it is committed to employing anyway. Hence a strong growth dynamism. And so on.

As for relational contracting between enterprises, there are three things to be said. First, the relative security of such relations encourages investment in supplying firms. The spread of robots has been especially rapid in Japan's engineering subcontracting firms in recent years, for example. Second, the relationships of trust and mutual dependency make for a more rapid flow of information. In the textile industry, for example, news of impending changes in final consumer markets is passed more rapidly upstream to weavers and yarn dyers; technical information about the appropriate sizing or finishing for new chemical fibres is passed down more systematically from the fibre firms to the beamers and dyers. Third, a by-product of the system is a general emphasis on quality. What holds the relation together is the sense of mutual obligation. The butcher shows his benevolence by never taking advantage of the fact that the customer doesn't know rump from sirloin. If one side fails to live up to his obligations, the other side is released from his. According to the relational contract ethic, it may be difficult to ditch a supplier because, for circumstances for the moment beyond his control, he is not giving you the best buy. It is perfectly proper to ditch him if he is not giving the best buy and not *even trying* to match the best buy. The single most obvious indicator of effort is product quality. A supplier who consistently fails to meet quality requirements is in danger of losing even an established relational contract. I know that even sociologists should beware of anecdotal evidence, but single incidents can often illustrate national norms and I make no apology for offering two.

1. The manager of an automobile parts supplier said that it was not uncommon for him to be rung up at home in the middle of the night by the night-shift supervisor of the car factory 60 miles away. He might be told that they had already found two defective parts in the latest batch, and unless he could get someone over by dawn they were sorry, but they'd have to send the whole lot back. And he would then have to find a foreman whom he could knock up and send off into the night.
2. The manager of a pump firm walking me round his factory explains that it is difficult to diagnose defects in the pump-castings before machining though the founders are often aware when things might have gone wrong. 'I suspect', he said cheerfully, 'our supplier keeps a little pile of defective castings in the corner of his workshop, and when he's got a good batch that he thinks could stand a bit of rubbish he throws one or two in'.

I leave the reader to guess which is the Japanese and which the British story.

HOW *UNIQUELY* JAPANESE?

So if it is the case that relational contracting has some X-efficiency advantages which compensate for allocative inefficiencies, what lessons should we draw from all this about how to run an efficient economy and build a decent society? The first thing to do is to look around at our economies and take stock of the ways in which benevolence/goodwill actually modify the workings of the profit motive in daily practice. So far I have referred to relational contracting as something the Japanese have an *unusual* preference for. But that is far from saying that they are *uniquely* susceptible to it. If we look around us we will find far more evidence of relational contracting than we think. This is so even in America where capitalism seems generally to be more hard-nosed than in Europe. In an interesting article written 20 years ago, Stewart Macaulay examined the relative importance of personal trust and enforceable legal obligation in business contracts in the USA. He found many businessmen talking of the need for give-and-take, for keeping accountants and lawyers, with their determination to press every advantage, out of direct dealings with other firms.[23] Among those with experience of large projects in the civil construction industry it is a truism that successful work requires a bond of trust between client and contractor. Engineers, as fellow-professionals, sharing a commitment to the project's success, can create that trust. Their firms' lawyers can endanger it by the confrontational stance with which they approach all potential conflicts of interest. Recently I got a simple questionnaire answered by seven managers or owner-managers of weaving mills in Blackburn asking them about their trading practices, and found a strong preference for stable long-term relationships with give-and-take on the price, and a claim that, on average, two-thirds of their business already was that way. In the British textile trade, of course, Marks and Spencers is well known for its relational contracting, squeezing suppliers a bit in times of trouble but not ditching them as long as they are maintaining quality standards, and accepting some responsibility for helping them technically. In the supermarket world, Sainsbury's have the same reputation, supposedly very different from that of Tesco's which believes that frequent switching of suppliers encourages the others to keep the price down.

QUALITY, AFFLUENCE AND RELATIONAL CONTRACTING

There may be something very significant in the nature of these examples. Try adding together the following thoughts.

1. Marks and Spencers is well known for one thing besides relational contracting, namely that it bases its appeal on product quality more than on price.
2. There is also an apparent relation between a quality emphasis and relational contracting in Japan.
3. Sainsburys is up-market compared with Tesco which is for keen pricers.
4. Japan's consumer markets are *generally* reckoned to be more middle-class, more quality sensitive and less price sensitive than Britain's. (Textile people, for instance, have given me rough estimates that if

one divides the clothing market crudely into the AB groups, fastidious about quality and not too conscious of price, and the rest who look at price and superficial smartness rather than the neatness of the stitching, in Britain the proportions are: 25:75; in Japan 60:40.)

5. Japan of the 1920s, and again in the postwar period, was much more of a cut-throat jungle than it is today. Not the ethics of relational contracting nor the emphasis on product quality nor the life-time employment system, seem to have been at all characteristic of earlier periods of Japanese industrialization.

Add all these fragments together and an obvious hypothesis emerges that relational contracting is a phenomenon of affluence, a product, Hobhouse would say, of moral evolution. It is when people become better off and the market-stall haggle gives way to the world of *Which*, where best buys are defined more by quality than by price criteria, that relational contracting comes into its own.

It does so for two reasons: first because quality assurance has to depend more on trust. You always *know* whether the butcher is charging you sixpence or sevenpence. But if you don't know the difference between sirloin and rump, and you think your guests might, then you *have* to trust your butcher: you have to depend on his benevolence. Also, I suspect, when affluence reduces price pressures, any tendencies to prefer a relationship of friendly stability to the poker-game pleasures of adversarial bargaining—tendencies which might have been formerly suppressed by the anxious concern not to lose a precious penny—are able to assert themselves. Japan's difference from Britain, then, is explained both by the fact that the cultural preferences, the suppressed tendencies, are stronger *and* by the fact that the price pressures have been more reduced by a much more rapid arrival at affluence, and consequently a greater subjective sense of affluence.

The fragmentary evidence about relational contracting in interfirm trading relations in Britain, is much more easily complemented by evidence of its growth in the labour market. Not only Britain, but Europe in general—even the USA to a lesser extent—are no longer countries where employers hire and fire without compunction. Statutory periods of notice gradually lengthen. National redundancy payment schemes recognize the expectation of continuance of an employment contract as a property right. In industries like steel, job tenures are valued at well over a year's wages. More generally, labour mobility has been falling for 15 years. Factory flexibility agreements take the employment contract further away from the original rate-for-the-specific-job basis. More attention to career-promotion systems within the firm, managerial doctrines about 'worker involvement' in the affairs of the enterprise and, intermittently, talk of, and even occasional moves towards, enterprise-based industrial democracy all exemplify the transformation of the employment contract into a more long-term, more diffuse commitment.

RELATIONAL CONTRACTING, RIGIDITIES
AND ECONOMIC POLICY

Economists have occasionally noted these trends, but have generally treated them as market imperfections, basically lag problems of the long and the short run—for in the end, habit always succumbs to the pursuit of profit. And among imperfection problems they have found them less interesting to analyse than other kinds like monopoly. And those bold souls among them who *have* taken aboard the new phenomenon of stagflation, and tried to explain the tendency for contraction in demand to lead to a contraction in output not a fall in price, to increased unemployment but only slow, delayed and hesitant deceleration in the rate of wage increase, have rarely recognized the importance of a general growth in relational contracting—of the effects on the effectiveness of fiscal and monetary regulators of the fact that more and more deals are being set by criteria of fairness not by market power. More commonly, they speak of the growth of oligopoly on the one hand and on the other of trade union monopoly consequent on statutory job protection and higher welfare benefits. They have explained stagflation, in other words, not as the result of creeping benevolence—the diffusion of goodwill and mutual consideration through the economy—but as the result of creeping malevolence, increasing abuse of monopoly power. And the cure which our modern believers in the supreme virtues of the market have for these 'rigidities', is a deflation stiff enough to restore the discipline of market forces, to make firms competitive again and force the inefficient out of business, to weaken trade union monopolies and get firms hiring and firing according to their real needs.

A few people have given relational contracting and its growth the importance it is due. Albert Hirschman, first in this as in so many things, described the general syndrome of voice and loyalty taking over from exit and entry as the characteristic disciplining force of advanced capitalism.[24] More recently Arthur Okun developed before his untimely death a similarly comprehensive view of relational contracting and, moreover, explained in his *Prices and Quantities* its connection to worsening stagflation.[25] He wrote of the tendency in capital goods and intermediate markets, and to some extent in consumer markets, for what he called 'customer markets', to grow at the expense of 'auction markets', and of the corresponding growth of 'career labour markets'—employment characterized by an implicit contract of quasi-permanence—the invisible handshake is one of his phrases—all adding up to what he called a 'price-tag economy' as opposed to the 'auction economy' of orthodox text books. What I do not think he fully took aboard is the way in which social relations in customer markets and career-labour markets take on a moral quality and become regulated by criteria of fairness. Consequently, his remedies, apart from being far more imaginatively interventionist, are not so very different in kind from the more common marketist prescriptions for dealing with the rigidities of stagflation. That is to say, he also concentrates on devices to change (a) incentives and (b) expectations under the unchanged assumption that economic behaviour will continue to be guided solely by short-run income-maximizing considerations.

There is no mention of Japan in his index, and none that I have discovered in his book. But if we do think of Japan, a society which has far more developed forms of relational contracting than ours and glories in it, *and* achieves high growth and technical progress, we might think of a different prescription.

It would run something like this. First, recognize that the growth of relational contracting can provide a very real enhancement of the quality of life. Not many of us who work in a tenured job in the academic career market, for example, would relish a switch to freelance status. I hear few academics offering to surrender their basic salary for the freedom to negotiate their own price for every lecture, or even demanding personally negotiated annual salaries in exchange for tenure and incremental scales. And if you overhear a weaving mill manager on the telephone, in a relaxed friendly joking negotiation with one of his long-standing customers, you may well wonder how much more than the modest profits he expects would be required to tempt him into the more impersonal cut-and-thrust of keen auction-market-type competition.

But the second point is this. Having recognized that relational contracting is something that we cannot expect to go away, and that inevitably a lot of allocative efficiency is going to be lost, try to achieve the advantages of X-efficiency which can compensate for the loss.

This prescription has a macro-part and a micro-part. The macro-part includes, first of all, maintaining the conditions for free competition in the one set of markets which remain impersonally competitive—the markets for final consumer goods. This is necessary to provide the external stimulus for the competing chains or pyramids of relational-contract-bound producers to improve their own internal inefficiency. It means on the one hand an active competition policy, and on the other, where monopoly is inevitable, the organization of countervailing consumer watchdog groups. Also included in the macro-part are first, an incomes policy, since if it *is* now criteria of fairness rather than the forces of supply and demand which determine wages in career labour markets, those fairness criteria had better be institutionalized. Second it means an attempt, if you like, to tip the ideology towards benevolence; in Fred Hirsch's terms, to try to revive an 'ethos of social obligation' to replenish the 'depleting moral legacy' which capitalism inherited from an earlier more solidary age,[26] not least by stressing the importance of quality and honest thoughtful service, the personal satisfactions of doing a good job well as a source of pride and self-respect—letting profits be their own reward, not treated as if they were a proxy measure of social worth. The Department of Industry's recent announcement of an £8 million programme of subsidies for improvement in quality assurance systems in British factories is at least a recognition of the enhanced importance of quality in the modern world, even if there are no signs of a recognition that this might entail new attitudes and values (or a new affirmation of old ones now lost), a move away from the spirit of *caveat emptor*.

The micro-part of the prescription involves a better specification of the ethics of relational contracting; perhaps, as the French have been contemplating, criteria for deciding what constitutes unfair dismissal of a subcontractor, parallel to those for employees, with protection depending on performance, including quality criteria and conscientious timing of deliveries. Second, at the enterprise level, it means taking the growth of job tenure rights not just as an unfortunate rigidity, but as an opportunity for developing a sense of community in business enterprises. It means, that is to say, reaping the production advantages which can come from a shared interest in the firm's success, from cooperation and free flow of information and a flexible willingness not to insist on narrow occupational roles. What those advantages can be we can see in Japan, but in Britain, where attitudes to authority are very different from those of Japan, the prescription probably means not manipulative policies of worker 'involvement' in existing hierarchies, but some real moves towards constitutional management, industrial democracy or what you will—anything *except* the extension of traditional forms of collective bargaining made for, and growing out of, the era of auction markets for labour.

I think Hobhouse would not have objected to a lecture in his honour being used as an occasion for preaching, though I am not sure that he would have approved of the contents. I am enough of an old-fashioned liberal, however, to hope that he might.

NOTES

1. A. Smith, *The Wealth of Nations*, London, J. M. Dent, 1910, p. 13.
2. R. H. I. Palgrave, *Dictionary of Political Economy*, ed. H. Higgs, London, Macmillan, 1923–6.
3. D. Greenwald, *McGraw-Hill Dictionary of Modern Economics*, New York, McGraw-Hill, 1973.
4. P. A. Samuelson, *Economics*, Eleventh Edition, New York, London, McGraw-Hill, 1980, pp. 121–2.
5. O. E. Williamson, 'The modern corporation: Origins, evolution, attributes', *Journal of Economic Literature*, vol. 19, no. iv, December 1981.
6. V. P. Goldberg, 'A relational exchange perspective on the employment relationship', Paper for SSRC Conference, York, 1981.
7. O. E. Williamson, 'Transaction-cost economics: the governance of contractual relations', *Journal of Law and Economics*, vol. 22, no. ii, 1979, pp. 233–61.
8. R. M. Solow, 'On theories of unemployment', *American Economic Review*, vol. 70, i, 1980.
9. Seni Torihiki Kindaika Suishin Kyogikai (Association for the Promotion of the Modernization of Trading Relations in the Textile Industry), *Nenji Hōkoku* (Annual Report), 1980.
10. R. Dore, *British Factory: Japanese Factory: The Origins of National Diversity in Industrial Relations*, Berkeley, University of California Press, 1973, pp. 269 ff.
11. H. Okumura, 'Masatsu o umu Nihonteki keiei no heisa-sei' (The closed nature of Japanese corporate management as a source of international friction), *Ekonomisuto*, 6 July 1982. H. Okumura, 'The closed nature of Japanese intercorporate relations', *Japan Echo*, vol. 9, no. iii, 1982.

12. H. Okumura, 'Interfirm relations in an enterprise group: The case of Mitsubishi', *Japanese Economic Studies*, Summer 1982. H. Okumura, *Shin Nihon no Rokudaikigyō-shūdan. (A new view of Japan's six great enterprise groups)*, Tokyo, Diamond, 1983.

13. Okumura in *Japan Echo*, 1982.

14. O. E. Williamson, 'Transaction-cost economics: the governance of contractual relations', *Journal of Law and Economics*, vol. 22, no. ii, 1979, pp. 233–261.

15. A. Macfarlane, *The Origins of English Individualism*, Oxford, Basil Blackwell, 1978.

16. I. Nakatani, *The Role of Intermarket keiretsu Business Groups in Japan*, Australia-Japan Research Centre, Research Paper, no. 97, Canberra, ANU. I. Nakatani, Risuku-shearingu kara mita Nihon Keizai, ('Risk-sharing in the Japanese economy'), 'Osak-adaigaku Keizaigaku', col. 32, nos. ii–iii, December 1982.

17. E. Durkheim, *De la Division du travail social*, Paris, Felix Alcan, 1893, tr. G. Simpson, *The Division of Labour in Society*, 1960.

18. L. T. Hobhouse, *Morals in Evolution*, London, Chapman & Hall, 1908, 7th ed., 1951.

19. Durkheim, op. cit., p. 222.

20. G. Becker, *Altruism in the Family and Selfishness in the Market Place*, Centre for Labour Economics, LSE, Discussion Paper No. 73, 1980.

21. H. Leibenstein, *Beyond Economic Man: A New Foundation for Micro Economics*, Cambridge, Mass., Harvard University Press, 1976.

22. L. De Alessi, 'Property rights transaction costs and X-efficiency: An essay in economic theory', *American Economic Review*, vol. 73, no. i, March, 1983.

23. S. Macaulay, 'Non-contractual relations in business: a preliminary study', *American Sociological Review*, vol. 28, no. i, February, 1963.

24. A. O. Hirschman, *Exit, Voice and Loyalty: Responses to Decline in Firms, Organizations and States*, Cambridge, Mass., Harvard University Press, 1970.

25. A. Okun, *Prices and Quantities*, Oxford, Basil Blackwell, 1981.

26. F. Hirsch, *Social Limits to Growth*, London, Routledge & Kegan Paul, 1977.

EDITORS' NOTES ON FURTHER READING: DORE

Ronald Dore has written extensively about Japanese society and especially its economy. *Taking Japan Seriously* (1987) further developed some of the themes in "Goodwill and the Spirit of Capitalism." In an earlier well-known work, *British Factory—Japanese Factory: The Origins of National Diversity in Industrial Relations* (1973), Dore gave a vivid picture of the differences and similarities between working life in Japan and England. The growing empirical literature on Japanese industry was summarized in James Lincoln and Karry McBride's "Japanese Industrial Organization in Comparative Perspective," *Annual Review of Sociology* 13 (1989):289–312 and linked to theory in James Lincoln's "Japanese Organizations and Organization Theory," *Research in Organizational Behavior* 12 (1990). Two works made systematic comparisons between the United States and Japan based on surveys in both countries: Robert E. Cole's *Work, Mobility, and Participation: A Comparative Study of American and Japanese Industry* (1979), which has an especially lucid chapter on the role of Japanese "culture" in Japanese organizations, and James Lincoln and Arne Kalleberg's *Culture, Control, and Commitment: A Study of Work Organization and Work Attitudes in the United States and Japan* (1990) (reviewed by Granovetter in *Contemporary Sociology* 19 [1990]:789–791). For a recent statistical study of the different sources of income inequality in Japan and the United States, see Arne Kalleberg and James Lincoln, "The Structure of Earnings Inequality in the United States and Japan,"

American Journal of Sociology (Supplement) 94 (1988):S121–S153. Fascinating ethnographic detail is found in Thomas P. Rohlen's account of the education of bank officials in *For Harmony and Strength: Japanese White-Collar Organization in Anthropological Perspective* (1974). For the concept of "relational contracting" in Dore's article, see the literature referred to after Stewart Macaulay's article (Chapter 10) in this anthology.

The role society outside the workplace has played in creating the differences between the United States and Japan is a much-debated subject. Early studies, such as James Abegglen's *The Japanese Factory* (1958), emphasized the influence of the distinct tradition of Japanese culture, an argument given especially clear formulation in Chie Nakane's *Japanese Society* (1970). This influence has been questioned on several grounds, including the idea that all industrial societies are increasingly becoming alike (see, e.g., Clark Kerr et al., *Industrialism and Industrial Man*, 1960) and that it is the social structure, rather than some general "culture," that accounts for the differences in question (see, e.g., the article by Gary Hamilton and Nicole Biggart [Chapter 7] in this anthology). That the Japanese state has played a key role in the successful growth of Japan's postwar economy is, however, clear; and on this point the reader is referred to Chalmers Johnson's *MITI and the Japanese Miracle: The Growth of Industrial Policy, 1925–1975* (1982) and to Richard T. Samuels's *The Business of the Japanese State: Energy Markets in Comparative and Historical Perspective* (1987).

For a brief analysis of the relationship between industrial policy and financial systems (including the Japanese case), see John Zysman, *Governments, Markets, and Growth: Financial Systems and the Politics of Industrial Change* (1983). For an introduction to the origins of the industrial revolution in Japan, see, for example, Frances Moulder, *Japan, China, and the Modern World Economy: Toward a Reinterpretation of East Asian Development, ca. 1600 to ca. 1918* (1977) and Ellen Kay Trimberger, *Revolutions from Above: Military Bureaucrats and Developments in Japan, Turkey, Egypt, and Peru* (1978).

7

Market, Culture, and Authority: A Comparative Analysis of Management and Organization in the Far East[1]

GARY G. HAMILTON
NICOLE WOOLSEY BIGGART

Several social science disciplines have been interested in the structure and functioning of economic organizations. This widespread interest is largely grouped around three perspectives. Especially in economics (Chandler 1977, 1981; Teece 1980; Williamson 1981, 1985) but also in anthropology (Orlove 1986) and sociology (White 1981), scholars have studied economic decision making in regard to the conditions under which business firms arise and operate in relation to market-mediated transactions. We call this general perspective the "market approach." The second perspective on economic organization is the "cultural approach," which suggests that cultural patterns shape economic behavior. This perspective was formerly a preserve of anthropologists (e.g., Benedict 1946; Douglas 1979; see also Orlove 1986) but is now widespread among a large number of scholars from diverse backgrounds. Studies of corporate culture (Deal and Kennedy 1982; Peters and Waterman 1982; Kanter 1983) and comparative culture studies of Japanese (Ouchi 1981, 1984; Pascale and Athos 1981; Vogel 1979), Swedish (Blumberg 1973; Foy and Gadon 1976), Yugoslavian (Adizes 1971), and other nations' industrial practices have increased manifold in the past 10 years. The third perspective is a political economy perspective, which we call the "authority approach." Scholars in all social science fields have worked on economic organization from this wide-ranging perspective, from the seminal work of Marx (1930) and Weber (1958, 1978) to such recent studies as Granovetter

From *American Journal of Sociology (Supplement)* 94 (1988):S52–S94. Copyright © 1988 by The University of Chicago. Reprinted by permission.

(1985), Perrow (1981, 1986), Portes and Walton (1981), Haggard and Cheng (1986), Reynolds (1983), and Mintz and Schwartz (1985).

This paper assesses the relative efficacy of each of these three approaches in explaining the industrial arrangements and strategies of three rapidly developing countries of the Pacific region—South Korea, Taiwan, and Japan. We argue that, while market and culture explanations make important contributions to understanding, neither is alone sufficient. A market explanation correctly draws our attention to state industrial policies and entrepreneurial responses. But a market explanation cannot account for the distinctive and substantially different organizational arrangements that have appeared in the three countries. A cultural explanation, however, enables us to see, correctly, organizational practices in Japan, South Korea, and Taiwan as generalized expressions of beliefs in the relative importance of such social factors as belongingness, loyalty, and submission to hierarchical authority. But looking at culture alone obscures the fact that business organizations, no matter how well they accord with cultural beliefs, are fundamentally responses to market opportunities and conditions. Enterprise may be culturally informed, but it remains enterprise. Moreover, cultural variables are insufficiently distinguishable in the region to have clear explanatory force.

In this paper, we argue that the political economy approach with a Weberian emphasis produces the best explanation of the three. This approach incorporates elements of the market and culture explanations but does so from the point of view of the historically developed authority relations that exist among individuals and institutions in each society. We argue that market opportunities do indeed lead to innovations in organizational design but that these innovations are not simply a rational calculus of the most efficient way to organize. Organizational practices, instead, represent strategies of control that serve to legitimate structures of command and often employ cultural understandings in so doing. Such practices are not randomly developed but rather are fashioned out of preexisting interactional patterns, which in many cases date to preindustrial times. Hence, industrial enterprise is a complex modern adaptation of preexisting patterns of domination to economic situations in which profit, efficiency, and control usually form the very conditions of existence.

We pursue this argument in the following sections. First, we introduce the recent economic history of the three countries of interest and describe their current patterns of industrial organization. South Korea, Taiwan, and Japan offer an unusual opportunity for comparative analysis. The economy of each was virtually destroyed by war, World War II in the cases of Japan and Taiwan and the Korean War in the instance of South Korea. In recent years, all three nations have rebuilt their economies and achieved extraordinary rates of economic growth, yet each has a different dominant form of organizational structure. Second, we employ in turn market, culture, and authority relations explanations, suggesting the distinctive contribution and limitation of each to analyzing the three cases and explaining their differential outcomes. Finally, we suggest how our analysis of these three East Asian economies, and the relative superiority of the authority relations approach, has implications for industrial analysis, including the American case as it is currently understood.

RECENT ECONOMIC DEVELOPMENT IN JAPAN, TAIWAN, AND SOUTH KOREA

Forty years ago, at the end of World War II, Japan lay in ruins, its industrial core shattered and its colonial empire of Korea and Taiwan severed. Taiwan, a largely agricultural society, was also leveled by the war, and "three-quarters of [its] industrial capacity was destroyed" (Little 1979, p. 454). Moreover, Taiwan absorbed fleeing migrants from the Chinese mainland, who arrived with Chiang Kai-shek's armies and government. Taiwan's population jumped from fewer than 6 million people in 1944 to 8 million in 1950, a more than one-third increase in about five years (Kuznets 1979, p. 32). Similarly, 32 years ago Korea emerged from a civil war that destroyed its economy and killed 1.3 million of its people. The southern agricultural portion of the country was separated from the industrial north. South Korea lost its supply of manufactured goods, hydroelectric power, and the bituminous coal that powered its railroads (Bunge 1982, p. 24).

Yet, in the 1980s, these three countries are the centerpiece of a rapidly industrializing Asia (Hofheinz and Calder 1982; Linder 1986). They have not only rebuilt their economies but have also become the wonder of the developing and developed worlds. Japan's success is the envy of American and European nations: in 1984, Japan's gross national product was the second highest in the capitalist world (Economist Intelligence Unit 1985*a*), with growth and investment rates double the United States' (Vogel 1979). Taiwan's GNP increased an average of 10.6% a year in the decade 1963–72, and in the decade 1973–82, a period that includes a world recession, it increased 7.5% a year (Myers 1984). In 1949, Taiwan's per-capita income was less than $50 U.S. In 1970, it was around $350, and, in 1984, $2,500 (Minard 1984, p. 36). South Korea's economic development did not accelerate until the 1960s, but in the decade 1963–72 manufacturing exports grew 52% a year (Little 1979), and between 1962 and 1984 industrial production increased at an average rate of 17% (Economist Intelligence Unit 1985*b*). In 1962, South Korea's per-capita GNP was $87 U.S., in 1980, $1,503 (Bunge 1982, p. 109), and in 1983, $1,709 (*Monthly Bulletin of Statistics* 1985). All three countries' economic success has largely been fueled by exports. Table [7.]1 shows the extraordinary growth in the countries' export sectors. In 1984, Japan's trade surplus to the United States was about $40 billion (*Direction of Trade Statistics* 1985, p. 242); Taiwan's was nearly $10 billion (more than twice Japan's on a per-capita basis) (*Taiwan Statistical Data Book* 1985, p. 205); and South Korea's was $3.2 billion (*Direction of Trade Statistics* 1985, p. 248). By any economic measure, the growth of these northeast Asian economies is unprecedented and has led many to refer to this economic success story as the "Asian Miracle."

TABLE [7.]1   Value of Exports in Japan, South Korea, and Taiwan
in Millions of U.S. Dollars

	Japan[a]	South Korea[b]	Taiwan[c]
1965	8,452	175	450
1970	19,318	835	1,481
1975	55,753	5,081	5,309
1980	129,807	17,505	19,810
1984	170,132[d]	29,253	30,456

[a]From *Abstract of Statistics on Agriculture, Forestry and Fisheries*, Japan, 1982.
[b]From *Korea Statistical Handbook*, National Bureau of Statistics, 1985.
[c]From *Statistical Yearbook of the Republic of China*, Directorate General of Budget, Accounting, and Statistics, 1984.
[d]From United Nations, *Monthly Bulletin of Statistics*, 1985.

The similarities of Japan, Taiwan, and South Korea go beyond economic recovery in the wake of wartime destruction; in fact, other similarities might seem to account for their common economic development (Cumings 1984; Hofheinz and Calder 1982). All three countries have few natural, especially mineral, resources. Their success cannot be explained by the discovery of oil reserves, as in some comparably successful developing nations in the Middle East. Nor is land the source of their wealth. Taiwan, South Korea, and Japan are among the most populated countries in the world in relation to cultivable land, "higher even than Egypt and Bangladesh and four times as high as India" (Little 1979, p. 450). Clearly, these are nations dependent on industry for wealth. They received economic aid and direction from the United States to repair and restart their economies, but the aid alone, which was given to other countries as well, cannot explain the rapid development there (Amsden 1979; Haggard and Cheng 1986; Little 1979; Hofheinz and Calder 1982; Barrett and Whyte 1982). Historically and culturally, the three are intertwined. Japan colonized Taiwan in 1895 and Korea in 1910, pursuing similar colonial policies in each (Cumings 1984; Myers and Peattie 1984). While each nation has its own language and ethnicity, China has, historically, had influences throughout the region. Korea and Japan, like Taiwan, have been deeply influenced by Confucian and Buddhist traditions. All three have relied on exports as a means for economic expansion.

In sum, the similarities are substantial. In fact, they are so great and the fate of the three countries so interlinked historically that Bruce Cumings (1984, p. 38) insightfully argues that "the industrial development in Japan, Korea, and Taiwan cannot be considered as an individual country phenomenon; instead it is a regional phenomenon. . . . " He further argues: "When one [country] is compared to another the differences will also be salient, but when all three are compared to the rest of the world the similarities are remarkable."

Despite these similarities, Japan, South Korea, and Taiwan have substantially different forms of enterprise or firm organization, particularly in the export sectors of there economies. Moreover, in each country the firm is embedded in a network of institutional relationships that gives each economy a distinctive character.[2] The important point here is that, if one looks only at individual firms, one misses the crucial set of social and political institutions that serves to integrate the economy. Taking advantage of Granovetter's very useful discussion (1985), we argue that the firm is "embedded" in networks of institutionalized relationships and that these networks, which are different in each society, have a direct effect on the types of firms that develop, on the management of firms, and on organizational strategies more generally. The particular forms of economic embeddedness in each society, particularly in relation to political institutions, allow for the activation of different organizational designs to achieve industrialization.

THREE PATTERNS OF INDUSTRIAL ORGANIZATION

In Japan, two interrelated networks of firms are crucial for understanding the operation of the Japanese economy, and particularly the export sector. These networks represent two types of what Caves and Uekusa (1976) call "enterprise groups." One type of enterprise group consists of linkages among large firms. These linkages are usually loosely coupled, basically horizontal connections among a range of large firms. Although such firms differ in terms of size and prestige (Clark 1979, p. 95), the linkages between them are what Dore (1983, p. 467) calls "relational contracting between equals." These groupings of firms are intermarket groups and are spread through different industrial sectors (Vogel 1979, p. 107). The second type of enterprise group connects small- and medium-sized firms to a large firm, creating what economists (e.g., Nakamura 1981; Ozawa 1979; Patrick and Rosovsky 1976) call a "dual structure," a situation of "relational contracting between unequals" (Dore 1983, p. 465). Both types of enterprise groups make centrally located large firms and associations of large firms the principal actors in the Japanese economy. As a result of these enterprise groups, assets are distributed throughout a range of different types of firms, as shown in Table [7].2.

The best-known networks of large firms, or *grūpu* are the *kigyo shudan*, or intermarket groups, which are the modern-day descendants of the pre-World War II *zaibatsu*. These networks are normally groups of firms in unrelated businesses that are joined together by central banks or by trading companies (Clark 1979; Caves and Uekusa 1976). In prewar Japan, these groups were linked by powerful holding companies that were each under the control of a family. The *zaibatsu* families exerted firm control over the individual firms in their group through a variety of fiscal and managerial methods. During the U.S. occupation, the largest of these holding companies were dissolved, with the member firms of each group becoming independent (Bisson 1954). After the occupation, however, firms (e.g., Mitsui, Mitsubishi, and Sumitomo) regrouped themselves, but this time allowing for only limited concentration of fiscal resources in banks and none whatsoever in family-run holding companies (Johnson 1982, p. 174; Caves and Uekusa 1976). In

TABLE [7.]2   Distribution of Assets of Large Japanese Corporations, by Group Affiliation

Affiliate Group	Percentage of Total Assets		
	1955	1962	1965
Public corporations whose capital is wholly or partly government owned	62.2	50.1	38.3
Affiliates of long-term credit banks whose capital is partly government owned	2.1	3.3	4.3
Affiliates of *zaibatsu* and large private banks	23.3	28.4	29.2
Mitsui	6.1	3.8	5.0
Mitsubishi	5.0	6.4	7.2
Sumitomo	3.2	5.9	5.4
Fuji Bank (Yasuda)	2.9	3.6	3.8
Dai-ichi Bank	3.1	3.5	3.2
Sanwa Bank	1.4	2.2	2.6
Giant industrial corporations with vertical and conglomerate structures of subsidiaries and affiliates	5.6	9.5	8.8
Foreign-owned enterprises	1.0	1.4	1.4
Companies outside the affiliate system	5.8	7.3	18.0
Total	100.0	100.0	100.0

Source: Caves and Uekusa (1976, p. 64).

addition to the former *zaibatsu*, another variant of the intermarket groups emerged in the postwar period. This is what Clark (1979, p. 72) calls the "bank group," which consists of "companies dependent for funds on a major bank" (e.g., Fuji, Dai-ichi, and Sanwa).[3]

The second type of enterprise group consists of vertical linkages between major manufacturers (*kaisha*) and their related subsidiaries (Abegglen and Stalk 1985; Clark 1979, p. 73), linkages that produce a dual structure in the Japanese economy (Yasuba 1976; Nakamura 1981). Major firms in Japan are directly connected to a series of smaller independent firms that perform important roles in the overall system of production.[4] According to Nakamura's analysis (1981, pp. 171–93), with the exception of some assembly industries (e.g., automobiles), "The prevailing pattern is that large firms are in charge of the raw materials sector while small firms handle the transformation of these materials into manufactured goods." This system of subcontracting allows large firms to increase their use of small firms during times of expansion and to decrease their use during times of business decline. So common are these relations between large and small firms that the "sub-contractorization" of small firms by the large has been seen as the "greatest problem" confronting the Japanese economy because of the inequality and dual-wage system that it spawns (Nakamura 1981, p. 175).

In sum, the Japanese economy is dominated by large, powerful, and relatively stable enterprise groups. These groups constitute a "society of industry" (Clark 1979, pp. 95–96), "where *zaibatsu* and other affiliations

TABLE [7.]3   Contribution to Gross Domestic Production in the Manufacturing Sector by *Chaebol* Groups in South Korea (in percentages)

Number of Chaebols	1973	1975	1978	1984–85
4 largest[a]	...	...	...	45.0
5 largest[b]	8.8	12.6	18.4	...
10 largest[b]	13.9	18.9	23.4	...
20 largest[b]	21.8	28.9	33.2	...
50 largest[c]	...	...	...	80.0

[a]From *Business Week* (1985).
[b]From Koo (1984, p. 1032).
[c]From *Hankook Ilbo* (1985).

link industrial, commercial, and financial firms in a thick and complex skein of relations matched in no other country" (Caves and Uekusa 1976, p. 59).

Unlike Japan, with its diversity in business networks, in South Korea, the dominant industrial networks are large, hierarchically arranged sets of firms known as *chaebol*. *Chaebol* are similar to the prewar *zaibatsu* in size and organizational structure. In 1980–81, the government recognized 26 *chaebol*, which together controlled 456 firms (Westphal et al. 1984, p. 510). In 1985, there were 50 *chaebol* that controlled 552 firms (*Hankook Ilbo* 1985). Their rate of growth has been extraordinary. In 1973, the top five *chaebol* controlled 8.8% of the GNP (Koo 1984, p. 1032), but by 1985 the top four *chaebol* controlled 45% of the GNP (*Business Week* 1985, p. 48). In 1984, the top 50 *chaebol* controlled about 80% of the GNP (*Hankook Ilbo* 1985).

While the *chaebol* resemble enterprise groups in Japan, the member firms of the *chaebol* are closely controlled by central holding companies, which are owned by an individual or a family. In turn, the central holding companies of the *chaebol* do not have the independence of action that the enterprise groups possess in Japan. Instead, they are directly managed by the South Korean state through planning agencies and fiscal controls. Whereas the intermarket groups in Japan are based on a central bank and trading company, in South Korea *chaebol* rely on financing from state banks and government-controlled trading companies. With this type of support, the *chaebol* have developed at a phenomenal rate, as shown in Table [7.]3. In addition, in contrast to Japan, outside the *chaebol* networks there are few large, successful independent firms and less subcontracting between large and small firms.[5]

In Taiwan, the family firm (*jiazuqiye*) and the business group (*jituanqiye*) are the dominant organizational forms throughout the economy, especially in the export sector. Unlike in either Japan or South Korea, in Taiwan there are relatively low levels of vertical and horizontal integration and a relative absence of oligarchic concentrations. Family firms predominate, and they are usually small to medium in size (i.e., fewer than 300 employees or total assets of less than $20 million U.S.). According to Zhao (1982), of the 68,898 firms registered in 1976, 97.33% were small to medium in size. These firms employed about 60% of Taiwan's workers and accounted for 46% of the

TABLE [7.]4 Contribution to Gross National Product by Firm Size in Taiwan (in percentages)

Number of Firms	1980	1981	1982	1983
5 largest	5.52	4.90	5.02	5.45
10 largest	8.70	7.91	7.69	8.23
20 largest	12.66	11.73	10.96	11.85

Source: *Tianxia zazhi* (World Journal), September 1, 1983, pp. 63–84.

TABLE [7.]5 Contribution to Gross National Product by the Largest 100 Business Groups in Taiwan

	1973	1974	1977	1979	1981	1983
Percentage of GNP	34.0	29.5	29.1	32.8	30.8	31.7
Percentage of employees	5.1	5.1	5.0	4.9	4.6	4.7

Source: Zhonghua Zhengxinso (1985, pp. 46–47).

GNP and 65% of Taiwan's exports. (For GNP contributions of the largest firms, see Table [7.]4.) Some of these firms form production, assembly, or distribution networks among themselves, often linking together through informal contracts. Other firms, however, perform subcontracting work for larger firms.

Jituanqiye, or large business groups, cross-cut family firms. Most groups are networks of firms controlled by a single family (Zhonghua Zhengxinso 1985). These networks, however, do not rival the size of business groups in Japan and South Korea. Instead, most consist of conglomerate holding of small, medium, and a few modestly large firms. As shown in Table [7.]5, a survey of the 100 largest business groups in Taiwan between the years 1973 and 1983 revealed remarkable stability in the overall economy, especially when compared with the rising corporate holdings in Japan and the phenomenal growth of the *chaebol* in South Korea (Zhonghua Zhengxinso 1985).

We develop the details of these patterns of business networks as we discuss the market, culture, and authority explanations for these differences.

THE MARKET EXPLANATION

The market explanation for organizational structure is associated most importantly with Alfred D. Chandler's analysis of the American business firm. *The Visible Hand* (1977) attempts to account for the development and rapid diffusion of the modern corporation. The invention of the corporation, what Chandler calls "multiunit" business enterprise, accelerated the rate of industrialization in the United States and, as American management ideas spread abroad, in the industrializing world generally. Although Chandler (1984) recognizes local differences in the spread of the multiunit firm to Western Europe and Japan, he attributes such differences largely to market characteristics. The United States was the "seed bed" of managerial capitalism, not Europe, because of "the size and nature of its domestic market" (1977, p. 498).

The logic of Chandler's analysis is a straightforward developmental thesis of institutional change based on changing market conditions.[6] Chandler shows that the preindustrial American economy was dominated by small, traditional organizations: partnerships or family-owned businesses with limited outputs. The traditional business typically received its raw materials and tools from a general merchant who in turn purchased at wholesale the business's finished goods and distributed them in nearby markets at retail prices. The general merchant was the kingpin of the colonial economy (1977, p. 18). After the colonial period and until the advent of the railways, traditional businesses became more specialized, with the general merchant giving way to the commission merchant. But even with these changes, the essential organization of the traditional firm stayed the same. They "remained small and personally managed because the volume of business handled by even the largest was not yet great enough to require the services of a large permanent managerial hierarchy" (1977, p. 48).

The development of a nation-spanning railroad network in the United States in the mid-1800s had two important consequences for industrial organization (1977, pp. 79–187). First, the railroads, the first geographically dispersed business, were compelled to develop innovative strategies of management; they developed the first multiunit firm organizations. Second, and more important, the railroad made it possible for small, traditional businesses to buy and sell in much larger markets, and larger markets made it possible for them to increase the volume of production manifold. Newly enlarged businesses now found it more efficient to perform under one corporate roof the multiple services performed by various commission merchants. Each business arranged the purchase of its own raw materials, the financing of its debts, the production of goods, and the location of and distribution to markets. Managerial or administrative coordination of these multiple activities "permitted greater productivity, lower costs, and high profits than coordination by market mechanisms" (1977, p. 6). Chandler argues for the technical superiority of administrative over market coordination under conditions of mass markets created by the development of transportation networks.

Chandler's argument rests largely on technological causes. A related but much more economy-oriented argument has been developed by Oliver E. Williamson (1975, 1981, 1983, 1985). Building on the work of earlier economists (Commons 1934; Coase 1937), Williamson argues that the basic unit of economic analysis is the economic transaction—the exchange of goods or services across technological boundaries (e.g., the transformation of raw materials into finished goods or the purchase of goods for money). Every transaction contains costs, and especially those costs associated with ensuring that each party to a transaction lives up to the terms of the agreement. The more the uncertainty within the marketplace, Williamson argues (1985, pp. 30–32, 47–50, 64–67), the greater the likelihood that some parties will cheat, "will act opportunistically with guile." The more such opportunistic behavior occurs, the less reliable, the less efficient, and the less profitable the marketplace becomes. At this point, businesses reorganize to correct the deficiencies of the marketplace; they expand their organization through vertical or horizontal integration, thereby creating a "governance structure" that internalizes transactions, reducing transaction costs and increasing efficiency (1985, pp. 68–162).

Using transaction-cost theory, Williamson develops a theory of modern business organization. Multiunit firms arise when internally conducted transactions cost less than market-mediated transactions. The more complex and uncertain the economic environment, the more likely it is that business will expand their organization. Expansion reduces uncertainty and transaction costs and maximizes efficiency. For Williamson, the forms of organization that survive in specific economic arenas are the ones that deliver products more efficiently.[7]

To Chandler, multiunit firms offer superior coordination; to Williamson, lower transaction costs. Chandler acknowledges the influence of historical factors in explaining organization; Williamson explains the variety of organizations according to transactions: "There are so many kinds of organizations because transactions differ so greatly and efficiency is realized only if governance structures are tailored to the specific needs of each type of transaction" (1981, p. 568). Both, however, are efficiency theorists and see organization structure as the calculated expression of economically rational persons pursuing profit (Perrow 1981; Perrow 1986, pp. 219–57).

Chandler's market explanation of multiunit businesses can be applied to Japan, Korea, and Taiwan in a straightforward fashion but with ambiguous results. Williamson's central concepts are more difficult to operationalize, particularly "transaction costs" and "contracts" (Perrow 1986, pp. 241–47). Although both Chandler and Williamson qualify their theories at various points, they restrict their explanations to decisive economic variables.[8] Therefore, differences in organizational structure necessarily would have to be explained in terms of crucial differences among the three countries. We find, however, that all three countries are very similar in regard to the crucial variables Chandler pinpoints. Moreover, even loosely applied, Williamson's theory does not seem to explain adequately the differences among the three.

First, in all three countries internal transportation and communication systems are well developed, modern, and certainly far beyond what they were in late 19th-century America (see, e.g., Ranis 1979, p. 225). External transportation and communication systems are also well developed. Second, the three countries possess substantial and growing internal mass markets, which have already risen above the level of early 20th-century America. But more important, all the countries have vast external markets. Third, Japan, South Korea, and Taiwan use, have available, or have developed, the most advanced technologies in the various industrial sectors. This level of technology, of course, is far advanced over that discussed by Chandler.

Fourth, business enterprises in all three countries operate on principles of profit in the marketplace. By any definition, they are capitalist enterprises; they practice cost accounting, depend on free labor, develop through invested capital, and, if unsuccessful, may go bankrupt.[9]

Yet, despite these extensive similarities, as well as the others discussed earlier, among the three countries on all macroeconomic variables, the organizational structures of business enterprises are quite different. Moreover, even when each country is considered individually without regard to the other two, the enterprise structure is only partially explained by the market approach.

On the surface, Japanese business enterprise would seem to satisfy the conditions of Chandler's interpretation the best. The intermarket groups now include firms ranked among the largest in the world. They are vast, complexly organized, multiunit enterprises. They are successful in the world economy, where each of them has a sizable share of the total market in their respective sectors. Moreover, as is well known, these enterprises attempt to control the marketplace through administrative means (e.g., cartelization) insofar as it is possible (Johnson 1982; Vogel 1979). When Americans speak of emulating Japanese management practices, it is the management techniques of the intermarket groups, such as Mitsubishi and Sumitomo, or the giant *kaisha*, such as Toyota, to which they refer. In fact, Chandler (1977, p. 499) acknowledges that Japanese corporations satisfy his definition of the modern managerial business enterprise.

The South Korean case fits the market explanation less well than the Japanese case seemingly does. But if one includes the state as an aspect of business organization, then the Korean case might be squeezed into a market explanation. East Asian political organization has, of course, been a "multiunit" organization for centuries, but if one ignores this fact, then one could argue that, because of market conditions and the circumstances of a late-developing economy, the rapid industrialization in South Korea favored the formation of a type of state capitalism.[10] Vertical integration in South Korea occurred both at the level of the *chaebol* and at the level of the state, and both forms of integration were structurally and causally linked. Therefore, unlike the firm in the United States and somewhat unlike the firm in Japan, the South Korean multiunit business firm is not independent from state organization. As we will discuss later, important functional operations of the firm are controlled by bureaucratic departments of government. The firm is not an independent creation of market forces, even though state organization and the managerial corps of the *chaebol* attempt administratively to control the marketplace.

If the South Korean case can be made to fit Chandler's thesis, the Taiwan case obviously cannot.[11] Here we find, relative to the other cases, a conspicuous lack of vertical integration and the absence of the oligarchic concentration that occurred in the United States, Japan, and especially South Korea. The unwillingness or inability of Taiwanese entrepreneurs to develop large organizations or concentrated industries appears to have defied even the encouragement of government. Ramon Myers (1984) cites an example: When the government persuaded a successful businessman, Y. C. Wang, to establish a plastics factory, the Chinese impulse was immediately to copy Wang's success. "Three other businessmen without any experience in plastics quickly built similar factories, and many more entered the industry later. Between 1957 and 1971 plastic production grew 45% annually. In 1957 only 100 small firms fabricated products from plastic supplied by Wang's company, but in 1970 more than 1,300 small firms bought from plastic suppliers" (1984, p. 516).

The plastics industry is one of the most concentrated in Taiwan's private sector. The tendency in this industry is the rule elsewhere: the "unusual feature of manufacturing and service firms in Taiwan is their limited size: each operation is usually owned by a single proprietor or family" (Myers 1984, p. 515). Moreover, the organization of such firms is usually of single units, functionally defined in relation to a finished product. These small firms join together in what is called the *weixing gongchang*, which is a system of satellite factories that join together to produce a finished product. Such interorganizational networks are based on noncontractual agreements sometimes made between family members who own related firms but more often between unrelated businessmen. On personalistic terms, these businessmen informally negotiate such matters as the quality and quantity of their products. For instance, in Taiwan, the world's leading exporter of bicycles, the bicycle industry is organized in a vast array of separate parts manufacturers and bicycle-assembly firms.[12] Similarly, Myers reports that Taiwan's television industry is composed of 21 major firms and hundreds of satellite firms: "Since this industry [requires] thousands of small parts such as picture tubes, tuners, transformers, loudspeakers, coils, and antennae, countless Chinese firms sprang up to supply these in ever greater quantities" (Myers 1984, p. 517).

Although there are exceptions, the small-to-medium size, single-unit firm is so much the rule in Taiwan that when a family business becomes successful the pattern of investment is not to attempt vertical integration in order to control the marketplace, but rather is to diversify by starting a series of unrelated firms that share neither account books nor management. From a detailed survey of the 96 largest business groups (*jituanqiye*) in Taiwan, we find that 59% of them are owned and controlled by family groups (Zhonghua Zhengxinso 1985). Partnerships among unrelated individuals, which, as Wong Sui-lun (1985) points out, will likely turn into family-based business organizations in the next generation, account for 38%. An example of such a family-controlled business group is the Cai family enterprise, until recently the second largest private holding in Taiwan.[13] The family business included over 100 separate firms, the management of which was divided into eight groupings of unrelated businesses run by different family members, each of whom kept a separate account book (Chen 1985, pp. 13–17).

Taiwan does not fit Chandler's evolutionary, technology-based model of modern business organization. But neither does it seem to fit Williamson's model of business organization. Although the variables for transaction-cost theory are more difficult to operationalize than the variables for Chandler's theory, it seems apparent that the growth of large business groups in Taiwan cannot be explained by either transaction-cost reduction or market uncertainty, two key factors contributing to the boundary expansion of firms.

In the first place, a normal pattern by which business groups acquire firms is to start or buy businesses in expanding areas of the economy. Often, these firms remain small to medium in size, are not necessarily integrated into the group's other holdings (even for purposes of accounting), and cooperate extensively with firms outside the holdings of the business group. As such, firm acquisitions represent speculation in new markets rather than attempts to reduce transaction costs between previously contracting firms.

Second, uncertainty is a constant feature in Taiwan's economic environment.[14] Family firms, many no larger than the extended household, usually do not have either the ability or the means to seek out or forecast information on demand in foreign export markets. They produce goods or, more likely, parts for contractors with whom they have continuing relationships and on whom they depend for subsequent orders. The information they receive on product demand is second- and thirdhand and restricted to the present. They have limited abilities to plan organizational futures and to determine whether their products will find a market and elicit continuing orders. In fact, misinformation and poor market forecasting are common, as is evident in the high rate of bankruptcy in Taiwan.

Conditions like these are the very ones that Williamson predicts should produce vertical integration. These conditions should prevail especially during business depressions in the world economy, such as those that occurred in 1974–78 and again in 1980–81. Tables [7.]4 and [7.]5, however, show no discernible trend in this direction. If anything, one might argue that in Taiwan uncertainty leads in the opposite direction, away from strategies of vertical integration and toward a strategy of spreading investment risks.

Chandler's and Williamson's theories do not explain the organizational structure of Taiwan business. But if one looks more closely at the Japanese and South Korean cases, then it becomes equally obvious that they, too, do not fit the market explanations well.[15] Intermarket business groups date from the beginning of Japanese industrialization, in some cases even before. Therefore, growing technology, expanding communication, and the increased volume of manufacturing transactions are not the *causes* of Japanese industrial structure because the structure precedes the economic growth.

In the Tokugawa era, from 1603 to 1867, a rising merchant class developed a place for itself in the feudal shogunate. Merchant houses did not challenge the traditional authority structure but subordinated themselves to whatever powers existed. Indeed, a few houses survived the Meiji Restoration smoothly, and one in particular (Mitsui) became a prototype for the *zaibatsu* (Bisson 1954, p. 7). Other *zaibatsu* arose early in the Meiji era from enterprises that had been previously run for the benefit of the feudal overlords, the *daimyo*. In the Meiji era, the control of such *han* enterprises moved to the private sphere where, in the case of Mitsubishi, former samurai became the owners and managers (Hirschmeier and Yui 1981, pp. 138–42). In all cases of the *zaibatsu* that began early in the Meiji era, the overall structure was an intermarket group. The member firms were legal corporations, were large multiunit enterprises, and could accumulate capital through corporate means. As Nakamura (1983, pp. 63–68) put it, "Japan introduced the [organizational] framework of industrial society first and the content afterward."

Zaibatsu clearly emerged from a traditional form of enterprise. Although they adapted spectacularly well to an international, capitalist economy, they did not develop in response to it. Therefore, Chandler's assertion that the United States is the "seedbed of managerial capitalism" (1977, p. 498), that this form of organization "spread" to Japan (p. 500), is dubious and at the very least must be substantially qualified.

The organizational structure preceded economic development in South Korea as well. The organizational structure of *chaebol*, as well as state capitalism in general, although encouraged and invigorated by world economic conditions, can be traced more persuasively to premodern political practices, to pre–World War II Japanese industrial policy (Myers and Peattie 1984, pp. 347–452), and to the borrowing of organizational designs for industrialization from Japan than to those factors specified by either Chandler or Williamson. At the very best, causality is unclear.

The market explanation neither explains the organizational differences among the three countries nor offers an unqualified explanation for any one country. Still, at one level the market explanation is certainly correct. Transportation systems, mass markets, advanced technology, and considerations of profit all influence the organization of modern business, and it is inconceivable that modern business firms would have developed, as they have in fact developed, in the absence of these factors. Nonetheless, to equate these factors with organizational structure, to make them the sole causes of organizational design, is not only theoretically and substantively to misinterpret business organization but also to make a serious methodological blunder. Chandler and Williamson, each in his own way, concentrate their entire causal argument on proximate factors. Their cases are analogous to arguing that the assassination of Archduke Ferdinand caused World War I or that the possession of handguns causes crime. Clearly, important causal links are present in all these relationships, but secondary factors play crucial roles in shaping the patterns of unfolding events. To banish all secondary factors, such as political structures and cultural patterns, is to fall into what David Hackett Fischer (1970, p. 172) calls the "reductive fallacy," reducing "complexity to simplicity, or diversity to uniformity. . . . This sort of error appears in causal explanations which are constructed like a single chain and stretched taut across a vast chasm of complexity." This is what Chandler and Williamson do in their attempts to derive organizational structure solely from economic principles.

THE CULTURE EXPLANATION

Cultural explanations for the diversity of organizational structures and practice are many. Smircich (1983) identifies no fewer than five ways researchers have used the culture framework. Some analysts, for example, see culture as an independent variable, exerting pressure on organizational arrangements (e.g., Harbison and Meyer 1959; Crozier 1964), or as a dependent variable in comparative management studies (Peters and Waterman 1982). Most important recent approaches see culture as socially created "expressive forms, manifestations of human consciousness. Organizations are understood and analyzed not mainly in economic or material terms . . . " (Smircich 1983, p. 347). While market analysis sees organizations striving toward maximum efficiency, cultural theorists probe the nonrational, subjective aspects of organizational life.

Culture studies tend to link organizational patterns with the cultural practices of the larger society. For example, Nakane's classic study, *Japanese Society* (1970), combines cultural and structural analyses to show how the group relations of the Japanese family serve larger social institutions, including Japanese enterprise: ". . . the characteristics of Japanese enterprise as a social group are, first, that the group is itself family-like and, second, that it pervades even the private lives of its employees, for each family joins extensively in the enterprise" (1970, p. 19). Swedish shop-floor democracy can be traced to strong socialist sentiments in the country (Blumberg 1973). Worker self-management in Yugoslavia is linked to an ideology of social ownership (Tannenbaum et al. 1974). Americans' strong central values of individualism and free enterprise lead to segmentalist organizations (Kanter 1983) and fear of central planning by government (Miles 1980).

Most culture studies do not concern themselves with the economic implications of corporate culture, but a few more popular works do, often to critique economic approaches to management. Peters and Waterman's *In Search of Excellence* (1982, pp. 29–54) repudiates the "rational model" of organizations, citing, as more successful, organizations that promote shared values and productivity through people-centered policies.

William Ouchi's recent works (1980, 1984) are important links between culture studies and the economic tradition.[16] Whereas Williamson describes organizational structures ("governance structures") as emerging from market transactions, Ouchi claims that cultural values such as "trust" influence whether individuals will resort to contracts and other devices of control of mediate transactions (see Maitland, Bryson, and Van de Ven 1985).

If the market explanation errs by emphasizing proximate causes, then the culture explanation of organization errs in the opposite direction. By concentrating on secondary causes, primordial constants that undergird everything, the cultural explanation works poorly when one attempts to examine a changing organizational environment or to analyze differences among organizations in the same cultural area. Therefore, to use this explanation to account for differences among organizational structures of enterprise in Japan, South Korea, and Taiwan, one must demonstrate cultural differences that would account for different organizational patterns. Such cultural differences, we argue, are difficult to isolate.

The first step in locating cultural differences is to ask what factors would be included in a cultural explanation and what factors would not (see, e.g., Gamst and Norbeck 1976). Many scholars define culture as the socially learned way of life of a people and the means by which orderliness and patterned relations are maintained in a society. While the concept of order suggests its link to a sociological authority-relations understanding of society, in practice culture theorists tend to be concerned with the symbolic, rather than the material, impulse behind social life—with norms, values, shared meanings, and cognitive structures (see Harris [1979] for an exception). Basic culture ideals, and myths and rituals in relation to those ideals, are explored for their ability to integrate persons and to reinforce and celebrate common understandings.[17] Recent works about corporate culture, for example, refer to "weak" versus "strong" corporate cultures: how engaging and encompassing corporate life is for employees. While culture may be understood as universal to the society and changing only slowly, culture theory tends not to look beyond a culture of immediate interest, and especially not at long-term historical trends. In organizational analysis, culture study is social science writ small: either rich, detailed ethnographies of a single people during a relatively short historical period or, at most, the comparison of a limited number of bounded cases. Without a wider scope, such an approach is of only limited use in explaining differences in business organization among societies. Fortunately, in regard to the cases at hand, there have been numerous attempts to develop more broadly based cultural explanations.

The culture explanation has been used often to understand Japanese corporate practices (see Abegglen 1958; Benedict 1946). Although a number of points of departure have been taken, many share the belief that it is the central Japanese value of *wa*, or harmony, that explains Japanese organizational arrangements. *Wa* denotes a state of integration, a harmonious unity of diverse parts of the social order. The organizational consequences of *wa* are numerous, but most important is the subordination of the individual to the group and the practices to which that leads: the necessity to check with colleagues during contract negotiations; the routine and calculated movement of personnel among functional areas to promote wider understanding at the expense of specialization; the promotion of cohorts, not individuals, up the organization ladder; and the development of lifetime employment, internal labor markets, and seniority systems (*nenkō*) to maintain the integrity of the group. The wearing of uniforms, the performance of group exercises, the singing of corporate anthems, and even intercorporate cooperation have been explained as expressions of *wa*. At the societal level, cooperation is orchestrated by the state: "The Japanese government does not stand apart from or over the community; it is rather the place where *wa* deals are negotiated" (Sayle 1985, p. 35).

As persuasive as the culture approach seems in explaining the Japanese case, it has suffered substantial attack. An analysis of one practice, *nenkō* (seniority system), suffices to suggest the nature of the critique. *Wa* and its expression in practices such as *nenkō* have been described by culture theorists as part of a cultural continuity extending to preindustrial times. But there are many examples of different practices and of discontinuity. For instance, labor turnover rates were high before 1920 and very high in the late 1930s and early 1940s (Evans 1971; Taira 1970). Why, then, were apparently expensive lifetime employment and seniority preferences offered by enterprise group firms? Economics provides the alternative explanation that it is economically rational to maintain a stable work force and protect training investments. "It appears that some of the industrial features thought to be traditionally Japanese . . . are in fact fairly recent innovations, supported by traditional values to be sure, but consciously designed for good profit-maximizing reasons" (Dore 1962, p. 120). Jacoby further argues that, although economic interests are important in understanding the institution of lifetime employment and its adoption before World War II, they cannot explain why it exists only in some firms and not others, applies only to some worker groups in the same organization, and appeared at a given historic juncture. He suggests an explanation in line with an authority relations approach: "More careful historical research on the circumstances surrounding the introduction of internal labor markets in Japan indicates the importance of the increase in firm size and complexity, the change in skilled labor organization, and the desire to forestall unionization. These factors are causally connected to the emergence of an emphasis on stability and control in input markets, as well as the creation of new pressures to maintain employee effort and loyalty" (1979, p. 196). That *wa* provides a socially accepted justification for *nenkō* and that *nenkō* accords easily with Japanese culture cannot be denied. Culture constants, however, are insufficient to explain changing organizational practices.[18]

Similar culture arguments have been made for Chinese management practices (Chen 1984; Chen and Qiu 1984; Hou 1984; Huang 1984; Silin 1976; Zeng 1984). For the most part, they focus on the Confucian belief system and its expression in enterprise. Confucianism promotes individual self-control and dutiful conduct to one's superiors and particularly to one's family. At some level, modern Chinese organizations reflect these patterns. Comparative management studies show that Chinese entrepreneurs maintain more distance from workers than do the Japanese and are likely to promote competitive relations, not cooperation, among subordinates (who may be family members) (Fukuda 1983). But, unlike in Japan, where loyalty to the firm is important, Chinese loyalty is not firm specific and may extend to a network of family enterprises. Because a Chinese businessman can with some assurance trust that people in his family network will respect the Confucian obligation to act with honor toward relatives whenever possible, business is conducted with members of one's kinship network (Chan 1982; Huang 1984; Chen and Qiu 1984; Omohundro 1981; Redding 1980). Moreover, Confucianism has been described as a system that promotes strong bonds at the local level when face-to-face relations are paramount but that, in mediating broader relations, is a weak form of social control.

Despite an appearance of cohering, the Confucian culture argument, if pressed, falls apart. It is used to explain the conduct in large factories (Silin 1976) as well as in small, premodern commercial activities (Yang 1970). The question here is why today's enterprise organization in Taiwan is composed of relatively small to medium-sized, family-run firms. The Confucian culture argument alone will not work well because the culture is a broadly based underlying cognitive factor (Redding 1980) that affects the society in general and for that reason explains nothing in particular.

This criticism of the cultural explanation gains force especially when one considers that both South Korea and Japan have been deeply influenced by Confucianism, as well as by Buddhism and various folk religions, which China also shares. In fact, in regard to underlying cultural values, Japan, South Korea, and Taiwan are not three separate cultures, but rather parts of the same great tradition. All societies in East Asia have many cultural traits in common, which can be traced to the long-term interaction between the societies in the region. Some of the intermixing of cultures can be explained politically. Imperial China always considered Korea a tributary state and exacted submission during many long periods. More recently, Japan conquered and colonized both Korea and Taiwan and set out systematically to impose Japanese language and behavioral patterns on Taiwanese and Korean societies.

Intermixing due to politics is only part of the picture, however. A much more significant interaction occurred at the levels of language, elite culture, and religion. The direction of the cultural borrowing was usually from China to Japan and Korea. Both Korea and Japan borrowed and used Chinese script. Chinese was the written language of the Korean court until *hangul* was introduced in the 16th century. In Japan, the court language was a mixture of Chinese and Japanese, which itself had been adapted to written expression through the use of Chinese script. Scholars in both locations learned classical Chinese and used it in government and in arts. Beyond the Chinese script, poetry, painting styles, motifs on all artifacts, literature of all types, elite styles of dress and expression, architecture, and elements of cuisine—all these and more intermixed, so that no aspect of elite life in Japan or South Korea can be said to be untouched by cultural diffusion from China.

Besides politics and elite cultural intermixing, there was religious diffusion that permeated all levels in all three societies. Two religions are particularly important. Confucianism, which contains an elaborate ideology of familism and an equally elaborate ideology of statecraft, was supposed by the elites in all three societies. In imperial China, this was more or less the case from the time of the *Han* period (established in 221 B.C.) to the fall of the empire in A.D. 1911. Confucianism had less continuous influence and came later in the other two societies but was extremely important in Korea and Japan during the most recent dynastic periods. Buddhism entered China from India in the 2d and 3d centuries A.D. and later became very important before it was finally proscribed at the state level. Thereafter, Buddhism was primarily a local religion in China, merging with other folk practices. In Korea and Japan, after diffusing from China, Buddhism became an important religion at both the state and local levels. In all three societies, Buddhism and Confucianism continue to be important, with the symbolism and values of each being key components of modern life.

We are not arguing that these three societies have the same culture. In the same way that England and France do not have the same culture, these three societies do not either. But just as France and England belong to the same cultural complex (Western civilization) so do Japan, Korea, and China (Eastern civilization). The decisive point here is that we are not dealing with three distinct cases, but rather three societies that share many of the same cultural patterns. Therefore, using the cultural explanation, we can argue, as have others (Berger 1984; Tu 1984), that this common culture helps to explain common patterns in all three societies, such as the importance of the family, obedience to authority, high rates of literacy, the desire to achieve, and the willingness to work hard. What the culture explanation, however, is not able to do is to distinguish the many differences that exist among these societies, including the organizational structure of business enterprises. The culture explanation cannot explain changes and differences well because the causal argument is concentrated on secondary factors, especially in primordial constants, and thus the explanation only with difficulty deals with factors that underlie historical changes.

AUTHORITY STRUCTURE
AND ORGANIZATIONAL PRACTICE

The third approach to understanding organizations that we employ is a political economy approach primarily derived from the work of Max Weber (1978). One of the best examples of this approach is Reinhard Bendix's *Work and Authority in Industry* (1974), a historical study of the development of managerial ideology and practice in England, Russia, and the United States. Bendix covers some of the same territory as Chandler in *The Visible Hand* (1977) but provides an alternative explanatory framework.[19]

Briefly, in the Weberian view, many factors contribute to organizational structure. The structures of armies, tax collection, business enterprises, and officialdoms are influenced, most importantly, by the task at hand. But even when we consider task requirements, there is much room for variation, and historical and situational factors such as available technology, conditions of membership (Weber 1978, pp. 52–53), and the class and status composition of the group (1978, pp. 926–39) will have an influence.

But all organizations, no matter what their purpose or historical setting (although related to both), have an internal pattern of command and compliance. Organizations only exist insofar as "there is a probability that certain persons will act in such a way as to carry out the order governing the organization" (1978, p. 49). This probability rests in part on normative justifications that underlie given arrangements—who should obey and the distinctive mode of obedience owed to the powers that be. Weber called the underlying justifications "principles of domination."[20] In this context, principles of domination are not abstractions but rather serve as the substantive rationale for action. They provide guides, justifications, and interpretive frameworks for social actors in the daily conduct of organizational activity (Hamilton and Biggart 1984, 1985; Biggart and Hamilton 1984).

The Weberian approach incorporates economic and cultural factors and allows for historical diversity. Principles of domination are clearly related to culture but are not reducible to it. Bendix has shown how economically self-interested strategies of worker control were expressed as management ideologies in industrializing nations. These ideologies were based on an economic rationale, but "ideologies of management can be explained only in part as rationalizations of self-interest; they also result from the legacy of institutions and ideas which is adopted by each generation . . . " (1974, p. 444).

Recent extensions of Weberian views are found in the works of Karl Weick, John Meyer and W. Richard Scott, and Charles Perrow.[21] Weick (1979) discusses how people in organizations enact role-based strategies of organizational control; the enactments contain ritual, and tradition (organizational culture) builds around ritualized enactments. While enactments are certainly related to patterned behavior and the maintenance of predictable orders, they have no necessary connection with efficiency. Indeed, Meyer and Scott (1983) show that whole organizations adopt management practices for reasons of legitimacy; the organization enacts patterns understood and accepted by important constituents, not for reasons of economic rationality.[22] Perrow (1981, 1986) argues that firms are profitable not merely because they are efficient but because they are successful instruments of domination.

The market explanation concentrates on immediate factors and the culture explanation on distant ones. Both explanations are obviously important, but neither deals directly with organizations themselves; although both claim to account for organizations, they make organizations appear rather mysteriously out of a mix of economic variables or a brew of cultural beliefs. The authority explanation deals with organizations themselves and conceptualizes them broadly as patterned interactions among people, that is, as structures of authority. It aims at understanding how these structures came into being, how they are maintained, and to what consequence. As such, it attempts historically adequate explanations and therefore differs from both general cultural theories and specified, predictive economic models.

In applying this approach to account for business organization in East Asia, one must demonstrate decisive differences among the three societies in terms of the structures of authority and further demonstrate that these differences affect organizational practices. Two factors seem particularly important and in need of explanation. First, What are the relationships established between the state and the business sector in the three societies? And second, given that relationship between state and enterprise, What are the structures of authority in each type of business network?

In each of the three societies, the state has pursued similar policies promoting industrialization. Economists describe these policies in terms of a product-cycle industrialization pattern (Cumings 1984) in which import substitution was gradually replaced by aggressive, export-led growth policies (Ranis 1979). What is apparent but left unanalyzed is that such state policies are administered in very different political contexts.

In South Korea, government/business relations follow in the form of what can be called the "strong state" model. In South Korea, the state actively participates in the public and private spheres of the economy and is in fact the leading actor (SaKong 1980). The state achieves its central position through centralized economic planning and through aggressive implementation procedures. The entire government is "geared toward economic policy-making and growth. . . . Economic decision making [is] extremely centralized, and the executive branch dominate[s]" (Bunge 1982, p. 115; Mason et al. 1980, p. 257). Implementation procedures aim at controlling the entire economy. For public enterprises, control is direct and bureaucratic. This sector of the economy, which is relatively small but rapidly expanding, is run as departmental agencies of the state with civil servants as managers. Although not in as direct a fashion as occurs in the public sector, the state controls the private sector "primarily from its control of the banking system and credit rationing" (Westphal et al. 1984, p. 510) and through other financial controls. The state, however, does not hesitate to use noneconomic means to achieve compliance with policy directives. "A firm that does not respond as expected to particular incentives may find that its tax returns are subject to careful examination, or that its application for bank credit is studiously ignored, or that its outstanding bank loans are not renewed. If incentive procedures do not work, government agencies show no hesitation in resorting to command backed by compulsion. In general, it does not take a Korean firm long to learn that it will 'get along' best by 'going along'" (Mason et al. 1980, p. 265).

These procedures apply to all sizes of firms but especially to medium and large firms, which are in fact favored by such planning and implementation procedures (Koo 1984, p. 1032). This is particularly the case for business groups, the *chaebol*. State policies support business concentration, and statistics indeed reveal a rapid change in this direction (Jones and SaKong 1980, p. 268; Koo 1984; *Hankook Ilbo* 1985). In addition, many medium and all large firms are tethered by government-controlled credit, by government regulation of the purchase of raw materials and energy, and by government price-setting policies for selected commodities (Weiner 1985, p. 20).

In Japan, the government has developed quite a different relationship with business. The state policy toward business is one of creating and promoting strong intermediate powers, each having considerable autonomy, with the state acting as coordinator of activity and mediator of conflicting interests (Johnson 1982).[23] In business, the most important of these strong intermediate powers are the intermarket groups of large firms. The *zaibatsu* rose to great power in the pre–World War II era, and, because of their link to Japan's imperial past and because of their monopoly characteristics, American occupation authorities legally dissolved them and attempted to set up a new economic system based on the U.S. model. They promoted a union movement and encouraged small- and medium-sized competitive enterprises (Bisson 1954). After the American occupation ended, however, the Japanese government, through both action and strategic inaction, has allowed a maze of large and powerful intermarket groups to reappear.

These business networks and member firms are independent of direct state control, although they may acquiesce to the state's "administrative guidance." This administrative guidance has no statutory or legal basis. Rather, it "reflects above all a recognized common interest between MITI (Ministry of International Trade and Industry) and the leading firms in certain oligopolistic industries, the latter recognizing that guidance may occasionally impair their profits but in the long run will promote joint net revenues in the industry" (Caves and Uekusa 1976, p. 54). As Johnson (1982, p. 196) points out, this political system has led "to genuine public-private cooperation."

The strong state model in South Korea and the strong intermediate power model in Japan contrast sharply with what might be called the strong society model of state/business relations in Taiwan. The state in Taiwan is by no means weak. It is omnipresent, and, ceremonially at least, it repeatedly exacts obeisance. But, in regard to the export business sector, the Taiwan government promotes what Little (1979, p. 475) identifies as "virtually free trade conditions" and what Myers (1984, p. 522) calls "planning within the context of a free economy." Such policies have allowed familial patterns to shape the course of Taiwan's industrialization; this has in turn led to decentralized patterns of industrialization, a low level of firm concentration, and a predominance of small- and medium-sized firms.

Before we explain the strong society model further, three aspects of active state/business relations should be stressed. First, the state owns and manages a range of public enterprises that provide import-substituting commodities (e.g., petroleum, steel, and power) and services (e.g., railways and road and harbor construction) and that have been very important to Taiwan's economic development (Gold 1986; Amsden 1985). Unlike this sector in South Korea, public enterprises in Taiwan have steadily decreased in importance, and the government shows no signs of reversal (Gold 1986; Myers 1984). Second, the state imposes import controls on selected products and promotes industrial development in export products through special tax incentive programs and the establishment of export processing zones (Gold 1986; Amsden 1985). These incentives for export production, while they have certainly encouraged industrialization, have not favored industrial concentration, as has occurred in South Korea. Third, as in Japan and South Korea, the state in Taiwan exerts strong controls over the financial system, which includes the banking, insurance, and saving systems. Having one of the highest rates of savings in the world, Taiwan has also developed what Wade (1985) calls a "rigid" fiscal policy of high interest rates to control inflation, a preference for short-term loans, and an attitude of nonsupport for markets in equity capital (e.g., the stock market). Unlike Japan's and South Korea's, however, this financial system favored the development of a curb market, "an unregulated, semi-legal credit market in which loan suppliers and demanders can transact freely at uncontrolled interest rates" (Wade 1985, p. 113). Because most small- and medium-sized firms require only moderate to little investment capital and because such firms have difficulty obtaining bank loans, the curb market has played an extremely important role in financing Taiwan's industrial development (Yang 1981).

The difference in the role of the state between Taiwan and the other two societies is revealed in state planning. Like the South Korean state, Taiwan's government develops economic plans, but unlike South Korea there are no implementation procedures. State planning is done in a "loose, noncommand style," is "unsupported by controls," has no credibility in its economic projections, and has "no importance" in determining economic behavior (Little 1979, p. 487). This unimportance of planning, Little (1979, pp. 487–89) further believes, is even true in public sector enterprises. Moreover, of great importance in Taiwan's pattern of industrialization has been the absence, until recently, of spatial planning, including industrial zoning, at the municipal, provincial, and state levels. Considered together, these factors have led Little (1979, p. 488) to argue "that Taiwan planning has not even been intended to be indicative (authoritative). The mechanism usually associated with indicative planning is lacking. There are no standing consultative committees with private industry; any consultations are ad hoc. There are virtually no teeth either."

The lack of strong government intervention in the domestic economy, unlike that in South Korea, and the absence of active support for large firms, unlike that in Japan, has left the economy in Taiwan, especially the export sector, free to work out its own patterns. Using either Chandler's or Williamson's model, one would expect rapid concentration and the development of managerial capitalism. What has in fact emerged is something quite different, almost the opposite of what either theorist would predict: a low level of business concentration and a decentralized pattern of industrial development. And with this approach, Taiwan's sustained rate of economic growth during the past 30 years is one of the highest in the world.

Why did the state officials in each case choose one form of business relationship over other possible alternatives? For each society, it is clear that their choices were neither random nor inevitable. In each case, there was latitude. For instance, after the American occupation, the Japanese government could have supported and built on the system the Americans established, which was based on competition among small- and medium-sized firms. But instead they opted for creating strong intermediate powers, in terms of both economic and social controls (Johnson 1982, pp. 198–241). South Korea could have chosen the Japanese route, by building on the *zaibatsu* model they had inherited from the Japanese. Or they could have adopted the model found in Taiwan, by supporting the small-to-medium-sized private-sector firms that had developed in Korea before World War II (Juhn 1971) and still operate there to some extent. Instead, they opted for a strong state. Finally, Taiwan could have followed the other courses as well. In the early fifties, in fact, Taiwan clearly was moving toward the strong state model: the state had incorporated the former *zaibatsu* into the state apparatus, had aggressively forced the landowning class to accept sweeping land reform policies, and with a strong military presence was making ready to return to the mainland. On the other hand, the state could have supported a strong business class, as the Chiang Kai-shek regime had done with the Shanghai industrialists in the early thirties on the mainland. But, after some hesitation, the Nationalist government developed and since then has pursued a non-favoritist policy of "letting the people prosper." In each case, the decisions about the state/business relations were not inevitable, and certainly for the case of Taiwan it takes no imagination to envision a different course, because another outcome occurred across the Taiwan straits, in mainland China.

Therefore, what determined the choice? Many factors were important, but it seems likely that the most important were not economic factors at all. Rather, the key decisions about state/business relations should be seen in a much larger context, as flowing from the attempt on the part of political leaders to legitimize a system of rule. Each regime was at a crucial point in its survival after wars and occupations and needed to establish a rationale for its existence. In fashioning such a rationale, each regime in the end resorted to time-tested, institutionally acceptable ways of fashioning a system of political power. In each case, the first independent regime of the postwar era attempted to legitimize state power by adopting a reformulated model of imperial power of the kind that had existed before industrialization began. Such a model built on the preexisting normative expectations of political subjects and contained an ideology of rulership. Moreover, some of the institutions to support these models were still in place.

In Japan, the decisive factor was the presence of the emperor, who continues to stand as a symbol of political unity (Bendix 1977, p. 489). But the emperor was above politics and so was a weak center. The American-installed legislature also was a weak center, a place of haggling as opposed to unity. Gradually, successive decisions allowed for the creation of a modern version of the decentralized structure of the Tokugawa and Meiji periods: the center (in Tokugawa, the *shogun*, and, in Meiji, the emperor) coordinates strong and, in normative terms, fiercely loyal independent powers. In turn, the independent powers have normative responsibility for the people and groups who are subordinate to them. The symbolism of the past shaped the reality of the present.

The economic consequences of this type of legitimation strategy were to create large, autonomous enterprises. These enterprises needed to legitimize their own conduct and, accordingly, to develop distinctive "personalities." Such efforts to build corporate cultures traded heavily on established systems of loyalty—the family, community, and paternalism—but also added mythologies of their own. In addition, given their size and status, these business enterprises needed to secure oligarchic positions in the marketplace and did so through a variety of economic tactics with which we are now familiar (Vogel 1979; Abegglen and Stalk 1985). But the theoretically important point is that Japanese intermarket groups are not creations of market forces. In the middle fifties when they reappeared, they began large, they began prestigious, and their economic integration followed from those facts, rather than being simply the cause of them. They enacted and, in due course, institutionalized a managerial structure that, from the outside, looks like a corporation but, on the inside, acts like a fiefdom.

In South Korea, the present form of government arose in a time of crisis, during a brutal war in which over 1 million Koreans died and 5.5 million more were dislocated (Cole and Lyman 1971, p. 22). Social disruption on an extraordinary scale, destruction of rural society, and the historical absence of strong intermediary institutions placed great power in the hands of a state structure propped up by U.S. aid and occupying forces. The authoritarian postwar government of Syngman Rhee shaped the basic institutions that the Park government later gained control of and turned in the direction of economic development. The legitimizing strategy for both governments, although articulated quite differently, centered on the imagery of the strong Confucian state: a central ruler, bureaucratic administration, weak intermediate powers, and a direct relationship between ruler and subjects based on the subject's unconditional loyalty to the state. As Henderson writes (1968, p. 5), "The physics of Korean political dynamics appears to resemble a strong vortex tending to sweep all active elements of the society upward toward central power. . . . Vertical pressures cannot be countered because local or independent aggregations do not exist to impede their formation or to check the resulting vortex once formed."

South Korean firms draw their managerial culture from the same source, the state, and from state-prompted management policies; they do not have the local character of the corporate culture of Japanese firms. Instead, they have developed an ideology of administration, an updated counterpart to the traditional Confucian ideology of the scholar-official (Jones and SaKong 1980, p. 291). For this reason, American business ideology has had an important effect in South Korea, far more than in either Japan or Taiwan. In the late 1950s, the South Korean government, with a grant from the U.S. State Department, instituted American management programs in South Korean universities (Zo Ki-zun 1970, pp. 13–14). South Korea now has a generation of managers trained in American business practice, including persons at the top levels of the state. In 1981, South Korea's prime minister and deputy prime minister (who was chief of the Economic Planning Board) were U.S.-trained economists (Bunge 1982, p. 115).

In Taiwan the state/business relationship also results from a basic legitimation strategy undertaken by the state. The Chiang Kai-shek government, after an initial attempt to create a military state in preparation for a return to the mainland, tried to secure the regime's legitimacy on a long-term basis. Composed largely of northern Chinese, Chiang Kai-shek's forces virtually conquered and totally subordinated the linguistically distinct Taiwanese. This created much resentment and some continuing attempts to create a Taiwanese independence movement. When a return to the mainland became unlikely, Chiang began creating a stable, long-term government. He actively promoted an updated Confucian state based on the model of the late imperial system. Unlike the more legalistic model of the Confucian state developed in Korea, Chiang attempted to make the state an exemplary institution and its leader a benevolent ruler: a state that upholds moral principles (*dedao*), that explicitly allows no corruption and unfair wealth, and that "leaves the people at rest." In this role, the state supervises internal moral order and takes care of foreign affairs. This policy militates against the emergence of favorite groups, which had been a weakness of the Nationalist regime in the 1930s and 1940s. This policy also limits participation of the state in which was seen in late imperial times as the private sector (*sishi*), an area that includes not only people's economic livelihood but also all aspects of family and religious life. Taiwan's state policy toward business operates within the limits established by Chiang's legitimation strategy (Peng 1984).

The consequences of this state policy have been to allow society, unfettered by the state, to respond to the economic opportunities that existed in the world economy and for which the state offered incentives. The Chinese of Taiwan, using traditional commercial practices and customary norms, quickly adapted to modern economic conditions. This outcome should not be surprising, because Chinese business practices have for some time operated competitively in the world economy. In 19th-century China, there was a thriving commercial system that functioned well in the absence of a legal framework, even in the deteriorating political conditions of the time (Hao 1970, 1986; Hamilton 1985; Feuerwerker 1984; Myers 1980; Chen and Myers 1976, 1978). The Chinese used the same patterns of business relations to gain industrial and commercial control of the economies in Southeast Asia (Wickberg 1965; Omohundro 1981; Hamilton 1977) and, more recently, to develop highly industrial societies in Hong Kong and Singapore (Nyaw and Chan 1982; Redding 1980; Ward 1972). Therefore, when we consider the similar free-market conditions that exist in these other locations, the Chinese economic success in Taiwan is perhaps not surprising but needs to be examined nonetheless.

The industrial patterns in Taiwan reflect the same invigoration of Chinese commercial practices found in late imperial China and in Southeast Asia. As analysts have noted (e.g., Wong 1985; Chan 1982; Omohundro 1981), in all these locations Chinese businesses develop on the basis of small family-run firms and personalistic networks linking firms backward to sources of supply and forward to consumers. Two sets of factors account for the prevalence of these small family firms. The first set concerns the nature of the Chinese family system.[24] The Japanese family system is based on a household unit and on primogeniture; younger sons must start households of their own. In contrast, the Chinese system is based on patrilineage and equal inheritance among all sons. The eldest son has seniority but no particular privileges in regard to property or authority over property. Because all males remain in the line of descent, the patrilineage quickly expands within just a few generations. Adoption of a son into any household is considered improper, and the only approved way is to adopt the son of a kinsman (cf. Watson 1975a). Equally privileged sons connected to networks of relatives create a situation of bifurcated loyalties, with wealth itself becoming a measure of one's standing in the community of relatives. Accordingly, conflict between sons is ubiquitous, intralineage rivalries are common, and lineage segmentation is the rule (Baker 1979, pp. 26–70). Hence, the argument goes, besides the lineage and the state, there is no central integrating unit in Chinese society, and the lineage itself breeds as much conflict as unity. Therefore, it is difficult in Chinese society to build a large cohesive group.

This leads to a closely related set of explanations of how Chinese businesses are run.[25] The Chinese firm duplicates family structure; the head of the household is the head of the firm, family members are the core employees, and sons are the ones who will inherit the firm.[26] If the firm prospers, the family will reinvest its profits in branch establishments or more likely in unrelated but commercially promising business ventures (see, e.g., Chen 1985). Different family members run the different enterprises, and at the death of the head of household the family assets are divided (*fenjia*) by allocating separate enterprises to the surviving sons, each of whom attempts to expand his own firm as did the father. In this way, the assets of a Chinese family are always considered divisible, control of the assets is always considered family business, and decisions (in normative terms) should be made in light of long-term family interests. This pattern leads to what might be described as a "nesting box" system of Chinese management (see, e.g., Omohundro 1981; Huang 1984; Redding 1980). In the small, innermost box are those core family members who own or will inherit the business; in the next box are more distant relatives and friends who owe their positions to their connection with the owners and who are in a position to influence and be influenced by them; in the next outer boxes are ranks of unrelated people who work in the firm for money. Depending on the size of the firm, the outer boxes may contain ranks of professional managers, technicians, supervisors, and other craftspeople. The outermost box would include unskilled wage laborers. This pattern of business organization is most stable when the business is fairly small. Loyalty among unrelated employees is often low, which makes personalistic connections an essential part of management strategy (Huang 1984). The preference is always to begin one's own small business if one has sufficient capital to do so; as the Chinese saying goes, "It is better to be a rooster's beak than a cow's tail!"

Because everyone works in small- to medium-sized firms, Chinese have historically developed techniques to aid forward and backward linkages. These techniques include putting-out systems, satellite factory systems, and a variety of distribution networks often based on personalistic ties (see, e.g., Willmott 1972; Hamilton 1985). In fact, so complex and all-encompassing are these various techniques, and seemingly so efficient (Ho 1980), that they contribute to keeping businesses fairly small and investment patterns directed toward conglomerate accumulations rather than vertical integration (cf. Chan 1982).

In summary, as illustrated in Table [7.]6, in each of the three societies, a different combination of present and past circumstances led to the selection of a strategy of political legitimation. This strategy, in turn, had direct consequences for the relations between state and business sectors and for the formation of economic institutions.

Finally, we should note that the three types of business networks that developed in these three countries are usually not in direct competition with one another, except in a few product areas (e.g., electronics). Each possesses different economic capabilities, and each seems to fill a different niche in the world economy. Much more research needs to be done on this topic, but it appears that the following division is occurring: Taiwan's system of small family firms, which can flexibly shift from producing one commodity to another, has become a dominant producer of an extensive range of medium- to high-quality consumer goods (e.g., clothes, small household items) of the kind that fill the modern home and office but that require very little research and development. Large Japanese corporations specialize in a product area and, through research, development, and marketing strategies, attempt to create new commodities and consumers for those commodities (Abegglen and Stalk 1985). Exploiting their competitive advantage in technology and mass production, Japanese businesses operate on the frontiers of product development. With the entire economy orchestrated by the state, South Korean businesses are attempting to become important producers of commodities that require extensive capital investment but for which markets already exist (e.g., steel, major construction materials, automobiles). Such ventures require large amounts of capital and coordination but relatively little research and development. Each of these three strategies of industrialization may well be, in the economist's terminology, "least-cost" strategies in their respective niches of the world economy. But that fact does not make these strategies any less the outcomes of noneconomic factors. Moreover, a strategy of efficiency can only be calculated in terms of an existing array of economic and social institutions.

CONCLUSION

The theoretical question underlying this paper is, What level of analysis best explains organizational structure? We argue that, on the one hand, profit and efficiency arguments are too specific and too narrow to account for different organizational forms. Economic models predict organizational structure only at the most superficial level (e.g., successful businesses seek profit). On the other hand, cultural arguments seize on such general,

TABLE [7.]6 Firm Structure and Firm/State Relationships

	State/Business Relations	Principal Corporate Actors	Intrafirm Managerial Strategies	Extrafirm Market Strategies
Japan	Cooperative partnership	Intermarket groups	Company ideologies; consensus building; peer group controls	High R & D; manufacture and marketing of new products
South Korea	Political capitalism	Chaebol	State Confucianism; impersonal management; strong, centralized control	High capital ventures in established markets
Taiwan	Separation of spheres	Family firms	"Family-style" management; control through personal ties	Low capital; low R & D; manufacture of consumer expendables

omnipresent value patterns as to make it difficult to account for historical and societal variations occurring within the same cultural area. Culture pervades everything and therefore explains nothing. The authority explanation provides the most successful explanation because it aims at a middle level, at explanations having historical and structural adequacy. We argue that enterprise structure represents situational adaptations of preexisting organizational forms to specific political and economic conditions. Organizational structure is not inevitable; it results from neither cultural predispositions nor specific economic tasks and technology. Instead, organizational structure is situationally determined, and, therefore, the most appropriate form of analysis is one that taps the historical dimension.

Given this conclusion, then, this analysis suggests that the key factors in explaining economic organization may not be economic, at least in economists' usual meaning of that term. Economic and cultural factors are clearly critical in understanding the *growth* of markets and economic enterprise, but the *form* or structure of enterprise is better understood by patterns of authority relations in the society. This suggests further that the economic theory of the firm may in fact be a theory based on, and only well suited to, the American firm as it has developed historically in American society. Chandler's analysis of firm formation in the United States concentrates on how firm development permitted the lowering of costs under changing market conditions. It is important to note, however, that firm development also allowed the concentration of economic interests and market control by private parties. The American state (in both the 19th and 20th centuries) exists to allow the market to function in the service of private interests; it intervenes only to prevent market breakdowns or overconcentration. This state role was not an inevitability dictated by the market, however, and emerged from a historically developed vision about the "correct" state/industry relation. The American vision has always been that of a weak state and powerful private institutions (Hamilton and Sutton 1982). Industrialists of the 19th century, unfettered by transportation and communications impediments, realized that vision with the aid of a laissez-faire government. But the American firm, like the firms in Japan, South Korea, and Taiwan, had no inevitable developmental sequence in traverse.

NOTES

1. Versions of this paper have been presented in the following locations: Pan Pacific Conference in Seoul; Tunghai University Seminar Series in Taiwan; Stanford University Organizational Studies Seminar Series; Regional Seminar on Chinese Studies, University of California, Berkeley; and the All-University of California Conference in Economic History at Asilomar, California. We greatly appreciate the helpful comments from many who attended these sessions and thank the following people who carefully read one or more drafts of this paper: Howard Aldrich, Manuel Castells, Tun-jen Cheng, Donald Gibbs, Thomas Gold, Chalmers Johnson, Cheng-shu Kao, Earl Kinmonth, John W. Meyer, Ramon Myers, Marco Orrù, Charles Perrow, William Roy, W. Richard Scott, and Gary Walton. We also wish to acknowledge and

thank the following individuals for their help in some part of the research: Wei-an Chang, Ben-ray Jai, Hsien-heng Lu, Hwai-jen Peng, Cindy Stearns, Moon Jee Yoo, and Shuenn-der Yu. Hamilton also wishes to acknowledge the support of the Fulbright Foundation and the National Science Foundation (SES-8606582), which made this research possible.

2. Although true for all three societies, Japan is best known for these extrafirm networks. So prevalent and important are these networks in Japan that Clark (1979, pp. 95–96) suggests that they constitute a "society of industry": "No discussion of the Japanese company can disregard this context. The society of industry circumscribes, for example, the organization and administration of the company."

3. Usually, overlapping networks founded on banks are the networks of firms linked by general trading companies (*sōgō shōsha*) (Young 1979; Kunio 1982). These trading companies market and distribute the products of the firms that are affiliated with them. Some companies handle as many as 20,000 individual items and have offices in over 100 locations outside Japan (Krause and Sueo 1976, p. 389). Each bank-based network has its own trading company that supports its affiliate firms. Otherwise unaffiliated companies, usually small- to medium-sized businesses, also form their own trading-company cartels to market their products overseas as well as in Japan (Ozawa 1979, pp. 30-32).

4. Many of these major firms are independent of the established *keiretsu*. According to Abegglen and Stalk (1985, pp. 189–90), these firms represent the fastest growing sector of the Japanese economy. As these firms grow larger, however, they come to resemble the *keiretsu*: "Some have become so large and successful that through subsidiaries and affiliates they now control groups of their own."

5. Public sector enterprises are important in South Korea, even in export manufacturing. This sector continues to grow in importance in tandem with the *chaebol*, at the same time that the public sectors in Japan and Taiwan are declining both in size and in their involvement in export manufacturing. As in Japan, in South Korea there also are large associations of firms: the Korean Federation of Small Business, the Korean Traders' Association, the Federation of Korean Industries. But these associations do not have the influence of their Japanese counterparts, and "they have been accused of meekly obeying government directives" (Bunge 1982, p. 122).

6. In a personal comment, William G. Roy reminded us that Chandler's explanation is economic only in a narrow sense. Chandler considers mainly the flow of goods within and between firms. He does not include in his explanation the dynamics of money and finance. Inflation and deflation, busts and booms, credit and capital—none of these factors are a part of his explanation for the rise of modern corporations.

7. This idea is a central thesis in the work of other economists as well: "Absent fiat, the form of organization that survives in an activity is the one that delivers the product demanded by customers at the lowest price while covering costs" (Fama and Jensen 1983, p. 327).

8. Writing with Ouchi, Williamson acknowledges that different societies may have preferences for either a "hard" or a "soft" form of making contracts (Williamson and Ouchi 1981). Chandler (1977, pp. 498–500) implicitly qualifies his theory by noting that in some other societies there were social factors blocking what would otherwise be the natural development of managerial capitalism.

9. Although state/business cooperation is greater in Japan and South Korea than in the United States, these countries do not protect enterprise from business failure.

10. There is now a considerable literature on the Gerschenkron (1962) thesis that, among developing societies, strong states are able to promote industrialization better than those having different state formations (see Evans, Rueschemeyer, and Skocpol [1985] for a survey of this literature).

11. For another, related treatment of Taiwan as a deviant case, see Barrett and Whyte's (1982) insightful use of Taiwan data to criticize dependency theory.

12. Information based on interview material.

13. The family enterprise was rocked by scandals in the early months of 1985. The scandal forced the family to open their books and to account for their economic success. For one of the better descriptions of the Cai family enterprise, see Chen (1985).

14. Very little research has been done on the business environment in which small- and medium-sized firms in Taiwan operate. Some hints are found in Myers (1984), Peng (1984), Hu (1984), and DeGlopper (1972). In the popular press, however, the topic is discussed frequently, particularly in the very good business magazines, which are among the most widely read magazines in Taiwan. The following discussion draws particularly on Chen (1983).

15. See Dore (1983) for an excellent critique of Williamson's theory as it would be applied to Japan.

16. It is important to note the collaborative work of Williamson and Ouchi (1981), which is an attempt to introduce a cultural variable concerning trust into Williamson's transaction and Chandler's visible-hand theories.

17. From a cultural perspective, organizations can be seen in two ways: first, as culture-producing entities and, second, as expressions of the larger culture of the society. Recent studies of corporate culture reflect the first approach, but the second holds more promise for understanding the development of organizational arrangements in a given society.

18. For a very persuasive argument, in line with the one we present here, assessing the contribution of culture to Japanese corporate practices, see Dore (1973, pp. 375–403); also, see Johnson (1982, p. 307).

19. First published in 1956, Bendix's work has long been noted as one of the most important attempts to analyze management structure in modern industry. For this reason, it is more than surprising that Chandler seems totally to have ignored the one key work in which a clear alternative hypothesis to his own work could be found. For a recent expression of his thesis, see Bendix (1984, pp. 70–90).

20. For Weber's chief statements on a sociology of domination, see Weber (1978, pp. 941–1211; 1958, pp. 77–128). For general works commenting on Weber's sociology of domination, see Bendix and Roth (1971) and Schluchter (1981); on Weber's sociology of domination in regard to Asia, see Hamilton (1984).

21. After this article had been revised for publication, two articles appeared that independently call for the kind of institutional analysis of culture that we attempt to develop with the authority approach. Swidler (1986) calls for a "culture in action." "Cultural end values," she argues (1986, p. 284) do not "shape action in the long run. Indeed a culture has enduring effects on those who hold it, not by shaping the ends they pursue, but by providing the characteristic repertoire from which they build lines of action." Arguing for an institutional approach, Wuthnow (1985) applies a very similar line of reasoning in his critique of the "ideological" model of state structure.

22. It is, of course, true that, for purposes of legitimizing authority in modern industry, concepts of profit and efficiency are extremely important, as important in political as in economic ways. On this point, see Bendix (1974) and particularly Zucker (1983) and Perrow (1986).

23. The best analysis of state/business relations is found in Johnson (1982, pp. 196–97, 310–11). He notes that, of the various types of state/business relationships occurring in the past 50 years, "that of public-private cooperation is by far the most

important. . . . The chief mechanisms of the cooperative relationship are selective access to governmental or government-guaranteed financing, targeted tax breaks, government-supervised investment coordination in order to keep all participants profitable, the equitable allocation by the state of burdens during times of adversity (something the private cartel finds very hard to do), governmental assistance in the commercialization and sale of products, and governmental assistance when an industry as a whole begins to decline."

24. The material on Chinese kinship is extensive. The best general treatments are Baker (1979), Freedman (1966), Hsu (1971), Watson (1982), and Cohen (1970).

25. For treatments of the Chinese kinship system in relation to Taiwan's business development, see Lin (1984), Chen and Qiu (1984), Chen (1984), Hu (1984), and Huang (1984). For the role of an extended lineage in modern commercial ventures, see Cohen (1970), Watson (1975b), and Wong (1985).

26. The literature on large business enterprises in Japan often cites the family as having an important influence on how the firms are run. In comparison with the Chinese case, however, the Japanese family provides much more a metaphor for organization than an actual model. In Taiwan, the family structure and enterprise organization cannot be readily distinguished in many cases, so much so that the effect of the family on business in Taiwan is not metaphorical but actual and of great significance. Moreover, although the data are limited, the role of the family in modern business in Taiwan seems very similar to the role of the family in traditional agriculture (Baker 1979).

REFERENCES

Abegglen, James C. 1958. *The Japanese Factory.* Glencoe, Ill.: Free Press.

Abegglen, James C., and George Stalk, Jr. 1985. *Kaisha: The Japanese Corporation.* New York: Basic.

Adizes, Ichak. 1971. *Industrial Democracy: Yugoslav Style.* New York: Free Press.

Amsden, Alice H. 1979. "Taiwan's Economic History: A Case of *Étatisme* and a Challenge to Dependency." *Modern China* 5:341–80.

———. 1985. "The State and Taiwan's Economic Development." Pp. 78–106 *Bringing the State Back In,* edited by Peter B. Evans, Dietrich Rueschemeyer, and Theda Skocpol. Cambridge: Cambridge University Press.

Baker, Hugh. 1979. *Chinese Family and Kinship.* New York: Columbia University Press.

Barrett, Richard E., and Martin King Whyte. 1982. "Dependency Theory and Taiwan: Analysis of a Deviant Case." *American Journal of Sociology* 87:1064–89.

Bendix, Reinhard. 1974. *Work and Authority in Industry.* Berkeley: University of California Press.

———. 1977. *Kings or People.* Berkeley: University of California Press.

———. 1984. *Force, Fate, and Freedom.* Berkeley and Los Angeles: University of California Press.

Bendix, Reinhard, and Guenther Roth. 1971. *Scholarship and Partisanship: Essays on Max Weber.* Berkeley: University of California Press.

Benedict, Ruth. 1946. *The Chrysanthemum and the Sword: Patterns of Japanese Culture.* Boston: Houghton-Mifflin.

Berger, Peter. 1984. "An East Asian Development Model." *The Economic News,* no. 3079, September 17–23, pp. 1, 6–8.

Biggart, Nicole Woolsey, and Gary G. Hamilton. 1984. "The Power of Obedience." *Administrative Science Quarterly* 29:540–49.

Bisson, T. A. 1954. *Zaibatsu Dissolution in Japan.* Berkeley: University of California Press.

Blumberg, Paul. 1973. *Industrial Democracy: The Sociology of Participation.* New York: Schocken.

Bunge, Frederica M. 1982. *South Korea: A Country Study.* Washington, D.C.: Government Printing Office.

Business Week. 1985. "The Koreans Are Coming." *Business Week,* no. 2926, December, pp. 46–52.

Caves, Richard E., and Masu Uekusa. 1976. *Industrial Organization in Japan.* Washington, D.C.: Brookings Institution.

Chan, Wellington K. K. 1982. "The Organizational Structure of the Traditional Chinese Firm and Its Modern Reform." *Business History Review* 56:218–35.

Chandler, Alfred D., Jr. 1977. *The Visible Hand: The Managerial Revolution in American Business.* Cambridge, Mass.: Harvard University Press.

———. 1981. "Historical Determinants of Managerial Hierarchies: A Response to Perrow." Pp. 391–402 in *Perspectives on Organizational Design and Behavior,* edited by A. Van de Ven and William Joyce. New York: Wiley.

———. 1984. "The Emergence of Managerial Capitalism." *Business History Review* 58:473–502.

Chen, Chengzhong. 1985. "Caijia ti dajia shangle yike" (The Ts'ai Family Gives Everyone a Lesson). *Lianhe Yuekan* 44 (March): 13–17.

Chen, Fu-mei Chang, and Ramon Myers. 1976. "Customary Law and Economic Growth of China during the Qing Period," pt. 1. *Ch'ing-shih Wen-ti* 3, no. 5 (November): 1–32.

———. 1978. "Customary Law and Economic Growth of China during the Qing Period," pt. 2. *Ch'ing-shih Wen-ti* 3, no. 10 (November): 4–27.

Chen, Mingzhang. 1983. "Woguo xian jieduan zhongxiao qiye de fudao wenti" (The Difficulty in Assisting Taiwan's Present Day Small and Medium Businesses). *Tianxia zazhi* 29:137–41.

———. 1984. "Jiazu wenhua yu qiye guanli" (Family Culture and Enterprise Organization). Pp. 487–510 in *Zhongguo shi guanli* (Chinese-style Management). Taipei: Gongshang Shibao.

Chen, Qinan, and Shuru Qiu. 1984. "Qiye zuzhi de jiben xingtai yu chuantong jiazu zhidu" (Basic Concepts of Enterprise Organization and the Traditional Family System). Pp. 487–510 in *Zhongguo shi guanli* (Chinese-style Management). Taipei: Gongshang Shibao.

Clark, Rodney. 1979. *The Japanese Company.* New Haven, Conn.: Yale University Press.

Coase, R. H. 1937. "The Nature of the Firm." *Economica* 4 (November): 386–405.

Cohen, Myron L. 1970. "Developmental Process in the Chinese Domestic Group." Pp. 21–36 in *Family and Kinship in Chinese Society,* edited by Maurice Freedman. Stanford, Calif.: Stanford University Press.

Cole, David C., and Princeton N. Lyman. 1971. *Korean Development: The Interplay of Politics and Economics.* Cambridge, Mass.: Harvard University Press.

Commons, John R. 1934. *Institutional Economics.* Madison: University of Wisconsin Press.

Crozier, Michel. 1964. *The Bureaucratic Phenomenon.* Chicago: University of Chicago Press.

Cumings, Bruce. 1984. "The Origins and Development of the Northeast Asian Political Economy: Industrial Sectors, Product Cycles, and Political Consequences." *International Organizations* 38:1–40.

Deal, Terrence E., and Allan A. Kennedy. 1982. *Corporate Cultures*. Reading, Mass.: Addison-Wesley.

DeGlopper, Donald R. 1972. "Doing Business in Lukang." Pp. 97–326 in *Economic Organization in Chinese Society*, edited by W. E. Willmott. Stanford, Calif.: Stanford University Press.

Direction of Trade Statistics. 1985. Yearbook. Washington, D.C.: International Monetary Fund.

Dore, Ronald. 1962. "Sociology in Japan." *British Journal of Sociology* 13:116–23.

———. 1973. *British Factory-Japanese Factory: The Origins of National Diversity in Industrial Relations*. Berkeley: University of California Press.

———. 1983. "Goodwill and the Spirit of Market Capitalism." *British Journal of Sociology* 34:459–82.

Douglas, Mary, with Baron Isherwood. 1979. *The World of Goods*. New York: Basic.

Economist Intelligence Unit. 1985a. *Quarterly Economic Review of Japan*. Annual supplement.

———. 1985b. *Quarterly Economic Review of South Korea*. Annual supplement.

Evans, Peter B., Dietrich Rueschemeyer, and Theda Skocpol, eds. 1985. *Bringing the State Back In*. Cambridge: Cambridge University Press.

Evans, Robert, Jr. 1971. *The Labor Economics of Japan and the United States*. New York: Praeger.

Fama, Eugene F., and Michael Jensen. 1983. "Agency Problems and Residual Claims." *Journal of Law and Economics* 36:327–49.

Feuerwerker, Albert. 1984. "The State and the Economy in Late Imperial China." *Theory and Society* 13:297–326.

Fischer, David Hackett. 1970. *Historians' Fallacies*. New York: Harper.

Foy, Nancy, and Herman Gadon. 1976. "Worker Participation: Contrasts in Three Countries." *Harvard Business Review*, 54 (May–June): 71–83.

Freedman, Maurice. 1966. *Chinese Lineage and Society: Fujian and Guangdong*. London: Athlone.

Fukuda, K. John. 1983. "Transfer of Management: Japanese Practices for the Orientals?" *Management Decision* 21:17–26.

Gamst, Frederick C., and Edward Norbeck, eds. 1976. *Ideas of Culture*. New York: Holt, Rinehart & Winston.

Gerschenkron, Alexander. 1962. *Economic Backwardness in Historical Perspective*. Cambridge, Mass.: Harvard University Press.

Gold, Thomas B. 1986. *State and Society in the Taiwan Miracle*. New York: Sharpe.

Granovetter, Mark. 1985. "Economic Action and Social Structure: The Problem of Embeddedness." *American Journal of Sociology* 91:481–510.

Haggard, Stephen, and Tun-jen Cheng. 1986. "State and Foreign Capital in the 'Gang of Four.'" Pp. 84–135 in *The New East Asian Industrialization*. edited by Frederick Deyo. Ithaca, N.Y.: Cornell University Press.

Hamilton, Gary G. 1977. "Ethnicity and Regionalism: Some Factors Influencing Chinese Identities in Southeast Asia." *Ethnicity* 4:335–51.

———. 1984. "Patriarchalism in Imperial China and Western Europe: A Revision of Weber's Sociology of Domination." *Theory and Society* 13:393–426.

———. 1985. "Why No Capitalism in China? Negative Questions in Historical, Comparative Research." *Journal of Asian Perspectives* 2:2.

Hamilton, Gary, and Nicole Woolsey Biggart. 1984. *Governor Reagan, Governor Brown: A Sociology of Executive Power*. New York: Columbia University Press.

———. 1985. "Why People Obey: Theoretical Observations on Power and Obedience in Complex Organizations." *Sociological Perspectives* 28:3–28.

Hamilton, Gary G., and John Sutton. 1982. "The Common Law and Social Reform: The Rise of Administrative Justice in the U.S., 1880–1920." Presented at the annual meeting of the Law and Society Association, Toronto, June.

Hankook Ilbo. 1985. *Pal ship O nyndo hankook ui 50 dae jae bul* (The 50 Top *Chaebol* in Korea). Seoul, Korea.

Hao, Yen-p'ing. 1970. *The Comprador in Nineteenth-Century China.* Cambridge, Mass.: Harvard University Press.

————. 1986. *The Commercial Revolution in Nineteenth-Century China.* Berkeley and Los Angeles: University of California Press.

Harbison, Frederick H., and Charles A. Meyer. 1959. *Management in the Industrial World: An International Analysis.* New York: McGraw-Hill.

Harris, Marvin. 1979. *Cultural Materialism: The Struggle for a Science of Culture.* New York: Random House.

Henderson, Gregory. 1968. *Korea: The Politics of the Vortex.* Cambridge, Mass.: Harvard University Press.

Hirschmeier, Johannes, and Tsunehiko Yui. 1981. *The Development of Japanese Business 1600–1980.* London: Allen & Unwin.

Ho, Yhi-min. 1980. "The Production Structure of the Manufacturing Sector and Its Distribution Implications: The Case of Taiwan." *Economic Development and Cultural Change* 28:321–43.

Hofheinz, Roy, Jr., and Kent E. Calder. 1982. *The Eastasia Edge.* New York: Basic.

Hou, Jiaju. 1984. "Xianqin rufa liangjia guanli guannian zhi bijiao yanjiu" (Comparative Research on Management Concepts in Confucian and Legalist Philosophy in Early Ch'in). Pp. 59–74 in *Zhongguo shi guanli* (Chinese-style Management). Taipei: Gongshang Shibao.

Hsu, Francis L. K. 1971. *Under the Ancestors' Shadow: Kinship, Personality and Social Mobility in China.* Stanford, Calif.: Stanford University Press.

Hu, Tai-li. 1984. *My Mother-in-law's Village: Rural Industrialization and Change in Taiwan.* Taipei: Institute of Ethnology, Academia Sinica.

Huang, Guangkuo. 1984. "Rujia lunli yu qiye zuzhi xingtai" (Confucian Theory and Types of Enterprise Organization). Pp. 21–58 in *Zhongguo shi guanli* (Chinese-style Management). Taipei: Gongshang Shibao.

Jacoby, Sanford. 1979. "The Origins of Internal Labor Markets in Japan." *Industrial Relations* 18:184–96.

Johnson, Chalmers. 1982. *Miti and the Japanese Miracle.* Stanford, Calif.: Stanford University Press.

Jones, Leroy P., and Il SaKong. 1980. *Government, Business, and Entrepreneurship in Economic Development: The Korean Case.* Cambridge, Mass.: Council on East Asian Studies, Harvard University.

Juhn, Daniel Sungil. 1971. "Korean Industrial Entrepreneurship, 1924–40." Pp. 219–54 in *Korea's Response to the West,* edited by Yung-Hwan Jo. Kalamazoo, Mich.: Korean Research and Publications.

Kanter, Rosabeth Moss. 1983. *The Change Masters: Innovation and Productivity in the American Corporation.* New York: Simon & Schuster.

Koo, Hagen. 1984. "The Political Economy of Income Distribution in South Korea: The Impact of the State's Industrialization Policies." *World Development* 12:1029–37.

Krause, Lawrence, and Sekiguchi Sueo. 1976. "Japan and the World Economy." Pp. 383–458 in *Asia's New Giant,* edited by Hugh Patrick and Henry Rosovsky. Washington, D.C.: Brookings Institution.

Kunio, Yoshihara. 1982. *Sogo Shosha.* Oxford: Oxford University Press.

Kuznets, Simon. 1979. "Growth and Structural Shifts." Pp. 15–131 in *Economic Growth and Structural Change in Taiwan,* edited by Walter Galenson. Ithaca, N.Y.: Cornell University Press.

Lin, Xiezong. 1984. "Riben de qiye jingying—shehui zuzhi cengmian de kaocha" (Japanese Industrial Management: An Examination of Levels of Social Organization). *Guolijengjrtaxue xuebao,* no. 49, April, pp. 167–99.

Linder, Staffan B. 1986. *The Pacific Century.* Stanford, Calif.: Stanford University Press.

Little, Ian M. D. 1979. "An Economic Reconnaissance." Pp. 448–507 in *Economic Growth and Structural Change in Taiwan,* edited by Walter Galenson. Ithaca, N.Y.: Cornell University Press.

Maitland, Ian, John Bryson, and Andrew Van de Ven. 1985. "Sociologists, Economists and Opportunism." *Academy of Management Review* 10:59–65.

Marx, Karl. 1930. *Capital.* London: Dent.

Mason, Edward S., Mahn Ke Kim, Dwight H. Perkins, Kwang Suk Kim, and David C. Cole. 1980. *The Economic and Social Modernization of the Republic of Korea.* Cambridge, Mass.: Council of East Asian Studies, Harvard University.

Meyer, John W., and W. Richard Scott. 1983. *Organizational Environment: Ritual and Rationality.* Beverly Hills, Calif.: Sage.

Miles, Robert H. 1980. *Macro Organization Behavior.* Glenview, Ill.: Scott-Foresman.

Minard, Lawrence. 1984. "The China Reagan Can't Visit." *Forbes,* May 7, pp. 36–42.

Mintz, Beth, and Michael Schwartz. 1985. *The Power Structure of American Business.* Chicago: University of Chicago Press.

Monthly Bulletin of Statistics. 1985. March. New York: United Nations.

Myers, Ramon H. 1980. *The Chinese Economy, Past and Present.* Belmont, Calif.: Wadsworth.

———. 1984. "The Economic Transformation of the Republic of China on Taiwan." *China Quarterly* 99:500–528.

Myers, Ramon, and Mark R. Peattie, eds. 1984. *The Japanese Colonial Empire, 1895–1945.* Princeton, N.J.: Princeton University Press.

Nakamura, Takafusa. 1981. *The Postwar Japanese Economy.* Tokyo: University of Tokyo Press.

———. 1983. *Economic Growth in Prewar Japan.* New Haven, Conn.: Yale University Press.

Nakane, Chie. 1970. *Japanese Society.* Berkeley: University of California Press.

Nyaw, Mee-kou, and Chan-leong Chan. 1982. "Structure and Development Strategies of the Manufacturing Industries in Singapore and Hong Kong: A Comparative Study." *Asian Survey* 22:449–69.

Omohundro, John T. 1981. *Chinese Merchant Families in Iloilo.* Athens: Ohio University Press.

Orlove, Benjamin S. 1986. "Barter and Cash Sale on Lake Titicaca: A Test of Competing Approaches." *Current Anthropology* 27:85–106.

Ouchi, William. 1980. "Markets, Bureaucracies, and Clans." *Administrative Science Quarterly* 25:129–42.

———. 1981. *Theory Z.* Reading, Mass.: Addison-Wesley.

———. 1984. *The M-form Society.* Reading, Mass.: Addison-Wesley.

Ozawa, Terutomo. 1979. *Multinationalism, Japanese Style.* Princeton, N.J.: Princeton University Press.

Pascale, Richard Tanner, and Anthony G. Athos. 1981. *The Art of Japanese Management.* New York: Warner.

Patrick, Hugh, and Henry Rosovsky. 1976. "Japan's Economic Performance: An Overview." Pp. 1–62 in *Asia's New Giant*, edited by Hugh Patrick and Henry Rosovsky. Washington, D.C.: Brookings Institution.

Peng, Huaijen. 1984. *Taiwan jingyan de nanti* (The Difficult Problems of Taiwan's Experience). Taipei.

Perrow, Charles. 1981. "Markets, Hierarchies and Hegemony." Pp. 371–86 in *Perspectives on Organization Design and Behavior*, edited by A. Van de Ven and William Joyce. New York: Wiley.

———. 1986. *Complex Organizations*, 3d ed. New York: Random House.

Peters, Thomas J., and Robert H. Waterman, Jr. 1982. *In Search of Excellence*. New York: Warner.

Portes, Alejandro, and John Walton. 1981. *Labor, Class, and the International System*. New York: Academic.

Ranis, Gustav. 1979. "Industrial Development." Pp. 206–62 in *Economic Growth and Structural Change in Taiwan*, edited by Walter Galenson. Ithaca, N.Y.: Cornell University Press.

Redding, S. C. 1980. "Cognition as an Aspect of Culture and Its Relation to Management Processes: An Exploratory View of the Chinese Case." *Journal of Management Studies* 17:127–48.

Reynolds, Lloyd G. 1983. "The Spread of Economic Growth to the Third World: 1850–1980." *Journal of Economic Literature* 21:941–80.

SaKong, Il. 1980. "Macroeconomic Aspects of the Public Enterprise Sector." Pp. 99–128 in *Macroeconomic and Industrial Development in Korea*, edited by Chong Kee Park. Seoul: Korea Development Institute.

Sayle, Murray. 1985. "Japan Victorious." *New York Review of Books* 33 (5): 33–40.

Schluchter, Wolfgang. 1981. *The Rise of Western Rationalism: Max Weber's Developmental History*. Berkeley and Los Angeles: University of California Press.

Silin, Robert H. 1976. *Leadership and Values: The Organization of Large-scale Taiwanese Enterprises*. Cambridge, Mass.: East Asian Research Center, Harvard University.

Smircich, Linda. 1983. "Concepts of Culture and Organizational Analysis." *Administrative Science Quarterly* 28:339–58.

Swidler, Ann. 1986. "Culture in Action: Symbols and Strategies." *American Sociological Review* 51:273–86.

Taira, Koji. 1970. *Economic Development and the Labor Market in Japan*. New York: Columbia University Press.

Taiwan Statistical Data Book. 1985. Council for Economical Planning and Development, Republic of China.

Tannenbaum, Arnold S., Bogdan Kavcic, Menachem Rosner, Mino Vianello, and Georg Weiser. 1974. *Hierarchy in Organizations*. San Francisco: Jossey-Bass.

Teece, David. 1980. "Economics of Scope and the Scope of the Enterprise." *Journal of Economic Behavior and Organization* 1:223–48.

Tu, Wei-ming. 1984. "Gongye dongya yu rujia jingshen" (Industrial East Asia and the Spirit of Confucianism). *Tianxia zazhi* 41 (October 1): 124–37.

Vogel, Ezra. 1979. *Japan as Number One: Lessons for America*. Cambridge, Mass.: Harvard University Press.

Wade, Robert. 1985. "East Asian Financial Systems as a Challenge to Economics: Lessons from Taiwan." *California Management Review* 27:106–27.

Ward, Barbara E. 1972. "A Small Factory in Hong Kong: Some Aspects of Its Internal Organization." Pp. 353–86 in *Economic Organization in Chinese Society*, edited by W. E. Willmott. Stanford, Calif.: Stanford University Press.

Watson, James L. 1975*a*. "Agnates and Outsiders: Adoption in a Chinese Lineage." *Man* 10:293–306.

———. 1975*b*. *Emigration and the Chinese Lineage*. Berkeley: University of California Press.

———. 1982. "Chinese Kinship Reconsidered: Anthropological Perspectives on Historical Research." *China Quarterly* 92 (December): 589–627.

Weber, Max. 1958. *From Max Weber*. New York: Oxford University Press.

———. 1978. *Economy and Society*, edited by Guenther Roth and Claus Wittich. Berkeley: University of California Press.

Weick, Karl. 1979. *The Social Psychology of Organizing*. Reading, Mass.: Addison-Wesley.

Weiner, Steve. 1985. "K-Mart Apparel Buyers Hopscotch the Orient to Find Quality Goods." *Wall Street Journal*, March 19, pp. 1, 20.

Westphal, Larry E., Yung W. Rhee, Lin Su Kim, and Alice H. Amsden. 1984. "Republic of Korea." *World Development* 12:505–33.

White, Harrison. 1981. "Where Do Markets Come From?" *American Journal of Sociology* 87:517–47.

Wickberg, Edgar. 1965. *The Chinese in Philippine Life, 1850–1898*. New Haven, Conn.: Yale University Press.

Williamson, Oliver E. 1975. *Markets and Hierarchies*. New York: Free Press.

———. 1981. "The Economics of Organization." *American Journal of Sociology* 87:548–77.

———. 1983. "Organization Form, Residual Claimants and Corporate Control." *Journal of Law and Economics* 36:351–66.

———. 1985. *The Economic Institution of Capitalism*. New York: Free Press.

Williamson, Oliver E., and William G. Ouchi. 1981. "The Markets and Hierarchies and Visible Hand Perspective." Pp. 347–370, 387–390 in *Perspectives on Organization Design and Behavior*, edited by Andrew Van de Ven and William Joyce. New York: Wiley.

Willmott, W. E., ed. 1972. *Economic Organization in Chinese Society*. Stanford, Calif.: Stanford University Press.

Wong, Siu-lun. 1985. "The Chinese Family Firm: A Model." *British Journal of Sociology* 36, no. 1 (March): 58–72.

Wuthnow, Robert. 1985. "State Structures and Ideological Outcomes." *American Sociological Review* 50:799–821.

Yang, Jinlung. 1981. "Zhongxiao qiye yinhang zhedu zhi tantao." *Jiceng jinrong* 30:58–63.

Yang, Lien-sheng. 1970. "Government Control of Urban Merchants in Traditional China." *Tsing Hua Journal of Chinese Studies* 8:186–206.

Yasuba, Yasukichi. 1976. "The Evolution of Dualistic Wage Structure." Pp. 249–98 in *Japanese Industrialization and Its Social Consequences*, edited by Hugh Patrick. Berkeley: University of California Press.

Young, Alexander K. 1979. *The Sogo Shosha: Japan's Multinational Trading Corporations*. Boulder, Colo.: Westview.

Zeng, Shiqiang. 1984. "Yi rujia wei zhuliu de chongguo shi guanli linian zhi shentao" (An In-depth Discussion of Using Confucian Philosophy as the Unifying Principle for Chinese-style Management Concepts). Pp. 101–20 in *Zhongguo shi guanli* (Chinese-style Management). Taipei: Gungshang shibao.

Zhao, Jichang. 1982. "Zhengfu ying ruhe fudao zhongxiao quye zhi fazhan" (How Should the Government Develop an Assistance Policy for Small and Medium Businesses?). *Qiyin jikan* 5:32–38.

Zhonghua Zhengxinso, comp. 1985. *Taiwan diqu jitua qiye yanjiu* (Business Groups in Taiwan). Taipei: China Credit Information Service.
Zo, Ki-zun. 1970. "Development and Behavioral Patterns of Korean Entrepreneurs." *Korea Journal* 10:9–14.
Zucker, Lynn G. 1983. "Organizations as Institutions." *Research in the Sociology of Organizations* 2:1–48.

EDITORS' NOTES ON FURTHER READING: HAMILTON AND BIGGART

One of the strengths in the Hamilton and Biggart article is their clear outline of three contrasting perspectives on economic organizations—the market approach, the cultural approach, and the authority approach. A similar test of these three hypotheses can also be found in Gary Hamilton's "Chinese Consumption of Foreign Commodities: A Comparative Perspective," *American Sociological Review* 42 (1977):877–891. For a thoughtful defense of the cultural approach, see Viviana Zelizer, "Beyond the Polemics on the Market: Establishing a Theoretical and Empirical Agenda," *Sociological Forum* 3 (1988):614–634. Other useful readings on economics and culture are cited after Zelizer's article (Chapter 11) in this anthology. For additional material on the market approach, see the literature cited after the article by Alfred Chandler (Chapter 5), and on the authority approach, see the Editors' Notes on Further Reading for Alexander Gerschenkron's article (Chapter 4). Max Weber's work provides the best examples of the authority approach, and the reader is again referred to his *General Economic History* (Eng. tr. 1927) and Hans Gerth and C. Wright Mills, eds., *From Max Weber* (1946).

Since the appearance of the article reprinted in this anthology, Hamilton, Biggart, and their collaborators have produced a series of important papers that draw back from the emphasis placed here on the importance of the state, in favor of greater attention to the historical circumstances under which capitalist economies emerged in different Asian countries. See Hamilton and Kao Cheng-Shu, "The Institutional Foundations of Chinese Business: The Family Firm in Taiwan," in Craig Calhoun, ed., *Comparative Social Research*, Vol. 12, *Business Institutions* (1991). Also in the Calhoun book is Biggart's "Institutionalized Patrimonialism in Korean Business." See also Marco Orrù, Gary Hamilton, and Mariko Suzuki, "Patterns of Inter-Firm Control in Japanese Business," in *Organization Studies* 10, no. 4 (1989):549–574; Marco Orrù, Biggart, and Hamilton, "Organizational Isomorphism in East Asia: Broadening the New Institutionalism," in Walter Powell and Paul DiMaggio, eds., *The New Institutionalism in Organizational Analysis* (1991); Hamilton, William Zeile, and Wan-Jin Kim, "The Network Structures of East Asian Economies," pp. 63–77, in S. R. Clegg and S. G. Redding, eds., *Capitalism in Contrasting Cultures* (1989); and Hamilton, "Patterns of Asian Capitalism," Working Paper 28, Program in East Asian Culture and Development Research, University of California at Davis.

A useful book on Taiwan is Edwin Winckler and Susan Greenhalgh's *Contending Approaches to the Political Economy of Taiwan* (1988). See especially Greenhalgh's chapter, "Families and Networks in Taiwan's Economic Development." For background on Taiwanese social structure, see Greenhalgh's "Networks and their Nodes: Urban Society on Taiwan," *The China Quarterly* 99 (September 1984):529–552. For the role of the state, see Thomas Gold, *State and Society in the Taiwan Miracle* (1985) and Alice H. Amsden, "The State and Taiwan's Economic Development," pp. 78–106 in Peter Evans, Dietrich Rueschemeyer, and Theda Skocpol, eds., *Bringing the State Back In* (1985).

The most comprehensive source in English on Japanese interfirm alliances is Michael Gerlach's *Alliance Capitalism: The Social Organization of Japanese Business* (1991). A fascinating account of university/government/business/kinship linkages is given in Koji Taira and Teiichi Wada's "Business-Government Relations in Modern Japan: A Todai-Yakkai-Zakai Complex?" pp. 264–297 in Mark S. Mizruchi and Michael Schwartz, eds., *Intercorporate Relations: The Structural Analysis of Business* (1987); on the school/work linkage see James Rosenbaum and Takehiko Kariya, "From High School to Work: Market and Institutional Mechanisms in Japan," *American Journal of Sociology* 94 (1989):1334–1365. Other references on Japan follow Ronald Dore's article (Chapter 6) in this anthology.

For a quick introduction to how economists view the economies in Japan, Taiwan, and South Korea, see "Lessons for Development from the Experience in Asia," *Supplement to the American Economic Review* 80 (1990):104–121. An excellent critique of neoclassical economists' explanations of the comparative success of different newly industrializing countries (NICs) can be found in Stewart Clegg, Dexter Dunphy, and S. G. Redding's "Organization and Management in East Asia," in these authors' *The Enterprise and Management in East Asia* (University of Hong Kong, Centre of Asian Studies, Occasional Papers and Monographs, no. 69, 1986). A collection of papers that compare the different routes to industrialization taken by Asian and Latin American countries can be found in Gary Gereffi and Donald Wyman's *Manufacturing Miracles: Paths of Industrialization in Latin America and East Asia* (1990).

PART III

The Sociology of Economic Institutions

8

The Bazaar Economy: Information and Search in Peasant Marketing

CLIFFORD GEERTZ

There have been a number of points at which anthropology and economics have come to confront one another over the last several decades—development theory; preindustrial history; colonial domination. Here I want to discuss another where the interchange between the two disciplines may grow even more intimate; one where they may come actually to contribute to each other rather than, as has often been the case, skimming off the other's more generalized ideas and misapplying them. This is the study of peasant market systems, or what I will call bazaar economies.

There has been by now a long tradition of peasant market studies in anthropology. Much of it has been merely descriptive—inductivism gone berserk. That part which has had analytical interests has tended to divide itself into two approaches. Either the bazaar is seen as the nearest real world institution to the purely competitive market of neoclassical economics—"penny capitalism"; or it is regarded as an institution so embedded in its sociocultural context as to escape the reach of modern economic analysis altogether. These contrasting approaches have formed the poles of an extended debate between economic anthropologists designated "formalists" and those designated "substantivists," a debate that has now rather staled for all but the most persevering.

Some recent developments in economic theory having to do with the role of information, communication, and knowledge in exchange processes (see Michael Spence; George Stigler; Kenneth Arrow; George Akerlof; Albert Rees) promise to mute this formalism-substantivism contrast. Not only do they provide us with an analytic framework more suitable to understanding how bazaars work than do models of pure competition; they also allow the

---

From *Supplement to the American Economic Review* 68 (May 1978):28–32. Reprinted by permission of the American Economic Association.

incorporation of sociocultural factors into the body of discussion rather than relegating them to the status of boundary matters. In addition, their actual use on empirical cases outside the modern "developed" context may serve to demonstrate that they have more serious implications for standard economic theory and are less easily assimilable to received paradigms than at least some of their proponents might imagine. If this is so, then the interaction of anthropology and economics may come for once to be more than an exchange of exotic facts for parochial concepts and develop into a reciprocally seditious endeavor useful to both.

I

The bazaar economy upon which my discussion is based is that of a town and countryside region at the foot of the Middle Atlas in Morocco I have been studying since the mid-1960s. (During the 1950s, I studied similar economies in Indonesia. See the author, 1963.) Walled, ethnically heterogeneous, and quite traditional, the town is called Sefrou, as is the region, and it has been there for a millenium. Once an important caravan stop on the route south from Fez to the Sahara, it has been, for about a century, a thriving market center of 15,000–30,000 people.

There are two sorts of bazaar there: 1) a permanent one, consisting of the trading quarters of the old town; 2) a periodic one, which meets at various spots—here for rugs, there for grain—outside the walls on Thursdays, as part of a very complex regional cycle involving various other market places and the other days of the week. The two sorts of bazaar are distinct but their boundaries are quite permeable, so that individuals move freely between them, and they operate on broadly the same principles. The empirical situation is extremely complex—there are more than 600 shops representing about forty distinct commercial trades and nearly 300 workshops representing about thirty crafts—and on Thursdays the town population probably doubles. That the bazaar is an important local institution is beyond doubt: two-thirds of the town's labor force is employed there.

Empirical detail aside (a full-scale study by the author is in press), the bazaar is more than another demonstration of the truth that, under whatever skies, men prefer to buy cheap and sell dear. It is a distinctive system of social relationships centering around the production and consumption of goods and services—that is, a particular kind of economy, and it deserves analysis as such. Like an "industrial economy" or a "primitive economy," from both of which it markedly differs, a "bazaar economy" manifests its general processes in particular forms, and in so doing reveals aspects of those processes which alter our conception of their nature. Bazaar, that Persian word of uncertain origin which has come to stand in English for the oriental market, becomes, like the word market itself, as much an analytic idea as the name of an institution, and the study of it, like that of the market, as much a theoretical as a descriptive enterprise.

II

Considered as a variety of economic system, the bazaar shows a number of distinctive characteristics. Its distinction lies less in the processes which operate and more in the way those processes are shaped into a coherent form. The usual maxims apply here as elsewhere: sellers seek maximum profit, consumers maximum utility; price relates supply and demand; factor proportions reflect factor costs. However, the principles governing the organization of commercial life are less derivative from such truisms than one might imagine from reading standard economic textbooks, where the passage from axioms to actualities tends to be rather nonchalantly traversed. It is those principles—matters less of utility balances than of information flows—that give the bazaar its particular character and general interest.

To start with a dictum: in the bazaar information is poor, scarce, maldistributed, inefficiently communicated, and intensely valued. Neither the rich concreteness or reliable knowledge that the ritualized character of nonmarket economies makes possible, nor the elaborate mechanisms for information generation and transfer upon which industrial ones depend, are found in the bazaar: neither ceremonial distribution nor advertising; neither prescribed exchange partners nor product standardization. The level of ignorance about everything from product quality and going prices to market possibilities and production costs is very high, and much of the way in which the bazaar functions can be interpreted as an attempt to reduce such ignorance for someone, increase it for someone, or defend someone against it.

III

These ignorances mentioned above are *known* ignorances, not simply matters concerning which information is lacking. Bazaar participants realize the difficulty in knowing if a cow is sound or its price right, and they realize also that it is impossible to prosper without knowing. The search for information one lacks and the protection of information one has is the name of the game. Capital, skill, and industriousness play, along with luck and privilege, as important a role in the bazaar as they do in any economic system. They do so less by increasing efficiency or improving products than by securing for their possessor an advantaged place in an enormously complicated, poorly articulated, and extremely noisy communication network.

The institutional peculiarities of the bazaar thus seem less like mere accidents of custom and more like connected elements of a system. An extreme division of labor and localization of markets, heterogeneity of products and intensive price bargaining, fractionalization of transactions and stable clientship ties between buyers and sellers, itinerant trading and extensive traditionalization of occupation in ascriptive terms—these things do not just co-occur, they imply one another.

The search for information—laborious, uncertain, complex, and irregular—is the central experience of life in the bazaar. Every aspect of the bazaar economy reflects the fact that the primary problem facing its participants (that is, "bazaaris") is not balancing options but finding out what they are.

IV

Information search, thus, is the really advanced art in the bazaar, a matter upon which everything turns. The main energies of the bazaari are directed toward combing the bazaar for usable signs, clues as to how particular matters at the immediate moment specifically stand. The matters explored may comprise everything from the industriousness of a prospective coworker to the supply situation in agricultural products. But the most persistent concerns are with price and quality of goods. The centrality of exchange skills (rather than production or managerial ones) puts a tremendous emphasis on knowing what particular things are actually selling for and what sorts of things they precisely are.

The elements of bazaar institutional structure can be seen in terms of the degree to which they either render search a difficult and costly enterprise, or facilitate it and bring its costs within practical limits. Not that all those elements line up neatly on one or another side of the ledger. The bulk have effects in both directions, for bazaaris are as interested in making search fruitless for others as they are in making it effectual for themselves. The desire to know what is really occurring is matched with the desire to deal with people who don't but imagine that they do. The structures enabling search and those casting obstructions in its path are thoroughly intertwined.

Let me turn, then, to the two most important search procedures as such: clientelization and bargaining.

V

Clientelization is the tendency, marked in Sefrou, for repetitive purchasers of particular goods and services to establish continuing relationships with particular purveyors of them rather than search widely through the market at each occasion of need. The apparent Brownian motion of randomly colliding bazaaris conceals a resilient pattern of informal personal connections. Whether or not "buyers and sellers, blindfolded by a lack of knowledge simply grop[ing] about until they bump into one another" (S. Cohen, quoted in Rees, p. 110), is, as has been proposed, a reasonable description of modern labor markets, it certainly is not of the bazaar. Its buyers and sellers, moving along the grooved channels clientelization lays down, find their way again and again to the same adversaries.

"Adversaries" is the word, for clientship relations are not dependency relations, but competitive ones. Clientship is symmetrical, egalitarian, and oppositional. There are no "patrons" in the master and man sense here. Whatever the relative power, wealth, knowledge, skill, or status of the participants—and it can be markedly uneven—clientship is a reciprocal matter, and the butcher or wool seller is tied to his regular customer in the same terms as he to them. By partitioning the bazaar crowd into those who are genuine candidates for his attention and those who are merely theoretically such, clientelization reduces search to manageable proportions and transforms a diffuse mob into a stable collection of familiar antagonists. The use of repetitive exchange between acquainted partners to limit the costs of search is a practical consequence of the overall institutional structure of the bazaar and an element within that structure.

First, there is a high degree of spatial localization and "ethnic" specialization of trade in the bazaar which simplifies the process of finding clients considerably and stabilizes its achievements. If one wants a kaftan or a mule pack made, one knows where, how, and for what sort of person to look. And, since individuals do not move easily from one line of work or one place to another, once you have found a particular bazaari in whom you have faith and who has faith in you, he is going to be there for awhile. One is not constantly faced with the necessity to seek out new clients. Search is made accumulative.

Second, clientelization itself lends form to the bazaar for it further partitions it, and does so in directly informational terms, dividing it into overlapping subpopulations within which more rational estimates of the quality of information, and thus of the appropriate amount and type of search, can be made. Bazaaris are not projected, as for example tourists are, into foreign settings where everything from the degree of price dispersion and the provenance of goods to the stature of participants and the etiquette of contact are unknown. They operate in settings where they are very much at home.

Clientelization represents an actor-level attempt to counteract, and profit from, the system-level deficiencies of the bazaar as a communication network—its structural intricacy and irregularity, the absence of certain sorts of signaling systems and the undeveloped state of others, and the imprecision, scattering, and uneven distribution of knowledge concerning economic matters of fact—by improving the richness and reliability of information carried over elementary links within it.

VI

The rationality of this effort, rendering the clientship relation dependable as a communication channel while its functional context remains unimproved, rests in turn on the presence within that relation of the sort of effective mechanism for information transfer that seems so lacking elsewhere. And as that relation is adversary, so is the mechanism: multidimensional intensive bargaining. The central paradox of bazaar exchange is that advantage stems from surrounding oneself with relatively superior communication links, links themselves forged in sharply antagonistic interaction in which information imbalances are the driving force and their exploitation the end.

Bazaar bargaining is an understudied topic (but see Ralph Cassady), a fact to which the undeveloped state of bargaining theory in economics contributes. Here I touch briefly on two points: the multidimensionality of such bargaining and its intensive nature.

First, multidimensionality: Though price setting is the most conspicuous aspect of bargaining, the bargaining spirit penetrates the whole of the confrontation. Quantity and/or quality may be manipulated while money price is held constant, credit arrangements can be adjusted, bulking or bulk breaking may conceal adjustments, and so on, to an astonishing range and level of detail. In a system where little is packaged or regulated, and everything is approximate, the possibilities for bargaining along nonmonetary dimensions are enormous.

Second, intensiveness: I use "intensive" in the way introduced by Rees, where it signifies the exploration in depth of an offer already received, a search along the intensive margin, as contrasted to seeking additional offers, a search along the extensive. Rees describes the used car market as one in which intensive search is prominent as a result of the high heterogeneity of products (cars driven by little old ladies vs. taxicabs, etc.) as against the new car market, where products are considered homogeneous, and extensive search (getting new quotations from other dealers) predominates.

The prominence of intensive bargaining in the bazaar is thus a measure of the degree to which it is more like a used car market than a new car one: one in which the important information problems have to do with determining the realities of the particular case rather than the general distribution of comparable cases. Further, it is an expression of the fact that such a market rewards a "clinical" form of search (one which focuses on the diverging interests of concrete economic actors) more than it does a "survey" form (one which focuses on the general interplay of functionally defined economic categories). Search is primarily intensive because the sort of information one needs most cannot be acquired by asking a handful of index questions of a large number of people, but only by asking a large number of diagnostic questions of a handful of people. It is this kind of questioning, exploring nuances rather than canvassing populations, that bazaar bargaining represents.

This is not to say that extensive search plays no role in the bazaar; merely that it is ancillary to intensive. Sefrou bazaaris make a terminological distinction between bargaining to test the waters and bargaining to conclude an exchange, and tend to conduct the two in different places: the first with people with whom they have weak clientship ties, the second with people with whom they have firm ones. Extensive search tends to be desultory and to be considered an activity not worth large investments of time. (Fred Khuri reports that in the Rabat bazaar, bazaaris with shops located at the edge of the bazaar complain that such shops are "rich in bargaining but poor in selling," i.e. people survey as they pass, but do their real bargaining elsewhere.) From the point of view of search, the productive type of bargaining is that of the firmly clientelized buyer and seller exploring the dimensions of a particular, likely to be consummated transaction. Here, as elsewhere in the bazaar, everything rests finally on a personal confrontation between intimate antagonists.

The whole structure of bargaining is determined by this fact: that it is a communication channel evolved to serve the needs of men at once coupled and opposed. The rules governing it are a response to a situation in which two persons on opposite sides of some exchange possibility are struggling both to make that possibility actual and to gain a slight advantage within it. Most bazaar "price negotiation" takes place to the right of the decimal point. But it is no less keen for that.

REFERENCES

G. A. Akerhof, "The Market for 'Lemons': Quality, Uncertainty and the Market Mechanism," *Quart. J. Econ.*, Aug. 1970, *84*, 488–500.

Kenneth J. Arrow, *The Limits of Organization*, New York 1974.

R. Cassady, Jr., "Negotiated Price Making in Mexican Traditional Markets," *Amer. Indigena*, 1968, *38*, 51–79.

Clifford Geertz, *Peddlers and Princes*, Chicago 1963.

———, "Suq: The Bazaar Economy in Sefrou," in Lawrence Rosen et al., eds., *Meaning and Order in Contemporary Morocco: Three Essays in Cultural Analysis*, New York forthcoming.

F. Khuri, "The Etiquette of Bargaining in the Middle East," *Amer. Anthropologist*, July 1968, *70*, 698–706.

A. Rees, "Information Networks in Labor Markets," in David M. Lamberton, ed., *Economics of Information and Knowledge*, Hammondsworth 1971, 109–18.

M. Spence, "Time and Communication in Economic and Social Interaction," *Quart. J. Econ.*, Nov. 1973, *87*, 651–60.

G. Stigler, "The Economics of Information," in David M. Lamberton, ed., *Economics of Information and Knowledge*, Hammondsworth 1971, 61–82.

EDITORS' NOTES ON FURTHER READING: GEERTZ

This article, together with the introductory reading by Karl Polanyi, illustrates the common ground between economic anthropology and economic sociology. For other studies of bazaar economies, see the substantivist-oriented papers in Paul Bohannan and George Dalton, eds., *Markets in Africa* (1982); and the two formalist monographs, Sol Tax, *Penny Capitalism: A Guatemalan Indian Economy* (1953) and Ralph Beals, *The Peasant Marketing System of Oaxaca, Mexico* (1975). (For what happens when one tries to bargain in the United States, see Harold Garfinkel, *Studies in Ethnomethodology* [1967], pp. 68–70.) A much more detailed account of Geertz's argument can be found in his elaborate and subtle "Suq: The Bazaar Economy in Sefrou," pp. 123–263 in Clifford Geertz, Hildred Geertz, and Lawrence Rosen, *Meaning and Order in Moroccan Society: Three Essays in Cultural Analysis* (1979). A related and more extensive (though less intensive) study by Geertz is his brilliant *Peddlers and Princes: Social Development and Economic Change in Two Indonesian Towns* (1963). Also of interest to economic sociologists are Geertz's *Agricultural Involution: The Process of Ecological Change in Indonesia* (1963) and "Ports of Trade in Nineteenth Century Bali," *Research in Economic Anthropology* 3 (1980):109–120. For a general introduction to Geertz's work, see Ronald G. Walters, "Signs of the Times: Clifford Geertz and Historians," *Social Research* 47 (1980):537–556.

Richard Posner, the noted economist, legal scholar, and federal judge, uses Geertz's material to support a "law and economics" argument that personalized trading is an efficient, functional substitute for well-developed, modern legal guarantees in economic exchange in his "A Theory of Primitive Society with Special Reference to Law," *Journal of Law and Economics* 23 (1980):1–56. For related arguments, see Yoram Ben-Porath, "The F-Connection: Families, Friends, and Firms in the Organization of Exchange," *Population and Development Review* 6, no. 1 (1980):1–30; Janet Landa, "A Theory of the Ethnically Homogeneous Middleman Group: An Institutional Alternative to Contract Law," *Journal of Legal Studies* 10 (1981):349–362; and, posing the argument in especially stark form, Sumner LaCroix, "Homogeneous Middleman Groups: What Determines the Homogeneity?" *Journal of Law, Economics, and Organization* 5, no. 1 (1989):211–222. For a critique of this effort, and an account of the conditions under which peasant and tribal economies may be expected to be organized around personalized trading, see Mark Granovetter, chapter 3, "Society and Economy," draft manuscript.

Geertz's article illustrates the creative import of economic concepts (here, the search for information) into a different discipline with a different viewpoint. For other examples of such import by economic sociologists, see Carol Heimer, *Reactive Risk and Rational Action: Managing Moral Hazard in Insurance Contracts* (1985); Arthur Stinchcombe and Carol Heimer, *Organization Theory and Project Management: Administering Uncertainty in Norwegian Offshore Oil* (1985); Arthur Stinchcombe, *Information and Organizations* (1990); and Ronald Burt, "Structural Holes: The Social Structure of Competition," draft manuscript (1991).

9

The Sociological
and Economic Approaches
to Labor Market Analysis:
A Social Structural View

MARK GRANOVETTER

I. INTRODUCTION: THE SOCIOLOGICAL AND
ECONOMIC APPROACHES TO LABOR MARKETS

This chapter reviews recent economic and sociological work on labor markets, concentrating on studies whose comparison is particularly revealing of differences in strategies and underlying assumptions between the disciplines. The sociological studies reviewed are especially those stressing the embeddedness (Granovetter, 1985) of labor market behavior in networks of social interaction and demographic constraints. Most of these studies share with microeconomics the stance of "methodological individualism" (see Blaug, 1980:49–52) that attempts to ground all explanations in the motives and behaviors of individuals, but they differ in emphasizing social structural constraints and in avoiding the functionalist arguments now common in neoclassical work.

From a sociological viewpoint, it is an exaggerated version of methodological individualism that often appears in economics, in which individual actors are analyzed as if atomized from the influence of their relations with others, of these others' decisions and behaviors, and from the past history of these relations.[1] This atomized view of economic action has a long history in classical and neoclassical economics. Aside from leading to incorrect understanding of how labor market institutions actually function, it also makes it difficult to give an adequate account, even within a strictly methodologically individualist framework, of how individual actions can aggregate up to the level of institutions, since that aggregation takes place

From George Farkas and Paula England, eds., *Industries, Firms, and Jobs: Sociological and Economic Approaches* (New York: Plenum Press, 1988), pp. 187–216. Reprinted by permission.

through networks of relationships. Because of the unavailability, in this atomized view, of a persuasive causal account of how institutions arise, there is a powerful temptation to trot out "culture" as a *deus ex machina*, or to make the classic functionalist assumption that those institutions arise that are best suited to the circumstances at hand. When functionalist assumptions are defended—and usually they are not—it is asserted that inefficient arrangements will have failed the test of the marketplace, and surviving ones are thus the result of some sort of "natural selection."[2] Though the mechanism of this selection is usually vague, the most common account is that suboptimal arrangements are short-lived because they present the opportunity for beneficial trade or profit to those who develop more efficient ones. But this arbitrage-type argument, when developed in detail, depends crucially on stylized assumptions about information, productivity, and motivation that can be accurate only in the absence of social structure— i.e., in the presence of atomized actors.

A second major difference between economic and sociological work on labor markets is the general failure in the economic literature to consider the intertwining of economic and noneconomic motives. When we seek economic goals in our interactions with others, these are usually combined with striving for sociability, approval, status, and power as well. Though such motives have largely been absent from economic thinking since Adam Smith (see Hirschman, 1977), it does not follow that their pursuit is nonrational. Though there may be more sociologists than economists who *study* nonrational behavior, the study of rational action has nevertheless often been central in sociological work (Blau, 1964; Heath, 1976; Homans, 1974; Tilly, 1978; Weber, 1968). While it is an interesting intellectual exercise to construct models that assume *only* economic motives, to see how far such a position can be pushed before its limits of explanation are reached— and to ferret out self-interest in altruistic guise—much neoclassical work goes beyond this, insisting on principle that no other motives "significantly" affect the economic sphere. This insistence is sometimes defended by the imprecise and unfalsifiable assertion that noneconomic motives are "randomly distributed" among units of interest and may thus be assumed to "cancel out" in their overall effects.

In the following account, I shall try to show in some detail how these disciplinary differences affect the interpretation and explanation of concrete economic action and institutions.

II. SHIFTING ECONOMIC APPRAISALS OF LABOR MOBILITY

The classical economic appraisal of labor mobility was favorable. Mobility reallocates labor from locations of lower to those of higher demand; hence, Adam Smith's denunciation of legal institutions restricting free movement (1776/1976, Book I:Chap. 10). But when early 20th-century institutional economists confronted the extent of turnover costs, the evaluation changed and the word *turnover* came into vogue. While *mobility* and *turnover* have slightly different denotations, one having the individual and the other the firm as unit of analysis, the connotations diverge more widely. *Turnover* almost invites the suffix applied to it by Sumner Slichter in his 1920 article, "The Scope and Nature of the Labor Turnover Problem"; Paul Brissenden and Emil Frankel (1922:46) went so far as to assert that 54 to 86% of job changes in firms they surveyed had been "unnecessary."

The pendulum shifted back with the landmark SSRC volume *Labor Mobility and Economic Opportunity* (Bakke, 1954). The title could hardly have been *Turnover and Economic Opportunity*, and much of it sings the praises of mobility. The "free movement of labor," commented Bakke, "is in large part responsible for the flexibility with which millions of people and an amazing variety of jobs have been matched, for the vast potential of enterprise, initiative, incentive, invention and for the self-development and acquisition of skills which contributed greatly to our economic development" (1954:3). In 1954 mobility seemed relevant even to the Cold War: "Had the Marxists given appropriate attention to the human initiative, inventiveness and adaptive skill unleashed by the freedom of labor movement, they would have been less confident of the internal decay of a 'business civilization'" (Bakke *et al.*, 1954:3).

The 1970s saw still another shift, back to a negative view of labor mobility. This can be better understood by noting that an attitude to mobility entails a corresponding view of long job tenures and well-developed internal labor markets. Early institutionalists stressed the value of long-time employees to the firm, and the advantages of promoting from within. Slichter commented: "How much would the employment man not give to know as much concerning the skill, willingness to work, reliability and loyalty of applicants . . . as he already knows of the men on the force from his own acquaintance with them. . . . By promoting men who have made good on simple operations to more difficult ones and by hiring outsiders for the simple jobs the risk of a misfit is largely eliminated . . . where misfits are costly, and transferred to the simple jobs where they are less costly" (1919:290). By contrast, the post-World War II approval of mobility entailed a denunciation of long tenures in internal labor markets. Using medieval language, Clark Kerr described such markets as "manorial" (1954), and Arthur Ross summed up the prevailing fear in his article "Do We Have a New Industrial Feudalism?" (1958).

Mobility was deplored early in the century because it was perceived as exceptionally high, and applauded nostalgically in the 1950s when it seemed too low to ensure flexible responses to changes in economic needs (Doeringer and Piore, 1971; Hall, 1982; Ross, 1958). Both responses were critical of existing labor market conditions. The recent shift to approval of immobility in internal markets did not, however, result from a belief that mobility had become excessive; on the contrary, it resulted from a new trend in economics— broadly encapsulated by the term *new institutional economics*—that reclaims much of labor economics and other subjects from the "old" institutionalists by sophisticated demonstrations that what had appeared to be inefficiencies of historical, legal, or sociological origin could instead be interpreted as efficient solutions to economic problems more complex than initially recognized. In this new yet determinedly neoclassical spirit, internal labor markets, property rights, some unemployment, corporate hierarchy, and various legal arrangements have been rehabilitated as economically efficient.

Such a view makes criticism of observed trends unlikely. It is riddled with Panglossian pitfalls of the sort that Robert Merton warned against in his account of the difficulties in assuming that every social practice fills a well-defined function in an integrated whole (1947). Similar difficulties arise in biology, where Gould and Lewontin have recently complained about the tendency to explain behavioral traits as optimal by telling "adaptive stories" about what environmental exigency they can be viewed as meeting. They comment that evolutionists often "consider their work done when they concoct a plausible story. But plausible stories can always be told. The key to historical research lies in devising criteria to identify proper explanations among the substantial set of plausible pathways to any modern result" (1979:587–588).

Adaptive stories about long tenures and internal labor markets followed assertions that these were more prevalent than previously suspected (Hall, 1980, 1982; Main, 1982; Sekscenski, 1980). Rather than responding to this finding by further pursuit of the "industrial feudalism" concerns of the 1950s, economists have discovered the virtues in existing arrangements. Doeringer and Piore's 1971 book argued, much like the early 20th-century institutionalists, that given the costs of turnover, long tenures were economically rational. Growing attention to internal markets sparked an interest in "implicit labor contracts," to explain how rational individuals could produce institutional structures that seemed at first glance inconsistent with neoclassical assumptions (Azariadis, 1975; Baily, 1974).

With minor variations, the adaptive story line about long tenures goes as follows: Young workers "job-shop" (Johnson, 1978; Pencavel, 1972; Reynolds, 1951), trying out jobs to learn about the market and their own skills. By their mid-30s they settle into jobs that nicely match their tastes and abilities. The better the match, the longer the tenure will be. Most workers "do wind up in lifetime work . . . multiple tries eventually succeed" (Hall, 1982:720–721). Length of tenure is taken as a proxy for quality of a match (e.g., Bartel and Borjas, 1981:66; Jovanovic, 1979b:1257). High mobility is seen as suitable only in the job-shopping stage. Mincer and Jovanovic suggest that workers highly mobile prior to current job have little investment in firm-specific human capital, and one reason for this is "inefficiency in job-matching" (1981:35). When mobility persists beyond the job-shopping stage, it is pathological and ought to be designated "persistent turnover denoting little investment in specific capital" (Mincer and Jovanovic, 1981:38).

I will assess the "stories," old and new, about labor mobility by juxtaposing sociological and economic accounts, and stressing the embeddedness of mobility in social structural constraints. I consider various factors that determine mobility, beginning with those closest to the individual worker and proceeding to broad features of market organization. I neglect the current macroeconomic situation—e.g., the rate of unemployment—though this is widely acknowledged to affect the rate of mobility (see Ross, 1958).

III. MODELS OF "INDIVIDUAL PROPENSITY"
IN LABOR MARKETS

It is a frequent empirical observation that individuals who have already experienced an event (such as mobility or unemployment) are more likely than others to do so again. This observation could be due to those individuals' having high but stable probabilities for the event ("heterogeneity") or to each recurrence's making the next more likely ("state-dependence") (see Heckman, 1978). Which is the case matters a great deal. If current unemployment makes that state more likely in the future, then policies that reduce it reduce future unemployment as well, and the benefits are amplified by a hidden multiplier effect, not present if only heterogeneity explained differential chances of unemployment.

Though the concept of "heterogeneity" has no intrinsic theoretical content, it has been treated in the economic literature as indexing personal "propensities" exogeneous to the economic frame of reference. Stayers are, in effect, "sticks in the mud" and movers have "ants in their pants." Corcoran and Hill (1980), for example, attribute heterogeneity in the "propensity to work" to differences in "personal preferences, motivations and talents" and counsel that to reduce unemployment we must "identify and alter those skills, attitudes and habits which influence work stability" (1980:41, 54). They go on to attribute persistence in observed unemployment to "unmeasured personal differences in the propensity for unemployment" (1980:54). The word *propensity* unfortunately strongly connotes voluntary behavior with little sense of constraints; one might as well say that big-game hunters have a high propensity to be eaten by lions. Sociologists discussing heterogeneity have been more eclectic, suggesting that it may index not only personal differences but also those in characteristics of jobs and local labor markets and of the attachments between employers and employees (DiPrete, 1981:290; March and March, 1977:399–403; Tuma, 1976:357–358).

Not only are "heterogeneity" and "state-dependence" without intrinsic theoretical content, but which of these applies may depend crucially on model specification. Flinn and Heckman note that heterogeneity may include unobserved state-dependent components. If being unemployed has no effect on the probability of future unemployment, yet people vary in their chance of unemployment, we have pure heterogeneity. If it affects everyone's probability of future unemployment to exactly the same extent, we have pure state-dependence. But the economic losses caused by unemployment, that affect future behavior, may vary across workers in ways not fully measured: Flinn and Heckman call this interaction effect "state-dependent heterogeneity" (1982a:112).

What accounts for this variation in losses? The "unmeasured personal differences" approach to heterogeneity would suggest that individual characteristics are the reason. But variations in local labor markets might also create this outcome. Unemployment stemming from a plant's closing in a company town inflicts worse losses than temporary layoffs in a large city. But the crude specification of states in a stochastic model as "employed" and "unemployed" aggregates these situations. With more distinctions among states, individuals might no longer appear heterogeneous in how these states affected them, and data that had been taken to show heterogeneity would be reinterpreted as indicating state-dependence.

The category "employed" also conceals enormous differences among individuals' jobs. If these differences lead to different chances of mobility, this variation will appear to indicate unmeasured heterogeneity of individuals. Defining the states in a stochastic model is thus not a theoretically neutral procedure. When states are crudely specified, the dice are loaded for a finding of heterogeneity. This predisposition may result from the unspoken assumption, typical in economics, but also to some extent in sociological work on "status attainment," that personal differences underlie variation in individual outcomes. If one thinks, by contrast, that jobs and careers are embedded in social and bureaucratic structures that strongly affect the chances of mobility or unemployment, it is appropriate to define the state space in more detail. Such a specification would be more likely to produce findings of state-dependence.

The distinction between heterogeneity and state-dependence as influences on transition probabilities is thus arbitrary; more important, the attention focused on choosing between these deflects theoretical interest from the actual process of transition. Knowing what variables are nonspuriously correlated with these probabilities hardly gives a sufficient account of how transitions are accomplished, though it may be a valuable starting point for such an account and can cast doubt on explanations statistically inconsistent with the findings. As with many methodological innovations the danger lies in mistaking a starting point for the end of the theoretical road.

These considerations enter a discussion of labor mobility on account of the frequent observation that length of tenure and separation probability have a strong inverse relation. The question is whether this is the causally spurious result of heterogeneity, since, as Rosen points out, "those with greater propensities to move will always exhibit greater separation rates and lower tenure than those with the opposite propensities" (Rosen, 1981:3). Unless carefully formulated, the attribution of mobility "propensity" to heterogeneity may undercut the claim that job tenure is a good proxy for the quality of a match, since this attribution implies that long tenures result instead from a low propensity to move. Mincer and Jovanovic (1981) attempt to surmount this dilemma by interpreting heterogeneity as closely related to quality of job matches. They measure heterogeneity by the extent of mobility prior to current job, and relate the resulting estimate of "propensity to move" to current separation probability. This is justified by interpreting prior mobility as reflecting the level of specific human capital investment, which is, in turn, determined in part by the quality of previous job matches. They conclude that heterogeneity "biases the steepness of the tenure-turnover profile upward by 50% on average," with the effect growing with age since prior mobility is a better predictor of separation for older workers (Mincer and Jovanovic, 1981:35).

In Flinn and Heckman's terminology, "state-dependent heterogeneity" is asserted here. Differences in jobs lead individuals to different levels of specific human capital investment that affect future separation probabilities. With more detail on what the differences are in jobs or matches that shape these investments, a statistical finding of state-dependence might thus emerge. But either is consistent with the human capital argument offered, showing again that the statistical distinction between heterogeneity and state-dependence is of little direct theoretical import.

I suggest here a sociological interpretation of mobility history. The meaning of individuals' history of mobility is inadequately captured by human capital arguments. As one moves through a sequence of jobs, one acquires not only human capital but also, and more difficult to interpret as an investment phenomenon (though see Boorman, 1975) a series of co-workers who necessarily become aware of one's abilities and personality. This awareness occurs without cost, as a by-product of the interactions necessary for work; this costless feature is difficult to reconcile with most economic models in which investment assumes direct or opportunity costs. Because of the often-documented fact that employers acquire a great deal of information about prospective employees from individuals known to both (Granovetter, 1974, 1983), one's market situation changes significantly with the number of individuals who know one's characteristics and with the number of firms in which they are located.

The former has to do with the number of jobs one has held, the latter with the number held by one's contacts—since their immobility would concentrate them in a small number of firms that, *ceteris paribus*, would have fewer vacancies than a larger number. When economic action is embedded in social structure in this way, the usual distinction between heterogeneity and state-dependence is inadequate; both implicitly assume atomized actors. This can be seen in terms of the urn models used to represent these processes (e.g., Heckman, 1981:94–96)—where each individual has an urn containing red and black balls (corresponding to two states such as mobility and immobility). In each period one randomly draws a ball from the urn and is assigned to the corresponding state. In pure heterogeneity, each individual has an urn with a different proportion of red and black balls. The contents of the urn "are unaffected by actual outcomes and in fact are constant" (Heckman, 1981:95). State dependence means that the contents of the urn change as a consequence of outcomes. For example, "if a person draws a red ball, . . . additional new red balls are added to his urn" (Heckman, 1981:95). But in neither case are the contents of one's urn affected by what other individuals draw from their urns. As in most economic models, independent individuals are assumed, not directly affected by the behavior of others. My theoretical account requires precisely, however, that the composition of each person's urn change depending on what color balls are drawn by others: One's mobility depends on that of others. Nor would it suffice to model the interdependence by simple aggregation rules, such as modifying one's urn according to the average outcome of others. Urn composition is changed only by the draws of those others with whom one has direct connections; thus, the overall structure of this network of connections is implicated in total system functioning.[3]

Correspondingly, the mobility of the random sample of professional, technical, and managerial job-changers I studied was heavily mediated by personal contacts acquired at various stages of the career, and before. Their "mobility appears to be self-generating; the more different work and social settings one moves through, the larger reservoir of personal contacts . . . who may mediate further mobility. It is because ties from past jobs and from before work are as likely to be used as more recent ones that we have a cumulative effect, as if individuals "stockpile" their contacts. If only strong or recent ties mediated mobility, this could not be true, but since relatively weak ones may be crucial, working on a job for two or three years may be sufficient to build a tie that will later be useful (though this is generally unanticipated). Too short a time may not be enough, since one's contact must have a definite impression of one's abilities and personality; staying too long in one's jobs, on the other hand, may foreclose future mobility by truncating the pool of personal contacts one might otherwise have built up" (Granovetter, 1974:85).

I found, correspondingly, that those whose average job tenure over the career was intermediate were much more likely to have found the current job through contacts than those with short or long tenures. Moreover, the modal categories for proportion of jobs in career found through contacts, in my sample, were none and all, suggesting strong individual differences in the extent to which contacts have been "stockpiled" (Granovetter 1974:90). This outcome may result from a stochastic process in which early events are crucial: Initial mobility generates contacts, who facilitate further mobility, and so on. Branching processes, a reasonable analogue for this "snowball" sequence of events, yield bimodal results under relatively simple assumptions (see, e.g., Feller, 1957:274–276).

Many job separations may thus be voluntary and may reflect perception of better opportunities, rather than otherwise unexplained personal "propensities" to move. This suggestion is supported by cases in my sample where long tenures reduced mobility. I was struck by the dilemma of individuals whose long tenures were interrupted by conglomerate acquisition of their firm and attendant "housecleaning." Despite what appeared excellent qualifications, they were enormously disadvantaged in the job market because they knew almost no one in other firms and were consequently not taken seriously by employers accustomed to recruiting via personalized information.

These individuals were typically in firms where others also had long tenures; thus, those who knew them well had themselves never moved to other firms where they might be in a position to help. This points up that tenure length is a characteristic of firms, not only of individuals, and thus results in part from organizational characteristics (see Granovetter, 1974:88–90; Pfeffer, 1983). My argument is inconsistent both with assertions that long tenures represent a "good match" and a high "propensity" to "stay put." Instead, long tenures may indicate a deficiency of opportunity attributable in part to the details of previous mobility history; short tenures may, conversely, result from ample opportunity rather than poor matches or "ants in the pants."

What does other empirical evidence show? Mincer and Jovanovic (1981:38ff) found that prior mobility does not influence current wages for younger men but reduces them for older. But they did not distinguish between voluntary and involuntary mobility. Sorenson (1974:55–60) showed, with longitudinal data, better gains in income and occupational prestige, for voluntary than for involuntary moves. Bartel and Borjas's (1981) analysis of the NLS indicated that older men have negative and younger men positive returns to quits. At first glance this supports the story of job-shopping and increasingly better matches but they then disaggregate quits into those caused by "pushes" (job dissatisfaction) and "pulls" (better opportunities). When older men quit to pursue a better opportunity, their wage growth is positive, and greater than that of younger men who do so. The overall lower return to quits for older men results from the higher proportion of "dissatisfaction" quits they report; these do not create wage growth because most workers in this category "gave reasons relating to nonwage aspects of the job. Thus there is no obvious reason to expect any kind of wage increase for this group" (Bartel and Borjas, 1981:69). These findings are consistent with my sociological argument, and they show the need to disaggregate mobility events rather than assuming that all mobility at a given career stage is similar. Some studies consider explicitly the relation between contact networks and economic returns. In my own data, voluntary mobility among older men is overwhelmingly in response to better opportunities offered through contacts. I cannot assess wage growth, but it is clear in cross section that those who found their current jobs through contacts reported substantially higher wages than those using other methods (Granovetter, 1974:14–16). Corcoran, Datcher, and Duncan (1980:33–36) use PSID data and show positive wage returns to the use of contacts only for some groups and in certain specifications. But the levels of aggregation used in their analysis of men and women under 45, from all occupational groups, were too high to sort out the impact of contacts: Only distinctions of race and sex were made. Since information found via contact networks carries the main burden of allocating workers among jobs, we cannot expect that higher wages will invariably result; the variety of circumstances where contacts are used is simply too great. Important distinctions beyond race, sex, and age are as follows. (1) Voluntary versus involuntary immobility. When mobility is involuntary, individuals are much more likely to take the first job that comes along, and may then use personal contacts less well placed than those they might access from a position of greater security (Granovetter, 1974:44). This suggests the importance of (2) the kinds of resources available to individuals through their contacts. There is mounting evidence, hardly surprising, but important in any general account, that resources available from one's contact network will not exceed those characteristic of it. Thus, Mostacci-Calzavara (1982:153), in her Toronto sample, found that blue-collar, same-ethnic-group ties often led to jobs even in ethnic groups with low incomes, but the lower the income in one's group, the less advantage in income from using one's same-group contact network over other means of finding jobs. Also important is (3) the characteristics of the relationship that mediates mobility. Mostacci-Calzavara (1982) and Ericksen and Yancey (1980:24–25) found that jobs located through weak ties have higher incomes than those resulting from strong ties. This is explained by my 1973 argument that since one's acquaintances are less likely to know one another than are one's close friends, information received from them is less likely to be redundant (see also Granovetter, 1981, 1983). Lin, Ensel, and Vaughn (1981) showed that the use of weak ties in finding jobs has a strong association with occupational standing achieved, but only insofar as these ties connected respondents to others well placed in the occupational structure, a connection achieved with much greater probability through weak than strong ties. This combination of factors (2) and (3) may explain why the income advantage associated with weak ties in the Ericksen and Yancey study is found only for those with a high school diploma or greater, and increases in size with education. Finally, some implications of my general argument are consistent with results from studies of unemployment. Some unemployment is made up of those out of work for long periods (Akerlof and Main, 1980; Clark and Summers, 1979; Disney, 1979; Feldstein, 1973; Stern, 1979). For such workers, my argument suggests reasons different from the usually cited personal disabilities. The bimodality in size distribution of labor-market contacts and the self-sustaining character of job mobility imply that certain workers will have contacts to "signal" their productivity (cf. Spence, 1974). Their continuing failure in the labor market dampens their prospects not only by hurting their reputations (cf. Ghez, 1981) but also by continuing to prevent acquisition of contacts.

The process may begin early in the career. Economists Meyer and Wise (1982) found that the number of hours worked in high school is strongly related to weeks worked after high school—even four years after graduation. Effects on wages are weaker but positive. They comment that the strength and duration of this effect suggests that it results less from what is learned at the early jobs than from "personal characteristics not gained through work but leading to work in high school as well as greater labor force participation following graduation" (Meyer and Wise, 1982:306). These personal characteristics are identified as "ill-defined attributes associated with working hard and 'doing well,'" such as the "work ethic" and a high "propensity to work" (Meyer and Wise, 1982:327).

Though not so cast explicitly, this is yet another heterogeneity-state-dependence formulation that interprets the former as a matter of personal characteristics. To fall back on the "work ethic" is not exactly a neoclassical argument, but it is consistent with an atomized view of behavior. A more sociological interpretation would be that those who work in high school are indeed "heterogeneous," but that their difference consists of being those whose families and friends have offered significant help in finding jobs. This would help explain why, net of parents' income and education, nonwhites work much less in high school than whites (Meyer and Wise, 1982:309): Nonwhites are less connected to the structure of jobs and have less influence on hiring even when they are connected. This interpretation is consistent with Clark and Summers's (1982:204) argument that "for many teenagers, job search is a passive process in which the main activity is waiting for a job to be presented." In their data, while "only about a third of the unemployed find a job within a month, almost two-thirds of [teenage] labor-force entrants are successful within a month. This strongly suggests that many people only enter the labor force when a job is presented" (Clark and Summers, 1982:204–205). They also conclude that racial differences in youth unemployment rates are not due to blacks' being laid off or quitting but rather to their difficulty in initially entering the labor force (Clark and Summers, 1982:218). Thus, long-term unemployment may be traceable for some to a weak early start, making it difficult for contacts to snowball over time as they do in successful careers. Each period of failure feeds on the previous one. Not only unemployment but underemployment may have this effect since poor matching of one's abilities to jobs will make it difficult for one's actual skills to become widely known even to those in one's own workplace.

The empirical studies reviewed here present substantial evidence consistent with my sociological arguments on labor mobility, but since most were not directly addressed to arguments of this kind, this is not a conclusive demonstration. More studies are needed that directly consider the social embeddedness of labor mobility as a determinant of labor market outcomes.

IV. IMPLICIT CONTRACTS, EFFICIENCY WAGES, AND EMPLOYEE BEHAVIOR

Many of the perplexing puzzles of recent labor economics involve the existence of employee "loyalty" to firms. Of special interest is the impact of such loyalty on employee work effort, and on decisions to remain in or leave a firm. Two branches of the economic literature on these questions are those on "implicit contracts" and on "efficiency wages."

By "implicit contracts" is meant nonbinding commitments from employers to offer such advantages as continuity of wages, employment, and working conditions, and from employees to forgo such temptations as shirking and quitting for better opportunities (Akerlof and Miyazaki, 1980; Azariadis, 1975; Baily, 1974). Such "contracts" are said to stem mistrust: Long-term relationships require employees and employers to believe that the other will not act against one's interest at every opportunity to do so. Arthur Okun

(1980:84), who refers to implicit contracts as the "invisible handshake," comments that it "neither explicit nor implicit contracts could be developed that curbed the role of distrust, firms would be obliged to pursue the strategy of hiring casual workers." Much of this literature finds that apparently inefficient practices such as wage stickiness, seniority, and worker attachment to firms result from implicit contracts that are (by various criteria) optimal.

Efficiency wage arguments (see the useful summary in Yellen, 1984) have a less Panglossian tone. They address the much neglected aspect of labor supply that concerns individual work effort. All the models assume that workers' productivity depends in part on their wage—a major departure from the orthodox assumption that the productivity of labor is simply given by the technical conditions summarized by a production function. Some efficiency-wage models nevertheless stay on firm neoclassical ground, by assuming that the relation between wage and productivity is a matter of how incentives are arranged: Higher than market-clearing wages for some results in involuntary unemployment for others, and these conditions raise the cost of being fired, thus discouraging the low productivity that is called "shirking" in this literature. But some efficiency-wage arguments depart from purely economic motivations, arguing that higher wages may encourage worker loyalty to the firm, and thereby affect production by their impact on group output norms (Akerlof, 1982, 1984).

Here I focus on the social context in which employers and employees actually *develop* expectations about one another's behavior. Arguments about implicit contracts and efficiency wages depict workers' behavior in too atomized a way to capture the most important forces in the labor situation that affect loyalty and effort. My criticism has two main aspects. First, both literatures treat the relations between employers and employees as occurring between individuals whose information about one another is limited to formal education signals or generalized employer reputation. Second, both take the relations between employer and employee, and that among members of a work group, out of their context in a larger work organization, and thus neglect the way relations *among* groups and cascades of effects from group to group affect individual behavior and social relations, and vice versa.

There is substantial empirical evidence that employers and employees do not face one another as strangers, thus needing to rely on institutional arrangements to determine incentives. Rather, they often know a great deal about one another before ever entering the employment relationship. In my study of newly hired professional, technical, and managerial workers, nearly one in five reported having found out about the current job directly from the employer, whom he already knew. Another one in three heard from someone who worked in the same firm or from a business friend of the employer (Granovetter, 1974:46). Though these data do not reveal how many of those contacts who worked in the firm actually knew the employer, responses from a more intensively studied subsample indicate that about three out of four did (Granovetter, 1974:57). It thus appears that 80 to 90%

of the cases where contacts are used involve the employer or the employer's own contacts. If learning of a job through contacts mainly meant that information came from friends or friends of friends of employers—long diffusion chains—this information would not differ much in quality from what could be found through want ads or the employment service. In fact, however, diffusion chains were overwhelmingly short, indicating focused and reliable information connecting employers and employees before hiring occurs.

From evidence in other studies (Corcoran *et al.*, 1980; Langlois, 1977; Shack-Marquez and Berg, 1982) it appears that, depending on the exact question asked, from one-sixth to one-half of those entering new employment contracts have prior information about, and/or relations with, the other party that are bound to affect expectations and trust. In small firms the actual employer is highly likely to be part of this prior information, and since workers are substantially more likely to enter small firms than large through personal contacts (Granovetter, 1974:128—where "small" means less than 100), we may surmise that many "new" employer-employee relations in small firms are actually continuations of earlier dealings. Such small firms are more important in economic life than suggested by the image of typical employees as working in large manufacturing firms. Various estimates put the proportion of private sector U.S. employees in establishments of 100 workers or fewer at between 49 and 60%, and 26 to 38% are in those of 20 or fewer (Granovetter, 1984:327). Of particular interest for the present argument, there is evidence that the smallest firms, of 20 or fewer, generate from one-half to two-thirds of all new jobs (Greene, 1982).

In larger firms, employees' prior information may be less likely to be *directly* about those with authority to alter implicit or explicit agreements, but it still has implications for expectations of employer behavior, for worker effort, and for likely job tenure; this is because those entering a workplace through personal contacts have a ready entree to the informal relations that not only create a comfortable social niche but also smooth the way for learning "the ropes"—the subtle and idiosyncratic features of jobs whose understanding may spell the difference between success and failure.

Furthermore, the fact that employees have begun their jobs with personal information about the firm, the employer, or other employees should reduce the chance of separation by making unlikely gross mismatches due to ignorance. It should also enhance the level of trust, not only because of previous knowledge but also because of social relationships that have become overlaid on initially economic ones. Difficulties and grievances may be a source of separation where no mechanism exists for resolving them, as has been shown in the effect of unions in reducing quit rates (Freeman, 1980). Reservoirs of trust and interpersonal knowledge may serve a similar function, especially in small nonunion firms. Empirical evidence is generally supportive of these arguments (e.g., Bluedorn, 1982:89; Granovetter, 1974:15; Price, 1977:70–73; Shack-Marquez and Berg, 1982:20–21; Shapero, Howell, and Tombaugh, 1965:50).

It is also misleading to suppose that expectations, wage and separation decisions, and level of worker loyalty and effort evolve entirely as the result of pairwise relations—between employees and employers—or even from the norms of a work group, taken in isolation from other work groups. Particularly in organizations characterized by long tenures, and this is especially where implicit contract and efficiency wage arguments are directed, it is inappropriate to view employees as engaged in separate agreements that do not impinge on one another. Such a conception is more appropriate to spot markets. Solow (1980:9) notes that "the stability of the labor pool makes it possible for social conventions to assume some importance. There is a difference between a long-term relationship and a one-night stand, and acceptable behavior in one context may be unacceptable in another." When many employees have long tenures, the conditions are met for a stable network of relationships, shared understandings, and political coalitions to be constructed (see Homans, 1950, 1974, for relevant social psychological discussions). Lincoln (1982) notes that in Max Weber's conception of bureaucracy, formal organizations are "designed to function independently of the collective actions which can be mobilized through interpersonal networks. Bureaucracy prescribes fixed relationships among positions through which incumbents flow, without, in theory, affecting organizational operations." He goes on to summarize sociological studies, however, showing that "when turnover is low, relations take on additional contents of an expressive and personal sort which may ultimately transform the network and change the directions of the organization" (Lincoln, 1982:26).

Such internal organizational "atmospheres" (Williamson, 1975), "cultures," or "esprit de corps" may themselves make an important further contribution to individual attachments and relate closely to expenditure of effort. Though concepts like these have become popular in the economic literature, there is rarely an attempt to show how such cultural phenomena originate; rather, they are treated as givens, with some impact in situations where more purely economic variables have failed to explain all behavior. My claim is that these "atmospheres" are the accumulated outcome of social relations whose structure and history must be analyzed to understand what has occurred. William Foote Whyte (1955:Chap. 11), for example, tells the story of industrial relations at the Chicago Inland Container plant that resulted in a substantial rise in productivity from 1946 to 1948. What was crucial was the development of good relations between low- to mid-level management and union officials; these relations then acted as bridges to higher management to lever changes in how time rates were set. Once this happened, the "atmosphere" in the plant changed and production rose "phenomenally." Yet there had been only minor changes in the incentive rates—the object of wage-efficiency theories. While the level of abstract analysis offered by Whyte of the process by which this occurred is not adequate to lead to a general argument about the conditions under which this takes place, it is clear from the account that a neglect of social relations and their accumulated results would leave us with no understanding whatever of the crucial changes that occurred.

It is similarly problematic to call on the "norms" of a work group to explain its productivity in the absence of some account of whence those norms derive. Akerlof (1982, 1984), in his arguments about "partial gift exchange" and efficiency wages, attempts to ground these norms in employer wage policy, suggesting that "in most jobs, keeping busy makes the time go faster. . . . Payment of a fair wage legitimizes for the worker the use of this busyness for the advantage of the firm" (Akerlof, 1984:82). This statement is apt as far as it goes, but it leaves up for grabs the crucial issue of how groups decide what is a fair wage, and assumes that industrial work groups are merely passive recipients of whatever wage employers offer. In fact, highly paid work groups and categories may have this high wage as the result of concerted political activity, especially in unionized settings. It is clear that some work groups are characteristically much more involved in such concerted action than others (Sayles, 1958), and the groups that are successful in this action are often highly productive. One might then look in cross section at their high wages and argue that these wages have led to loyalty. But Sayles suggests instead that groups that have successfully pursued their own economic interests develop, for this reason, a sense of efficacy, cohesion, and esprit de corps that shows up in higher productivity (Sayles, 1958:112–113).

The question of which groups in large industrial firms are active in forwarding their own economic interests is one that can be successfully answered only by considering the place of a group in the firm's overall social structure. In Sayles's comprehensive study of 300 work groups in 22 plants (1958), there were two identifying characteristics of such groups. One was that they consisted of members whose work was similar to one another's, as opposed to complementary and interdependent, but who worked together; the other was that their relative status in the firm was ambiguous. In explaining why highly interdependent groups have difficulty mounting collective action, Sayles (1958:76) points out that the intensity of interaction in such groups can reduce its ability to combine with other groups with similar economic interests. "Each crew or short assembly line . . . can become really a world to itself. The close ties of the members to this work unit make loyalty to some larger interest group difficult to sustain." In terms of an argument I have made, the strong ties within highly interdependent groups close the group off, making difficult the formation of weak ties to other groups of the sort that have the potential to channel activity from one part of the social structure to another (Granovetter, 1973, 1983).

Furthermore, active groups tended to be in the middle range of the plant hierarchies, in jobs neither "obviously and inevitably undesirable" nor "manifestly the most superior available" (Sayles, 1958:49), so there was some room to seek a change in relative status. They were also often jobs not well defined by the local labor market. Being in the middle of the hierarchy, they were not hiring-in jobs like many jobs at the bottom or the top, but steps on an internal promotional ladder. "As a result, what are fair and equitable wage rates, in terms of the 'going rate' in the community, tend to be substantially more ambiguous for the middle range of occupations" (Sayles 1958:49).[4]

As a general matter, the question of how workers make the wage comparisons that determine whether they think they are fairly paid has received little research attention (see Gartrell, 1982, for one important exception). Yet as far back as the 1940s, labor economist John Dunlop and his students had noticed that certain jobs are "key jobs" in that if their wages change, this sets off a chain reaction of other changes in associated jobs, which, all together, make up a "job cluster"; and among firms, certain ones are key firms in this sense and there are correspondingly sets of firms that make up a "wage contour" (Dunlop, 1957). Doeringer and Piore (1971:89) later noted that jobs "which involve wide contacts with other workers acquire a strategic position in the internal wage structure which makes it impossible to change their wages without adjustments throughout the system." There is here an implicit social structural argument that workers are more likely to compare their wages to those of workers they frequently interact with. Sayles's general argument that these patterns of interaction are mainly determined by what he calls "technology"—including the way the firm arranges the flow of work within and between groups—remains to be investigated fully. Gartrell's (1982) empirical study indicates that there are a substantial number of wage comparisons made between workers in *different* internal labor markets, and that these comparisons are generally not, in the nature of the case, based on work interactions but rather follow the contours of existing social networks. He suggests that by "ignoring social networks outside of internal labor markets and the wage information which is conveyed through them, the institutional literature underestimates the extent of interdependence between wage-determining units" (Gartrell, 1982:29–30).

V. INTERNAL LABOR MARKETS AND PROMOTION

One of the major factors that affects worker performance and the likelihood of mobility between firms is the chances of promotion within internal labor markets. Labor economists have treated promotion as an important aspect of implicit contracts, which matches revealed productivity to wages. Jovanovic asserts that individual "contracting creates a structure of rewards that provides proper signals for the attainment of optimal matches. . . . a widely prevalent example is a system of promotion . . . based on the quality of workers' performance" (Jovanovic, 1979a:974; see also Malcolmson, 1984). Williamson, Wachter, and Harris (1975:275–276 believe that though wages and marginal productivity may not correspond closely at "ports of entry," "productivity differentials will be recognized over time and a more perfect correspondence can be expected for high level assignments in the internal labor market job hierarchy."

A different—though equally functionalist—interpretation is the Marxist argument that fine distinctions among jobs and multiplication of levels serve mainly to create artificial barriers among workers, via competition for promotion, thus avoiding a united working class (Gordon, Edwards, and Reich, 1982). Edwards's related account of "bureaucratic control" has in common with the neoclassical version that it assumes promotions to result principally from workers' performing according to bureaucratically stated criteria.

All of these accounts neglect the embeddedness of promotion judgments and actions in social structure. I will first argue that even if productivity were easily measurable it would not be the sole or even main explanation of promotion chances. I then discuss some of the difficulties in measuring productivity. Among the bases for promotion unrelated to productivity are seniority and ethnicity. Abraham and Medoff (1983:8) surveyed 392 firms and estimate that about 60% of private sector, nonagricultural employees are in settings where senior employees are favored for promotion even over junior ones thought more productive. In one-third of firms employing mainly unionized hourly employees, respondents asserted that junior employees are *never* promoted ahead of senior ones, regardless of the size of productivity differential (Abraham and Medoff, 1983:9).

Evidence on ethnic and personal bases for promotion is mostly anecdotal. Dalton's (1959:184) data on a midwestern chemical plant show, for example, that "ethnics composing probably less than 38% of the community filled 85% of . . . advisory and directive forces." Informants described the situation less politely: "Nearly all the big boys are in the Yacht Club, and damn near all of 'em are Masons. . . . Hell, these guys all play poker together. Their wives run around together. . . . Seniority, knowledge or ability don't count. You've got to be a suckass and a joiner" (Dalton, 1959:154). But even here Dalton stresses the importance of minimal qualifications and the desire of superiors to recruit and promote individuals politically useful to them in the complex coalitions that have so much impact on what gets done in the plant.

Promotion by seniority may have similar roots: More senior employees will have had a longer time to develop pivotal roles in networks of political influence and coalition within workplaces, and to have performed important services over the years for those in a position to promote. Supervisors who promote do not merely winnow talent but also act politically to place strategically those loyal to their personal aims and procedures. This may help explain why even in nonunion settings, more than half the firms responding to Abraham and Medoff's survey indicated promotion preference for more senior employees. Such an account sees the preference for promotion by seniority as the result of actors with strategic motives pursuing their aims—some economic, some noneconomic—in established networks of social relations, rather than merely as an exercise of union power on behalf of older employees, or as part of some elaborate structure of incentives in an unobservable implicit contract.

Rosenbaum has extensively studied promotions in a large investor-owned company having "offices in many cities and towns in one region of the United States" (Rosenbaum, 1979a,b, 1981, 1984). Conceding that promotions do serve the need to recruit to higher levels and thus will be decided on productivity criteria in part, he also points out the importance of promotions in the social comparisons workers make. Since "promotions are . . . one of the most important rewards in an organization, . . . they must be allocated in a way that gives hope and motivation to the maximum number of employees." Promotion chances, that is, "are likely to be an effective way of controlling employees, offering the possibility of material rewards and symbolic status to a far larger number of people than can possibly receive the actual promotions" (Rosenbaum, 1979a:27).

A pure productivity criterion might limit promotion to younger employees with more years to contribute, who are likely to be recognized as deserving soon if at all. But an age cutoff would depress the motivation of older employees; Medoff and Abraham (1980:732) note that within a grade level, those with most experience are behind their cohort in relative advancement and thus are likely to doubt they are on the "fast track," with consequent reduction in effort. Rosenbaum (1979a:28) thus suggests that sharp age discontinuities in the distribution of those promoted are avoided so "no age group suddenly perceives itself disproportionately deprived relative to its immediately younger cohort." His analysis of promotions from 1962 to 1972, based on personnel data, substantiates this argument. He finds, further, that periods of high growth increase promotion chances only for older employees, whose chances decline correspondingly in downturns. This further suggests the discretionary and motivational component of such promotions. The importance of social comparisons thus makes promotion policy a way to affect productive effort even among those not promoted—a more complex process than envisioned in wage-efficiency arguments.

Another determinant of promotion independent of productivity is demographic: the sheer availability of advancement opportunities. White (1970) points out that opportunity occurs in chains: A retirement or the creation of a new job creates a vacancy that pulls someone in. This new incumbent creates a vacancy in his previous job, which pulls in another person, and so on. The chain of vacancies ends when an individual enters without having previously held a job (e.g., a student) or when the job in which the vacancy appears is left unfilled. Rates of retirement or labor force entry have to do with general population demographics (see also Sorensen and Tuma, 1981), whereas rates of creation and abolition of jobs depend on the business cycle. These four rates, determining the lengths of "vacancy chains," closely determine the number of promotion opportunities. Stewman and Konda (1983) have shown that formal models in demography can be adapted to help explain promotion rates; this effort indicates complex interactions between the structure of organizational hierarchies and the sizes of various cohorts moving through them.

Now consider some problems in measuring productivity. March and March (1978) develop a model of "performance sampling," where skill exists unambiguously, but those in charge of promotion cannot observe it continuously but only take occasional samples, either because they are not in constant contact or because situations that indicate competence only arise from time to time. This argument is statistically related to the literature on quality control and implies that even in a skill-homogeneous population, career success would result in part from sampling variation. This suggests one reason why tenure is related inversely to chances of separation: Early in the job, samples of performance will be small, so the proportion of successes inferred to be characteristic will err substantially on the high or low side, leading to promotion or dismissal. Those with longer tenures will have larger samples of performance with less variance, and thus will not be promoted or dismissed for these statistical reasons alone (March and March, 1978:450–451).[5] Some "stars" will thus be thrown up by the promotion system without regard to actual ability. Stewman and Konda (1983:672) obtain a similar result from purely demographic considerations of cohort size.

In his empirical study, Rosenbaum correspondingly found great importance in early promotion histories. As in high school curriculum tracking, early winners are "seen as 'high-potential' people who can do no wrong, and who are given additional opportunities and challenges while those who do not win the early competition are given little or no chance to prove themselves again." By the "third year of employment, an employee's eventual career chances have been fundamentally affected" (Rosenbaum, 1981:236, 238). In Rosenbaum's account, productivity seems less a fixed trait of individuals than an outcome of social expectations and interactions endogenous to promotion history. *The parallel to infirm mobility, where I also argued early mobility to be self-sustaining, is important.*

Where productivity is ambiguous, those in charge of promotion must rely on various signals. Rosenbaum (1981:112) finds that the quality of college attended has substantial net effects, and that having attended a local college has greater impact than could be expected from its quality level alone. I suggest that this entails the role of key personal contacts acquired in local colleges who have connections to this corporation; the role of such contacts in conferring initial and continuing advantages in promotion deserves further investigation. The importance of contacts between educational institutions and corporate settings for early career advantage has been extensively documented for Japan (Taira and Wada, 1987). Pfeffer (1977:556) argues that certain situations make productivity evaluation especially hard: staff rather than line positions, small rather than large organizations, and industries where "personal contact is likely to be more important" in one's work, such as financial services as opposed to manufacturing. He finds that in such situations, socioeconomic origins affect salary more, for a sample of business school graduates at a "large, prestigious state university."

Ample evidence shows that productivity is rarely measured well except in certain well-defined and individualized jobs such as typing (e.g., Medoff and Abraham, 1981). The difficulties of measurement are not merely technical. Rather, the productivity of individual workers is inextricably intermeshed in a network of relations with other workers. Slichter pointed out in 1919 that inadequate instruction "in how to do the work frequently causes men to appear to be incompetent, when, if properly taught, they could do the new job easily" (Slichter, 1919:207). But why should training be inadequate? Economists have suggested some institutional reasons. Freeman and Medoff (1980:77) assert that under unionism, rewards depend less on performance and more on seniority, so competition among individuals is mitigated and workers will give one another more informal assistance. Thurow (1975:81) suggests that competition for jobs is typically limited to the entry level and employment security provided beyond that level, so workers will not be afraid to provide on-the-job training to those less experienced.

These arguments are apt but recognize insufficiently the embeddedness of helping relationships in a network of informal exchanges closely tied to status distinctions, friendships, and sponsor-protégé relations. Since the Western Electric studies first demonstrated the intimate relation between productivity and group structure (Homans, 1950; Roethlisberger and Dickson, 1939; Sonnenfeld, 1980), this connection has been pursued vigorously by industrial sociologists (Sayles, 1958; Whyte, 1955). Some of the processes are subtle and might easily escape attention. Dalton describes the case of a black worker in a chemical plant who had the seniority to operate some delicate and complex equipment, and the necessary experience with similar but less intricate machines. His promotion was resisted by the group of all white workers he would have joined, who did not want such a "precedent" set. He filed a successful grievance with the union and was promoted, but was told that "he would be 'entirely' on his own and would 'assume all responsibility for the job'. [This] meant that he would not receive the usual preliminary guidance given to others taking these jobs. The processes in this department were dangerous in that both the product and chemicals used . . . were either corrosive, lethal to inhale or highly inflammable and explosive" (Dalton, 1959:128–129). The worker withdrew from the promotion.

The white workers had violated no explicit rule but had made clear that the social position of the black worker was such that he would not receive the usual assistance necessary to perform the job properly. His "productivity" in the job was thus shown to be not the individual attribute of human capital formulations but rather the result of a structure of social relations oriented to noneconomic as well as economic aims. This example should not be pigeonholed into the category of "discrimination"; it is only a variant of group processes that affect the productivity of all workers where informal on-the-job training is significant.

To sum up this section: Even if productivity were easily gauged, promotions often result from motives or causes not clearly related to it, but easily understandable when relevant social structures and motives are analyzed. When one adds to this consideration the evidence of problems in measuring productivity, and that such measurement is ambiguous in part because of the strong effects of the social context of production, it seems naive to suppose that promotion systems are nothing more than efficient talent sieves and that firms can thus be in a position to promise implicitly or explicitly that employees' productive efforts will always be appropriately rewarded.

VI. INTERNAL LABOR MARKETS, INTERFIRM MOBILITY, AND THE OPTIMALITY OF LABOR ALLOCATION

The prevalence of large internal labor markets with extensive promotion ladders and implicit or explicit promises of long tenures must discourage interfirm mobility. This implies that internal markets have a self-perpetuating character quite independent of their efficiency characteristics, which casts doubt on adaptive stories that trumpet the optimality of these employment arrangements. The dynamics of this self-perpetuation have to do in part simply with the relative proportions of positions inside and outside such internal labor markets. Doeringer and Piore (1971:38) comment that "the relative security of an open market is a function of its size and of the diversity of industries within it. If any employer withdraws jobs from a competitive market and allocates them internally, the job security of workers in other establishments is thereby reduced and the value of an internal market to them is correspondingly enhanced." The structure of contact networks generated in systems with large internal markets also contributes to their perpetuation. This is so because interfirm mobility generates contacts who make possible further mobility; thus, in systems with little such movement one knows mainly others in one's own firm and is thus less able to move to other firms since one's ability cannot be certified there with the confidence that comes through personalized information.

These arguments, rather than widely alleged "cultural" differences, may help explain why, comparing the individual mobility experiences of Yokohama versus Detroit workers, Cole found that, in every cohort, the proportion never changing employer in Yokohama is two or three times greater than in Detroit, and that those who do change employers in Yokohama do so significantly less often than those in Detroit (Cole, 1979:64, 68). The self-perpetuation of internal markets seems especially likely in a large urban location like Yokohama, where the large firms that contain such markets are much more important than in other parts of Japan.

But if internal markets perpetuate themselves and workers move within and among firms for reasons having more to do with social structure than with how well they are matched to jobs, it becomes hard to credit the equation of long tenure to good job matches current in neoclassical labor economics. Moreover, the very notion of the "quality" of a job match is poorly developed. For this concept to have clear denotation requires well-developed theory and evidence on the comparative advantage of workers in the set of available jobs, similar to the concept of comparative advantage in the theory of international trade.

The few discussions of this kind in the economics literature are extremely stylized (Rosen, 1978; Roy, 1953; Sattinger, 1980; Willis and Rosen, 1979), and the empirical prospects of assessing quality of matches in comparative advantage terms are dim. In the section on promotion I suggested the difficulty of measuring productivity on account of its embeddedness in a structure of social relations. Comparative advantage calculations require us to know not only one's productivity in the current job but also that in all other jobs one might have filled but did not. The theoretical literature in labor economics takes such calculations to involve the imputing of one or more dimensions of "ability" to workers and various levels of requirements for these dimensions to jobs. But this is precisely to ignore the empirical reality that productivity does not result from the characteristics of individuals and jobs alone. Individuals in jobs are not atomized from individuals in other jobs, but all together they make up a system that must be treated as such. Nor is it reasonable to take the set of jobs available as given independently of the population of workers. Many job accessions represent the filling of entirely new positions rather than of previously held vacancies. This was true of more than one in three for my sample of professional, technical, and managerial workers (Granovetter, 1974:15); many of these new jobs had in fact been tailored to the needs, preferences, and abilities of the workers recruited. Correspondingly, jobs found through personal contacts were much more likely than those found through other means to have been newly created (44% vs. 24%) and made up 70% of all newly created jobs in the sample (1974:15). Difficulties of this kind may explain why the theoretical literature on comparative advantage of workers in jobs has not yet been systematically linked with assertions about match quality in the empirical literature on labor mobility.

Some skepticism is thus warranted as to whether the praise of labor mobility in classical and postwar economics could have been utterly and completely misplaced. It seems too good to be true that after a period of job shopping ending around age 35, most workers will have found an optimal match. This is even less credible when workers are in a system of lifetime employment, so that the firm where one begins must be asserted to be just the one where his or her talents can be best utilized in the entire economy. Further, considerations of both equity and efficiency should lead us to ask whether any match advantages that do accrue to that part of the labor force in long tenures might be at the expense of others not able to take advantage of such arrangements. Firms that normally subcontract part of their operations may be able to guarantee employment to regular workers in a downturn only because of the possibility of dropping the subcontracts (Okun, 1980:107). Strong firms with well-developed internal labor markets can thus transfer the risk of cyclical fluctuations to weaker "peripheral" firms that depend on their subcontracts and must engage in large layoffs when demand falls off (Doeringer and Piore, 1971:173; Gordon et al., 1982:191, 200–201).

Japanese "permanent employment" conceals large numbers of temporary subcontract workers, whose numbers are underreported and who receive poor benefits and little job security. Many such workers are actually relatively long-term employees classified as temporary precisely to save the firm the expense of benefits and job security (Somers and Tsuda, 1966; Taira, 1970:161–162). In the 1974–1975 recession large firms dismissed temporary workers, and as many as 600,000 women may have left the labor force. "In short," remarks Cole, "employment security is much better for white-collar workers than blue-collar workers, for young workers than older workers . . . for employees in large firms than small firms . . . for male workers than female workers. . . . This overall system, with its ascriptive age and sex discrimination and dualistic labor market practices, hardly represents a model for the solution of the problems facing the United States" (Cole, 1979:263).

At the level of the firm, the efficiency of internal labor markets has been challenged. The 1950s emphasis on inflexibility of systems with low mobility is echoed for the Japanese case by Cole, who argues that internal labor markets were inefficient in recent periods of rapid technological change: "The education and training costs associated with having to upgrade established employees (who did not have the requisite skills) relative to recruitment on the external market may have been substantial" (Cole, 1979:120) but could be borne because of the expanding economy and the dominant position of these firms in their product markets.

Whether turnover adversely affects efficiency of firms is the subject of a complex literature. Price summarizes sociological studies indicating that the level of turnover is positively related to formalization and bureaucratization in firms, because without long-term relations a web of informal understandings is less likely to develop (Price, 1977:96–102). Increased turnover is associated also with increases in the ratio of administrative to productive employees, in part because of the increase in supervision, recruitment, and training activity, and in part because new administrators attempt to bring in additional staff loyal to themselves (Price, 1977:93–96). But the impact of formalization and increased proportions of administrators on productivity cannot be determined on abstract grounds lone; it is rather embedded in the particular history of the firm. In Gouldner's (1954), classic study of a gypsum mining and processing plant, managerial turnover resulted in bureaucratization that replaced an inefficient set of informal arrangements. One cannot conclude in general, however, that informal coalitions are less efficient than clear-cut formal procedures; if anything, the former are more often reported as having been adopted to escape the rigidities of the latter (Blau, 1963; Dalton, 1959).

In organizations where turnover is variable among units, those with lower turnover become more powerful because their continuity of personnel gives them advantages in understanding and manipulating the system (Bluedorn, 1982:108–109). In this connection one thinks of the French Third and Fourth Republics, where it was widely asserted that the civil bureaucracy was the real center of power since it stayed in place while governments came and went at revolving-door speed. Such unplanned devocation of power on persisting units may be efficient and adaptive in stable periods but they produce rigid resistance to change when it is needed. Pfeffer (1983) suggests that firms with long-term employment may become ingrown and that industries composed of such firms may suffer by losing the coordination that results from extensive interfirm mobility. By contrast, the frequent movement of personnel among firms may generate an industry-wide perspective since managers in each firm will know managers in most others from having once worked with them (Granovetter, 1974: Chap. 8; Pfeffer, 1983).

All in all, the impact of labor mobility and turnover at the level of firms, industries, and the economy as a whole cannot be easily assessed, and it presents far more complex questions than have yet been appreciated in the more microscopically oriented economic literature. One must agree with economist Robert Hall's comment that economists "have only just begun to examine the issues in the efficient movement of workers among firms" (Hall, 1980:108). Despite their potential to do so, sociologists have contributed even less to assessment of this question. I believe this is in large part because the general discrediting of structural-functional theory in macro-sociology has discouraged them from asking questions about efficiency. Healthy suspicion of Panglossian pitfalls and hidden value judgments has created an intellectual climate in which scholars do not even think of asking whether systems are functioning well; but this can be asked with reference to clearly stated criteria of efficient functioning and need not be oriented to showing that all is for the best.

VII. CONCLUSIONS

I have tried to show that the characteristically atomistic explanatory approaches of neoclassical economic theory to problems of labor markets give inadequate accounts both of individual economic action and of how this action cumulates into larger patterns, some of which come to be called "institutions." The failure to consider the embeddedness of individual behavior in networks of social and economic relations, and the mixture of economic and noneconomic motives, leads to the use of "adaptive stories" and appeal to "cultures" or "atmospheres" where institutional developments cannot be otherwise derived. Yet the use of such stories and appeals is broadly inconsistent with the usual methodological and individualist stance of most economists; closer attention to social structure would provide a more satisfactory account of how economic patterns arise.

For analytical purposes let me separate the two main issues I have raised: the embeddedness of economic action in networks of relations, and the intertwining of economic with noneconomic motives. Suppose that actors had only the economic motives and goals attributed to them in most economic analyses and, in addition, could be conceived as perfectly rational, given the information at hand. Then at least some of the spirit of neoclassical analysis could carry over to a treatment that took seriously the embeddedness of these actors in a network of relations. If, for example, as I have argued, the number of contacts one has in other firms who know one's characteristics both depends on one's past mobility and influences one's chance of future moves, it would be natural to construct models for "investment" in contacts and perhaps to assess optimal stopping rules for number of job changes. Such models would yield predictions of turnover and would also make the structure of networks partially endogenous to the economic process. Boorman's interesting model of investment in contacts for the purpose of acquiring job information (1975) has been amplified by Delany (1980) in a dynamic setting (see my further comments, Granovetter, 1981:25–26).

But while formal models may well be useful in elucidating such problems, I am skeptical as to what extent the usual neoclassical apparatus will be suitable. In particular, it is problematic whether utility functions—originally developed to represent an isolated individual's ordinal preferences over a universe of goods—can easily capture network effects. While Becker (1976) and others have used interdependent utility functions, where the utility of some other becomes an argument of your own function, this usage is usually confined to pairs of individuals, and the structure of a broader network of relations can probably not easily be incorporated, at least not in the current state of technical development.

The example of investment in contacts also points up to the extent to which noneconomic motives are mixed with economic ones. One's interaction with others is generally not confined to "economic investment activity": As with other aspects of economic life, striving for sociability, approval, status, and power also enter in. Indeed, a perception by others that one's interest in them is mainly a matter of "investment" will make this investment less likely to pay off; we are all on the lookout for those who only want to use us. Whether noneconomic motives can easily be incorporated into the typical formal models of neoclassical economics is again problematic, though there are some interesting attempts in this direction (Iannaccone, 1986; Kuran, 1986).

Whatever turns out to be the best methodology, better models of the labor market will result from a merger of the economists' sophistication about instrumental behavior and concerns with efficiency, and the sociologists' expertise on social structure and relations and the complex mixture of motives present in all actual situations. By laying economic and sociological models side by side for detailed comparison, I hope here to have clarified the advantages of, and obstacles to, such a merger, and thus to have brought it closer to fruition.

ACKNOWLEDGMENTS

I am indebted to Robert Averitt, Paula England, George Farkas, Randy Hodson, Kevin Lang, and Oliver Williamson for their helpful comments.

NOTES

1. For an extended argument on atomization in economic discourse see Granovetter, 1985.

2. For critical views of this neo-Darwinian argument see Blaug (1980:114–120) and Elster (1979:133–137).

3. Stochastic processes with a network component are more complex than those involving independent units, and resulting mathematical arguments would have to

be correspondingly recast (see Boorman, 1975; Erdos and Renyi, 1960; Kleinrock, 1964).

4. Compare the similar difficulty of determining transfer prices for intermediate goods with no external market (Eccles, 1985).

5. But note that this explanation assumes individuals' true ability to lie in the moderate range, suitable for retention, but not promotion or dismissal.

REFERENCES

Abraham, Katharine, and James Medoff. 1983. "Length of Service and the Operation of Internal Labor Markets." Sloan School of Management Working Paper, 1394–83. Massachusetts Institute of Technology.

Akerlof, George. 1982. "Labor Contracts as Partial Gift Exchange." *Quarterly Journal of Economics* 97:543–569.

Akerlof, George. 1984. "Gift Exchange and Efficiency-Wage Theory: Four Views." *American Economic Review* 74:79–83.

Akerlof, George, and Brian Main. 1980. "Unemployment Spells and Unemployment Experience." *American Economic Review* 70:885–893.

Akerlof, George, and H. Miyazaki. 1980. "The Implicit Contract Theory of Unemployment Meets the Wage Bill Argument." *Review of Economic Studies* 47:321–338.

Azariadis, C. 1975. "Implicit Contracts and Underemployment Equilibria." *Journal of Political Economy* 83:1183–1202.

Baily, Martin. 1974. "Wages and Unemployment Under Uncertain Demand." *Review of Economic Studies* 41:37–50.

Bakke, E. W., editor. 1954. *Labor Mobility and Economic Opportunity*. Cambridge, MA: MIT Press.

Bartel, Ann, and George Borjas. 1981. "Wage Growth and Job Turnover: An Empirical Analysis." Pp. 65–90 in *Studies in Labor Markets*, edited by S. Rosen. Chicago: University of Chicago Press.

Becker, Gary. 1976. *The Economic Approach to Human Behavior*. Chicago: University of Chicago Press.

Blaug, Mark. 1980. *The Methodology of Economics*. New York: Cambridge University Press.

Blau, Peter. 1963. *The Dynamics of Bureaucracy*. Chicago: University of Chicago Press.

Blau, Peter. 1964. *Exchange and Power in Social Life*. New York: Wiley.

Bluedorn, Allen. 1982. "The Theories of Turnover: Causes, Effects and Meaning." Pp. 75–128 in *Research in the Sociology of Organizations*, Vol. 1, edited by S. Bacharach. Greenwich, CT: JAI Press.

Boorman, Scott. 1975. "A Combinatorial Optimization Model for the Transmission of Job Information Through Contact Networks." *Bell Journal of Economics* 6:216–249.

Brissenden, Paul, and Emil Frankel. 1922. *Labor Turnover in Industry: A Statistical Analysis*. New York: Macmillan.

Clark, Kim, and Lawrence Summers. 1979. "Labor Market Dynamics and Unemployment." *Brookings Papers on Economic Activity* 1:13–60.

Clark, Kim, and Lawrence Summers, 1982. "The Dynamics of Youth Unemployment." Pp. 199–234 in *The Youth Labor Market*, edited by R. Freeman and D. Wise. Chicago: University of Chicago Press.

Cole, Robert. 1979. *Work, Mobility and Participation: A Comparative Study of American and Japanese Industry*. Berkeley: University of California Press.

Corcoran, Mary, Linda Datcher, and Greg Duncan. 1980. "Information and Influence Networks in Labor Markets." Pp. 1–37 in *Five Thousand American Families: Patterns of Economic Progress*, Vol. 8, edited by Greg Duncan and James Morgan. Ann Arbor: Institute for Social Research.

Corcoran, Mary, and Martha Hill. 1980. "Persistence in Unemployment among Adult Men." In Five Thousand American Families: Patterns of Economic Progress, Vol. 8, edited by Greg Duncan and James Morgan. Ann Arbor: Institute for Social Research.

Dalton, Melville. 1959. *Men Who Manage*. New York: Wiley.

Delany, John. 1980. Aspects of Donative Resource Allocation and the Efficiency of Social Networks: Simulation Models of Job Vacancy Information Transfers Through Personal Contacts. Unpublished doctoral dissertation, Yale University, Department of Sociology.

DiPrete, Thomas. 1981. "Unemployment over the Life Cycle." *American Journal of Sociology* 87:286–307.

Disney, R. 1979. "Recurrent Spells and the Concentration of Unemployment in Great Britain." *Economic Journal* 89:109–119.

Doeringer, Peter, and Michael Piore. 1971. *Internal Labor Markets and Manpower Analysis*. Lexington, MA: D. C. Heath.

Dunlop, John T. 1957. "The Task of Contemporary Wage Theory." Pp. 117–139 in *New Concepts in Wage Determination*, edited by G. Taylor and F. Pierson. New York: McGraw-Hill.

Eccles, Robert. 1985. *The Transfer Pricing Problem*. Lexington, MA: D. C. Heath.

Elster, Jon. 1979. *Ulysses and the Sirens*. New York: Cambridge University Press.

Erdos, P., and A. Renyi. 1960. "On the Evolution of Random Graphs." *Publications of the Mathematical Institute of the Hungarian Academy of Sciences* 5A:17–61.

Ericksen, Eugene, and William Yancey. 1980. "The Locus of Strong Ties." Mimeo, Department of Sociology, Temple University, Philadelphia.

Feldstein, Martin. 1973. "The Economics of the New Unemployment." *Public Interest* 33:3–42.

Feller, William. 1957. *An Introduction to Probability Theory and Its Applications*, Vol. 1. New York: Wiley.

Flinn, Christopher, and James Heckman. 1982a. "New Methods for Analyzing Individual Event Histories." Pp. 99–140 in *Sociological Methodology*, edited by S. Leinhardt. San Francisco: Jossey-Bass.

Freeman, Richard. 1980. "The Exit-Voice Tradeoff in the Labor Market: Unionism, Job Tenure, Quits and Separations." *Quarterly Journal of Economics* 94:643–676.

Freeman, Richard, and James Medoff. 1980. "The Two Faces of Unionism." *Public Interest* 39:69–93.

Gartrell, C. David. 1982. "On the Visibility of Wage Referents." *Canadian Journal of Sociology* 7:117–143.

Ghez, Gilbert. 1981. "Comment on Bartel and Borjas." Pp. 84–89 in *Studies in Labor Markets*, edited by S. Rosen. Chicago: University of Chicago Press.

Gordon, David, Richard Edwards, and Michael Reich. 1982. *Segmented Work, Divided Workers*. New York: Cambridge University Press.

Gould, Steven, and Richard Lewontin. 1979. "The Spandrels of San Marco and the Panglossian Paradigm: A Critique of the Adaptionist Programme." *Proceedings of the Royal Society of London* B205:581–598.

Gouldner, Alvin. 1954. *Patterns of Industrial Bureaucracy*. Glencoe, IL: Free Press.

Granovetter, Mark. 1973. "The Strength of Weak Ties." *American Journal of Sociology* 78:1360–1380.

Granovetter, Mark. 1974. *Getting a Job: A Study of Contacts and Careers.* Cambridge, MA: Harvard University Press.

Granovetter, Mark. 1981. "Toward a Sociological Theory of Income Differences." In *Sociological Perspectives on Labor Markets,* edited by I. Berg. New York: Academic Press.

Granovetter, Mark. 1983. "The Strength of Weak Ties: A Network Theory Revisited." *Sociological Theory* 1:201–233.

Granovetter, Mark. 1984. "Small is Bountiful: Labor Markets and Establishment Size." *American Sociological Review* 49:323–324.

Granovetter, Mark. 1985. "Economic Action and Social Structure: The Problem of Embeddedness." *American Journal of Sociology* 91:481–510.

Greene, Richard. 1982. "Tracking Job Growth in Private Industry." *Monthly Labor Review* 105 (9):3–9.

Hall, Robert. 1980. "Employment Fluctuations and Wage Rigidity." *Brookings Papers on Economic Activity* 1:91–123.

Hall, Robert. 1982. "The Importance of Lifetime Jobs in the U.S. Economy." *American Economic Review* 72:716–724.

Heath, Anthony. 1976. *Rational Choice and Social Exchange.* New York: Cambridge University Press.

Heckman, James. 1978. "Simple Statistical Models for Discrete Panel Data Developed and Applied to Test the Hypothesis of True State Dependence against the Hypothesis of Spurious State Dependence." *Annales de l'INSEE* 30–31:227–269.

Heckman, James. 1981. "Heterogeneity and State Dependence." Pp. 91–139 in *Studies in Labor Markets,* edited by S. Rosen. Chicago: University of Chicago Press.

Hirschman, Albert. 1977. *The Passions and the Interests.* Princeton: Princeton University Press.

Homans, George. 1950. *The Human Group.* New York: Harcourt Brace World.

Homans, George. 1974. *Social Behavior.* New York: Harcourt Brace Jovanovich.

Iannaccone, Laurence. 1988. "A Formal Model of Church and Sect." *American Journal of Sociology.*

Johnson, William. 1978. "A Theory of Job Shopping." *Quarterly Journal of Economics* 93:261–277.

Jovanovic, Boyan. 1979a. "Job Matching and the Theory of Turnover." *Journal of Political Economy* 87:972–990.

Jovanovic, Boyan. 1979b. "Firm-Specific Capital and Turnover." *Journal of Political Economy* 87:1246–1260.

Kerr, Clark. 1954. "The Balkanization of Labor Markets." Pp. 92–110 in *Labor Mobility and Economic Opportunity,* edited by E. W. Bakke, P. Hauser, G. Palmer, C. Myers, D. Yoder, and C. Kerr. Cambridge, MA: M.I.T. Press.

Kleinrock, L. 1964. *Communication Nets: Stochastic Message Flow and Delay.* New York: McGraw-Hill.

Kuran, Timur. 1986. "Preference Falsification, Policy Rigidity and Social Conservatism." Mimeo, Department of Economics, University of Southern California.

Langlois, Simon. 1977. "Les Reseaux Personnels et la Diffusion des Informations sur les Emplois." *Recherches Sociographiques* 2:213–245.

Lin, Nan, M. Ensel, and J. Vaughn. 1981. "Social Resources and Strength of Ties: Structural Factors in Occupational Status Attainment." *American Sociological Review* 46:393–405.

Lincoln, James. 1982. "Intra- (and Inter-) Organizational Networks." Pp. 1–38 in *Research in the Sociology of Organizations,* Vol. 1, edited by S. Bacharach. Greenwich, CT: JAI Press.

Main, Brian. 1982. "The Length of a Job in Great Britain." *Economica* 49 195:325–333.

Malcolmson, James M. 1984. "Work Incentives, Hierarchy and Internal Labor Markets." *Journal of Political Economy* 92:486–507.

March, James C., and James G. March. 1977. "Almost Random Careers: The Wisconsin School Superintendency, 1940–1972." *Administrative Science Quarterly* 22:377–408.

March, James C., and James G. March. 1978. "Performance Sampling in Social Matches." *Administrative Science Quarterly* 23:434–453.

Medoff, James, and Katharine Abraham. 1980. "Experience, Performance and Earnings." *Quarterly Journal of Economics* 95:703–736.

Medoff, James, and Katharine Abraham. 1981. "Are Those Paid More Really More Productive? The Case of Experience," *Journal of Human Resources* 16:186–216.

Merton, Robert. 1947. *Social Theory and Social Structure*. New York: Free Press.

Meyer, Robert, and David Wise. 1982. "High School Preparation and Early Labor Force Experience." Pp. 277–348 in *The Youth Labor Market Problem*, edited by R. Freeman and D. Wise. Chicago: University of Chicago Press.

Mincer, Jacob, and Boyan Jovanovic. 1981. "Labor Mobility and Wages." Pp. 21–63 in *Studies in Labor Markets*, edited by S. Rosen. Chicago: University of Chicago Press.

Mostacci-Calzavara, Liviana. 1982. Social Networks and Access to Job Opportunities. Doctoral dissertation, Department of Sociology, University of Toronto.

Okun, Arthur. 1980. *Prices and Quantities*. Washington, D.C.: Brookings Institution.

Pencavel, John. 1972. "Wages, Specific Training and Labor Turnover in U.S. Manufacturing Industries." *International Economic Review* 13:53–65.

Pfeffer, Jeffrey. 1977. "Toward an Examination of Stratification in Organizations." *Administrative Science Quarterly* 22:553–567.

Pfeffer, Jeffrey. 1983. "Organizational Demography." Pp. 299–357 in *Research in Organizational Behavior*, Vol. 5, edited by L. L. Cummings and B. Shaw, Greenwich, CT: JAI Press.

Price, James. 1977. *The Study of Turnover*. Ames: University of Iowa Press.

Reynolds, Lloyd. 1951. *The Structure of Labor Markets*. New York: Harper.

Roethlisberger, Fritz, and William Dickson. 1939. *Management and the Worker*. Cambridge, MA: Harvard University Press.

Rosen, Sherwin. 1978. "Substitution and the Division of Labour." *Economica* 45 179:235–250.

Rosen, Sherwin. 1981. "Introduction." In *Studies in Labor Markets*, edited by S. Rosen. Chicago: University of Chicago Press.

Rosenbaum, James. 1979a. "Organizational Career Mobility. Promotion Chances in a Corporation during Periods of Growth and Contraction." *American Journal of Sociology* 85:21–48.

Rosenbaum, James. 1979b. "Tournament Mobility: Career Patterns in a Corporation." *Administrative Science Quarterly* 24:220–241.

Rosenbaum, James. 1981. "Careers in a Corporate Hierarchy." In *Research in Social Stratification and Mobility*, Vol. 1, edited by D. Treiman and R. Robinson. Greenwich, CT: JAI Press.

Rosenbaum, James. 1984. *Career Mobility in a Corporate Hierarchy*. New York: Academic Press.

Ross, Arthur. 1958. "Do We Have a New Industrial Feudalism?" *American Economic Review* 48:903–920.

Roy, A. D. 1953. "Some Thoughts on the Distribution of Earnings." Oxford Economic Papers.

Sattinger, Michael. 1980. *Capital and the Distribution of Labor Earnings.* New York: North-Holland.

Sayles, Leonard. 1958. *The Behavior of Industrial Work Groups.* New York: Wiley.

Sekscenski, E. 1980. "Job Tenure Declines as Work Force Changes." Special Labor Force Report No. 235. Washington, D.C.: Bureau of Labor Statistics.

Shack-Marquez, Janice, and Ivar Berg. 1982. "Inside Information and the Employer-Employee Matching Process." Fels Discussion Paper 159, School of Public and Urban Policy, University of Pennsylvania.

Shapero, A., R. Howell, and J. Tombaugh. 1965. *The Structure and Dynamics of the Defense R and D Industry: The Los Angeles and Boston Complexes.* Menlo Park, CA: Stanford Research Institute.

Slichter, Sumner. 1919. *The Turnover of Factory Labor.* New York: Appleton.

Slichter, Sumner. 1920. "The Scope and Nature of the Labor Turnover Problem." *Quarterly Journal of Economics* 34:329–345.

Smith, Adam. 1976. *The Wealth of Nations.* Chicago: University of Chicago Press. (Originally published 1776).

Solow, Robert. 1980. "On Theories of Unemployment." *American Economic Review* 70:1–11.

Somers, G., and M. Tsuda. 1966. "Job Vacancies and Structural Change in Japanese Labor Markets." In *The Measurement and Interpretation of Job Vacancies*, edited by R. Ferber. New York: Columbia University Press.

Sonnenfeld, Jeffrey. 1980. "Hawthorne Hoopla in Perspective: Contextual Illumination and Critical Illusions." Working Paper No. HBS 81–60. Boston, Mass.: Harvard Business School.

Sorensen, Aage. 1974. "A Model for Occupational Careers." *American Journal of Sociology* 80:44–57.

Sorensen, Aage, and Nancy Tuma. 1981. "Labor Market Structures and Job Mobility." In *Research in Social Stratification and Mobility*, Vol. 1, edited by D. Treiman and R. Robinson. Greenwich, CT: JAI Press.

Spence, Michael. 1974. *Market Signaling.* Cambridge, MA: Harvard University Press.

Stern, Jon. 1979. "Who Bears the Burden of Unemployment?" In *Slow Growth in Britain*, edited by W. Beckerman. Oxford: Oxford University Press.

Stewman, Shelby, and Suresh Konda. 1983. "Careers and Organizational Labor Markets: Demographic Models of Organizational Behavior." *American Journal of Sociology* 88:637–685.

Taira, Koji. 1970. *Economic Development and the Labor Market in Japan.* New York: Columbia University Press.

Taira, Koji, and Teiichi Wada. 1987. "The Japanese Business—Government Relations: A Todai-Yakkai-Zaikai Complex?" Pp. 264–297 in *The Structural Analysis of Business*, edited by M. Schwartz and M. Mizruchi. New York: Cambridge University Press.

Thurow, Lester. 1975. *Generating Inequality.* New York: Basic Books.

Tilly, Charles. 1978. *From Mobilization to Revolution.* Reading, MA: Addison-Wesley.

Tuma, Nancy. 1976. "Rewards, Resources and the Rate of Mobility: A Non-Stationary Multivariate Stochastic Model." *American Sociological Review* 41:338–360.

Weber, Max. 1968. *Economy and Society.* Translated and edited by G. Roth and C. Wittich. Totowa, NJ: Bedminster Press. (Originally published 1921.)

White, Harrison. 1970. *Chains of Opportunity: System Models of Mobility in Organizations.* Cambridge, MA: Harvard University Press.

Whyte, William F. 1955. *Money and Motivation.* New York: Harper.

Williamson, Oliver. 1975. *Markets and Hierarchies.* New York: Free Press.

Williamson, Oliver, M. Wachter, and J. Harris. 1975. "Understanding the Employment Relation: The Analysis of Idiosyncratic Exchange." *Bell Journal of Economics* 6:250–278.

Willis, Robert, and Sherwin Rosen. 1979. "Education and Self-Selection." *Journal of Political Economy* 87:S7–S36.

Yellen, Janet. 1984. "Efficiency-Wage Models of Unemployment." *American Economic Review* 74:200–210.

EDITORS' NOTES ON FURTHER READING: GRANOVETTER

Because this paper is constructed as a review and critique of existing literature, the interested reader can best pursue its themes by examining the many citations referred to in the text. A related paper by Granovetter, "Labor Mobility, Internal Markets, and Job-Matching: Comparison of the Economic and Sociological Approaches," which appeared in the 1986 volume of *Research in Social Stratification and Mobility*, pp. 3–39, has more detailed citations to empirical studies.

10

Non-Contractual Relations
in Business:
A Preliminary Study

STEWART MACAULAY

What good is contract law? who uses it? when and how? Complete answers
would require an investigation of almost every type of transaction between
individuals and organizations. In this report, research has been confined to
exchanges between businesses, and primarily to manufacturers.[1] Furthermore,
this report will be limited to a presentation of the findings concerning when
contract is and is not used and to a tentative explanation of these findings.[2]

This research is only the first phase in a scientific study.[3] The primary
research technique involved interviewing 68 businessmen and lawyers representing 43 companies and six law firms. The interviews ranged from a
30-minute brush-off where not all questions could be asked of a busy and
uninterested sales manager to a six-hour discussion with the general counsel
of a large corporation. Detailed notes of the interviews were taken and a
complete report of each interview was dictated, usually no later than the
evening after the interview. All but two of the companies had plants in
Wisconsin; 17 were manufacturers of machinery but none made such items
as food products, scientific instruments, textiles or petroleum products. Thus
the likelihood of error because of sampling bias may be considerable.[4]
However, to a great extent, existing knowledge has been inadequate to
permit more rigorous procedures—as yet one cannot formulate many precise

Revision of a paper read at the annual meeting of the American Sociological Association,
August, 1962. An earlier version of the paper was read at the annual meeting of the
Midwest Sociological Society, April, 1962. The research has ben supported by a Law and
Policy Research Grant to the University of Wisconsin Law School from the Ford Foundation.
I am grateful for the help generously given by a number of sociologists including Robert
K. Merton, Harry V. Ball, Jerome Carlin and William Evan.

From *American Sociological Review* 28 (1963):55–67.

questions to be asked a systematically selected sample of "right people." Much time has been spent fishing for relevant questions or answers, or both.

Reciprocity, exchange or contract has long been of interest to sociologists, economists and lawyers. Yet each discipline has an incomplete view of this kind of conduct. This study represents the effort of a law teacher to draw on sociological ideas and empirical investigation. It stresses, among other things, the functions and dysfunctions of using contract to solve exchange problems and the influence of occupational roles on how one assesses whether the benefits of using contract outweigh the costs.

To discuss when contract is and is not used, the term "contract" must be specified. This term will be used here to refer to devices for conducting exchanges. Contract is not treated as synonymous with an exchange itself, which may or may not be characterized as contractual. Nor is contract used to refer to a writing recording an agreement. Contract, as I use the term here, involves two distinct elements: (a) Rational planning of the transaction with careful provision for as many future contingencies as can be foreseen, and (b) the existence or use of actual or potential legal sanctions to induce performance of the exchange or to compensate for non-performance.

These devices for conducting exchanges may be used or may exist in greater or lesser degree, so that transactions can be described relatively as involving a more contractual or a less contractual manner (a) of creating an exchange relationship or (b) of solving problems arising during the course of such a relationship. For example, General Motors might agree to buy all of the Buick Division's requirements of aluminum for ten years from Reynolds Aluminum. Here the two large corporations probably would plan their relationship carefully. The plan probably would include a complex pricing formula designed to meet market fluctuations, an agreement on what would happen if either party suffered a strike or a fire, a definition of Reynolds' responsibility for quality control and for losses caused by defective quality, and many other provisions. As the term contract is used here, this is a more contractual method of creating an exchange relationship than is a home-owner's casual agreement with a real estate broker giving the broker the exclusive right to sell the owner's house which fails to include provisions for the consequences of many easily foreseeable (and perhaps even highly probable) contingencies. In both instances, legally enforceable contracts may or may not have been created, but it must be recognized that the existence of a legal sanction has no necessary relationship to the degree of rational planning by the parties, beyond certain minimal legal requirements of certainty of obligation. General Motors and Reynolds might never sue or even refer to the written record of their agreement to answer questions which come up during their ten-year relationship, while the real estate broker might sue, or at least threaten to sue, the owner of the house. The broker's method of *dispute settlement* then would be more contractual than that of General Motors and Reynolds, thus reversing the relationship that existed in regard to the "contractualness" of the *creation* of the exchange relationships.

TENTATIVE FINDINGS

It is difficult to generalize about the use and nonuse of contract by manufacturing industry. However, a number of observations can be made with reasonable accuracy at this time. The use and nonuse of contract in creating exchange relations and in dispute settling will be taken up in turn.

The creation of exchange relationships. In creating exchange relationships, businessmen may plan to a greater or lesser degree in relation to several types of issues. Before reporting the findings as to practices in creating such relationships, it is necessary to describe what one can plan about in a bargain and the degrees of planning which are possible.

People negotiating a contract can make plans concerning several types of issues: (1) They can plan what each is to do or refrain from doing; e.g., S might agree to deliver ten 1963 Studebaker four-door sedan automobiles to B on a certain date in exchange for a specified amount of money. (2) They can plan what effect certain contingencies are to have on their duties; e.g., what is to happen to S and B's obligations if S cannot deliver the cars because of a strike at the Studebaker factory? (3) They can plan what is to happen if either of them fails to perform; e.g., what is to happen if S delivers nine of the cars two weeks late? (4) They can plan their agreement so that it is a legally enforceable contract—that is, so that a legal sanction would be available to provide compensation for injury suffered by B as a result of S's failure to deliver the cars on time.

As to each of these issues, there may be a different degree of planning by the parties. (1) They may carefully and explicitly plan; e.g., S may agree to deliver ten 1963 Studebaker four-door sedans which have six cylinder engines, automatic transmissions and other specified items of optional equipment and which will perform to a specified standard for a certain time. (2) They may have a mutual but tacit understanding about an issue; e.g., although the subject was never mentioned in their negotiations, both S and B may assume that B may cancel his order for the cars before they are delivered if B's taxi-cab business is so curtailed that B can no longer use ten additional cabs. (3) They may have two inconsistent unexpressed assumptions about an issue; e.g., S may assume that if any of the cabs fails to perform to the specified standard for a certain time, all S must do is repair or replace it. B may assume S must also compensate B for the profits B would have made if the cab had been in operation. (4) They may never have thought of the issue; e.g., neither S nor B planned their agreement so that it would be a legally enforceable contract. Of course, the first and fourth degrees of planning listed are the extreme cases and the second and third are intermediate points. Clearly other intermediate points are possible; e.g., S and B neglect to specify whether the cabs should have automatic or conventional transmissions. Their planning is not as careful and explicit as that in the example previously given.

The following diagram represents the dimensions of creating an exchange relationship just discussed with "X's" representing the example of S and B's contract for ten taxi-cabs.

	Definition of Performances	Effect of Contingencies	Effect of Defective Performances	Legal Sanctions
Explicit and careful	X			
Tacit agreement		X		
Unilateral assumptions			X	
Unawareness of the issue				X

Most larger companies, and many smaller ones, attempt to plan carefully and completely. Important transactions not in the ordinary course of business are handled by a detailed contract. For example, recently the Empire State Building was sold for $65 million. More than 100 attorneys, representing 34 parties, produced a 400 page contract. Another example is found in the agreement of a major rubber company in the United States to give technical assistance to a Japanese firm. Several million dollars were involved and the contract consisted of 88 provisions on 17 pages. The 12 house counsel— lawyers who work for one corporation rather than many clients—interviewed said that all but the smallest businesses carefully planned most transactions of any significance. Corporations have procedures so that particular types of exchanges will be reviewed by their legal and financial departments.

More routine transactions commonly are handled by what can be called standardized planning. A firm will have a set of terms and conditions for purchases, sales, or both printed on the business documents used in these exchanges. Thus the things to be sold and the price may be planned particularly for each transaction, but standard provisions will further elaborate the performances and cover the other subjects of planning. Typically, these terms and conditions are lengthy and printed in small type on the back of the forms. For example, 24 paragraphs in eight point type are printed on the back of the purchase order form used by the Allis Chalmers Manufacturing Company. The provisions: (1) describe, in part, the performance required, e.g., "DO NOT WELD CASTINGS WITHOUT OUR CONSENT"; (2) plan for the effect of contingencies, e.g., ". . . in the event the Seller suffers delay in performance due to an act of God, war, act of the Government, priorities or allocations, act of the Buyer, fire, flood, strike, sabotage, or other causes beyond Seller's control, the time of completion shall be extended a period of time equal to the period of such delay if the Seller gives the Buyer notice in writing of the cause of any such delay within a reasonable time after the beginning thereof"; (3) plan for the effect of defective performances, e.g., "The buyer, without waiving any other legal rights, reserves the right to cancel without charge or to postpone deliveries of any of the articles covered by this order which are not shipped in time reasonably to meet said agreed dates"; (4) plan for a legal sanction, e.g., the clause "without waiving any other legal rights," in the example just given.

In larger firms such "boiler plate" provisions are drafted by the house counsel or the firm's outside lawyer. In smaller firms such provisions may be drafted by the industry trade association, may be copied from a competitor, or may be found on forms purchased from a printer. In any event, salesmen and purchasing agents, the operating personnel, typically are unaware of what is said in the fine print on the back of the forms they use. Yet often the normal business patterns will give effect to this standardized planning. For example, purchasing agents may have to use a purchase order form so that all transactions receive a number under the firm's accounting system. Thus, the required accounting record will carry the necessary planning of the exchange relationship printed on its reverse side. If the seller does not object to this planning and accepts the order, the buyer's "fine print" will control. If the seller does object, differences can be settled by negotiation.

This type of standardized planning is very common. Requests for copies of the business documents used in buying and selling were sent to approximately 6,000 manufacturing firms which do business in Wisconsin. Approximately 1,200 replies were received and 850 companies used some type of standardized planning. With only a few exceptions, the firms that did not reply and the 350 that indicated they did not use standardized planning were very small manufacturers such as local bakeries, soft drink bottlers and sausage makers.

While businessmen can and often do carefully and completely plan, it is clear that not all exchanges are neatly rationalized. Although most businessmen think that a clear description of both the seller's and buyer's performances is obvious common sense, they do not always live up to this ideal. The house counsel and the purchasing agent of a medium size manufacturer of automobile parts reported that several times their engineers had committed the company to buy expensive machines without adequate specifications. The engineers had drawn careful specifications as to the type of machine and how it was to be made but had neglected to require that the machine produce specified results. An attorney and an auditor both stated that most contract disputes arise because of ambiguity in the specifications.

Businessmen often prefer to reply on "a man's word" in a brief letter, a handshake, or "common honesty and decency"—even when the transaction involves exposure to serious risks. Seven lawyers from law firms with business practices were interviewed. Five thought that businessmen often entered contracts with only a minimal degree of advance planning. They complained that businessmen desire to "keep it simple and avoid red tape" even where large amounts of money and significant risks are involved. One stated that he was "sick of being told, 'We can trust old Max,' when the problem is not one of honesty but one of reaching an agreement that both sides understand." Another said that businessmen when bargaining often talk only in pleasant generalities, think they have a contract, but fail to reach agreement on any of the hard, unpleasant questions until forced to do so by a lawyer. Two outside lawyers had different views. One thought that large firms usually planned important exchanges, although he conceded that occasionally matters might be left in a fairly vague state. The other dissenter represents a large utility that commonly buys heavy equipment and buildings. The supplier's employees come on the utility's property to install the equipment or construct the buildings, and they may be injured while there. The utility has been sued by such employees so often that it carefully plans purchases with the assistance of a lawyer so that suppliers take this burden.

Moreover, standardized planning can break down. In the example of such planning previously given, it was assumed that the purchasing agent would use his company's form with its 24 paragraphs printed on the back and that the seller would accept this or object to any provisions he did not like. However, the seller may fail to read the buyer's 24 paragraphs of fine print and may accept the buyer's order on the seller's own acknowledgment-of-order form. Typically this form will have ten to 50 paragraphs favoring the seller, and these provisions are likely to be different from or inconsistent with the buyer's provisions. The seller's acknowledgment form may be received by the buyer and checked by a clerk. She will read the *face* of the acknowledgment but not the fine print on the back of it because she has neither the time nor ability to analyze the small print on the 100 to 500 forms she must review each day. The face of the acknowledgment—where the goods and the price are specified—is likely to correspond with the face of the purchase order. If it does, the two forms are filed away. At this point, both buyer and seller are likely to assume they have planned an exchange and made a contract. Yet they have done neither, as they are in disagreement about all that appears on the back of their forms. This practice is common enough to have a name. Law teachers call it "the battle of the forms."

Ten of the 12 purchasing agents interviewed said that frequently the provisions on the back of their purchase order and those on the back of a supplier's acknowledgment would differ or be inconsistent. Yet they would assume that the purchase was complete without further action unless one of the supplier's provisions was really objectionable. Moreover, only occasionally would they bother to read the fine print on the back of suppliers' forms. On the other hand, one purchasing agent insists that agreement be reached on the fine print provisions, but he represents the utility whose lawyer reported that it exercises great care in planning. The other purchasing agent who said that his company did not face a battle of the forms problem, works for a division of one of the largest manufacturing corporations in the United States. Yet the company may have such a problem without recognizing it. The purchasing agent regularly sends a supplier both a purchase order and another form which the supplier is asked to sign and return. The second form states that the supplier accepts the buyer's terms and conditions. The company has sufficient bargaining power to force suppliers to sign and return the form, and the purchasing agent must show one of his firm's auditors such a signed form for every purchase order issued. Yet suppliers frequently return this buyer's form *plus* their own acknowledgment form which has conflicting provisions. The purchasing agent throws away the supplier's form and files his own. Of course, in such a case the supplier has not acquiesced to the buyer's provisions. There is no agreement and no contract.

Sixteen sales managers were asked about the battle of the forms. Nine said that frequently no agreement was reached on which set of fine print was to govern, while seven said that there was no problem. Four of the seven worked for companies whose major customers are the large automobile companies or the large manufacturers of paper products. These customers demand that their terms and conditions govern any purchase, are careful generally to see that suppliers acquiesce, and have the bargaining power to have their way. The other three of the seven sales managers who have no battle of the forms problem, work for manufacturers of special industrial machines. Their firms are careful to reach complete agreement with their customers. Two of these men stressed that they could take no chances because such a large part of their firm's capital is tied up in making any one machine. The other sales manager had been influenced by a law suit against one of his competitors for over a half million dollars. The suit was brought by a customer when the competitor had been unable to deliver a machine and put it in operation on time. The sales manager interviewed said his firm could not guarantee that its machines would work perfectly by a specified time because they are designed to fit the customer's require-ments, which may present difficult engineering problems. As a result, contracts are carefully negotiated.

A large manufacturer of packing materials audited its records to determine how often it had failed to agree on terms and conditions with its customers or had failed to create legally binding contracts. Such failures cause a risk of loss to this firm since the packaging is printed with the customer's design and cannot be salvaged once this is done. The orders for five days in four different years were reviewed. The percentages of orders where no agreement on terms and conditions was reached or no contract was formed were as follows:

1953 . . . . 75.0%
1954 . . . . 69.4%
1955 . . . . 71.5%
1956 . . . . 59.5%

It is likely that businessmen pay more attention to describing the per-formances in an exchange than to planning for contingencies or defective performances or to obtaining legal enforceability of their contracts. Even when a purchase order and acknowledgment have conflicting provisions printed on the back, almost always the buyer and seller will be in agreement on what is to be sold and how much is to be paid for it. The lawyers who said businessmen often commit their firms to significant exchanges too casually, stated that the performances would be defined in the brief letter or telephone call; the lawyers objected that nothing else would be covered. Moreover, it is likely that businessmen are least concerned about planning their transactions so that they are legally enforceable contracts.[5] For example, in Wisconsin requirements contracts—contracts to supply a firm's requirements of an item rather than a definite quantity—probably are not legally enforceable. Seven people interviewed reported that their firms regularly used requirements contracts in dealings in Wisconsin. None thought that the lack of legal sanction made any difference. Three of these people were house counsel who knew the Wisconsin law before being interviewed. Another example of a lack of desire for legal sanctions is found in the relationship between automobile manufacturers and their suppliers of parts. The manufacturers draft a carefully planned agreement, but one which is so designed that the supplier will have only minimal, if any, legal rights against the manufacturers. The standard contract used by manufacturers of paper to sell to magazine publishers has a pricing clause which is probably sufficiently vague to make the contract legally unenforceable. The house counsel of one of the largest paper producers said that everyone in the industry is aware of this because of a leading New York case concerning the contract, but that no one cares. Finally, it seems likely than planning for contingencies and defective performances are in-between cases—more likely to occur than planning for a legal sanction, but less likely than a description of performance.

Thus one can conclude that (1) many business exchanges reflect a high degree of planning about the four categories—description, contingencies, defective performances and legal sanction—but (2) many, if not most, exchanges reflect no planning, or only a minimal amount of it, especially concerning legal sanctions and the effect of defective performances. As a result, the opportunity for good faith disputes during the life of the exchange relationship often is present.

The adjustment of exchange relationships and the settling of disputes. While a significant amount of creating business exchanges is done on a fairly noncontractual basis, the creation of exchanges usually is far more contractual than the adjustment of such relationships and the settlement of disputes. Exchanges are adjusted when the obligations of one or both parties are modified by agreement during the life of the relationship. For example, the buyer may be allowed to cancel all or part of the goods he has ordered because he no longer needs them; the seller may be paid more than the contract price by the buyer because of unusual changed circumstances. Dispute settlement involves determining whether or not a party has performed as agreed and, if he has not, doing something about it. For example, a court may have to interpret the meaning of a contract, determine what the alleged defaulting party has done and determine what, if any, remedy the aggrieved party is entitled to. Or one party may assert that the other is in default, refuse to proceed with performing the contract and refuse to deal ever again with the alleged defaulter. If the alleged defaulter, who in fact may not be in default, takes no action, the dispute is then "settled."

Business exchanges in non-speculative areas are usually adjusted without dispute. Under the law of contracts, if B orders 1,000 widgets from S at $1.00 each, B must take all 1,000 widgets or be in breach of contract and liable to pay S his expenses up to the time of the breach plus his lost anticipated profit. Yet all ten of the purchasing agents asked about cancellation of orders once placed indicated that they expected to be able to cancel orders freely subject to only an obligation to pay for the seller's major expenses such as scrapped steel.[6] All 17 sales personnel asked reported that they often had to accept cancellation. One said, "You can't ask a man to eat paper [the firm's product] when he has no use for it." A lawyer with many large industrial clients said,

> Often businessmen do not feel they have "a contract"—rather they have "an order." They speak of "cancelling the order" rather than "breaching our contract." When I began practice I referred to order cancellations as breaches of contract, but my clients objected since they do not think of cancellation as wrong. Most clients, in heavy industry at least, believe that there is a right to cancel as part of the buyer-seller relationship. There is a widespread attitude that one can back out of any deal within some very vague limits. Lawyers are often surprised by this attitude.

Disputes are frequently settled without reference to the contract or potential or actual legal sanctions. There is a hesitancy to speak of legal rights or to threaten to sue in these negotiations. Even where the parties have a detailed and carefully planned agreement which indicates what is to happen if, say, the seller fails to deliver on time, often they will never refer to the agreement but will negotiate a solution when the problem arises apparently as if there had never been any original contract. One purchasing agent expressed a common business attitude when he said,

> if something comes up, you get the other man on the telephone and deal with the problem. You don't read legalistic contract clauses at each other if you ever want to do business again. One doesn't run to lawyers if he wants to stay in business because one must behave decently.

Or as one businessman put it, "You can settle any dispute if you keep the lawyers and accountants out of it. They just do not understand the give-and-take needed in business." All of the house counsel interviewed indicated that they are called into the dispute settlement process only after the businessmen have failed to settle matters in their own way. Two indicated that after being called in house counsel at first will only advise the purchasing agent, sales manager or other official involved; not even the house counsel's letterhead is used on communications with the other side until all hope for a peaceful resolution is gone.

Lawsuits for breach of contract appear to be rare. Only five of the 12 purchasing agents had ever been involved in even a negotiation concerning a contract dispute where both sides were represented by lawyers; only two of ten sales managers had ever gone this far. None had ben involved in a case that went through trial. A law firm with more than 40 lawyers and a large commercial practice handles in a year only about six trials concerned with contract problems. Less than 10 percent of the time of this office is devoted to any type of work related to contracts disputes. Corporations big enough to do business in more than one state tend to sue and be sued in the federal courts. Yet only 2,779 out of 58,293 civil actions filed in the United States District Courts in fiscal year 1961 involved private contracts.[7] During the same period only 3,447 of the 61,138 civil cases filed in the principal trial courts of New York State involved private contracts.[8] The same picture emerges from a review of appellate cases.[9] Mentschikoff has suggested that commercial cases are not brought to the courts either in periods of business prosperity (because buyers unjustifiably reject goods only when prices drop and they can get similar goods elsewhere at less than the contract price) or in periods of deep depression (because people are unable to come to court or have insufficient assets to satisfy any judgment that might be obtained). Apparently, she adds, it is necessary to have "a kind of middle-sized depression" to bring large numbers of commercial cases to the courts. However, there is little evidence that in even "a kind of middle-sized depression" today's businessmen would use the courts to settle disputes.[10]

At times relatively contractual methods are used to make adjustments in ongoing transactions and to settle disputes. Demands of one side which are deemed unreasonable by the other occasionally are blocked by reference to the terms of the agreement between the parties. The legal position of the parties can influence negotiations even though legal rights or litigation are never mentioned in their discussions; it makes a difference if one is demanding what both concede to be a right or begging for a favor. Now and then a firm may threaten to turn matters over to its attorneys, threaten to sue, commence a suit or even litigate and carry an appeal to the highest court which will hear the matter. Thus, legal sanctions, while not an everyday affair, are not unknown in business.

One can conclude that while detailed planning and legal sanctions play a significant role in some exchanges between businesses, in many business exchanges their role is small.

TENTATIVE EXPLANATIONS

Two questions need to be answered: (A) How can business successfully operate exchange relationships with relatively so little attention to detailed planning or to legal sanctions, and (B) Why does business ever use contract in light of its success without it?

Why are relatively non-contractual practices so common? In most situations contract is not needed.[11] Often its functions are served by other devices. Most problems are avoided without resort to detailed planning or legal sanctions because usually there is little room for honest misunderstandings or good faith differences of opinion about the nature and quality of a seller's performance. Although the parties fail to cover all foreseeable contingencies, they will exercise care to see that both understand the primary obligation on each side. Either products are standardized with an accepted description or specifications are written calling for production to certain tolerances or results. Those who write and read specifications are experienced professionals who will know the customers of their industry and those of the industries with which they deal. Consequently, these customs can fill gaps in the express agreements of the parties. Finally, most products can be tested to see if they are what was ordered; typically in manufacturing industry we are not dealing with questions of taste or judgment where people can differ in good faith.

When defaults occur they are not likely to be disastrous because of techniques of risk avoidance or risk spreading. One can deal with firms of good reputation or he may be able to get some form of security to guarantee performance. One can insure against many breaches of contract where the risks justify the costs. Sellers set up reserves for bad debts on their books and can sell some of their accounts receivable. Buyers can place orders with two or more suppliers of the same item so that a default by one will not stop the buyer's assembly lines.

Moreover, contract and contract law are often thought unnecessary because there are many effective non-legal sanctions. Two norms are widely accepted. (1) Commitments are to be honored in almost all situations; one does not welsh on a deal. (2) One ought to produce a good product and stand behind it. Then, too, business units are organized to perform commitments, and internal sanctions will induce performance. For example, sales personnel must face angry customers when there has been a late or defective performance. The salesmen do not enjoy this and will put pressure on the production personnel responsible for the default. If the production personnel default too often, they will be fired. At all levels of the two business units personal relationships across the boundaries of the two organizations exert pressures for conformity to expectations. Salesmen often know purchasing agents well. The same two individuals occupying these roles may have dealt with each other from five to 25 years. Each has something to give the other. Salesmen have gossip about competitors, shortages and price increases to give purchasing agents who treat them well. Salesmen take purchasing agents to dinner, and they give purchasing agents Christmas gifts hoping to improve the chances of making sale. The buyer's engineering staff may work with the seller's engineering staff to solve problems jointly. The seller's engineers may render great assistance, and the buyer's engineers may desire to return the favor by drafting specifications which only the seller can meet. The top executives of the two firms may know each other. They may sit together on government or trade committees. They may know each other socially and even belong to the same country club. The interrelationships may be more formal. Sellers may hold stock in corporations which are important customers; buyers may hold stock in important suppliers. Both buyer and seller may share common directors on their boards. They may share a common financial institution which has financed both units.

The final type of non-legal sanction is the most obvious. Both business units involved in the exchange desire to continue successfully in business and will avoid conduct which might interfere with attaining this goal. One is concerned with both the reaction of the other party in the particular exchange and with his own general business reputation. Obviously, the buyer gains sanctions insofar as the seller wants the particular exchange to be completed. Buyers can withhold part or all of their payments until sellers have performed to their satisfaction. If a seller has a great deal of money tied up in his performance which he must recover quickly, he will go a long way to please the buyer in order to be paid. Moreover, buyers who are dissatisfied may cancel and cause sellers to lose the cost of what they have done up to cancellation. Furthermore, sellers hope for repeat for orders, and one gets few of these from unhappy customers. Some industrial buyers go so far as to formalize this sanction by issuing "report cards" rating the performance of each supplier. The supplier rating goes to the top management of the seller organization, and these men can apply internal sanctions to salesmen, production supervisors or product designers if there are too many "D's" or "F's" on the report card.

While it is generally assumed that the customer is always right, the seller may have some counterbalancing sanctions against the buyer. The seller may have obtained a large downpayment from the buyer which he will want to protect. The seller may have an exclusive process which the buyer needs. The seller may be one of the few firms which has the skill to make the item to the tolerances set by the buyer's engineers and within the time available. There are costs and delays involved in turning from a supplier one has dealt with in the past to a new supplier. Then, too, market conditions can change so that a buyer is faced with shortages of critical items. The most extreme example is the post World War II gray market conditions when sellers were rationing goods rather than selling them. Buyers must build up some reserve of good will with suppliers if they face the risk of such shortage and desire good treatment when they occur. Finally, there is reciprocity in buying and selling. A buyer cannot push a supplier too far if that supplier also buys significant quantities of the product made by the buyer.

Not only do the particular business units in a given exchange want to deal with each other again, they also want to deal with other business units in the future. And the way one behaves in a particular transaction, or a series of transactions, will color his general business reputation. Blacklisting can be formal or informal. Buyers who fail to pay their bills on time risk a bad report in credit rating services such as Dun and Bradstreet. Sellers who do not satisfy their customers become the subject of discussion in the gossip exchanged by purchasing agents and salesmen, at meetings of purchasing agents' associations and trade associations, or even at country clubs or social gatherings where members of top management meet. The American male's habit of debating the merits of new cars carries over to industrial items. Obviously, a poor reputation does not help a firm make sales and may force it to offer great price discounts or added services to remain in business. Furthermore, the habits of unusually demanding buyers become known, and they tend to get no more than they can coerce out of suppliers who choose to deal with them. Thus often contract is not needed as there are alternatives.

Not only are contract and contract law not needed in many situations, their use may have, or may be thought to have, undesirable consequences. Detailed negotiated contracts can get in the way of creating good exchange relationships between business units. If one side insists on a detailed plan, there will be delay while letters are exchanged as the parties try to agree on what should happen if a remote and unlikely contingency occurs. In some cases they may not be able to agree at all on such matters and as a result a sale may be lost to the seller and the buyer may have to search elsewhere for an acceptable supplier. Many businessmen would react by thinking that had no one raised the series of remote and unlikely contingencies all this wasted effort could have been avoided.

Even where agreement can be reached at the negotiation stage, carefully planned arrangements may create undesirable exchange relationships between business units. Some businessmen object that in such a carefully worked out relationship one gets performance only to the letter of the contract. Such planning indicates a lack of trust and blunts the demands of friendship, turning a cooperative venture into an antagonistic horse trade. Yet the greater danger perceived by some businessmen is that one would have to perform his side of the bargain to its letter and thus lose what is called "flexibility." Businessmen may welcome a measure of vagueness in the obligations they assume so that they may negotiate matters in light of the actual circumstances.

Adjustment of exchange relationships and dispute settlement by litigation or the threat of it also has many costs. The gain anticipated from using this form of coercion often fails to outweigh these costs, which are both monetary and non-monetary. Threatening to turn matters over to an attorney may cost no more money than postage or a telephone call; yet few are so skilled in making such a threat that it will not cost some deterioration of the relationship between the firms. One businessman said that customers had better not rely on legal rights or threaten to bring a breach of contract law suit against him since he "would not be treated like a criminal" and would fight back with every means available. Clearly actual litigation is even more costly than making threats. Lawyers demand substantial fees from larger business units. A firm's executives often will have to be transported and maintained in another city during the proceedings if, as often is the case, the trial must be held away from the home office. Top management does not travel by Greyhound and stay at the Y.M.C.A. Moreover, there will be the cost of diverting top management, engineers, and others in the organization from their normal activities. The firm may lose many days work from several key people. The non-monetary costs may be large too. A breach of contract law suit may settle a particular dispute, but such an action often results in a "divorce" ending the "marriage" between the two businesses, since a contract action is likely to carry charges with at least overtones of bad faith. Many executives, moreover, dislike the prospect of being cross-examined in public. Some executives may dislike losing control of a situation by turning the decision-making power over to lawyers. Finally, the law of contract damages may not provide an adequate remedy even if the firm wins the suit; one may get vindication but not much money.

Why do relatively contractual practices ever exist? Although contract is not needed and actually may have negative consequences, businessmen do make some carefully planned contracts, negotiate settlements influenced by their legal rights and commence and defend some breach of contract law suits or arbitration proceedings. In view of the findings and explanation presented to this point, one may ask why. Exchanges are carefully planned when it is thought that planning and a potential legal sanction will have more advantages than disadvantages. Such a judgment may be reached when contract planning serves the internal needs of an organization involved in a business exchange. For example, a fairly detailed contract can serve as a communication device within a large corporation. While the corporation's sales manager and house counsel may work out all the provisions with the customer, its production manager will have to make the product. He must be told what to do and how to handle at least the most obvious contingencies. Moreover, the sales manager may want to remove certain issues from future negotiation by his subordinates. If he puts the matter in the written contract, he may be able to keep his salesmen from making concessions to the customer without first consulting the sales manager. Then the sales manager may be aided in his battles with his firm's financial or engineering departments if the contract calls for certain practices which the sales manager advocates but which the other departments resist. Now the corporation is obligated to a customer to do what the sales manager wants to do; how can the financial or engineering departments insist on anything else?

Also one tends to find a judgment that the gains of contract outweigh the costs where there is a likelihood that significant problems will arise.[12] One factor leading to this conclusion is complexity of the agreed performance over a long period. Another factor is whether or not the degree of injury in case of default is thought to be potentially great. This factor cuts two ways. First, a buyer may want to commit a seller to a detailed and legally binding contract, where the consequences of a default by the seller would seriously injure the buyer. For example, the airlines are subject to lawsuits from the survivors of passengers and to great adverse publicity as a result of crashes. One would expect the airlines to bargain for carefully defined and legally enforceable obligations on the part of the airframe manufacturers when they purchase aircraft. Second, a seller may want to limit his liability for a buyer's damages by a provision in their contract. For example, a manufacturer of air conditioning may deal with motels in the South and Southwest. If this equipment fails in the hot summer months, a motel may lose a great deal of business. The manufacturer may wish to avoid any liability for this type of injury to his customers and may want a contract with a clear disclaimer clause.

Similarly, one uses or threatens to use legal sanctions to settle disputes when other devices will not work and when the gains are thought to outweigh the costs. For example, perhaps the most common type of business contracts case fought all the way through to the appellate courts today is an action for an alleged wrongful termination of a dealer's franchise by a manufacturer. Since the franchise has been terminated, factors such as personal relationships and the desire for future business will have little effect; the cancellation of the franchise indicates they have already failed to maintain the relationship. Nor will a complaining dealer worry about creating a hostile relationship between himself and the manufacturer. Often the dealer has suffered a great financial loss both as to his investment in building and equipment and as to his anticipated future profits. A cancelled automobile dealer's lease on his showroom and shop will continue to run, and his tools for servicing, say, Plymouths cannot be used to service other makes of cars. Moreover, he will have no more new Plymouths to sell. Today there is some chance of winning a lawsuit for terminating a franchise in bad faith in many states and in the federal courts. Thus, often the dealer chooses to risk the cost of a lawyer's fee because of the chance that he may recover some compensation for his losses.

An "irrational" factor may exert some influence on the decision to use legal sanctions. The man who controls a firm may feel that he or his organization has been made to appear foolish or has been the victim of fraud or bad faith. The law suit may be seen as a vehicle "to get even" although the potential gains, as viewed by an objective observer, are outweighed by the potential costs.

The decision whether or not to use contract—whether the gain exceeds the costs—will be made by the person within the business unit with the power to make it, and it tends to make a difference who he is. People in a sales department oppose contract. Contractual negotiations are just one more hurdle in the way of a sale. Holding a customer to the letter of the contract is bad for "customer relations." Suing a customer who is not bankrupt and might order again is poor strategy. Purchasing agents and their buyers are less hostile to contracts but regard attention devoted to such matters as a waste of time. In contrast, the financial control department—the treasurer, controller or auditor—leans toward more contractual dealings. Contract is viewed by these people as an organizing tool to control operations in a large organization. It tends to define precisely and to minimize the risks to which the firm is exposed. Outside lawyers—those with many clients—may share this enthusiasm for a more contractual method of dealing. These lawyers are concerned with preventive law—avoiding any possible legal difficulty. They see many unstable and unsuccessful exchange transactions, and so they are aware of, and perhaps overly concerned with, all of the things which can go wrong. Moreover, their job of settling disputes with legal sanctions is much easier if their client has not been overly casual about transaction planning. The inside lawyer, or house counsel, is harder to classify. He is likely to have some sympathy with a more contractual method of dealing. He shares the outside lawyer's "craft urge" to see exchange transactions neat and tidy from a legal standpoint. Since he is more concerned with avoiding and settling disputes than selling goods, he is likely to be less willing to rely on a man's word as the sole sanction than is a salesman. Yet the house counsel is more a part of the organization and more aware of its goals and subject to its internal sanctions. If the potential risks are not too great, he may hesitate to suggest a more contractual procedure to the sales department. He must sell his services to the operating departments, and he must hoard what power he has, expending it on only what he sees as significant issues.

The power to decide that a more contractual method of creating relationships and settling disputes shall be used will be held by different people at different times in different organizations. In most firms the sales department and the purchasing department have a great deal of power to resist contractual procedures or to ignore them if they are formally adopted and to handle disputes their own way. Yet in larger organizations the treasurer and the controller have increasing power to demand both systems and compliance. Occasionally, the house counsel must arbitrate the conflicting positions of these departments; in giving "legal advice" he may make the business judgment necessary regarding the use of contract. At times he may ask for an opinion from an outside law firm to reinforce his own position with the outside firm's prestige.

Obviously, there are other significant variables which influence the degree that contract is used. One is the relative bargaining power or skill of the two business units. Even if the controller of a small supplier succeeds within the firm and creates a contractual system of dealing, there will be no contract if the firm's large customer prefers not to be bound to anything. Firms that supply General Motors deal as General Motors wants to do business, for the most part. Yet bargaining power is not size or share of the market alone. Even a General Motors may need a particular supplier, at least temporarily. Furthermore, bargaining power may shift as an exchange relationship is first created and then continues. Even a giant firm can find itself bound to a small supplier once production of an essential item begins for there may not be time to turn to another supplier. Also, all of the factors discussed in this paper can be viewed as *components* of bargaining power—for example, the personal relationship between the presidents of the buyer and the seller firms may give a sales manager great power over a purchasing agent who has been instructed to give the seller "every consideration."

Another variable relevant to the use of contract is the influence of third parties. The federal government, or a lender of money, may insist that a contract be made in a particular transaction or may influence the decision to assert one's legal rights under a contract.

Contract, then, often plays an important role in business, but other factors are significant. To understand the functions of contract the whole system of conducting exchanges must be explored fully. More types of business communities must be studied, contract litigation must be analyzed to see why the nonlegal sanctions fail to prevent the use of legal sanctions and all of the variables suggested in this paper must be classified more systematically.

NOTES

1. The reasons for this limitation are that (a) these transactions are important from an economic standpoint, (b) they are frequently said in theoretical discussions to represent a high degree of rational planning, and (c) manufacturing personnel are sufficiently public-relations-minded to cooperate with a law professor who wants to ask a seemingly endless number of questions. Future research will deal with the building construction industry and other areas.

2. For the present purposes, the what-difference-does-it-make issue is important primarily as it makes a case for an empirical study by a law teacher of the use and nonuse of contract by businessmen. First, law teachers have a professional concern with what the law ought to be. This involves evaluation of the consequences of the existing situation and of the possible alternatives. Thus, it is most relevant to examine business practices concerning contract if one is interested in what commercial law ought to be. Second, law teachers are supposed to teach law students something relevant to becoming lawyers. These business practices are facts that are relevant to the skills which law students will need when, as lawyers, they are called upon to create exchange relationships and to solve problems arising out of these relationships.

3. The following things have been done. The literature in law, business, economics, psychology, and sociology has been surveyed. The formal systems related to exchange transactions have been examined. Standard form contracts and the standard terms and conditions that are found on such business documents as catalogues, quotation forms, purchase orders, and acknowledgment-of-order forms from 850 firms that are based in or do business in Wisconsin have been collected. The citations of all reported court cases during a period of 15 years involving the largest 500 manufacturing corporations in the United States have been obtained and are being analyzed to determine why the use of contract legal sanctions was thought necessary and whether or not any patterns of "problem situations" can be delineated. In addition, the informal systems related to exchange transactions have been examined. Letters of inquiry concerning practices in certain situations have been answered by approximately 125 businessmen. Interviews, as described in the text, have been conducted. Moreover, six of my students have interviewed 21 other businessmen, bankers and lawyers. Their findings are consistent with those reported in the text.

4. However, the cases have not been selected because they *did* use contract. There is as much interest in, and effort to obtain, cases of nonuse as of use of contract. Thus, one variety of bias has been minimized.

5. Compare the findings of an empirical study of Connecticut business practices in Comment, "The Statute of Frauds and the Business Community: A Re-Appraisal in Light of Prevailing Practices," *Yale Law Journal,* 66 (1957), pp. 1038–1071.

6. See the case studies on cancellation of contracts in *Harvard Business Review,* 2 (1923–24), pages 238–40, 367–70, 496–502.

7. *Annual Report of the Director of the Administrative Office of the United States Courts,* 1961, p. 238.

8. State of New York, The Judicial Conference, Sixth Annual Report, 1961, pp. 209–11.

9. My colleague Lawrence M. Friedman has studied the work of the Supreme Court of Wisconsin in contracts cases. He has found that contracts cases reaching that court tend to involve economically-marginal-business and family-economic disputes rather than important commercial transactions. This has been the situation since about the turn of the century. Only during the Civil War period did the court deal with significant numbers of important contracts cases, but this happened against the background of a much simpler and different economic system.

10. New York Law Revision Commission, *Hearings on the Uniform Code Commercial Code,* 2 (1954), p. 1391.

11. The explanation that follows emphasizes a *considered* choice not to plan in detail for all contingencies. However, at times it is clear that businessmen fail to plan because of a lack of sophistication; they simply do not appreciate the risk they are running or they merely follow patterns established in their firm years ago without reexamining these practices in light of current conditions.

12. Even where there is little chance that problems will arise, some businessmen insist that their lawyer review or draft an agreement as a delaying tactic. This gives the businessman time to think about making a commitment if he has doubts about the matter or to look elsewhere for a better deal while still keeping the particular negotiations alive.

EDITORS' NOTES ON FURTHER READING: MACAULAY

Stewart Macaulay's landmark 1963 paper inspired a conference celebrating its twentieth anniversary, and the conference proceedings were published in a special issue of *Wisconsin Law Review* in 1985. The articles, including Macaulay's own reflections on developments after 1963, discuss Macaulay's work as well as Ian Macneil's and Macneil's related concept of *relational contracting.* The most complete statement of Macneil's thesis—that contracting takes place over a period of time rather than instantaneously—can be found in his *The New Social Contract* (1980). For some interesting comparative material as well as a clear picture of the academic model of contracts, see Stewart Macaulay, "Elegant Models, Empirical Pictures, and the Complexities of Contract," *Law and Society Review* 11 (1977):507–528.

Both sociologists and economists have been influenced by the ideas of Macaulay and Macneil. Much of Ronald Dore's article (Chapter 6) in this anthology, for example, is cast in terms of relational contracting. Oliver Williamson has also tried to integrate Macneil's approach into his own work on transaction costs. See, for example, Oliver Williamson, chapters 2–3 in *The Economic Institutions of Capitalism* (1985) and "Transaction-Cost Economics: The Governance of Contractual Relations," *Journal of Law and Economics* 2 (1979):233–261.

The relationship between economics and law has been analyzed by many scholars. Durkheim's famous analysis of the contract ("in a contract not everything is contractual") can be found in *The Division of Labor in Society* (Eng. tr. 1984), pp. 154–

165. The reader may also look at Durkheim's account of the emergence of the modern contract in *Professional Ethics and Civic Morals* (Eng. tr. 1958) and compare it to Max Weber's in *On Law in Economy and Society* (Eng. tr. 1954). For some contemporary research in the sociology of law, which is of relevance here, see the literature cited in Lawrence M. Friedman, "Litigation and Society," *Annual Review of Sociology* 15 (1989):17–29. See, in addition, Arthur Stinchcombe, "Contracts as Hierarchical Documents," pp. 121–171 in Arthur Stinchcombe and Carol Heimer, *Organization Theory and Project Management* (1977). Some interesting research on law and society has also been made from a Marxist perspective; see especially Karl Renner, *The Institutions of Private Law and Their Social Functions* (Eng. tr. 1949) and Steven Spitzer, "Marxist Perspectives in the Sociology of Law," *Annual Review of Sociology* 9 (1983):103–124.

Finally, and generally posed in opposition to the "law and society" perspective, is the extensive literature on "law and economics." The reader may begin by consulting the articles on law and economics, property rights, and the Coase theorem in *The New Palgrave Dictionary of Economics*. Two major works in this genre are R. H. Coase's *The Firm, the Market, and the Law* (1988) and Richard Posner's *The Economics of Justice* (1981). A good general textbook account is *Law and Economics* (1988) by Robert Cooter and Thomas Ulen.

11

Human Values and the Market: The Case of Life Insurance and Death in 19th-Century America[1]

VIVIANA A. ZELIZER

For Durkheim and Simmel, one of the most significant alterations in the moral values of modern society has been the sacralization of the human being, his emergence as the "holy of holies" (Wallwork 1972, p. 145; Simmel 1900). In his *Philosophie des Geldes*, Simmel (1900) traces the transition from a belief system that condoned the monetary evaluation of life to the Judeo-Christian conception of the absolute value of man, a conception that sets life above financial considerations. The early utilitarian criterion was reflected in social arrangements, such as slavery, marriage by purchase, and the *wergeld* or blood money. The rise of individualism was the determining factor in the transition. "The tendency of money to strive after ever-growing indifference and mere quantitative significance coincides with the ever-growing differentiation of men . . . and thus money becomes less and less adequate to personal values" (Altmann 1903, p. 58).[2] For Simmel, money the equalizer became money the profaner. Considered "sub specie pecuniae," the uniqueness and dignity of human life vanished.

Only small fragments of Simmel's penetrating analysis of personal and monetary values have been translated, and, with a few exceptions, this work has been ignored in the sociological literature.[3] There has been much generalizing about the "cash nexus" but, strangely, very little work on the area. The problem of establishing monetary equivalences for such things as death, life, human organs, and generally ritualized items or behavior considered sacred and, therefore, beyond the pale of monetary definition is as intriguing as it is understudied. Perhaps the absorption of many social scientists with "market" models and the notion of economic man led them and others to disregard certain complexities in the interaction between the

From *American Journal of Sociology* 84 (1978):591–610. Copyright © 1978 by The University of Chicago. Reprinted by permission.

market and human values.[4] Market exchange, although perfectly compatible with the modern values of efficiency and equality, conflicts with human values which defy its impersonal, rational, and economizing influence. Titmuss's imaginative cross-national comparison of voluntary and commercial systems of providing human blood for transfusions stands as a lone effort to consider this conflict in depth. His study suggests that commercial systems of distributing blood are not only less efficient than voluntary blood donation but also, and more important, morally unacceptable and dangerous to the social order. Transform blood into a commercial commodity, argues Titmuss, and soon it will become "morally acceptable for a myriad of other human activities and relationships also to exchange for dollars and pounds" (1971, p. 198).[5] Dissatisfied with the consequences of market exchange, Titmuss is persuaded that only reciprocal or gift forms of exchange are suitable for certain items or activities: among others, blood transfusions, organ transplants, foster care, and participation in medical experimentation. His resistance to the laws of the marketplace is not unique. In his early writings, Marx was already concerned with the dehumanizing impact of money. In *The Economic and Philosophic Manuscripts* Marx deplored the fact that in bourgeois society human life is easily reduced to a mere salable commodity; he pointed to prostitution and the sale of persons which flourished in his time as ultimate examples of this degrading process (1964, p. 151).[6] Similarly, Blau, despite his predominantly "market" model of social behavior, states that "by supplying goods that moral standards define as invaluable for a price in the market, individuals prostitute themselves and destroy the central value of what they have to offer" (1967, p. 63). Using love and salvation as examples, Blau suggests that pricing intangible spiritual benefits inevitably leaves some unwholesome by-product; not love but prostitution, not spiritual blessing but simony.[7] The marketing of human organs presents a similar dilemma. Significantly, while organ donations have become more common, organ sales are still rare.[8] Parsons, Fox, and Lidz note that "regardless of how scientific the setting in which this transaction occurs may be, or how secularized the beliefs of those who take part in it, deep religious elements . . . are at least latently present in the transplant situation" (1973, p. 46). Likewise, even after the repeal of most prohibitions against the sale of corpses, the majority of medical schools still obtain corpses and cadavers through individual donations and unclaimed bodies from the morgue. People refuse to sell their bodies for "ethical, religious or sentimental reasons" ("Tax Consequences of Transfers of Bodily Parts," 1973, pp. 862–63). The law itself remains ambivalent. While the Uniform Anatomical Gift Act permits the gift of one's body or organs after death, "the state of the law on anatomical sales remains in a flux" ("Tax Consequences of Transfers of Bodily Parts," 1973, p. 854).

This paper uses data concerning the diffusion of life insurance in 19th-century America as a testing ground to explore the larger theoretical problem of establishing monetary equivalences for sacred things. Our hypothesis is that cultural resistance to including certain items in the social order—namely, those related to human life, death, and emotions—into a market-type of exchange introduces structural sources of strain and ambivalence into their marketing. Life insurance raises the issue in its sharpest terms by posing the question of how one establishes a fixed-dollar amount for any individual death.

Life insurance was part of a general movement to rationalize and formalize the management of death that began in the early part of the 19th century. In the 18th century, the widow and her orphans were assisted by their neighbors and relatives as well as by mutual aid groups that ministered to the economic hardships of the bereaved. In the 19th century, the financial protection of American families became a purchasable commodity. Trust companies, like life insurance companies, replaced more informal systems with professional management (White 1955). The funeral was another "family and neighborhood" affair that became a business. Previously, the physical care and disposal of the dead had been provided mostly be neighbors and relatives, but in the 19th century it became a financially rewarded occupational specialty (Bowman 1959; Habenstein and Lamers 1955). The process of formalization extended to the drafting of wills. The largely informal, generalized provisions drafted by a man shortly before his death turned into a highly structured system of estate planning in the 19th century (Friedman 1964).

The new institutions were primarily concerned with death as a major financial episode. Their business was to make people plan and discuss death in monetary terms. Life insurance defined itself as "the capitalization of affection. . . . Tears are nothing but salt water, to preserve a fresh grief. Insurance is business, genuine, old-fashioned sixteen-ounce precaution" (Phelps 1895, pp. 12–13). Its avowed goal was to encourage men to "make their own death the basis of commercial action" (Beecher 1870). This was no simple enterprise. Putting death on the market offended a system of values that upheld the sanctity of human life and its incommensurability. It defied a powerful normative pattern: the division between the nonmarketable and the marketable, or between the sacred and the profane. Durkheim has written, "The mind irresistibly refuses to allow the two [sacred and profane] . . . to be confounded or even merely to be put into contact with each other . . . " (1965, p. 55). Sacred things are distinguished by the fact that men will not treat them in a calculating, utilitarian manner.

I will argue that resistance to life insurance in this country during the earlier part of the 19th century was largely the result of a value system that condemned the materialistic assessment of death, and of the power of magical beliefs and superstitions that viewed with apprehension any commercial pacts dependent on death for their fulfillment. By the latter part of the 19th century, the economic definition of the value of death became finally more acceptable, legitimating the life insurance enterprise. However, our data suggest that the monetary evaluation of death did not desacralize it; far from "profaning" life and death, money became ritualized by its association with them. Life insurance took on symbolic values quite distinct from its utilitarian function, emerging as a new form of ritual with which to face death and a processing of the dead by those kin left behind.

The present study is based on a qualitative analysis of historical documentary sources. The attempt was made to include an extensive and diversified set of different kinds of data. Among the primary sources consulted were advertising booklets published by life insurance companies, insurance journals and magazines, early treatises and textbooks on insurance, life insurance agents' manuals and their memoirs. Although these sources represent predominantly the life insurance industry and not its customers, they provide important indicators of public opinion. For instance, the most prevalent objections against life insurance were repeatedly discussed and carefully answered by contemporary advertising copy. Primary sources outside the life insurance industry were consulted as well, among them 19th-century business periodicals and general magazines, widows' and marriage manuals, booklets written by critics of life insurance, and a series of government documents.

A BRIEF BACKGROUND

The first life insurance organizations in the United States were formed during the latter years of the 18th century to assuage the economic distress of the widows and orphans of low-paid Presbyterian and Episcopalian ministers. The idea soon appealed to the secular community, and by the early decades of the 19th century several companies had optimistically undertaken the business of insuring life. Legislatures were encouraging; special charters for the organization of the new companies were granted rapidly and eagerly by many states. Life insurance seemed the perfect solution to the increasing economic destitution of widows and orphans. The public, however, did not respond. Surprised and dismayed by their failure, many pioneering companies withdrew altogether or else turned to other businesses to compensate for their losses in life insurance. The contrasting success of savings banks and trust companies, as well as the prosperity of fire and marine insurance companies, attests to the fact that there was sufficient disposable income among the population at the beginning of the 19th century. In addition, the early companies offered a solid economic organization; no life insurance company failed before the 1850s. Epidemics and high mortality rates did not affect their stability; actuarial knowledge was sufficient to calculate adequate premium rates. Americans were offered sound policies which they needed and could well afford. They did not, however, want them.

After the 1840s there was a drastic reversal of trends, and life insurance began its fantastic history of financial success, becoming firmly established in the 1870s. Its sudden prosperity has puzzled insurance historians as much as the initial failure of the industry. The new companies were offering the same product; neither rates nor conditions of life insurance policies were significantly improved. Most analysts point to America's stage of economic growth as the major clue to the acceptance of life insurance. The great economic expansion that began in the 1840s and reached its peak in the

1860s explains the boom of life insurance at that time. The increased urbanization of mid-century America is also upheld as an explanation. Urban dependence on daily wages has been particularly linked to the growing acceptance of life insurance. Indeed, the acceleration of urbanization coincided in many states with the growth of life insurance. The percentage of people living in urban areas doubled between 1840 and 1860, with the greatest increase occurring in New York and Philadelphia, two cities in leading insurance states. The first life insurance companies were all organized in such heavily populated cities as New York, Philadelphia, Boston, and Baltimore.[9]

Other insurance historians, notably Stalson (1969), argue that the "rags-to-riches" transformation of life insurance in mid-century can be attributed unequivocally to the adoption of aggressive marketing techniques. Pioneer American life insurance companies used no agents, limited themselves to passive marketing tactics such as discreet announcement advertisements. In the 1840s, the new companies introduced person-to-person solicitation by thousands of active, high-pressure salesmen who went into the homes and offices of prospective customers. Marketing systems, however, do not develop in a sociological vacuum. Their structure and characteristics are deeply interrelated with such other variables as customers' social and cultural backgrounds. The struggles and victories of life insurance have remained enigmatic and misunderstood because existing interpretations systematically overlook the noneconomic factors involved in its acceptance and adoption. Indeed, economists and economic historians monopolize the field, while sociologists for the most part have ignored it.[10]

In the first place, the development of the insurance industry reflects the struggle between fundamentalist and modernistic religious outlooks that worked itself out in the 19th century. Contrasting theological perspectives divided the clergy into opposing groups; there were those who denounced life insurance to their congregations as a secular and sacrilegious device that competed against God in caring for the welfare of widows and orphans. Others, more attuned to the entrepreneurial spirit, supported the industry. The cultural incompatibility of life insurance with literalist and fundamentalist beliefs hindered its development during the first part of the century. In opposition, the emerging liberal theology tended to legitimate the enterprise. Religious liberals supported insurance programs for practical considerations as well. Congregations which had been unwilling to raise the meager salaries of their underpaid pastors and ministers were most easily persuaded to pay the relatively small premiums to insure the life of the clergymen.

Changing ideologies of risk and speculation also influenced the development of life insurance. Many practices considered to be deviant speculative ventures by a traditional economic morality were redeemed and transformed into legitimate, even noble investments by a different entrepreneurial ethos. Much of the opposition to life insurance resulted from the apparently speculative nature of the enterprise; the insured were seen as "betting" with their lives against the company. The instant wealth reaped by a widow who cashed her policy seemed suspiciously similar to the proceeds of a winning lottery ticket. Traditionalists upheld savings banks as a more honorable economic institution than life insurance because money was accumulated gradually and soberly. After the 1870s, as the notions of economic risk and rational speculation grew progressively more acceptable, the slower methods of achieving wealth lost some of their luster, and life insurance gained prominence and moral respectability.

The emergence of life insurance is also clearly tied to functional changes in the family system which resulted from urbanization. The urban family could no longer rely on informal, personal social arrangements in times of crisis. The care of widows and orphans, previously the responsibility of the community, became the obligation of the nuclear family with the assistance of formal, impersonal, bureaucratic mechanisms and paid professionals. Life insurance was the institutional response to the uncertain social and economic situation of a new commercial middle class without property and dependent exclusively on the money income of the father. Nineteenth-century writings clearly reflect the prevalent fear among businessmen of failure and downward mobility, if not for themselves, for their children.[11]

Finally, changing attitudes toward death made a major impact on the development of life insurance. Life insurance clashed with a value system that rejected any monetary evaluation of human life. However, by the latter part of the 19th century, a growing awareness of the economic value of death legitimated the life insurance business.

PROFANE MONEY

The resistance to evaluating human beings in monetary terms is among the major cultural factors either ignored by life insurance analysts or else dismissed in their historical accounts as a curious but certainly peripheral issue. Yet its centrality in Western culture is hardly disputable. Cultural aversion to treating life and death as commercial items is reflected in legal attempts to safeguard them from economic valuation. Roman law had early established the doctrine: Liberum corpus nullam recipit aestimationem (the life of a free man can have no monetary estimate) (Goupil 1905, pp. 32–33).[12] Successorial contracts were considered "stipulationes odiosae" and "contra bonos mores" because they surrounded death with financial considerations. Roman tradition was perpetuated in many countries, particularly in France, where the Civil Code ruled that "only things belonging to commerce can be the subject of a contract" (Pascan 1907, p. 2). Declaring that a man's life "cannot be the subject of commercial speculation," French jurists prohibited any contract on the lives of persons, such as life insurance, trusts, and successorial contracts. Wills, sufficiently surrounded by religious symbolism to remain untainted by commercial aspirations, remained the only legitimate vehicle to dispose of property after death (Goupil 1905, p. 139).

In the United States, the utilitarian treatment of human lives poses similar problems. American law protects human life from commerce, declaring that the human body is not property and may not be "bargained for, bartered or sold" (Schultz 1930, p. 5). Many social arrangements, regardless of their economic efficiency, have been condemned as offensive to the sacred qualities of life. Life insurance became the first large-scale enterprise in America to base its entire organization on the accurate estimate of the price of death. It was necessary to know the cost of death in order to establish adequate policy benefits and determine premiums. The economic evaluation of human life was a delicate matter which met with stubborn resistance. Particularly, although not exclusively, during the first half of the 19th century, life insurance was felt to be sacrilegious because its ultimate function was to compensate the loss of a father and a husband with a check to his widow and orphans. Critics objected that this turned man's sacred life into an "article of merchandise" (Albree 1870, p. 18). They asked, "Has a man the right to make the continuance of his life the basis of a bargain? Is it not turning a very solemn thing into a mere commercial transaction?" (Beecher 1870). Mennonites, who went to the extreme of excommunicating any member who insured his life, cited similar reasons: "It is equivalent to merchandising in human life; it is putting a monetary price on human life which is considered unscriptural since man is the 'temple of the Holy Ghost'" (*Mennonite Encyclopedia* 1957, p. 343). Life insurance benefits, however profitable, became "dirty money" (Knapp 1851).

MAGICAL MONEY

Whal notes the "remarkable paradox of an almost universal recourse to magic and irrationality" to handle death even among the most firm believers in science and the scientific method (1959, p. 17). But while examples of the relationship of magic to death in less-developed cultures are easily found (see Malinowski 1954; Haberstein and Lamers 1955; Simmons 1945; Blauner 1966), little is known about contemporary magic rituals.

For instance, few people make plans for their own death, largely because of magical fears that to do so will hasten it. Most wills are drafted shortly before death (Dunham 1963). Likewise, people rarely prearrange their own funerals despite the evidence that this reduces expenses considerably (Simmons 1975).

Its commercial intimacy with death made life insurance vulnerable to objections based on magical reasoning. A New York Life Insurance Co. newsletter (1869, p. 3) referred to the "secret fear" many customers were reluctant to confess: "the mysterious connection between insuring life and losing life." The lists compiled by insurance companies in an effort to respond to criticism quoted their customers' apprehensions about insuring their lives: "I have a dread of it, a superstition that I may die the sooner" (*United States Insurance Gazette* [November 1859], p. 19). Responding to the popular suspicion that life insurance would "hasten the event about which it calculates," Jencks urged the necessity to "disabuse the public mind of such nonsense" (1843, p. 111). However, as late as the 1870s, "the old feeling that by taking out an insurance policy we do somehow challenge an interview with the 'king of terrors' still reigns in full force in many circles" (*Duty and Prejudice* 1870, p. 3).

Insurance publications were forced to reply to these superstitious fears. They reassured their customers that "life insurance cannot affect the fact of one's death at an appointed time" (*Duty and Prejudice* 1870, p. 3). Sometimes they answered one magical fear with another, suggesting that not to insure was "inviting the vengeance of Providence" (Pompilly 1869). The audience for much of this literature was women. It is one of the paradoxes in the history of life insurance that women, intended to be the chief beneficiaries of the new system, became instead its most stubborn enemies. An Equitable Life Assurance booklet quoted wives' most prevalent objections: "Every cent of it would seem to me to be the price of your life. . . . It would make me miserable to think that I were to receive money by your death. . . . It seems to me that if [you] were to take a policy [you] would be brought home dead the next day" (June 1867, p. 3).

Thus, as a result of its commercial involvement with death, life insurance was forced to grapple with magic and superstition, issues supposedly remote from the kind of rational economic organization it represented.

SACRED MONEY

Until the late 19th century, life insurance shunned economic terminology, surrounding itself with religious symbolism and advertising more its moral value than its monetary benefits. Life insurance was marketed as an altruistic, self-denying gift rather than as a profitable investment. Most life insurance writers of this period denied the economic implications of their enterprise: "The term life insurance is a misnomer . . . it implies a value put on human life. But that is not our province. We recognize that life is intrinsically sacred and immeasurable, that it stands socially, morally, and religiously above all possible evaluation" (Holwig 1856, p. 4).

Later in the 19th century, the economic value of human life finally became a less embarrassing topic in insurance circles. The *United States Insurance Gazette* could suggest, "The life of every man has a value; not merely a moral value weighed in the scale of social affection and family ties but a value which may be measured in money" (May 1868, p. 2).[13] The Rev. Henry Ward Beecher (1870, p. 2) urged men to make their death "the basis of commercial action." The process of introducing the economic value of human life culminated in 1924 when the concept was formally presented at the annual convention of life underwriters: "The most important new development in economic thought will be the recognition of the economic value of human life. . . . I confidently believe that the time is not far distant when . . . we shall apply to the economic organization, management and conservation of life values the same scientific treatment that we now use in connection with property" (Huebner 1924, p. 18).

Death was redefined by the new economic terminology as "all events ending the human life earning capacity" (Huebner 1959, p. 22). It was neatly categorized into premature death, casket death, living death (disability), and economic death (retirement). From this perspective, disease was the "depreciation of life values" (Dublin and Lotka 1930, p. 112) and premature death an unnecessary waste of money. In 1930, Dublin and Lotka developed the first estimate of capital values of males as a function of their age. By establishing differential financial values for lives, they also set a new criterion for stratifying them. Exceptional lives were those that made the greatest contributions, while substandard lives burdened their communities with financial loss (Dublin and Lotka 1930, pp. 80–82). It is claimed that the rational-utilitarian approach to death typified by life insurance has deritualized and secularized death (Vernon 1970; Gorer 1965). Death, however, is not tamed easily. Keener observers deny the hypothesis of deritualization and see instead the secularization of religious ritual (Faunce and Fulton 1957; Pine and Phillips 1970; Blauner 1966). This "metamorphosis of the sacred" (Brown 1959, p. 253) does not exempt ritual but changes its nature. The dead can be mourned in very different ways. Paradoxically, money that corrupts can also redeem: dollars can substitute for prayers.

Brown (1959) criticizes traditional sociology for perpetuating a secular and rational image of money without paying due attention to its symbolic and sacred functions (pp. 239–48). There is a dual relationship between money and death, actual or symbolic. While establishing an exact monetary equivalence for human life represents a profanation of the sacred, the symbolic, unrestrained use of money may contribute to the sanctification of death. Durkheim briefly dwells on the sacred qualities of money. "Economic value is a sort of power of efficacy and we know the religious origins of the idea of power. Also richness confers mana, therefore it has it. Hence, it is seen that the ideas of economic value and of religious value are not without connection" (1965, p. 466). The widespread practice of spending large sums of money at times of death testifies to the existence of a powerful and legitimate symbolic association between money and death. Expensive funerals are held without regard to the financial position of the deceased (Dunham 1963). Accusing fingers point routinely at the undertakers, blaming unreasonable expenses on their exorbitant prices (Mitford 1963; Harmer 1963). Historical evidence, however, shows that high expenditures at the time of death preceded the rise of the professional undertaker in the 19th century. Haberstein and Lamers describe the "wanton lavishness" of 18th century funerals, when gloves, scarves, and all kinds of expensive gifts were distributed (1955, p. 203). The symbolic ties between money and death are also revealed by the norm that proscribes bargaining at times of death (Simmons 1975). Comparison shopping for funerals is strictly taboo, even though it reduces costs. Similarly, in the case of life insurance, "to count our pennies is tempting the Gods to blast us" (Gollin 1969, p. 210). Parsons and Lidz suggest that spending large sums of money may be an attempt to affect "the ultimate well being, or even the salvation of the deceased soul" (1967, p. 156).

When it comes to death, money transcends its exchange value and incorporates symbolic meanings. The dual relationship between money and death—actual as well as symbolic—is essential to the understanding of the development of life insurance. Sacrilegious because it equated cash with life, life insurance became on the other hand a legitimate vehicle for the symbolic use of money at the time of death. We will briefly examine three different aspects of the ritualization of life insurance: its emergence as a secular ritual, as an additional requirement for a "good death," and as a form of immortality.

LIFE INSURANCE AS RITUAL

Funeral expenditures have been defined as a secular ritual (Pine and Phillips 1970, p. 138; Bowman 1959, p. 118).[14] Our evidence suggests that life insurance became another one. Curiously, its critics and not its proponents have been particularly sensitive to the ritualistic overtones of life insurance. Among others, Welsh claims that life insurance is a way of coming to terms with death not only financially but also emotionally and religiously (1963, p. 1576).

The view of life insurance as ritual can be substantiated with firmer evidence. From the 1830s to the 1870s life insurance companies explicitly justified their enterprise and based their sales appeal on the quasi-religious nature of their product. Far more than an investment, life insurance was a "protective shield" over the dying, and a consolation "next to that of religion itself" (Holwig 1886, p. 22). The noneconomic functions of a policy were extensive: "It can alleviate the pangs of the bereaved, cheer the heart of the widow and dry the orphans' tears. Yes, it will shed the halo of glory around the memory of him who has been gathered to the bosom of his Father and God (Franklin 1860, p. 34).

LIFE INSURANCE AND THE "GOOD DEATH"

Most societies have some conception of what constitutes an appropriate death, whether that means dying on a battlefield or while working at a desk. A "triumphant" death in pre–Civil War America meant a holy death; it involved spiritual transportation and the "triumph" of the faith (Saum 1975). Religiosity and moral generosity alone, however, soon became dysfunctional to a changed social context. In the 18th and early 19th centuries, widows and orphans had generally inherited sufficient land to live on and support themselves. Urbanization changed this, making families exclusively dependent on the father's wage. If he did not assume responsibility for the economic welfare of his wife and children after his death, society would have to support them. The principle of testamentary freedom in American law exempted men from any legal obligation to their children after death. Moral suasion, therefore, had to substitute for legal coercion. It was crucial to instill in men a norm of personal financial responsibility toward their families that did not stop with death. More and more a good death meant the wise and generous economic provision of dependents. A man was judged posthumously by his financial foresight as much as by his spiritual qualities. Only the careless father left "naught behind him but the memory of honest, earnest work and the hopeless wish that loves ones . . . might somehow find their needed shelter from poverty. . . . " (*Insurance Journal*, October 1882, p. 313). Diamond (1955) and Goody (1962) point out how attitudes toward death and the dead serve as efficient mechanisms for controlling the behavior of the living. Newspaper obituaries or clergymen's eulogies, for instance, remind the living what behavior is sanctioned by a particular social system. The public reformulation of social norms after a man's death reaffirms their value for the living. Life insurance writings referred to the new standards of dying in America: "The necessity that exists for every head of family to make proper provision for the sustenance of those dear to him after his death, is freely acknowledged and there is no contingency whereby a man stand excused from making such a provision" (*Life Insurance*, journal of the Manhattan Life Insurance Co., 1852, p. 19).

As an efficient mechanism to ensure the economic provision of dependents, life insurance gradually came to be counted among the duties of a good and responsible father. As one mid-century advocate of life insurance put it, the man who dies insured and "with soul sanctified by the deed, wings his way up to the realms of the just, and is gone where the good husbands and the good fathers go" (Knapp 1851, p. 226). Economic standards were endorsed by religious leaders such as Rev. Henry Ward Beecher, who pointed out, "Once the question was: can a Christian man rightfully seek Life Assurance? That day is passed. Now the question is: can a Christian man justify himself in neglecting such a duty?" (1870). The new criteria for a "good death" emerge from this excerpt from a sermon delivered in the 1880s:

> I call to your attention Paul's comparison. Here is one man who through neglect fails to support his family while he lives or after he dies. Here is another who abhors the Scriptures and rejects God. . . . Paul says that a man who neglects to care for his household is more obnoxious than a man who rejects the Scriptures. . . . When men think of their death they are apt to think of it only in connection with their spiritual welfare. . . . It is meanly selfish for you to be so absorbed in heaven . . . that you forget what is to become of your wife and children after you are dead. . . . It is a mean thing for you to go up to Heaven while they go into the poorhouse. [T. DeWitt Talmage, quoted in Hull 1964, p. 240]

LIFE INSURANCE AND ECONOMIC IMMORTALITY

Theological concern with personal immortality was replaced in the 19th century by a growing concern with posterity and the social forms of immortality. Carl Becker (1932) points out that as early as the 18th century European *philosophes* replaced the Christian promise of immortality in the afterworld with the belief that good men would live in the memory of future generations. This shift was reflected in the changing nature of wills. Earlier wills were concerned primarily with the spiritual salvation of the dying. The testator regulated all the details of his burial, assuring his chances of salvation by donations to the poor who would pray for his soul and by funding hundreds of thousands of masses and religious services in his honor, often in perpetuity (Vovelle 1974). After the mid-18th century, wills were no longer concerned with matters of personal salvation; they became lay instruments for the distribution of property among descendants. Vovelle attributes the change in wills to the "de-Christianization" and deritualization of attitudes toward death in the mid-18th century. It is likely, however, that the new format of wills was less the reflection of a loss of religious belief than an indicator of a new set of ideas and beliefs on immortality.[15] Feifel describes the transition in America: "When we gave up the old ideas of personal immortality through an afterlife we created the idea of social immortality. It meant that I could not live on but I would live on [sic] my children" (1974, p. 34). The Puritan concern with individual salvation was pushed aside by the new emphasis on posterity. Men became preoccupied less with their souls and more with leaving an estate for their heirs. The concern with social immortality interacted with structural pressures generated by new economic conditions and the process of urbanization. The multiplication of people with no more capital than their personal incomes made the economic future of their children painfully precarious. The premature death of the breadwinner spelled economic disaster to his widow and orphans. The new institutions that specialized in the economic consequences of death, such as life insurance and trusts, responded to that economic plight by serving the practical needs of dependents. However, they went beyond mere functionality by also symbolizing a form of economic immortality.

The appeal of life insurance as a pathway to immortality was early recognized by the insurance companies, which used it very explicitly to attract their customers. Life insurance was described as "the unseen hand of the provident father reaching forth from the grave and still nourishing his offspring and keeping together the group" (United States Life Insurance Co. booklet, 1850, p. 5). The idea of rewards and punishments after death also served to reinforce the father's responsibility for his widow and orphans. Goody suggests that the belief in afterworld retribution, like other supernatural beliefs, reinforces the system of social control over the living by placing it beyond human questioning (1962, pp. 375–78). The uninsured could anticipate an uneasy afterlife. The dead also assumed a more active role than in the past; there was a shift from "service to serving" (Goody 1975, p. 4). They were no longer the passive recipients of their survivors' prayers; it was soon recognized that "the desire to outlive life in active beneficence is the common motive to which [life insurance] appeals" (Tyng 1881, p. 4).

CONCLUSION

My concern in this paper goes beyond a historical narrative of life insurance. Using previously unanalyzed aspects of that history, I explore the more general problem of establishing monetary equivalents for relations or processes which are defined as being beyond material concerns, a problem of long-standing interest in sociological thought. With life insurance, man and money, the sacred and the profane, were thrown together; the value of man became measurable by money. The purely quantitative conception of human beings was acceptable in primitive society where only the gods belonged to the sacred sphere while men remained part of the profane world. The growth of individualism resulted in a new respect for the infinite worth of human personality, displacing the earlier utilitarianism with an absolute valuation of human beings. In an increasingly industrialized market economy dominated by the "cash nexus," human life and human feelings were culturally segregated into their separate, incommensurable realm. Life insurance threatened the sanctity of life by pricing it. In the earlier part of the 19th century, the American public was not ready to commercialize death. Life insurance was rejected as a sacrilegious enterprise.

The task of converting human life and death into commodities is highly complex, creating inescapable sources of structural ambivalence in any enterprise that deals commercially with such sacred "products." Business demands profits for survival, yet profits alone remain a justification too base for an institution of its kind. I suggest that one solution, in the case of life insurance, was its "sacralization"; the transformation of the monetary evaluations of death into a ritual. Death yielded to the capitalist ethos—but not without compelling the latter to disguise its materialist mission in spiritual garb. For instance, life insurance assumed the role of a secular ritual and introduced new notions of immortality that emphasized remembrance through money. A "good death" was no longer defined only on moral grounds; the inclusion of a life policy made financial foresight another prerequisite. One finds, in addition to religious legitimation, attempts at moral and social legitimation of the industry. The public was assured that marketing death served the lofty social purpose of combating poverty, thereby reducing crime. At the individual level, there were moral rewards for the selfless and altruistic insurance buyer.

This religious, moral, and social legitimation was also true of American business in general until the 1870s. Sanford (1958) refers to the "psychic" factor of moral justification which distinguished America's industrial pioneers from their European counterparts. American industry was not justified by profits alone but as an agency of moral and spiritual uplift. Business was seen to serve God, character, and culture.[16] But if profit alone was an unacceptable motivation for most commercial enterprises, it was a particularly unseemly justification for a business, like life insurance, that dealt with human life and death. Indeed, by the latter part if the 19th century, when American business felt sufficiently confident to seek no other justification than the wealth it produced, life insurance still retained part of its religious camouflage. Even some of the most hard-bitten business leaders of the industry slipped into sentimentalism in speaking of life insurance as a "conviction first and then a business" (Kingsley 1911, p. 13).

298   *Viviana A. Zelizer*

We do not suggest that ingenious sales pitches alone were responsible for the adoption of life insurance. Its newly acquired legitimate status by the latter part of the 19th century was the result of profound economic, social, and cultural changes in America. Marketing techniques, however, can be useful indirect indicators of cultural values. In the case of life insurance, its earlier moralistic appeal reflected the powerful ideological resistance to commercializing death. As the economic definition of death became finally more acceptable by the latter part of the 19th century, life insurance could afford a more direct business-like approach to death without, however, fully discarding its ritualistic appeal. The pivotal role of the life insurance agent further confirms the cultural struggle of the industry. Life insurance sales began to improve in the 1840s when companies introduced personal solicitation. In sharp contrast to life policies, marine and fire insurance sold with only minor participation of agents. Customers who would not insure their lives unless pursued sought voluntarily the protection of their homes and ships. The distinctive role of the agent in life insurance was not simply an ingenious marketing device. It was a response to powerful client resistance. From the data available it is safe to hypothesize that the adoption of life insurance would have been much slower and far less successful without the agency system. Persuasive and persistent personal solicitation alone could break through the ideological and superstitious barriers against insuring life.[17] Indeed, historical evidence clearly attests to the failure of all experiments to sell life insurance directly in this country and abroad.[18] The agent was indispensable. His role, however, was ambiguous. The dilemma of marketing life was again evident in the ambivalent role definition of agents. Death could not be pushed and promoted as a common ware. Official rhetoric urged agents to remain above materialistic concerns, performing their task with the spiritual devotion of a missionary. The rewards, however, went to the successful salesman who solicited the most policies.

Other "businessmen" of death are caught in the same structural ambivalence as life insurance. To undertakers, as to life insurance salesmen, death is a money-making business. As "businessmen" of death they are differentiated from the "professionals" of death, physicians and clergymen, whose connection to death is made legitimate by their service orientation.[19] Parsons (1949) and Merton (1975) distinguish between individual motivational patterns and the institutional structures of business and the professions. Regardless of the individual motivations of the practitioners—their greed or beneficence—professions institutionalize altruism while businesses institutionalize self-interest. Particularly when it comes to death, to save and to heal is holier than to sell. The powerful normative stigma of the utilitarian association of money with death results in a negative evaluation of those involved in making money out of death. In sum, marketing death is what Hughes has instructively called "dirty work" (1958, pp. 49–52). As with life insurers, undertakers attempt to legitimate their business by transforming it into a sacred ritual. Warner describes the tendency on the part of the undertaker "to borrow the ritual and sacred symbols of the minister . . .

to provide an outward cover for what he is and does. His place of business is not a factory or an office but a 'chapel' or a 'home'" (1959, p. 317).

This paper has shown that the "profanation" of the sacred, such as making money out of death, creates sources of strain and ambivalence in its practitioners which can be assuaged but not resolved by "sacralizing" the profanation. This hypothesis would be enriched by further investigation of the marketing of other similarly "sacred" products such as human organs or even the recently expanding business of mercenary mothers and their "black-market" babies, in which human life is routinely handled as a commodity to be exchanged, as Titmuss feared, for "dollars and pounds."

NOTES

1. I am deeply grateful for the generous advice and support of Professors Sigmund Diamond and Bernard Barber. I also want to thank Professor Irving Louis Horowitz for his help, and an anonymous reviewer of the *American Journal of Sociology* for very useful suggestions.

2. Parsons and Lidz (1967, p. 163) also attach the conception of the sanctity of life to the stress on individualism.

3. For English versions of some portions of the book, see Becker (1959), Altmann (1903), Levine (1971), Lawrence (1976), and Etzkorn (1968).

4. On the "absolutization" of the market as an analytical tool for social analysis in most social science disciplines, and for a discussion of the types and functions of different forms of economic and social exchange, see Barber (1974).

5. According to a recent report, the nation appears to be shifting toward almost total reliance on volunteer, nonpaid donors (*New York Times*, June 19, 1977).

6. See also the *Manifesto of the Communist Party* (Marx 1971, p. 11). Above all, money for Marx (1964, pp. 165–69) destroys individuality by enabling its possessor to achieve objects and qualities which bear no connection to individual talents or capacities.

7. Cooley formulated another, different perspective on the "moral problem" created by the fact that "pecuniary values fail to express the higher life of society." Although he accepted the fact that human values such as love, beauty, and righteousness were not traditional market commodities, Cooley rejected the permanent segregation of pecuniary values into a special, inferior province of life. His alternative was the enhancement of monetary evaluation; precisely by encouraging "the translation into it of the higher values . . . the principle that everything has its price should be rather enlarged than restricted" (1913, pp. 202–3).

8. A recent policy-oriented analysis of organ transplants concludes that "if the body is to be made available to others for personal or societal research, it must be a gift" (Veatch 1976, p. 269).

9. On the impact of economic growth and urbanization on the development of life insurance, see, among others, Buley (1967). North and Davis (1971), and Mannes (1932).

10. There are a few exceptions. See, e.g., Riley (1963). An entire issue of the *American Behavioral Scientist* (May 1963) was devoted to social research and life insurance. Two doctoral dissertations have been written on the life insurance agent (Taylor 1958; Bain 1959).

11. On the fear of failure among 19th-century businessmen, see Katz (1975). For a fuller explanation of the cultural and sociostructural factors involved in the adoption of life insurance, see Zelizer (1979).

12. Only slaves were considered to have pecuniary value. This explains why countries that forbade life insurance in principle allowed the insurance of slaves. Their lack of human value justified economic equivalences without presenting serious moral difficulties (Reboul 1909, p. 23).

13. The greater acceptance of the economic value of a man's life did not include women. The *Insurance Monitor,* among others, was outspoken against insuring wives for the benefit of husbands: "The husband who can deliberately set a money value upon his wife, is so far destitute not only of affection for her, but of respect for himself. . . . To him she is but a chattel . . . " ("The Insurable Value of a Wife" [September 1870]. p. 712d). The insurance of children was similarly opposed by many individuals and organizations who objected to the economic evaluation of a child's life. In the 1870s, industrial insurance companies began insuring the poor. For the first time children under 10 years of age were insured on a regular basis. There were at least 70 legislative attempts in various states to prohibit it as being against public policy and the public interest. The *Boston Evening Transcript* reflected their prevalent feeling that "no manly man and no womanly woman should be ready to say that their infants have pecuniary value" (March 14, 1895).

14. Ariès (1975) sees the contemporary American funeral rite as a compromise between deritualization and traditional forms of mourning. Group therapy and family reunions have also been suggested as secular rituals (Patterson 1975).

15. Ariès's interpretation of Vovelle's data may have some bearing on this hypothesis. Ariès uses the rise of the family and of new family relationships based on feelings and affection in the mid-18th century to explain the change in wills. The dying person no longer used legal means to regulate the rituals of his burial because he now trusted his family to remember him voluntarily (1974, pp. 64–65). The growing importance of family ties may have encouraged religious belief in posterity and social forms of immortality.

16. The accumulation of great fortunes was justified by the ultimate social and philanthropic purposes to which the money was put (Diamond 1955, pp. 13–15). On this subject, see also Hofstadter (1963, p. 251).

17. For the impact of personal influence on the diffusion of innovations, see Rogers and Shoemaker (1971); on marketing, see Katz and Lazarsfeld (1955).

18. Savings bank life insurance, e.g., which has offered low-price quality policies since 1907, has never been very successful. Interestingly, one of the few commercial failures of the Sears Roebuck catalogue business was an attempt in the 1930s to sell life insurance directly.

19. Parsons (1951, p. 445) suggests that even medical students need certain rites to justify their association to death, such as the ritualistic dissection of cadavers in the early stages of medical training.

REFERENCES

Albree, George. 1870. *The Evils of Life Insurance.* Pittsburg: Bakewell & Mathers.
Altmann, S. P. 1903. "Simmel's Philosophy of Money." *American Journal of Sociology* 9 (July): 46–68.
Ariès, Philippe. 1974. *Western Attitudes toward Death.* Baltimore: Johns Hopkins University Press.

――――. 1975. "The Reversal of Death: Changes in Attitudes toward Death in Western Society." Pp. 134–58 in *Death in America*, edited by David E. Stannard. Philadelphia: University of Pennsylvania Press.

Bain, Robert K. 1959. "The Process of Professionalization: Life Insurance Selling." Ph.D. dissertation, University of Chicago.

Barber, Bernard. 1974. "The Absolutization of the Market: Some Notes on How We Got from There to Here." Paper read at the conference on Markets and Morals, Battelle Institute, Seattle.

Becker, Carl. 1932. *The Heavenly City of Eighteenth-Century Philosophers*. New Haven, Conn.: Yale University Press.

Becker, Howard. 1959. "On Simmel's Philosophy of Money." Pp. 216–32 in *Georg Simmel*, edited by Kurt H. Wolff. Columbus: Ohio State University.

Beecher, Henry Ward. 1870. *Truth in a Nutshell*. New York: Equitable Life Assurance Co.

Blau, Peter M. 1967. *Exchange and Power in Social Life*. New York: Wiley.

Blauner, Robert. 1966. "Death and Social Structure." *Psychiatry* 29 (November): 378–94.

Bowman, Leroy. 1959. *The American Funeral*. Washington, D.C.: Public Affairs Press.

Brown, Norman O. 1959. *Life against Death*. Middletown, Conn.: Wesleyan University Press.

Buley, R. Carlyle. 1967. *The Equitable Life Assurance Society of the United States*. New York: Appleton-Century-Crofts.

Cooley, Charles H. 1913. "The Sphere of Pecuniary Valuation." *American Journal of Sociology* 19 (September): 188–203.

Diamond, Sigmund. 1955. *The Reputation of the American Businessman*. Cambridge, Mass.: Harvard University Press.

Dublin, Louis I., and Alfred J. Lotka. 1930. *The Money Value of Man*. New York: Ronald.

Dunham, Allison. 1963. "The Method, Process and Frequency of Wealth Transmission at Death." *University of Chicago Law Review* 30 (Winter): 241–85.

Durkheim, Émile. 1965. *The Elementary Forms of the Religious Life*. New York: Free Press.

Duty and Prejudice. 1870. New York: J. H. & C. M. Goodsell.

Etzkorn, Peter. 1968. *Georg Simmel: Conflict in Modern Culture and Other Essays*. New York: Teachers College Press.

Faunce, William A., and Robert L. Fulton. 1957. "The Sociology of Death: A Neglected Area of Research." *Social Forces* 36 (October): 205–9.

Feifel, Herman. 1974. "Attitudes towards Death Grow More Realistic." *New York Times* (July 21).

Franklin, Morris. 1860. "Proceedings from the First Annual Session of the Convention of Life Insurance Underwriters." *American Life Assurance Magazine* 1 (January): 34–39.

Friedman, Lawrence M. 1964. "Patterns of Testation in the 19th Century: A Study of Essex County (New Jersey) Wills." *American Journal of Legal History* 8 (January): 34–53.

Gollin, James. 1969. *Pay Now, Die Later*. New York: Penguin.

Goody, Jack. 1962. *Death, Property and the Ancestors*. Stanford, Calif.: Stanford University Press.

――――. 1975. "Death and the Interpretation of Culture: A Bibliographic Overview." Pp. 1–8 in *Death in America*, edited by David E. Stannard. Philadelphia: University of Pennsylvania Press.

Gorer, Geoffrey. 1965. *Death, Grief and Morning in Contemporary Britain*. London: Cresset Press.

Goupil, René. 1905. *De La Considération de la mort des personnes dans les actes juridiques*. Caen: Université de Caen.

Habenstein, Robert, and William M. Lamers. 1955. *The History of American Funeral Directing*. Milwaukee: Bulfin Printers.

Harmer, Ruth. 1963. *The High Cost of Dying*. New York: Crowell.

Hofstadter, Richard. 1963. *Anti-Intellectualism in American Life*. New York: Vintage.

Holwig, David. 1886. *The Science of Life Assurance*. Boston: Provident Life & Trust Co.

Huebner, S. S. 1924. *Proceedings of the 35th Annual Convention of the National Association of Life Underwriters*. New York: National Association of Life Underwriters.

————. 1959. *The Economics of Life Insurance*. New York: Crofts.

Hughes, Everett Cherrington. 1958. *Men and Their Work*. Glencoe, Ill.: Free Press.

Hull, Roger. 1964. "Immortality through Premiums." *Christian Century* 81 (February): 239–40.

Jencks, T. R. 1843. "Life Insurance in the United States." *Hunt's Merchants' Magazine* 8 (February): 109–30.

Katz, Elihu, and Paul F. Lazarsfeld. 1955. *Personal Influence*. Glencoe, Ill.: Free Press.

Katz, Michael B. 1975. *The People of Hamilton*. Cambridge, Mass.: Harvard University Press.

Kingsley, Darwin P. 1911. *Militant Life Insurance*. New York: New York Life Insurance Co.

Knapp, Moses L. 1851. *Lectures on the Science of Life Insurance*. Philadelphia: E. J. Jones & Co.

Lawrence, P. A. 1976. *Georg Simmel: Sociologist and European*. New York: Harper & Row.

Levine, Donald, ed. 1971, *Georg Simmel on Individuality and Social Forms*. Chicago: University of Chicago Press.

Malinowski, Bronislaw. 1954. *Magic, Science, and Religion*. New York: Doubleday.

Mannes, Alfred. 1932. "Principles and History of Insurance." Pp. 30–47 in *International Encyclopedia of the Social Sciences*, vol. 8. New York: Macmillan.

Marx, Karl. 1964. *The Economic and Philosophic Manuscripts of 1844*. New York: International Publishers.

————. 1971. *Manifesto of the Communist Party*. New York: International Publishers.

Mennonite Encyclopedia, The. 1957. Scottdale, Pa.: Mennonite Publishing House.

Merton, Robert K. 1975. "The Uses of Institutionalized Altruism." In *Seminar Reports*, vol. 3, no. 6. New York: Columbia University.

Mitford, Jessica. 1963. *The American Way of Death*. Greenwich, Conn.: Fawcett.

North, Douglass C., and Lance E. Davis. 1971. *Institutional Change and American Economic Growth*. Cambridge: Cambridge University Press.

Parsons, Talcott. 1949. "The Professions and the Social Structure." Pp. 34–49 in *Essays in Sociological Theory*. Glencoe, Ill.: Free Press.

————. 1951. *The Social System*. Glencoe, Ill.: Free Press.

Parsons, Talcott, Renee C. Fox, and Victor Lidz. 1973. "The Gift of Life and Its Reciprocation." Pp. 1–49 in *Death in American Experience*, edited by Arien Mack. New York: Schocken.

Parsons, Talcott, and Victor Lidz. 1967. "Death in American Society." Pp. 133–40 in *Essays in Self Destruction*, edited by Edwin S. Schneidman. New York: Science House.

Pascan, Michel. 1907. *Les Pactes sur succession future.* Paris: Faculté de Droit, Université de Paris.

Patterson, Raul R. 1975. "Children and Ritual of the Mortuary." Pp. 86–99 in *Grief and the Meaning of the Funeral,* edited by Otto S. Margolis. New York: MAS Information Corp.

Phelps, James T. 1895. *Life Insurance Sayings.* Cambridge, Mass.: Riverside Press.

Pine, Vanderlyn R., and Derek L. Phillips. 1970. "The Cost of Dying: A Sociological Analysis of Expenditures." *Social Problems* 17 (Winter): 131–39.

Pompilly, Judah T. 1869. *Watchman! What Time of the Night? or Rejected Blessings for Wives and Mothers.* New York: English & Rumsey.

Reboul, Edmond. 1909. *Du Droit des enfants bénéficiaires d'une assurance sur la vie contractée par leur père.* Paris: Librairie Nouvelle de Droit.

Riley, John W. 1963. "Basic Social Research and the Institution of Life Insurance." *American Behavioral Scientist* 6 (May): 6–9.

Rogers, Everett M., and F. Floyd Shoemaker. 1971. *Communications of Innovations.* New York: Free Press.

Sanford, Charles L. 1958. "The Intellectual Origins and New-Worldliness of American Industry." *Journal of Economic History* 18 (1): 1–15.

Saum, Lewis O. 1975. "Death in the Popular Mind of Pre-Civil War America." Pp. 30–48 in *Death in America,* edited by David E. Stannard. Philadelphia: University of Pennsylvania Press.

Schultz, Oscar T. 1930. *The Law of the Dead Human Body.* Chicago: American Medical Assoc.

Simmel, Georg. 1900. *Philosophie des Geldes.* Leipzig: Duncker & Humblot.

Simmons, Leo W. 1945. *The Role of the Aged in Primitive Society.* New Haven, Conn.: Yale University Press.

Simmons, Marilyn G. 1975. "Funeral Practices and Public Awareness." *Human Ecology Forum* 5 (Winter): 9–13.

Stalson, Owen J. 1969. *Marketing Life Insurance.* Bryn Mawr, Pa.: McCahan Foundation.

"Tax Consequences of Transfers of Bodily Parts." 1973. *Columbia Law Review* 73 (April): 842–65.

Taylor, Miller Lee. 1958. "The Life Insurance Man: A Sociological Analysis of the Occupation." Ph.D. dissertation, Louisiana State University.

Titmuss, Richard M. 1971. *The Gift Relationship.* New York: Vintage.

Tyng, Stephen H. 1881. "Life Insurance Does Assure." *Harper's Monthly Magazine* 62 (April): 754–63.

Veatch, Robert M. 1976. *Death, Dying and the Biological Revolution.* New Haven, Conn.: Yale University Press.

Vernon, Glenn. 1970. *The Sociology of Death.* New York: Ronald.

Vovelle, Michel. 1974. *Piété baroque et déchristianisation en Provence au XVIII siècle.* Paris: Plon.

Wallwork, Ernest. 1972. *Durkheim: Morality and Milieu.* Cambridge, Mass.: Harvard University Press.

Warner, Lloyd W. 1959. *The Living and the Dead: A Study of the Symbolic Life of Americans.* New Haven, Conn.: Yale University Press.

Welsh, Alexander. 1963. "The Religion of Life Insurance." *Christian Century* 80 (December 11): 1541–43, 1574–76.

Whal, Charles W. 1959. "The Fear of Death." Pp. 16–29 in *The Meaning of Death,* edited by Herman Feifel. New York: McGraw-Hill.

White, Gerald T. 1955. *A History of the Massachusetts Hospital Life Insurance Company.* Cambridge, Mass.: Harvard University Press.

Zelizer, Viviana A. 1979. *Morals and Markets: The Development of Life Insurance in the United States*. New York: Columbia University Press (in press).

EDITORS' NOTES ON FURTHER READING: ZELIZER

Viviana A. Zelizer's argument is elaborated in her *Morals and Markets: The Development of Life Insurance in the United States* (1979). The reader interested in sociological studies of insurance may also look at Carol Heimer's *Reactive Risk and Rational Action: Managing Moral Hazard in Insurance Contracts* (1985). Heimer's work reflects more of a rational choice tradition than does Zelizer's more culturally oriented type of analysis. Zelizer traces her idea that it is important to look at the intersection of human and economic values to Georg Simmel's *The Philosophy of Money* (Eng. tr. 1978); and this perspective also informs her *Pricing the Priceless Child: The Changing Social Value of Children* (1985) and "The Social Meaning of Money: 'Special Monies,'" *American Journal of Sociology* 95 (1989):342–377.

Zelizer's work ultimately addresses the relationship between morality and economics, as do such classic works as Max Weber's *The Protestant Ethic and the Spirit of Capitalism* (Eng. tr. 1930); Karl Marx's "The Power of Money in Bourgeois Society," in *Economic and Philosophic Manuscripts of 1844* (Eng. tr. 1964); and Benjamin Nelson's *The Idea of Usury: From Tribal Brotherhood to Universal Otherhood* (1969). That economics *must* take moral values into account is argued in Amitai Etzioni's *The Moral Dimension: Toward a New Economics* (1988). Many economists have dealt with moral questions; for some particularly outstanding examples, see Adam Smith, *The Theory of Moral Sentiments* (1759); Gunnar Myrdal, *The Political Element in the Development of Economic Theory* (Eng. tr. 1954); Kenneth Boulding, "Economics as a Moral Science," *American Economic Review* 49 (March 1969):1–12; and Amartya Sen, *On Ethics and Economics* (1987). The reader may also ponder Richard Titmuss's sociological study of different ways of organizing bloodgiving—voluntary or for profit—and his conclusion that the free market solution is costly and inefficient in *The Gift Relationship: From Human Blood to Social Policy* (1971). There exists a fascinating debate about "the moral economy," which was started by E. P. Thompson in "The Moral Economy of the English Crowd in the Eighteenth Century," *Past and Present* 50 (1971):76–136 and continued by James C. Scott in *The Moral Economy of the Peasant: Rebellion and Subsistence in Southeast Asia* (1976); Thompson and Scott argued that the political impact of free market capitalism depends on agreed moral standards which local actors believe economic systems must meet. This view was attacked from a rational choice standpoint by Samuel Popkin in *The Rational Peasant: The Political Economy of Rural Vietnam* (1979).

Other works on economics and morality include Michael Schudson's *Advertising, the Uneasy Persuasion: Its Dubious Impact on American Society* (1984); David Horowitz's *The Morality of Spending: Attitudes Towards the Consumer Society in America, 1875–1940* (1985); and Michael Walzer's thoughtful essay "Money and Commodities" in *Spheres of Justice* (1983).

PART IV

The Sociology of the Firm and Industrial Organization

12

Group Dynamics and Intergroup Relations[1]

GEORGE STRAUSS

This is the story of an experiment that failed because it succeeded too well.

The Hovey and Beard Company manufactured wooden toys of various kinds: wooden animals, pull toys, and the like. One part of the manufacturing process involved spraying paint on the partially assembled toys and hanging them on moving hooks which carried them through a drying oven. This operation, staffed entirely by girls, was plagued by absenteeism, turnover, and low morale.

A consultant, working with the foreman in charge, "solved" the problem. But the changes that were made in order to solve it had such repercussions in other parts of the plant that the company abandoned the new procedures, despite their obvious benefits to production in that local area.

THE PROBLEM

Let us look briefly at the painting operation in which the problem occurred.

The toys were cut, sanded, and partially assembled in the wood room. Then they were dipped into shellac, following which they were painted. The toys were predominantly two-colored; a few were made in more than two colors. Each color required an additional trip through the paint room.

Shortly before the troubles began, the painting operation had been reengineered so that the eight girls who did the painting sat in a line by an endless chain of hooks. These hooks were in continuous motion, past the line of girls and into a long horizontal oven. Each girl sat at her own painting booth so designed as to carry away fumes and to backstop excess paint. The girl would take a toy from the tray beside her, position it in a

"Group Dynamics & Intergroup Relations" by George Strauss, from *Money and Motivation: An Analysis of Incentives in Industry* by William Foote Whyte. Copyright © 1955 by Harper & Row, Publishers, Inc. Reprinted by permission of HarperCollins Publishers.

jig inside the painting cubicle, spray on the color according to a pattern, then release the toy and hang it on the hook passing by. The rate at which the hooks moved had been calculated by the engineers so that each girl, when fully trained, would be able to hang a painted toy on each hook before it passed beyond her reach.

The girls working in the paint room were on a group bonus plan. Since the operation was new to them, they were receiving a learning bonus which decreased by regular amounts each month. The learning bonus was scheduled to vanish in six months, by which time it was expected that they would be on their own—that is, able to meet the standard and to earn a group bonus when they exceeded it.

By the second month of the training period trouble had developed. The girls learned more slowly than had been anticipated, and it began to look as though their production would stabilize far below what was planned for. Many of the hooks were going by empty. The girls complained that they were going by too fast, and that the time-study man had set the rates wrong. A few girls quit and had to be replaced with new girls, which further aggravated the learning problem. The team spirit that the management had expected to develop automatically through the group bonus was not in evidence except as an expression of what the engineers called "resistance." One girl whom the group regarded as its leader (and the management regarded as the ringleader) was outspoken in making the various complaints of the group to the foreman. The complaints had all the variety customary in such instances of generalized frustration: the job was a messy one, the hooks moved too fast, the incentive pay was not being correctly calculated, and anyway it was too hot working so close to the drying oven.

INTRODUCING THE NEW APPROACH

The consultant who was brought into this picture worked entirely with and through the foreman. After many conversations with him, the foreman felt that the first step should be to get the girls together for a general discussion of the working conditions—something, incidentally, which was far from his mind originally and which in his own words would only have been "begging for trouble." He took this step with some hesitation, but he took it on his own volition.

The first meeting, held immediately after the shift was over at four o'clock in the afternoon, was attended by all eight girls. They voiced the same complaints again: the hooks went by too fast, the job was too dirty, the room was hot and poorly ventilated. For some reason it was this last item that they complained of most. The foreman promised to discuss the problem of ventilation and temperature with the engineers, and he scheduled a second meeting to report back to the girls. In the next few days the foreman had several talks with the engineers, and it seemed that the girls' cynical predictions about what the engineers would say were going to be borne out. They and the superintendent felt that this was really a trumped-up complaint, and that the expense of any effective corrective measure would be prohibitively high. (They were thinking of some form of air conditioning.)

The foreman came to the second meeting with some apprehensions. The girls, however, did not seem to be much put out, perhaps because they had a proposal of their own to make. They felt that if several large fans were set up so as to circulate the air around their feet, they would be much more comfortable. After some discussion the foreman agreed that the idea might be tried out. (Immediately after the meeting, he confided to the consultant that he probably shouldn't have committed himself to this expense on his own initiative; also, he felt that the fans wouldn't help much anyway.) The foreman and the consultant discussed the question of the fans with the superintendent, and three large propeller-type fans were purchased. The decision was reached without much difficulty, since it seemed that the fans could be used elsewhere after their expected failure to provide relief in the paint room.

The fans were brought in. The girls were jubilant. For several days the fans were moved about in various positions until they were placed to the satisfaction of the group. Whatever the actual efficiency of these fans, one thing was clear: the girls were completely satisfied with the results, and relations between them and the foreman improved visibly.

The foreman, after this encouraging episode, decided that further meetings might also be profitable. He asked the girls if they would like to meet and discuss other aspects of the work situation. The girls were eager to do this.[2] The meeting was held, and the discussion quickly centered on the speed of the hooks. The girls maintained that the time-study men had set them at an unreasonably fast speed and that they would never be able to reach the goal of filling enough of them to make a bonus.

The turning point of the discussion came when the group's leader frankly explained that the point wasn't that they couldn't work fast enough to keep up with the hooks, but that they couldn't work at that pace all day long. The foreman explored the point. The girls were unanimous in their opinion that they could keep up with the belt for short periods if they wanted to. But they didn't want to because if they showed that they could do this for short periods they would be expected to do it all day long. The meeting ended with an unprecedented request: "Let us adjust the speed of the belt faster or slower depending on how we feel." The foreman, understandably startled, agreed to discuss this with the superintendent and the engineers.

The engineers' reaction naturally was that the girls' suggestion was heresy. Only after several meetings was it granted grudgingly that there was in reality some latitude within which variations in the speed of the hooks would not affect the finished product. After considerable argument and many dire prophecies by the engineers, it was agreed to try out the girls' idea.

With great misgivings, the foreman had a control with a dial marked "low, medium, fast" installed at the booth of the group leader; she could now adjust the speed of the belt anywhere between the lower and upper limits that the engineers had set. The girls were delighted, and spent many lunch hours deciding how the speed of the belt should be varied from hour to hour throughout the day.

Within a week the pattern had settled down to one in which the first half hour of the shift was run on what the girls called medium speed (a dial setting slightly above the point marked "medium"). The next two and one-half hours were run at high speed; the half hour before lunch and the half hour after lunch were run at low speed. The rest of the afternoon was run at high speed with the exception of the last forty-five minutes of the shift, which was run at medium.

In view of the girls' reports of satisfaction and ease in their work, it is interesting to note that the constant speed at which the engineers had originally set the belt was slightly below medium on the dial of the control that had been given the girls. The average speed at which the girls were running the belt was on the high side of the dial. Few if any empty hooks entered the oven, and inspection showed no increase of rejects from the paint room.

Production increased, and within three weeks (some two months before the scheduled ending of the learning bonus) the girls were operating at 30 to 50 percent above the level that had been expected under the original arrangement. Naturally the girls' earnings were correspondingly higher than anticipated. They were collecting their base pay, a considerable piece-rate bonus, and the learning bonus which, it will be remembered, had been set to decrease with time and not as a function of current productivity. (This arrangement, which had been selected by the management in order to prevent being taken advantage of by the girls during the learning period, now became a real embarrassment.)

The girls were earning more now than many skilled workers in other parts of the plant. Management was besieged by demands that this inequity be taken care of. With growing irritation between superintendent and foreman, engineers and foreman, superintendent and engineers, the situation came to a head when the superintendent without consultation arbitrarily revoked the learning bonus and returned the painting operation to its original status: the hooks moved again at their constant, time-studied designated speed, production dropped again, and within a month all but two of the eight girls had quit. The foreman himself stayed on for several months, but, feeling aggrieved, then left for another job.

ANALYSIS OF SUCCESS AND FAILURE

It is not difficult to understand why installing the fans and permitting the speed of the hooks to be controlled by them should have affected the girls the way it did. No normal person is happy in a situation which he cannot control to some extent. The fans may not have actually changed the heat or the humidity, but they were a visible and daily reminder that worker ideas were given consideration.

About the speed of the hooks an additional observation may be made. The idea that efficient work results from proceeding at a constant rate derives certainly from the operations of machines and not from the characteristic operation of human beings. If anything is clear about human performance it is that it is characterized by changes of pace. Some production operations by their nature permit little variation in this respect, but even when the possibility exists it is not readily perceived by many engineers as a source of increased efficiency. From the operator's point of view, to be paced unvaryingly by a machine which he may not even shut down with impunity may be psychologically uncomfortable. In such a situation the only avenue left for the expression of any independence is that of complaint: the machine or its master, the engineer, must be shown to be wrong. Also, three appear to be inherent and unconscious defensive mechanisms which operate against the threat of being "stretched out."

Control over the speed of the hooks in this situation not only allowed changes of pace which were in themselves restful and refreshing, but also allowed the operator the natural enjoyment of operating at top speed without fear that he might be compelled to stay there. Of course, the manner in which the changes was instituted was significant. The opportunity to exercise initiative, the gratification of being listened to seriously, helped to bring about changes in the emotional overtones of the situation which were in themselves favorable to increased effort.

In the light of all this it is not surprising that the situation fell apart so completely when the management retrogressed. And the management's action, while it may not have been wise, was certainly an understandable response to what had become an uncomfortable situation. Along with improved production in the paint room had come a host of embarrassments. The extra production in the paint room had created a pile-up in front and a vacuum behind, and both results were unwelcome to the adjoining departments. The wage structure of the plant had been shaken. The prestige of the engineers had suffered, and some of the prerogatives of management were apparently being taken over by employees.

It is clear from this instance that *local* improvements can often be obtained by the methods described here; but it is also clear that they may not lead to benefits for the enterprise as a whole. Changes in one part of an integrated organization may require widespread changes elsewhere, and the cost of such readjustments may far outbalance the benefits received in the local situation.

The changes made in the paint room implied over-all managerial attitude and philosophy that were not in fact present. This being the case, there was no conceptual or philosophic resource for dealing with the eventual implications of what had been done in the paint room. The management neither expected nor was ready to make the kind of changes that seemed necessary. It would have been far better if the consultant had done with the relevant management group what he had done with the foreman in the initial discussions, so that there would have been some shared understandings of the long-range implications of the moves. In a real sense, the superintendent was justified in feeling that the foreman and the consultant between them had put him on the spot. True, his assent to the changes had been secured, but the consultant had not been sufficiently concerned with his genuine understanding of the possible consequences.

The factory is a social system, made up of mutually dependent parts. A drastic change in one part of the system—even a change that is viewed as highly successful within that part—may give rise to conflict reactions from other parts of the system. It may then be dangerous for management to try a new approach in one small part of the system unless it is prepared to extend this approach to the whole organization. . . .

NOTES

1. This chapter was written by George Strauss, based upon information furnished him by the consultant in the story, Alex Bavelas. The consultant also reviewed and revised the chapter.

2. These subsequent meetings were effective largely because of the reduced tension and the good will engendered by the original discussions.

EDITORS' NOTES ON FURTHER READING: STRAUSS

This article, like much midcentury industrial sociology, stresses that a work organization is a complex, interdependent social system and that the analyst will be grossly misled by attempting to understand the localized situation in isolation. This lesson has still scarcely been absorbed by the sociology and economics of the firm. One aspect that has received some recent attention is that workers from one unit compare their situations with those in others and make judgments about the fairness of the outcome. For a sociological treatment of perceived fairness of compensation, and the impact of social structure on these perceptions, see C. David Gartrell, "On the Visibility of Wage Referents," *Canadian Journal of Sociology* (1982):117–143 and his "Network Approaches to Social Evaluation," *Annual Review of Sociology* (1987).

Another key purpose of Strauss's article, as of much industrial sociology, was to debunk the idea that workers respond only to economic motivations. For a different but savage critique of that idea, see Gunnar Myrdal, *The Political Element in the Development of Economic Theory* (Eng. tr. 1954). Modifications of the traditional emphasis on economic motivations can be found in Gary Becker's *The Economic Approach to Human Behavior* (1976). Mancur Olson's argument about the free-rider in *The Logic of Collective Action: Public Goods and the Theory of Groups* (1965) is also highly important for a discussion of incentives and motivation. Finally, agency theory, with its emphasis on the difficulty in getting the self-interested agent to do what the principal wants, has led to a new concern about the effect of piece-rates versus ordinary salary. For a general reader in agency theory, which also touches on some of these other issues, see John W. Pratt and Richard J. Zeckhauser, eds., *Principals and Agents: The Structure of Business* (1985). For a critical view of the attempt to expand the traditional use of economic theory, see Amitai Etzioni's *The Moral Dimension: Toward a New Economics* (1988). Sociologists have a long tradition of looking at the sources of economic motivation, from Max Weber's *The Protestant Ethic and the Spirit of Capitalism* (Eng. tr. 1930) to Daniel Bell's *The Cultural Contradictions of Capitalism* (1976). For a discussion of contemporary sociological research on piece-rates, see

Mark Granovetter and Charles Tilly, "Inequality and Labor Processes," at pp. 206–207 in Neil Smelser, ed., *Handbook of Sociology* (1988).

The classic *Money and Motivation* by William Foote Whyte et al., from which the Strauss article is drawn, introduces the reader to some of the main themes of the "golden age" of industrial sociology that have to do with human relations in industry, such as quota restriction, "making out," and "rate busting." Many of these themes were worked out in the late 1920s and early 1930s in a series of studies of Western Electric Company's Hawthorne Works in Chicago. For a convenient summary of these, see George C. Homans, *The Human Group* (1950). Other classics in this genre include Melville Dalton, *Men Who Manage* (New York: John Wiley & Sons, 1959) (see Chapter 13 in this anthology); William F. Whyte, *Human Relations in the Restaurant Industry* (1948); and his *Men at Work* (1961). Some important early papers were collected by Whyte in *Industry and Society* (1946). A critical appraisal of the deficiencies in this "human relations" tradition is offered by Charles Perrow in his *Complex Organizations*, 3d ed. (1986), especially chapters 2–3.

For a time after the mid-1960s, industrial sociology was displaced by the sociology of organizations, as described in Paul Hirsch's "Organizational Analysis and Industrial Sociology: An Instance of Cultural Lag," *American Sociologist* 10 (February 1975):3–12. One work that combined the best of the two traditions was Alvin W. Gouldner's *Patterns of Industrial Bureaucracy* (1954). Recently there has been a revival in good industrial sociology, especially of the Marxist variety, and in some of these works there has also been a conscious attempt to further develop the ideas of Whyte, Strauss, and similar writers. This is, for example, the case with Michael Burawoy's *Manufacturing Consent: Changes in the Labor Process Under Monopoly Capitalism* (1979). Burawoy used participant observation and centered the analysis around the concept of "making out" (a way to defeat boredom and get the work done by turning the attempt to fulfill the day's quota into a kind of game). See also Burawoy's comparative studies, especially *The Politics of Production: Factory Regimes Under Capitalism and Socialism* (1985); for a related comparison of production and social organization in Hungary and the United States, see David Stark, "Rethinking Internal Labor Markets: New Insights from a Comparative Perspective," *American Sociological Review* 51 (1986): 492–504.

A good text on industrial sociology is Ivar Berg's *Industrial Sociology* (1979). Two recent overviews of relevant literature are Granovetter and Tilly's "Inequality and Labor Processes" and Joanne Miller's "Jobs and Work," pp. 175–221, 327–359 in Neil Smelser, ed., *Handbook of Sociology* (1988).

13

Men Who Manage

MELVILLE DALTON

The excerpt presented here from Melville Dalton's Men Who Manage *concerns the "Milo Fractionating Center," a chemical plant in the Midwest employing about 8,000 people. Dalton, a sociologist, was employed at Milo without top management knowing that he was conducting a study and with his co-worker informants knowing only in a general way of his interest in "personnel problems."*

Dalton analyzes the informal interaction in the plant contrasting it to what would be expected from the formal organization chart, and indicates the ways in which this informal structure, though deviant from what is expected, actually makes it possible for the plant's work to get done. The reader should be alert for Dalton's main point, which is that the cliques and political intrigues are not a sideshow and distraction from productive activities but instead an essential aspect of the way these activities are carried out. It is significant that "in terms of profits and dividends paid, Milo was definitely successful and presumably well managed" (Dalton, p. 190n). [Editor's note]

This chapter will cover only *one* set of struggles for dominance, that between managers of the production and maintenance branches of the line, and between the entire Milo unit and its Office over the same issue. . . .

THE MILO MANAGERS

To follow these struggles in Milo we must first identify key managers and rank them in terms of their observed daily working authority. Then, as outlined above, we will follow the developing conflicts between planned and actual ways of caring for maintenance costs inside Milo and between Milo and the Office as a series of controls were set up to prevent such conflicts. From our observations we can then sketch a working theory of cliques and their role in getting the job done under various conditions.

Excerpted from "Power Struggles in the Line," Chapter 3 in Melville Dalton, *Men Who Manage: Fusions of Feeling and Theory in Administration* (New York: John Wiley & Sons, 1959). Reprinted by permission of Dorothea Dalton.

FIGURE [13.1]   Milo formal chart simplified

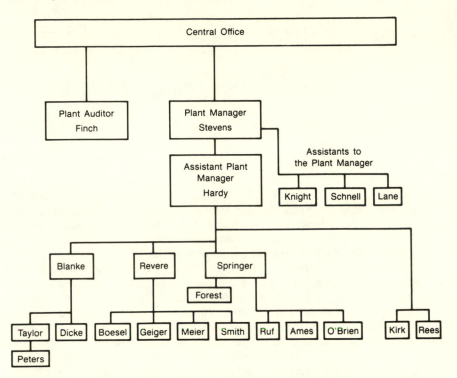

Official Versus Unofficial Authority

A rough picture of the disparity between the formal and informal authority of the major executives can be formed by comparing Figures [13.1] and [13.2]. Excepting Forest, Figure [13.2] shows the officers of Figure [13.1] reranked according to their unofficial weight or influence. An individual's influence was judged less by the response of subordinates to his officially spoken or written orders than by the relative deference of associates, superiors, and subordinates to his known attitudes, wishes, and informally expressed opinions, and the concern to respect, prefer, or act on them. . . .

Fifteen reliable Milo participants evaluated the officers in Figure [13.2]. All judges were, or had been, close associates of the managers they were rating. As only a staff member at Milo my part in the judging was confined largely to challenging the rankings. My criticisms were based on my own experience and many conversations with executives and their subordinates of all grades from the level of Taylor down.

In Figure [13.2] the central vertical, dropping from Hardy and Stevens through Rees, Springer, and Blanke, ranks these officers in that order. Rectangles on the same level and horizontal (Hardy-Stevens, Geiger-Revere, Kirk-Finch) indicate that the officers therein were considered to have equal

FIGURE [13.2]   Milo chart of unofficial influence

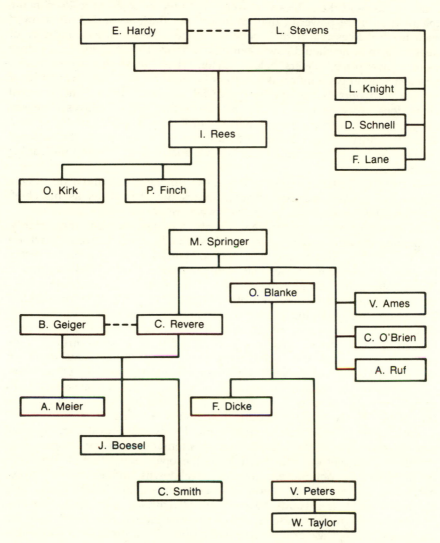

influence. At the same time each division is ranked according to the estimated power of its leader in plant affairs. That is, Springer is above Blanke, and Revere below, as least influential of the division chiefs. The department heads *inside* a given division are ranked in the same way but are not compared with those of other divisions.

As shown in Figure [13.1], Peters was not a department head. But all the judges agreed that he should be put on the informal chart, and thirteen ranked him above Taylor.

There were minor disagreements on the placement of a few officers. For example, some of the judges who were line[1] officers objected to Rees' being regarded as more powerful than Springer. But these same officers showed such fear[2] of Rees that if their behavior alone were taken as a measure of Rees' influence, he should have been placed above Hardy. Two of the judges would have placed Peters below Taylor. These dissenters were general foremen who apparently disliked Peters because he had been brought over from a staff organization by his powerful sponsor, Blanke. The informal chart does not of course measurably show that the executives exercised more or less than their given authority, but it does indicate that formal and actual authority differed. Scales and numbers were not used in the rankings because the judges opposed a formal device and believed it was a misleading overrefinement.

To develop the ties between informal executive position and actions, note that assistant plant manager, Hardy, shares the same level as his chief, Stevens. This ranking was given for several reasons.

In executive meetings, Stevens clearly was less forceful than Hardy. Appearing nervous and worried, Stevens usually opened meetings with a few remarks and then silently gave way to Hardy who dominated thereafter. During the meeting most questions were directed to Hardy. While courteous, Hardy's statements usually were made without request for confirmation from Stevens. Hardy and Stevens and other high officers daily lunched together. There, too, Hardy dominated the conversations and was usually the target of questions. This was not just an indication that he carried the greater burden of *minor* duties often assigned to assistants in some firms, for he had a hand in most issues, including major ones. Other items useful in appraising Hardy and Stevens were their relative (a) voice in promotions, (b) leadership in challenging staff projects, (c) force in emergencies, (d) escape as a butt of jokes and name-calling, (e) knowledge of subordinates, (f) position in the firm's social and community activities.

For example, informants declared that Hardy's approval, not Stevens' was indispensable in the more important promotions. In the struggle over maintenance incentives (discussed later) the open opposition to Rees was made by Hardy, not Stevens. During breakdowns and emergency stops, officers in charge showed concern to "get things going before Hardy gets out here," or "before Hardy hears about it," without reference to Stevens. In too many significant cases staff officers saw Hardy, not Stevens, as the top executive to please or to convince of a point. Even production employees felt the difference. Seeing Hardy and Stevens approach together on a walk through the plant, they often remarked, "Here comes the dog and his master," with reference to Hardy as the master.

Stevens was also called a "lone wolf" because he was "unsocial and distant," and "Simon Legree" as befitting a "slave driver." Especially active in civic life, the staff officials were outspoken against Stevens' "never participating in anything."

An assistant departmental superintendent pinpointed line feelings toward Stevens:

[Stevens] tried to stop us from bringing newspapers into the plant. He barred the paper boy in the bus station from selling papers, but the [worker's union] broke that up in a week. It all started when he saw a couple of fellows reading papers out in the plant. He's a damned old grouch and unreasonable as hell! He was taking a woman's club through the shops one day. He stepped on an oily spot on the floor and fell. Then he got up and called all the bosses of _____ department and bawled hell out of them right there in front of the women. That's a hell of a way for a man in his position to act. He's not big enough for his job—he's always blowing up about things that [Hardy or Springer] would never say a damn thing about. A couple of years ago the street outside the plant was tied up with traffic. I was just going into the office when [Stevens] came tearing out wild-eyed to see what the trouble was. He looked like a damn fool.

On the other hand, Hardy's social activities and occupational experience—and possibly even his personal appearance—were material to his prestige in Milo. In community gatherings he was something of a social lion. Under forty, he looked and moved like an athlete, which contrasted strikingly with his white temples. Wives of his associates called him "very handsome" without offending their husbands. Hardy was a member of the Masonic Order, as were most of the Milo managers . . . and community leaders.

The managers were impatient for the time when Stevens, a rejected non-Mason past sixty, would retire and be succeeded by Hardy. Hardy's tie with his subordinates was strong from his having been both a departmental and divisional superintendent at Milo, an experience Stevens lacked. This gave Hardy a personal knowledge of his associates that, with his other qualities, enabled him to outstrip Stevens as a power in the plant.

Though officially head of Industrial Relations and presumably only a consultant on such matters, I. Rees at times inspired more concern than any of the other managers. This was partly attributable to his being sent out from the Office to "strengthen" the department. Aged thirty-six, with a degree in aeronautical engineering, he replaced "weak" F. Lane who was made assistant-to Stevens. The following incident points the error of the formal chart as a gauge of Rees' place in Milo affairs.

For some time the most widespread struggle in Milo had been between line factions favoring and opposing the use of maintenance incentives.[3] Otis Blanke, head of Division A, opposed the incentives and persuaded Hardy that dropping them would benefit Milo. At a meeting to deal with the problem Hardy stated his position and concluded, "We should stop using maintenance incentives. They cause us too much trouble and cost too much."

Then as only a staff head, and one without vested interest in this issue or the formal authority to warrant threats or decisive statements, Rees arose and said:

I agree that maintenance incentives have caused a lot of trouble. But I don't think it's because they're not useful. It's because there are too many people not willing to toe the mark and give them a try. The [Office] put that system in here and by God we're going to make it work, not just tolerate it!

The surprise at these remarks broke the meeting up in embarrassment for everyone but Rees. His statement quickly spread to all of supervision. Since Industrial Engineering had set up the incentives, one of its supervisors asked the Maintenance Department to aid the pay plan by having its foreman, in addition to the inspectors, count the number of pieces done on various orders in their shops. The appeal was made with the thought that report of non-existent pieces might be a factor in making the plan "too costly." Rees learned of the request and described the idea as one that "would cause more trouble than it would be worth." This remark was similarly flashed through the plant. Early the following day all line executives who had been approached by the staff supervisor telephoned apologies for their inability to aid him, and they asked him to please consider their position in view of Rees' stand. These and other less overt incidents led Milo executives to see Rees as an unofficial spokesman for the Office. Because he had spent three years there as staff representative of Industrial Relations, local managers assumed he had been selected as "a bright young boy" and "groomed" for the Milo post. His predecessor, Lane, was regarded as "a grand old guy," but was removed to a "safe spot" for a few years until his retirement because he was "not sharp enough to deal over and under the table at the same time." Several of the executives explicitly stated their belief that Rees had powerful sponsors in the Office and that to provoke him would "just be suicide."

Although Hardy was overmatched by Rees on the issue of incentives, he is placed above Rees in Figure [13.2] because he dominated more areas of Milo life. Officially Hardy had authority over the line organization and six of the staffs, including Rees'. But they were at swords' points on any issue that Rees by loose interpretation could bring into the province of his department—and maintenance incentives as a stimulus to union-management friction was one of these. Hardy almost certainly exceeded his assigned authority over all plant processes except those which Rees interpreted as lying in his sphere. Here Hardy exercised less than his formal authority.

M. Springer, Superintendent of Division C and formally on a par with Blanke and Revere, is placed just below Rees in Figure [13.2]. Springer was thirty-six years old, held a degree in mechanical engineering, and had spent four years in the Office before coming to Milo as a processing superintendent in Division B. During the four years Springer was in this position, Hardy was head of Division B. They worked together as a clique in winning favors from a former plant chief. The understanding developed between them remained solid. Revere and Blanke recognized this. When seeking important favors from Hardy, they always first conferred with Springer, though all three had the same formal relation to Hardy. . . .

OPERATION VERSUS MAINTENANCE

Cost Pressures

Operating costs are a concern top management vehemently shares with all levels of supervision. At Milo, cost meetings were the point at which top officers relieved their feelings on the need for greater economy. Middle and lower officers learned that an excellent cost record was directly related to their future. By graphs on bulletin boards, and semimonthly newsletters, departmental operating costs were publicized in much the same way as lost-time accidents and charity drives. The more efficient heads were lauded, the others shamed. This scheme of reward and penalty led to ingenious distortions of records to more nearly approach ideal cost figures. And divergent social rivalries hindered the hope that lower officers would compete with each other for rank on the efficiency scale.

For example, the maintenance department received an appropriation of $200,000 to cover installation of new equipment in one of the production units, but "lost" $130,000 of the allocation before it could be used for that purpose. According to a maintenance chief, eight operation heads applied pressure "for a divvy because Maintenance was always getting them into a jam." By the time work started on the project, only $70,000 remained. The eight chiefs then "tried to outdo each other" in the following months by redecorating their offices, installing luxurious plastic and tile floors or wall-to-wall carpeting, sumptuous furniture, and only electrically operated office machines. To a query as to how this could be done, the informant stated:

> Part of it was just taking money out of one pocket and putting it in another. Supposing a guy [department chief] wanted to paint his office. Well, he wrote out an order for it and charged it against his cut of the $200,000. . . . He had an order number for it and he had a deal with Maintenance, so they had to do the job for him. He could go on charging things to that same number that had nothing to do with painting. He could go in the storehouse with that order number and get anything they had that he wanted as long as his honey [buying power that had been transferred to him] from Maintenance held out. I've seen a bench from the carpenter shop cost $400 [as a result of other work added to the order number for the bench]. If Auditing got to snooping around, what the hell could they find out? And if they did find anything, they'd know a damn sight better than to say anything about it. How could they prove that a bench didn't cost $400? [Hardy] might bawl hell out of somebody but he can't do anything about something that everybody does— especially when it's already done. All the work of installing the stuff was done by Maintenance. Buying the stuff was easy. All those guys [department heads] have got lines through Cost Accounting. That's a lot of bunk about Auditing being independent.[4]

The informant's inclusion of "everybody" was an exaggeration. Obviously those executives unsuccessful in such participation were under a burden of concern about costs and the need of comparing favorably with others. And as the covert nature of informal arrangements gave no assurance that one would be equally successful at all times, most of the executives did compete to please higherups and to win aid from them. These conditions bore directly on the struggles between Operation and Maintenance as production chiefs searched for loopholes in the tightening cost system.

R. Forest, assistant-to Springer, periodically called meetings of all operation heads. He went around the circle calling on each for an estimate of his working costs for the following month. The Standard Cost section of the Auditing Department recorded these estimates. All heads knew that Hardy and Stevens expected the estimates to be justified and consistently not exceeded.

To keep his record straight, each head was given a series of order numbers which constituted his "account." The Auditing Department prepared the wage and salary record of all employees in a given department. Consumption of utilities was recorded with similar precision. But upkeep of present equipment, purchase of new and replacement of old materiel, and the unforeseen costs attending expansion were all more difficult to control. Hence this area of upkeep was used by the department chief as one means of relieving cost pressures on himself. In using the escape he of course competed obscurely with other heads groping for similar devices. Hence at times calculating alliances were formed to share an expedient. As pressures for economy increased, many operation executives placed low short-run production costs above concern for equipment. That is, they favored continuous use of equipment with shutdowns only for breakdowns followed by minimum repair and quick resumption of production. Maintenance chiefs argued that long-run costs would be less, and equipment safer and more lasting, if thorough periodic overhauls were made. Each sought to achieve his goal without losing favor with Hardy.

For a decade the records of all repair work were prepared by the maintenance shops in which the work was done. This record included time and materials for doing the work. The shops sent a copy to the Auditing Department which charged the cost to the given head. Over a period of several years friction developed between operation and maintenance groups. Some heads of Operation complained about the backlog of over 1500 uncompleted orders in the various shops, while foremen of Maintenance protested about being "pushed around" by operation executives.

Hardy and the assistants-to Stevens investigated and found that some heads had hundreds of unfinished orders while others had none. The condition was hushed to prevent invidious ascription of good or poor leadership, when obviously there could be no poor leaders.

The backlog belonged almost entirely to the less aggressive and less astute heads. Once their orders and worn equipment were delivered to the shops, they assumed that the work would be done as soon as possible, and attended to more urgent matters. Or if they did inquire at the shops they put no pressure on maintenance foremen. On the other hand, the chiefs abreast of their repair work were there because they checked constantly on the progress of their orders. They expedited the work by use of friendships, by bullying, and implied threats. As all the heads had the same formal rank, one could say that an inverse relation existed between a given officer's personal influence and his volume of uncompleted repairs.

For example, a dominant chief would appear in person and tell the maintenance foreman that certain jobs were "hot" and were holding up production. Some operation chiefs threatened to block their flow of informal favors to maintenance officers. These favors included (1) cooperation to "cover up" errors made by maintenance machinists, or at least to share responsibility for them; (2) defense for the need of new maintenance personnel; (3) support in meetings against changes recommended by staff groups that maintenance forces opposed; (4) consideration, and justification to top management, of material needed by Maintenance for its success and survival in meeting the demands of Operation.

Confronted by an aggressive executive demanding special service, the foreman would look about his shop for machines with jobs that could be removed with least danger of offending other executives concerned. He would "pull" the partially repaired job of some less bellicose supervisor and replace it with that of the demanding head.

The use of fear to coerce favored service and its effect on foremen is illustrated by Revere's behavior at the same time he was a department head. According to one of the foremen

> Charlie would come out here snorting that "By God I want this done and I want that done!" He'd throw his brass around here till he'd have everybody shaking in their boots. We all knew that if he got anything on us it would be just too damn bad—he was that kind of guy. If you tried to humor him and tell him you'd get around to it as soon as you could, he'd yell, "What d' you mean as soon as you can? Jesus Christ! I can see a dozen men settin' on their asses doing nothing! Get 'em to work!"
>
> His idea of a man not doing anything was all wrong. He'd see a lathe hand settin' on a box and say he was loafing. Well hell, you know as well as I do that a man can be taking a long cut that may take an hour before he makes another change. Why the hell should he stand up all that time? Yesterday the man might have had a job that made him ball the jack all day—and he might have one just like it tomorrow. So why not take it easy when he can? But that was Charley. Always riding you and always on the lookout to get something on you. I'll bet he ain't changed a damn bit, either.

Once the damage of maintenance tie-up to production was admitted by all, there was further dispute concerning the cause. Hinting at the play of personal relations, some executives declared that "politics" was the factor. Others held that maintenance mechanics were "laying down on the job" and that a piecework incentive plan would "clear the jam" and prevent such blocks in the future. This view appealed to the division chiefs and Stevens' group. They were reluctant to believe that supervisory behavior alone could have precipitated the problem. The new staff of industrial engineers agreed, for they would set up the pay plan and thereafter have a larger voice in all related matters. After many conferences, a faction of Milo and Office managers agreed on a twofold plan to harmonize different views. One part of the project was a control to prevent friction between the two line branches; the other was a wage scheme to speed up maintenance work.

The Control

The new system was called the Field Work Department (FWD). To tap all available knowledge, its personnel was drawn from a pool of experienced operation and maintenance men. In addition to having a broad knowledge of Milo technology and intimacy with blueprints, shop mathematics, and materials, each officer was a specialist in at least one of the areas such as pipe fitting, welding, machine operation, carpentry, boiler repair, motor repair, electrical maintenance, bricklaying, layout, statistics, and accounting. Several men were former supervisors. Administrators of the FWD were at least second level managers from both Operation and Maintenance. The whole body, nearly one hundred personnel, was under a Superintendent of Maintenance who had earlier been in Operation. He was surrounded by a corps of consultants.

In theory, all members of the FWD would be working in a fresh atmosphere unhampered by the coerced cooperation or friendly ties of earlier jobs. Housed in a new, isolated building, the FWD was both the point of entry and termination for maintenance orders. And between these points the orders would flow in a circuit around the shops without the previous difficulties.

A scheme was introduced to lessen contacts between the personnel of Operation and Maintenance and to assure a fixed numerical and chronological sequence in processing the orders. The old system of "order numbers" and "accounts" was converted to give each department a specific annual series of numbers for use in writing maintenance orders. A department's series would run from say 5000 to 10,000. Any order in that range would identify the department and would take priority over any higher number from that department. The chronological sequence of an order from any department was determined on a time clock as it entered the FWD. Each order was then classified as an aid to rapid location of the job in process.

Frequently a job analyst visited the production site to get additional and confirmatory data on the newly registered order. Then the order was given to the proper specialists who determined the cost of materials and labor to do the job, and indicated the shops and routes among machines and operations that the job should follow. The FWD estimate of costs was then submitted to the executive who had issued the order. This enabled him to see how well he was remaining inside the budget he had submitted to Forest. . . . He had a certain freedom to bargain for a smaller or larger estimate, but in the end he had to sign it, which gave him no justification for wide departures. Once he did, the order was placed in a pouch with blueprints and instructions and sent to the assigned shop. There again the order was clocked, recorded, filed; then completed as specified by the FWD.

As the job traveled about the shop, the time and course of each movement were recorded. On completion, a copy of the record was retained, another was sent to the Auditing Department, and one to the FWD where the "exact" cost of the job was analyzed and recorded for future reference. Throughout the job journey the FWD apparatus was expected to protect shop foremen from pressure by operation heads and to end recurring problems with the union over job placement.

The FWD in Practice

The new control was successful in permanently breaking the jam of maintenance orders. However, in a few months inconsistencies began to develop. The FWD discovered a mounting number of gaps between its estimates and actual costs as computed from the completed job records. Some differences were expected, but not multiples of the estimate or, as in some cases, jobs completed with no charge at all against them.

The social relations behind these unexpected results were complex, but due largely to the persisting cost pressures and the play of old enmities and friendships that the FWD had not considered and certainly had not erased. We can see this quickly by analyzing executive actions and regroupings. In group A were those chiefs who formerly dominated the shops and enjoyed priority on their orders: Geiger, Dicke, Boesel, Meier, Ames, and Revere before his promotion. In group B were those who paid for this advantage by having their repair work neglected: Smith, Taylor, O'Brien, Ruf, and others not on the chart.

Now, officers of group A covertly charged that work of the FWD was "slowing down production" because of the "red tape" and "no-good" estimates. They told jokes of the "soft jobs," "pencil pushing," "coffee-drinking," "loafing," and "sham work" of FWD personnel. Behind a mask of humor they asked FWD personnel if they were able to look the Paymaster's assistants in the face when receiving their checks. Finally, officers of group A became reluctant to sign estimates made by the FWD. Privately they indicated a fear that Hardy and Stevens would draw threatening inferences from comparing FWD estimates with (a) their actual costs and with (b) the advance estimate each of them submitted to Forest. Research showed a tie between their fear and the fact that their actual costs were markedly greater than FWD estimates.

In time the executives of group B also became averse to signing the estimates, but for a different reason: they were getting their jobs done for less, and sometimes so much less, than the estimates, that they, too, feared questions.

In terms of low maintenance costs and "smooth" operation, the two groups were reversing the positions they held before entry of the FWD. From a place of dominance, group A executives were in process of losing face with their division chiefs, while those of group B were moving from a condition of "poor management" to commendable efficiency in terms of cost figures. As group A was losing control over its repair costs, group B was gaining command, with some members reducing their costs by half. The major factor in this radical shift was action by new informal alignments *among* the executives and especially *between them and maintenance foremen.* The unplanned reorganization grew out of old friendships and enmities, and experiment to find loopholes in the FWD controls. It was reflected in the more startling gaps between estimated and actual costs.

These gaps—and jibes from maliciously perceptive cost analysts who had failed to "get in the brain department"—threw the FWD on the defensive. Several of its members visited the shops but learned little except that foremen were evasive and that some jobs were not on machines to which they had been routed. As members of the FWD, the investigators were seen, even by old acquaintances in the shops, as "dangerous" to the extent they might "make a slip" to key figures in the FWD.

Collaboration between group B executives and foremen to charge various amounts of group B work time to accounts of group A executives was the chief factor in the hiatus between estimates and final costs. The foremen were indispensable in this arrangement. They of course had to be willing participants—and were in most cases. Not only as individuals had they been bullied by many operations heads for years, but they had suffered the abasement peculiar to most foremen over the past two or three decades, losses of authority to unions and expanding staff organizations. The cooperative maintenance foremen now derived a new sense of power from unexpected arrangements growing out of the FWD. They found themselves confronted by operation executives who could beg for favors but could not coerce them because of the buffer supplied by the FWD.

The physical details of charging time incorrectly were simple. The foreman had only to enter the pouch number (assigned by the FWD) of any uncompleted job in the shop on the time card of a mechanic. If a foreman remembered an enemy head, usually a member of group A, he could take revenge and simultaneously reward a friendly head by entering a job number of the enemy on the time cards of repairmen doing his friend's work. All "elapsed time" between clock punches was thereby charged to his enemy.

As competition developed to hold down costs and remain inside the agreed estimates, several of the smaller departments were cooperating with each other as well as with maintenance foremen to poach on accounts of the larger departments headed by executives of group A.

Other contradictory but interlocked social and technical practices helped clear a path for the developing evasion. All estimates, for example, assumed that maintenance equipment was in top working order. But this is rarely true in any shop and was not at Milo. Hence the FWD's allotted time was inadequate for some jobs. Also unavoidable change in mechanics, with different skill levels and motivations, frequently held a prior order to a given machine so long that the routing of other orders was thrown off schedule. This of course initiated departures. Again, some situations demanded that foremen substitute other job numbers, quite apart from agreements with friends in operation. For example, when a job was completed and all papers "closed out," it was established practice to regard it as "dead." However, a completed piece might be passed by Inspection and sent to its department only to be rejected there because it had been machined to fit *perfect* rather than the *worn* with which it engaged. Because the old order could not be reopened without embarrassment to the people who would have to make decisions and protect those responsible for the failure in communication, and because all time had to be charged to some account, someone's job number had to be used. Knowing the cost pressures on operation heads, and having power to assign a number, the foreman's sentiments toward executives who had been "reasonable" with him repeatedly influenced his choice of a number. Though relatively infrequent, this condition set a precedent for other deviations, whether demanded by work conditions or friendships.

A third long-standing job arrangement also afforded group B executives some escape from the FWD. The larger departments (group A chiefs) had more repetitive maintenance work than did the other departments. For use with only this class of repair service, they were given "standing order numbers." These numbers were always "open" in the shops. The new shuffle of strictures and freedoms made these numbers a useful but limited device that the foremen used to reward group B and to penalize group A chiefs.

At the height of the struggle among operation chiefs, Geiger learned by his own intrigues that the unnamed head, Whymper, in Springer's division was having much of his maintenance costs charged to Geiger's account. Geiger telephoned Whymper, gave enough details to show his knowledge of the poaching, and told him, "By God, you'd better pay up!" Expecting Geiger to go to Hardy, Whymper was terrified. He had shortly before received a $35,000 appropriation with which Maintenance was to enlarge a section of his department. Now he transferred the uncommitted portion— $3900—to Geiger's account. This was evidently more than he had poached, for according to staff informants Geiger used much of it for "fancy new storm windows, ten new fans, and a 9000 square foot paint job" in his own department.

Reactions of Top Management

Inevitably Stevens' office learned enough to respond by calling the heads with excessive costs to account. Some officers charged that "padding of books" by unnamed groups, was responsible for their costs. All groups denied responsibility and professed ignorance of how the condition had developed.

Above suspicion at top levels, the FWD nevertheless elaborated the obvious fact that its data for actual costs came from the shops, and that its interest was to bring the two figures together, not separate them. The Auditing Department cleared itself by showing that its computations were based on only the workmen's time cards and the accompanying shop order numbers supported by the foremen's signature. The shop foremen declared that they always followed instructions to the letter and had not confused shop order numbers when assigning jobs. A similar defense was made by the shop clerical force which transcribed and dispatched the records. And some of group B heads even praised the FWD, maintaining that for the first time the more efficient executives were free to show their superiority. Hardy and Stevens were not convinced that they had the facts—or could get them inside the limitations governing everyone.

To uncover the maze of expanding innovations would have been a formidable task. Just the problem of gathering initial evidence, with the full cooperation of everyone, would require that hundreds of pouch numbers, continuing active for weeks on complex jobs, be compared with hundreds of time cards having five to twelve job entries daily, etc. Certainly the situation could not be brought out into the open for all to see without danger of exposing the involvement of close associates and dredging up old issues that would outweigh the current ones. Enough was suspected, however, to warrant their making changes. For some time several departments had had small maintenance forces of their own to care for trifling repairs. These groups were known collectively as *Departmental Maintenance*, as distinct from the larger system of shops dealing with the major work of all departments, called *Field Maintenance*. Several steps were now taken.

First, departmental maintenance crews were enlarged so that each department could do nearly all of its own repair work. At the same time the department head would have direct authority over his repairs and all personnel involved, including foremen. This was to prevent interdepartmental conflict. To expedite the change a large shop was closed and its tools distributed among the departments on the basis of individual needs. With union cooperation the personnel from this shop was similarly distributed among the various departments. Finally, the FWD was reduced to a "skeleton crew" of less than a dozen, and its forces were similarly absorbed around the plant.

Though no official charges of malfeasance were made from above, Operation and Maintenance covertly blamed each other for breakup of the FWD. Maintenance officers held that *their* wage plan had been effective in turning out repair work, and with less than half the men required before use of the incentives. Operation agreed, but declared that the financial cost was prohibitive. Under the money incentives some mechanics had so improved their skills after guaranteed pay rates had been set up on certain types of work that later they were able to perform at remarkable levels. Operation heads regarded these costs of repair as so great that they hoped to cut outlays by using certain machine parts until they were worn beyond repair and replacing them when possible with less expensive parts, thus eliminating the repair aspect of maintenance on these items.

The real issue–the wish to escape cost pressures and the resultant poaching of operation heads on each other's maintenance accounts—was not discussed, as both sides made a red herring of the incentive system. Operation forces convinced Hardy that their position was just. This led him to denounce maintenance incentives, and then to lose face in the unexpected clash with Rees mentioned earlier.

The FWD was theoretically sound as far as the knowledge on which it was based. But that knowledge was too limited. Created to reduce costs, speed repair work, and check "politics," it was undone by politics because such relations were not understood and were officially rejected as improper, which blocked understanding. At the same time the FWD actually increased cost pressures but did nothing to change the disparity in rewards which gave applause, prestige, and more income to Operation for "producing," and only toleration to Maintenance as a necessary evil. The failure was largely one of not adapting the control to what actually existed. . . .

THE OFFICE VERSUS MILO

Managers in the Office had learned that some of the local chiefs wished to eliminate maintenance incentives, or at least to be free to buy certain parts outside when and if repair costs for these items became too great as a result of the incentives. As an unofficial agent, Rees presumably gave the Office helpful details on factors and persons. Hence the Office sought to fit its scheme to these attitudes, but at the same time to shift more control of Maintenance into its own hands. This approach changed the emphasis from concern about *who* in Milo would be responsible for maintenance costs, to developing a record of all replacement parts on hand so that each department head would have to *justify purchase of new parts*. This developing tactic of containment in response to covert evasions in Milo initiated new realignments. Struggle for dominance among groups of Milo managers shifted to one between Milo and Office managers as local chiefs saw their accustomed control of the plant being usurped by "chair-warmers" of the Office.

Dynamic steps were followed in developing and introducing the Office plan. It was shaped by exploratory interplays between groups of the Office and Milo. The Office pushed its logic with an eye to Milo morale, while Milo parried moves that threatened its authority and its social arrangements.

First, departmental maintenance was greatly reduced but, like the FWD, continued as a framework that could not be entirely dropped without encouraging potential rivalries and disrupting the newer productive practices. While details of the plan were being settled, repair work would be done wherever most expedient.

The plan itself can be discussed under (1) cost aspects and (2) personnel reorganization.

Cost Aspects

The major item to cut expenses was a "surplus parts program." This was aimed at compiling a record of all reserve equipment on hand in each department and developing a permanent system for keeping the record up-to-date. Next, the purchase of new parts was to be taken largely out of the hands of Milo chiefs, though the plan was introduced so that they would seem to have a voice in the purchases.

To get the program going the Office requested a listing from Milo of the number of parts on hand that cost $500 or more, and of those parts currently needed or that would be needed by the end of a given period. The intent was to start with the more expensive parts and then systematically lower the figure as experience grew.

Personnel Reorganization

It was believed in the Office that a simple request for such information, to be reported in writing, was unlikely to accomplish its purpose. The realistic move, it was held, would be to create new specific duties and assign able men to enforce them. After collapse of the elaborate FWD, however, simplicity and directness were seen as basic to any reorganization, so only two new supervisory positions were set up in Milo.

Office representatives held conferences with a few Milo executives to work out details of the change. When the department chiefs learned of the developing plan, group A executives wished a voice in selection of the two new officers who would be liaison men between Milo and the Office. They were supported by their assistants as well as Blanke, Revere, and Springer. After conferences among themselves, these eleven executives worked as a clique to convince Hardy that the choice should be made *entirely* by Milo. Hardy was quite clear to his intimates that he regarded the pending control as interference with local authority, and he agreed with the executive clique that "we should pick some good men."

In the meantime the Office, ignorant of his attitude among local executives, was searching for a device to soften the shock of its plan. Failure of the FWD was seen by the Office as leaving Milo chiefs sensitive about the whole subject of cost control—and even indisposed to be cooperative. Hence the Office made a bland approach and voluntarily asked Stevens to suggest candidates from his own ranks.

The request precipitated meetings to choose candidates. Hardy met with the clique, some of the group B chiefs, and a few supervisors. These last two named no one but did stress the need for "able men." With Hardy still silent, the clique designated two persons who were generally regarded as *not able* men. Quickly it was seen that the clique of group A chiefs wanted only amenable candidates. When Hardy added his voice to theirs, the decision was made. The officers nominated were W. Taylor and F. Bingham. This was the Taylor who was out-maneuvered for the superintendency of Division A by the clique of Blanke, Dicke, and Peters. Both men were accepted by the Office. Opponents of the cause led by Hardy, including some of those who praised the FWD, ridiculed the appointments. They saw both candidates as "weak" and "impossible" in the roles given them. Taylor's failure to win the post of division head was considered proof of unfitness to "act on his own." They considered his private life as further proof. His wife had "disgraced" him and Milo by a noisy divorce in the local community. His heavy drinking and repeated defeats in clashes with the union were also evidence of his having "nothing on the ball" and of his "willingness to go along with any policy" of his superiors. Bingham, too, was regarded as a "soft touch." A low ranking staff supervisor, he was near retirement and pension and allegedly so fearful of losing these payments that he fell in with any demands by higherups. It was agreed that he lacked confidence and avoided responsibility. Without voice on this issue, many staff officers analyzed the choice of Taylor and Bingham as "manipulation by the top brass for their own ends."

In the assignment of duties, Taylor was to be responsible to no one in Milo but Hardy. And this was qualified accountability, for Taylor was expected to communicate *freely* and *directly* with the Office, a privlege that not over three of all the Milo managers possessed. Taylor's duties were to inspect and approve each "parts report" turned into his office and to verify its correctnmess by personal count of parts if necessary. He was the only officer in the plant with power to authorize the order of new parts.

Bingham was to assist Taylor, but he was responsible *only* to the Office for his duties. He was to initiate the reports periodically by requesting statements from each head of Operation. Thus he, not Taylor, made the face-to-face contacts. After obtaining the statements, Bingham turned them over to Taylor who approved them by signature and returned them to Bingham who mailed them to the Office. The Office then issued the superintendent in question a certificate of authorization which for a specified time enabled him to buy necessary parts from the outside without going through the Office, though each purchase, during any period, required Taylor's approval. By thus focusing on two individuals, neither of whom had authority over the other and both of whom had direct access to the Office to escape local pressures, the control was regarded as simple, direct, and manageable.

THE CONTROL IN PRACTICE

Initial Executive Reaction

Following introduction of the parts program, Bingham notified the heads that he was ready to receive statements. When two weeks passed with no response, he made further requests. A few officers gave excuses of being shorthanded, of having prior problems, emergency work, etc., but no records of parts.

The clique supported by Hardy had now compromised most of the executives, and they coerced the others to ignore and resists the control as long as possible while studying it "to find ways to make it work." Despite some oppositions in the past, Dicke, Meier, and Smith, with their assistants, favored compliance with the Office, but feared the outcome of not going along with the others. During meetings and in private arguments with members of the Hardy group, their vocal resistance was beaten down and they were finally frightened into silence. The arguments used against them showed the issue to be primarily one of *who* exercised authority in the plant—Milo executives or the Office. Hardy's remark was the keynote of the resisters: "The program, is too inflexible and causes too much trouble." Blanke spelled out the dominant sentiments:

The thing I've got against the whole damn setup is procedures. Every time you turn around you run into a rule that stymies you. Some chairwarmer in [the Office] cooks up a crack-pot notion of how things ought to be done. Maybe he was never in the plant but he don't let that bother him. He writes it up and sends it out. Then by God it's up to us to make it work. The way I feel about it is this: if the setup is so damned farfetched that you can't make it work, why bother with it at all? What the hell do they think we're out here for? We know our jobs. If they'd leave us alone we'd never have any trouble.

Statements of this kind and knowledge of Hardy's attitude indicated to the minority that their problems would multiply if they met Bingham's request at this time.

In the meantime, Bingham was increasingly disturbed by his failure but was helpless to *do* anything. He told confidants, "I need a psychiatrist. I'm so damned fidgety I don't know what to do with myself. I'd rather be out in the shop than sitting at this damn desk all day with nothing to do. I like to be doing something." After six weeks of growing distress over his inability to bridge the gap between expectations of the Office and the anonymous note from the local executives *that he was to do nothing,* Bingham received a letter from the Office asking for a progress report. Devoted to the letter of official directives, and still having no statements, he notified the Office that the superintendents "refused to cooperate."

Response of the Office

On learning of Bingham's rebuff, the Office sent several investigators to Milo. Tightness of the informal bloc eluded their inquiry, but they prepared a statement praising Bingham's efforts and censuring the heads "for failure to cooperate" with him. Copies of the report were distributed at the Office and among local top managers.

Bingham's desperation and resulting action had not been foreseen by the executives. This open support by the Office meant that despite Bingham's docility, new devices were necessary to control him. Part of the assumed incentive of his new role was that he would enjoy the leisure of what was really a sinecure. But in his dilemma about what to do his leisure was spent in anxiety, and thus failed to be a reward.

Now supported by nearly all the heads, Hardy's group searched for indirect ways of winning him over. They sought to inflate his self-importance by installing him in a larger office with an immense desk, giving him a secretary, dictaphone, filing cabinets, etc. Need to control the character of his communications to the Office led the executives to reinforce these trappings of rank with a flattering personal appeal. Several of them including Taylor, went to his new quarters and proposed that "we work this thing out together. After all, we don't want to do anything to stir up trouble." Apparently these inducements, with fear of reprisals, and the assurance that he would be protected by appearances, prevailed on Bingham. He agreed to go along.

Tactics of Escape

Though some of the superintendents continued to fear the Office, they cooperated to thwart an accurate tally of their extra parts. The motivation to prevent a count was complex. Probably satisfaction in outwitting authority was a minor factor. Certainly the managers felt an obscure urge to preserve their "right" to command the plant. However, judging from actions and spontaneous remarks, the major factor was their wish to keep a margin of funds beyond operating costs in the narrow sense. As we shall see in a later chapter [not included here], there are operating costs in the broad sense that include use of funds to meet the demands of daily personal relations—*the maintenance of a good fellowship structure as well as material equipment.* The financial costs of keeping social mechanisms in repair merge with those of the physical. If cataloged at Milo they would include such entries as (1) part or full time employment of relatives or friends of associates from both plant and community; (2) the executive's wish to have plush offices in his department; (3) possible emergencies in a period of change; and (4) use of plant services and materials . . . to get more cooperation from subordinates and colleagues.

Before the executives showed resistance to the Office, Bingham's instructions were to make formal requests for a record of parts. To limit the evasion, the Office notified Taylor that his job would now include surprise inspections and count of parts in each department. He and Bingham were alarmed by this new directive for neither had the front or address to carry out the order as intended. After conferences with the executives, their solution was not to make unannounced counts, but to telephone various heads before a given inspection telling them the starting point, time, and route that would be followed. By varying these conditions on successive tours, Taylor and Bingham made each inspection *appear* to catch the chiefs off guard.

This use of official form as a mask was not new in the plant. Nominal surprise was a common device in Milo and between Milo and the Office in other actions also. For example, visits from members of the Office were planned but given a camouflage of spontaneity that served the needs of both groups. This spared Office managers the unpleasantness of seeing a condition of which they should be officially ignorant, and of feeling embarrassment in possessing knowledge that presupposed corrective action by them. The condition and the potential consequence of action would of course sully the friendly call and hence should be avoided. For their part, Milo officers reduced the time, cost, and interference with routine of setting up acceptable appearances by deciding in advance the specific path through the plant that the tour would follow. Then just on the fringes of the entire route, equipment was cleaned and possibly painted, walks and driveways were cleared and swept, and everything "put in order."

Inside Milo nominal surprise was also a preventive of conflict. For example, safety and health inspectors usually telephoned in advance of visits so that they would not see unsafe practices or conditions they would feel obliged to report. They thus escaped present embarrassment for themselves and avoided incurring hostility that might persist to a time when the good will of associates could be personally helpful in the ongoing and elusive structure of personal claims in which all the executives unavoidably moved. This fiction of surprise enabled the managers to preserve the official dignity so essential for any rules of the game, and to give the appearance of following formal procedures despite inevitable obstacles and frequent impossibility. They were experimenting to find workable means of dealing with problems too elusive to trap in a formal procedure.

Notice that a count of parts was to begin provoked a flurry among the executives to hide certain parts and equipment, and thus save the faces of Taylor and Bingham. Motor and hand trucks, with laborers and skilled workers who could be spared, were assembled in a given department. Then the materials *not* to be counted were moved to: (1) little-known[5] and inaccessible spots; (2) basements and pits that were dirty and therefore unlikely to be examined; (3) departments that had already been inspected and that could be approached circuitously while the counters were en route between official storage areas; and (4) places where materials and supplies might be used as a camouflage for parts. Though complete inspections were required only four times a year, Bingham and Taylor had other duties so that with the size of Milo, inspections continued for longer periods than would be expected. Various evasive answers were given to questions raised by the work force involved. And in most cases the break in their routine was to them more of a lark than a question-provoking situation.

As the practice developed, cooperation among the chiefs to use each other's storage areas and available pits became well organized and smoothly functioning. Joint action of a kind rarely, if ever, shown in carrying on official activities enabled the relatively easy passage of laborers and truckers from one work area to another without serious complications for formal arrangements.

The inspections were meant to be both a control and a supplementary count. Once a month reports of parts were to be submitted to Bingham by each chief. The list of course should conform closely to Bingham's quarterly count. The reports now arrived regularly at his desk. Probably in no case were they accurate. But Taylor approved them, and Bingham dispatched them to the Office.

Thus a working adjustment was reached. The Office received its required flow of documents, which, though only roughly accurate, allowed planning within workable limits. Able to work behind a screen of assured formalities, Bingham and Taylor escaped nervous breakdown. Friction between Operation and Maintenance subsided to a low level. Finally, the Milo chiefs preserved their conception of local rights and at the same time raised morale. Conflict between principle and action in the area had not, of course, "ended," but it was contained and existed latently. . . .

CLIQUES AS FOUNTAINHEADS OF ACTION

Although the term "clique" *denotes* a small exclusive group of persons with a common interest, it too often *connotes* a group concerned with questionable activity. Without these moral overtones, the term can aptly apply to the initiating nucleus of many group activities in and out of industry. Certainly the negative feeling associated with the term is carried too far, for cliques and secrets are inseparable and essential for group life. We would question, for example, whether parents covertly checking on their children's activities in school and community are "conspirators"; whether the indirect attempts all of us make to learn more of our acquaintances than they voluntarily tell us is "immoral"; and whether the widespread "manipulations" by both leaders and followers in all areas of life in competitive societies to win ends is "villainy." Villainy may develop in all these cases, but not necessarily. Cliques may work for moral as well as immoral ends. Whether or not we are able to preach what we practice, the organization will fall apart without sustaining action by some clique. All organizations must have "privy councils" similar in some sense to the meaning of that phrase in feudal times. One may well ask, what organization is without secrets held by some members, usually the more responsible, from other members with the intent and eventual result of helping all *loyal* members? Too often uncertainty hallows and hides the developing defects of official doctrine for changing situations. Responsible members must nevertheless try to fit the department, or firm, to inescapable conditions. And in doing this they necessarily "socialize" and "discuss problems," which is easily seen by opponents as "clique" activity "undermining" the organization.

More of this later, but for now let us think of a clique as the informal association of two or more persons to realize some end. The end is usually a calculated one, but it may be multiple and differ for some members. Typical ends in an industrial plant are: to increase the status and reward of one or all members; to get more support in job activities; to find social satisfactions; to hide facts or conditions that would be frowned on by superiors; to escape unpleasant situations or annoyances; to get more privileges, especially those peculiar to higherups; and to share the limelight with superiors. . . .

TYPES OF CLIQUES

Though cliques arise from dynamic situations and engage in many actions, they can be classified roughly. Typing may be in terms of their recurrence, what they do, the situations they spring from, or their effects. Probably the simplest relevant scheme, however, is to label cliques chiefly on the basis of their relation to the formal chart and the services they give to members. Such a scheme is, of course, not exhaustive or exclusive.

Approached in this way, cliques fall into three general groups: *vertical*, *horizontal*, and *random*. Vertical cliques can be broken down to vertical *symbiotic*[6] and vertical *parasitic*; and horizontal; to horizontal *aggressive* and horizontal *defensive* cliques. Vertical cliques usually occur in a single department. The tie is between the top officer and some of his subordinates.

It is vertical in the sense that it is an up-and-down alliance between formal unequals. It could be represented as a rectangle with the altitude greater than the base, e.g., □. Horizontal cliques, on the other hand, cut across more than one department and embrace formal equals for the most part. The horizontal clique can be symbolized as a rectangle with a base greater than its altitude, e.g., □.

Vertical Symbiotic Clique

In this relation, the top officer is concerned to aid and protect his subordinates. He does this by concealing or minimizing their errors, occasional lapses, etc. He does what favors he can to meet their immediate needs and to solidify their future in the firm. He interprets their behavior favorably to critical members of the department and to his own superiors. He humanizes the painful impersonal situations and the demands he must make.

The subordinates fully advise him of real or rumored threats to his position. They tell him of current work situations, confer on ways of dealing with "troublemakers" outside the clique, and discuss interdepartmental maneuvers. When urgency demands action and the chief is unavailable or there is no time for consultation, lower members confer and make moves with the chief's welfare in mind, and in terms of his known attitudes. Thus for all levels involved, there is a satisfying exchange of services. This is the most common and enduring clique in large structures. It is more than "team work" because only a nucleus of departmental personnel is involved. As it sweeps other members along they may follow gratefully, indifferently, or with some hostility. It is most effective when lower members are relatively indifferent about promotion or reasonably patient in waiting.

Vertical symbiotic cliques formed the real power centers in Milo, and they occurred at the divisional as well as the departmental level. Though not quite ideal because of Taylor's resentment, the Blanke-Dicke-Peters clique was an example extending into the divisional level, and the Hardy-Springer-Ames clique was another. However, several things make the clique less important at divisional levels. Personal ambitions and opportunities to move to other plants, for example, make the clique less stable there than at departmental levels. More subject to direct claims from the top, too, division heads usually want no official knowledge or part in taboo activities below them that they are sure department heads can contain. The latter understand that they are to serve as screening stations for conversion of unavoidable irregularities into reports befitting divisional dignity. . . .

Vertical Parasitic Clique

This is *the clique* of popular thought, the one that writers of supervisory manuals have in mind when they make such statements as, "No person may work under the direct or indirect supervision of an officer to whom he is related by blood or marriage."

This is a negative approach which assumes that collusive behavior is inevitable among persons with kinship ties who are in certain job relations.

Apparently the implied dangers are thought to be confined to such persons and situations. This is not the case, and the approach explains nothing about how the clique works, or of its relation to other unmentioned cliques that may preserve it in some form. If this kind of clique is regarded as organizationally harmful, it deserves more study.

The term "parasitic" is used because the exchange of services between lower and higher clique members is unequal. The lower ranked person or persons receive more than they give and may greatly damage the higher officer. This clique need not be a family affair. It may be based on a friendship developed earlier in the plant or elsewhere, when the current higher and lower ranking officers were on the same job level. The subordinate person owes his position to one of his superiors. He reports to this person what he regards as pertinent facts in his work area. His information may be of use to the superior, but often its importance is exaggerated. It is useful where it is accurate and the higher officer has real need of it—but in such cases the clique relation moves toward the symbiotic type. The problem arises when the lower member is thought to "carry tales" to the higher, whether he does or not. In this event his rejection by the group leads him to resentful distortion and overstatement.

Since management theoretically places members on merit only, the belief that special aid is given the lower member of the clique obviously inspires fear in associates that he has advantages they lack and will win still more by informing on them. Where this feeling is widespread, the group resists the chief and misinterprets his best efforts. He may exchange aid with the lower member, but group alertness to hide things from the lower member cuts the volume of favors he can send up as compared with that coming down to him. Much of the harm of this clique to the firm stems from its interference with operation of the symbiotic type. Given the values of personnel, the fringe identification of some members, and the incentives applied by higher management, *a symbiotic clique is essential for a given department to compete on a par with other departments* for favors from higherups and to set up workable arrangements with other departments.

The uneven exchange holds when the clique includes members of the work groups. In at least two cases in Milo, workmen informed to general foremen with whom they had been intimate before the foremen entered management. The foremen granted favors that eluded vigilance of the union and were repaid with information and cooperation on rush jobs. But the exchange showed a more tangible balance in favor of the workmen.

Formal regulations against the action we ascribe to this clique are evaded in various ways to allow the soliciting member to receive special aid and favors. An arrangement used at Milo, similar to what is described below as an aggressive horizontal clique, worked in effect to establish the parasitic clique in at least six situations. That is, two or more higher officers on comparable levels agreed to aid each other's relatives or friends on an exchange basis. One officer made a place in his department for the solicitee of the other, or promoted the person ahead of others, or gave him more

FIGURE [13.3]   Horizontal clique

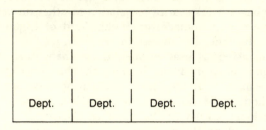

desirable work or more freedom from regulations in exchange for like aid for *his* protégé from a colleague. This cooperation, of course, promotes other understandings and joint action across departments.

HORIZONTAL CLIQUES

Horizontal Defensive Clique

Cutting across departments and including officers, as we noted, of nearly the same rank, this clique is usually brought on by what its members regard as crises. Threatened reorganization, introduction of disliked methods or a control such as that of the FWD or the Office, efforts by lower and middle management to shift responsibility to each other for problems that have developed, or opposition among the same groups as reassignment of duties is made after a reorganization, are all conditions that bring on crises. This clique may also arise across departments when day and night supervision hold each other responsible as the source of illegal strikes, serious accidents, rejection of the product by a customer, etc.

Usually this clique is strong for only the limited time necessary to defeat or adjust to a threat. Since nothing is served by its persisting longer, it lapses to dormancy until another crisis, but when active it forces the symbiotic cliques into quiescence. However, it is inherently weak because of the vertical breaks likely to occur from action by resurgent symbiotic cliques. That is, as a horizontal structure the clique is made up of departmental segments, each restrained temporarily by the chief's preoccupation with interdepartmental action. [See Figure 13.3.]

Horizontal Aggressive Clique

This type is distinguished from the defensive clique chiefly by its goals and the direction of its action. Its members are the same, and they are likely to have some ties based on past cooperative victories in getting favors and outwitting others. Their action is a cross-departmental drive to effect changes rather than resist them, to redefine responsibility, or even directly shift it. As with defensive action, interdepartmental friction subsides as the clique becomes a mutual aid bloc. Its goals may be to get increased operating allowances; to bring on advantageous reorganization or to win favored consideration over other units of the corporation; to obtain an advantage in forthcoming union-management negotiations; to check the expansion of some staff group; or to advance some member to a higher post so he can help the clique. And of course any executive level, top management, division chiefs, department heads, spontaneously forms this clique when it sets out to correct extreme action by other cliques at lower levels.

When advancement of some member is successful his placement graphically distorts the clique toward the vertical form, but this does not of course necessarily destroy old horizontal ties. For in his new post, the promoted officer frequently finds that his present assistants do not measure up to his earlier ones.[7] He may then contrive to bring one of his former associates closer to him formally. Obviously the continuation of old ties and understandings hinders adjustment to a new circle. Where the promoted officer does work to draw advantages from earlier associations, he and its members behave remarkably like campaigning politicians. They introduce praise and blame into the stream of plant gossip where it will bring highest returns. If conditions allow, the upgraded officer criticizes the state of the product as it enters his department. He attributes defects to laxity under the responsibility of the person to be discredited. He cooperates with his favorite chiefs to decrease their costs at the expense of others. He talks and exchanges favors with intimates among the superiors of those he wishes to aid, as in the cases above where rules against nepotism were reinterpreted. To aid his own candidates he may omit the subtleties of faint praise and positively damn the chances of others by attacks on their personal untidiness, excessive drinking, extramarital activities; or their disgraceful family squabbles, unmanageable children, impossible personality, and the like. Or, if the condition is known to exist, he may stress the person's stomach ulcers as proof of his shortcomings.

Blanke, Geiger, Meier, and Boesel were an aggressive horizontal clique. At one time they were all in the same division. As we noted, Blanke was then departmental chief with Geiger as his assistant. Meier and Boesel were assistant heads in other departments. When Blanke moved to head another division, Geiger succeeded him. Then with two other officers eligible in service and experience, Boesel became the next department head. Conversations with Geiger and others indicated that Blanke and Geiger greatly aided Boesel and that the three of them worked for Meier who came last to full superintendency. As superintendents, Meier, Boesel, and Geiger then cooperated closely to win favors from Revere. Through strong support from Boesel and Meier, Geiger had as much influence in the division as Revere. Although Blanke was in a different division and all faced new distractions, the old ties were revived on occasion to surmount official barriers.

The Random Clique

This clique is called *random* because its members usually cannot be classified in terms of formal rank, duties, or departmental origin, though they associate intimately enough to exchange confidences. Typically they have no consciously shared formal goal in the plant or point of company policy they are working to change, but the attraction is clearly friendship and social satisfaction. This can of course also exist in the other cliques, but friendship is not their end and may hardly be present. As compared with the more functional cliques this one is random in the sense that its members may come from any part of the personnel, managers and managed, and that they do not anticipate important consequences of their association.

As a rule, members of the random clique are not solidly in any of the more functional cliques. And usually they have never been in them, or if so, they are rejectees for indiscreet talk and failure in action. They are most often apathetic persons who are not sure why they are in the department. But being there they are given things to do, including the less desirable tasks, and they mechanically follow the routines. Consequently they resent, and do not fit into, the changing informal arrangements around them. They would like to escape the confusion to find simpler and more permanent recreational relations. As a result they get away from their jobs when possible to indulge in unguarded talk about people and events.

Their friends are like themselves. From the cafeteria to the showers they meet and gossip about their home departments and their dissatisfactions. Though only on the rim of events they do interact superficially with members of the other cliques. As would be expected, they learn few if any important secrets because of the barriers between themselves and these pivotal groups. And they may miss the meaning for larger issues of what they do learn. Nevertheless this relatively aimless association is important in plant affairs. As small unattached gossip groups moving freely around the firm, these cliques are both a point of leaks from the functional groups as well as a source of information for them. As such, the random clique intensifies informal activities in the plant.[8] The incomplete bits of information members exchange may mean little out of their larger context to an apathetic person, but much to an alert member of some functional clique. Discrete items supplied by a random clique on, for example, cost manipulation, or "gentlemen's agreements" at some level of union-management trading, may fit so well into the puzzle of an interested action clique that its members will clinch or change their pending action.

Instances from Milo show the circuitous routes of information leaks and the effects on others. The assistant chief chemist, Miller, received a confidential monthly salary "adjustment" of a hundred and twenty-five dollars. He wished to hide this from his subordinates, who were also pressing for salary increases to maintain the gap between themselves and the surging unionized stillmen and samplers. However, Miller did tell his wife, who belonged to a woman's club in the community. She told members of the club, one of whom was the wife of Sand, a line foreman from a third department. Sand was intimate in the plant with Wheeler, one of the samplers. Wheeler played golf with Sand and spent considerable time in Sand's office. Sand eventually passed the secret from his wife to Wheeler. Apparently seeing it as a joke on the chemists, Wheeler told them. Angered at Miller's "unfairness," some of the chemists wanted to face him with their knowledge and use it as a lever. Others overruled this, but "to get even" all cooperated with the samplers to conceal line errors and deviations from Miller, and to reduce the number of their own analyses.

In another case, superintendent Smith learned from his neighbor, Haller, a Milo employee whose loquacity was guarded against in his own department and encouraged elsewhere, that Boesel had arranged with his grievance committeeman to promote a workman contrary to the seniority record. Smith sought a similar deal with his own grievance man but was refused.[9] Smith's anger struck fear in Boesel and his union ally that Hardy and the president of the union local might be called in. They returned the promoted workman to his old position temporarily, though later both Boesel and Revere made deals with the union adverse to seniority principle. This incident made enemies of Smith and Boesel, and Boesel never learned the source of the leak.

CONTROL OF CLIQUES

Given the nature of personnel, and the official frameworks they create, even the cliques essential for intertwining official and informal actions occasionally get out of hand and must be curbed. These are the vertical symbiotic and the two horizontal forms. They normally function (a) to build working harmony from the differing skills and abilities, private feuds, and shifting identifications of employees in endless turnover; and (b) to adapt the personnel and changing technology to each other. But when this function fails, or other factors give one department a force in events unwarranted by its contributions, eventual action by a high level horizontal aggressive clique corrects the distortion. . . .

As implied earlier, almost never would an able executive be discharged for clique activity. Higher managers value these skills as necessary for cutting a way through or around chaotic situations. Public relations and the equalitarian ideology may require denial, but top managers are more disposed to pardon than punish occasional excesses of the social skill required for organizational coherence and action.

SUMMARY

In every administrative group, gaps appear between granted and exercised authority. Symptoms in a sense of disorganization, these divergences are inherent in a continuing process of reorganization, authorized or not.

As executive roles are changed by pressures inside and outside the firm, the role of "assistant-to" is utilized for formal as well as unofficial purposes. As an unofficial jack-of-all-roles, it gives the flexibility to executive positions and actions that formal theory and planning usually cannot. It serves as a reward, as an unofficial channel of information, as an informal arm of authority, as a safety valve for the pressures generated by a necessary surplus of able and ambitious developing executives, as a protective office for loyal but aging members rendered unfit by changes they cannot meet or from other failures, as a training post, etc.

The logically conceived plans of one executive level are variously altered by subordinate levels to fit their shifting social relations, as well as the emergencies at work. Inspired by fear of unofficial reprisals, the alterations are usually concealed and therefore not incorporated into future planning, so that the organization is always out-of-date in some sense. Therefore while planning must in general be logical, it must also be abbreviated, and even loose, in some areas to allow latitude for social contingencies. Achievement of organizational goals intertwines with individual and group ends near and remote from those of the firm. Much confusion among personnel stems from disagreement over the distance that can legitimately exist between the two. Persons able to deal with the confusion come to the fore as leaders, with or without the official title. They become the nucleus of cliques that work as interlocking action centers, and as bridges between official and unofficial purposes.

Springing from the diverse skills, attitudes, and turnover of personnel, cliques are both an outgrowth and instrument of planning and change. They fall into recognizable types shaped by, and related to, the official pattern of executive positions. Cliques are the indispensable promoters and stabilizers—as well as resisters—of change; they are essential both to cement the organization and to accelerate action. They preserve the formalities vital for moving to the goal, and they provoke but control the turmoil and adjustment that play about the emerging organization.

NOTES

1. This resentment was typical of line attitudes toward staff people. . . .

2. This was frequently expressed clearly as, "What he could do to you if you crossed him!"

3. That is, the application of piece-rate pay systems to maintenance and repair work.

4. The nonindustrial reader should not regard these practices as peculiar to Milo. In the Fruhling Works, in Mobile Acres, a plant of 20,000 employees including 984 full members of management, much the same thing occurred on a larger scale. Fred Jessup, a division head, had sought for two years to get acceptance of his idea for changes in a refinement process, but was resisted by the Fruhling chief on the ground that Jessup's proposal was "phony." Taking a new tack, Jessup justified an increase of 20 new production and clerical personnel in his division and won appropriations to cover their payroll. Actually they were fictitious, but he created names and roles for them, and by his relations with the Auditing and Time departments he was able to use the funds for secret purchase of new equipment and experimentation in a vacant building. By support from associates (see "horizontal aggressive clique") the experiment was carried on for many months and established as successful. When the plant manager shortly retired, the new technology was brought into the open, acclaimed, and labeled the "[Jessup] process."

Jessup declared that his "operations" were "really small stuff," that he had got the idea of "underground" action from the "shenanigans" of his retiring chief. According to Jessup, his late chief had several years earlier directed a major modernization of Fruhling. Only after the most careful planning, $30,000,000 had been appropriated for the program. But as the change advanced, the appropriation "came up short by $7,000,000 because of smart pencils and fattened payrolls." That is, a total of $37,000,000 was used, but nearly one-fifth of it was consumed to reduce social rivalries, to accommodate "empire-building," etc., and skillfully attributed to extraneous factors. Jessup incidentally illustrates the possible breach between given and exercised authority.

5. Milo covered over a square mile and was broken into many units and subunits connected by numbered walkways and zoned driveways.

6. The term *symbiotic* is adapted from the biological term *symbiosis* (*syn*, together, and *bios*, life) which refers to a mutually beneficial *internal* partnership between two different kinds of organisms. This is related to the term *commensalism* (*con*, together; and *mensa*, table) which is reserved by some students for *external* associations between two quite different kinds of animals, who live together in effect as messmates or fellow boarders. Examples of commensalism are the tie between the Dor beetle and its blind mite partner, the hermit crab (some) and sea-anemones, the Nile crocodile and one of the plovers, and the "tuatara" lizard and the petrel. Symbiotic relations include those between heather and its fungus partner, and termites and their flagellates. Our aim is not to force rigid parallels or to precisely follow biological usage. See R. W. Hegner, *College Zoology*, The Macmillan Company, New York, 1942, 5th edition, pp. 155, 702–703, and use of the term by sociologists: R. E. Park, "Symbiosis and Socialization: A Frame of Reference for the Study of Society," *American Journal of Sociology*, 45: 1–25, July, 1939; E. Gross, "Symbiosis and Consensus as Integrative Factors in Small Groups," *American Sociological Review*, 21: 174–179, April, 1956.

7. Frequently there is reluctance to break old emotional ties and to face the problems of developing new ones. His feeling is understandable if there are strong differences in attitude between his earlier and present associates on the issue of literal or loose interpretation of official doctrine. He may also be committed to aid one or more of his earlier associates. This last is related to a kind of spoils system and has been observed by numerous executives. See H. Frederick Willkie, *A Rebel Yells*, D. Van Nostrand Company, New York, 1946, pp. 186–88, and Eli Ginzberg, ed., *What Makes an Executive?* Columbia University Press, New York, 1955, p. 156, where it is noted that changes in top leadership often mean that the "new man promoted his own associates" to the detriment of other well-qualified individuals. Sometimes correction of this evil creates others.

8. The random clique is not, of course, the only source of leaks. Under stress, members of the functional cliques may tell things they would not normally, and for calculated purposes they may deliberately pass a secret to a known "two-way funnel."

9. It is common . . . for grievance officers and managers to pair off in cliques and to oppose like cliques as all pursue peaceful informal adjustments with small concern for their official roles under the contract.

EDITORS' NOTES ON FURTHER READING: DALTON

Melville Dalton's *Men Who Manage* (New York: John Wiley & Sons, 1959) is one of the great classics of industrial sociology and should be read in its entirety. Dalton explains the background to this work and how he used participant observation to get the information he wanted in "Preconceptions and Methods in *Men Who Manage*," pp. 58–110 in Phillip E. Hammond, ed., *Sociologists at Work: Essays on the Craft of Social Research* (1964). The reader of this essay should imagine what modern committees on "human subjects" would think of some of Dalton's techniques for obtaining information! Other examples of fieldwork in an industrial setting are discussed in William Foote Whyte's *Learning from the Field: A Guide from Experience* (1984).

Another important study of power relations in industry from this period is Michael Crozier's *The Bureaucratic Phenomenon* (1963), which reports his findings on several industrial settings in France with speculation about cultural differences. A fine survey is Jeffrey Pfeffer's *Power in Organizations* (1981). Two excellent general treatments of organizations that place power on the analytic center stage are Charles Perrow's *Complex Organizations: A Critical Essay,* 3d ed. (1986) and Stewart Clegg's *Modern Organizations: Organization Studies in the Postmodern World* (1990). Another study of the conflict between different departments in a corporation is Perrow's "Departmental Power and Perspectives in Industrial Firms," pp. 59–89 in Mayer Zald, ed., *Power in Organizations* (1979). Perrow's assertion that the marketing department tends to dominate once manufacturing is routinized has been challenged on the ground that depending on the situation, different departments will dominate the firm; see Neil Fligstein, "The Spread of the Multidivisional Form Among Large Firms," *American Sociological Review* 50 (1985):377–391 and his *The Transformation of Corporate Control* (1990).

14

Bureaucratic and Craft Administration of Production: A Comparative Study

ARTHUR L. STINCHCOMBE

Administration in the construction industry depends upon a highly professionalized manual labor force.[1] The thesis of this paper is that the professionalization of the labor force in the construction industry serves the same functions as bureaucratic administration in mass production industries and is more rational than bureaucratic administration in the face of economic and technical constraints on construction projects.

Specifically we maintain that the main alternative to professional socialization for workers is communicating work decisions and standards through an administrative apparatus. But such an apparatus requires stable and finely adjusted communications channels. It is dependent on the continuous functioning of administrators in official statuses. Such continuous functioning is uneconomical in construction work because of the instability in the volume and product mix and of the geographical distribution of the work. Consequently the control of pace, manual skill, and effective operative decision (the essential components of industrial discipline) is more economical if left to professionally maintained occupational standards.

After presenting evidence and argument for these assertions, we will try to show why work on large-scale tract construction of houses continues to be administered on a nonbureaucratic, craft basis. Tract housing turns out to be a major revision in the *marketing* of construction products, rather than a revision in the *administration of work*.

Our method will be to reanalyze certain published demographic and economic data for their administrative implications. Since the data were collected for other purposes, they fit the requirements of our problem only roughly. The gaps in the information and the gross character of the categories

From *Administrative Science Quarterly* 4 (1959):168–187. Reprinted by permission of Arthur L. Stinchcombe.

make it necessary, therefore, to use very rough statistical procedures and to limit the data to a suggestive role.

On the basis of the empirical findings, we will re-examine Max Weber's model of bureaucracy, showing that some elements of that model are not correlated with other elements. This will provide a basis for constructing a model of bureaucracy as a subtype of rational administration, with professionalization another main subtype. A general model of rational administration will be built out of the common elements of these subtypes.

BUREAUCRATIC ADMINISTRATION
AND CRAFT ADMINISTRATION

Craft institutions in construction are more than craft trade unions; they are also a method of administering work. They include special devices of legitimate communications to workers, special authority relations, and special principles of division of work, the "jurisdictions" which form the areas of work defining labor market statuses. The distinctive features of craft administration may be outlined by contrasting it with mass production manufacturing administration.[2] The object of this section is to show that craft institutions provide a functional equivalent of bureaucracy.

Mass production may be defined by the criterion that *both* the product *and* the work process are planned in advance *by persons not on the work crew.* Among the elements of the work process planned are: (1) the location at which a particular task will be done, (2) the movement of tools, of materials, and of workers to this work place, and the most efficient arrangement of these work-place characteristics, (3) sometimes the particular movements to be performed in getting the task done, (4) the schedules and time allotments for particular operations, and (5) inspection criteria for particular operations (as opposed to inspection criteria for final products).

In construction all these characteristics of the work process are governed by the worker in accordance with the empirical lore than makes up craft principles. These principles are the content of workers' socialization and apply to the jobs for which they have preferential hiring rights.

This concentration of the planning of work in manual roles in construction results in a considerably simplified communications system in the industry; but the simplification does not markedly reduce the number of people in administrative statuses. Administrative statuses are roughly equivalent to occupations in census categories: proprietors, managers, and officials; professional, technical, and kindred workers; and clerical and kindred workers.

The proportion of administrative personnel in the labor force in various fabricating industries does not vary widely. In construction the proportion of the labor force in the three administrative occupations is 15.5 percent; in manufacturing as a whole it is 20.6 percent; in iron and steel primary extraction, 15.5 percent; motor vehicles and motor vehicle equipment, 17.6 percent; in chemicals and allied industries, 33.4 percent.[3] But these rough similarities in proportion of administrative personnel conceal wide differences in the internal structure of the communications system.

TABLE [14.]1   The proportion of administrative personnel[a] who are clerks in selected fabricating industries, U.S., 1950

Industry or Industry Group	Administrators' Clerks
Manufacturing	53%
Motor vehicles and accessories	63%
Iron and steel primary extraction	60%
Chemicals and allied	45%
Construction	20%

[a]Proprietors, managers, and officials; professional, technical and kindred workers. *Characteristics of the Population, Part 1*, pp. 290–291.

To provide a rough index of one of these differences in the internal structure of the authority systems, we have computed the proportion of clerical positions in the administration. This should provide an index of the proportion of people in administration who do not legitimate by their status the communications they process (e.g., typists, filing clerks, bookkeepers). They file the communications; they do not initiate them. Authority structures with special communications-processing positions may be called "bureaucratic" structures.[4] They provide for close control of the work process farther up the administrative hierarchy, and hence facilitate the control and planning of the work process in large enterprises. They decrease the dependence of the enterprise on empirical lore and self-discipline at the work level and allow technical and economic decisions to be concentrated. Finally, they allow the processing of information and communications from distant markets, enabling the enterprise to be less dependent on the geographical location of clients.

The proportion of administrative personnel who are clerks in various fabricating industries is presented in Table [14.]1.

Clearly the proportion of all administrative personnel who are clerks is considerably greater in manufacturing generally than it is in construction, and the typical mass production industries tend to have even greater development of specialized communications processing structures. The centralized planning of work is associated with this development of filed communications, with specialized personnel processing them.

Another type of internal differentiation of authority structures (systems of originating and processing communications legitimately directing workers) concerns the status and training of the originators. In some authority structures in fabricating industries, people in authority are largely defined by ownership and contract institutions, while in others their status derives from professional institutions. That is, communications from a position in the authority system may be considered legitimate because of the special competence of the originator, a professional; or they may be legitimate because of the special responsibility of the originator, as owner or official, for economic decisions.

We may contrast administrations by the proportion of people in authority whose status derives from special education. This may be denoted as "the

TABLE [14.]2   The proportion of top administrators[a] who are professionals in various industries, U.S., 1950

Industry or Industry Group	Professional Authority Positions
Manufacturing	50%
Motor vehicles and accessories	63%
Iron and steel primary extraction	64%
Chemicals and allied	65%
Construction	31%

[a]Proprietors, managers, and officials; and professional, technical and kindred workers. *Characteristics of the Population, Part 1*, pp. 290–291.

professionalization of authority." The proportion of all "top" administrative personnel (proprietors, managers, and officials; *and* professionals) who are professionals in the selected industries is presented in Table [14.]2.

The contrast in the degree of professionalization of authority between manufacturing and construction, and more especially between mass production and construction, is just as clear as was the case with bureaucratization.

The engineering of work processes and the evaluation of work by economic and technical standards take place in mass production in specialized staff departments, far removed from the work crew in the communications system. In the construction industry these functions are decentralized to the work level, where entrepreneurs, foremen, and craftsmen carry the burden of technical and economic decision.

This decentralization of functions of the firm to the work level in construction, and the relative lack of information about and professional analysis of work processes at administrative centers, is accompanied by a difference in the types of legitimate communication.

In the construction industry, authoritative communications from administrative centers carry only specifications of the product desired and prices (and sometimes rough schedules). These two elements of the communication are contained in the contract; first, the contract between the client (with the advice of architects or engineers) and the general contractor,[5] and, second, between the general contractor and subcontractors. Subcontractors do the work falling within the "jurisdiction" of the trade they specialize in.

In mass production, where both the product and the work process are centrally planned, we find a system of legitimated advice on work and legitimate commands from line officials to foremen and workers to do particular work in particular ways. This more finely adjusted communications system depends on the development of specialized communications positions (clerks) and staff advice departments (professionals). These differences in administration are shown in Charts [14.]1 and [14.]2.

Craft administration, then, differs from bureaucratic administration by substituting professional training of manual workers for detailed centralized

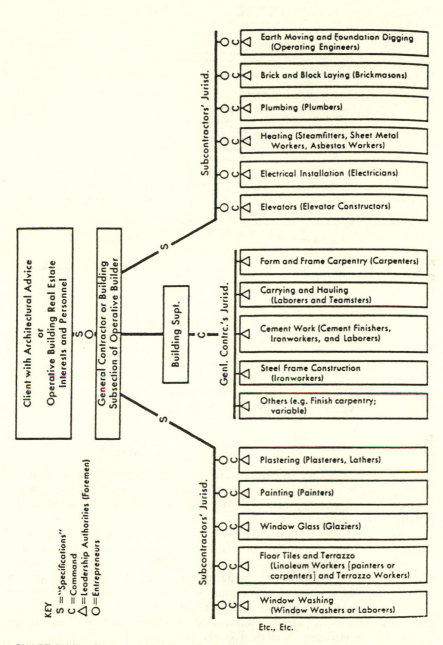

CHART [14.]1   Site administration of a construction project

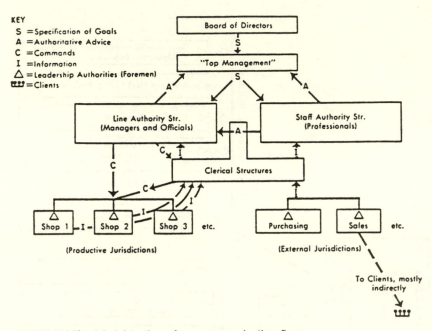

KEY
S =Specification of Goals
A =Authoritative Advice
C =Commands
I =Information
△ =Leadership Authorities (Foremen)
☡☡☡ =Clients

CHART [14.]2   Administration of a mass production firm

planning of work. This is reflected in the lack of clerical workers processing communications to administrative centers and less complex staffs of professionals planning work. It is also reflected in the simplification of authoritative communications from administrative centers.

VARIABILITY AND BUREAUCRATIZATION

In this section we try to demonstrate that professionalization of manual labor is more efficient in construction because bureaucratic administration is dependent on stability of work flow and income, and the construction industry is economically unstable.

Bureaucratization of administration may be defined as a relatively permanent structuring of communications channels between continuously functioning officials. This permanent structuring of channels of legitimate communications, channels defined by the permanent official status of the originator of the communication and of its receiver, permits the development of routine methods of processing information upward and authoritative communication downward. That is, it permits administration on the basis of files and the economical employment of clerical workers.

Routine processing of administrative communications and information is economical only when the overhead cost of specialized information-processing structures is highly productive; this productivity will be high only if rules concerning the route of communication can be taught to clerks. Otherwise, if it is necessary to use discretion in the choice of the receiver of a communication, it is cheaper to rely on visual supervision and executive or professional discretion.

The Case of Mass Production

Bureaucratization of administration depends therefore on the long-term stability of the administration. Of bureaucratic industrial administrations Peter Drucker says,

> The central fact of industrial economics is not "profit" but "loss"—not the expectation of ending up with a surplus . . . but the inevitable and real risk of ending up with an impoverishing deficit, and the need, the absolute need, to avoid this loss by providing against the risks. . . . The economic activity of an industrial economy is not "trade" taking place in the almost timeless instant of exchange, but production over a very long period. *Neither the organization* (the human resources) nor the capital investment (the material resources) *are productive in the "here and now" of the present.* It will be years before the organization or the investment will begin to produce, and many more years before they will have paid for themselves.[6]

It is clear that he cannot be talking about construction organizations, which have to be productive "here and now."

This association between orientation to stability and large-scale bureaucratized firms reflects the social requirements of complex communications systems between designated officials. Administrations faced with critical problems of instability and flexibility, such as those in the construction industry, will not find it economical to teach clerks rules for channeling communications. For it is impossible to hire a clerk on the labor market who will know the firm's communications channels, so clerks have to be kept on even when they are not productive.[7] And it is difficult to specify rules for channeling communications in advance when volume, product mix, and work-force composition change rapidly, as they do in construction.

The Case of Construction

The variability of the construction industry, its intimate dependence on variations in local markets, makes the development of bureaucracy uneconomical. Table [14.]3 shows the relationship between one type of variability and the employment of clerks.

Data are for some types of construction firms, for all firms in Ohio large enough to have to report to the State Employment Office (those normally employing 3 or more persons). In the first column the mean size of firms in the branch is reported (computed here), and the branches are classified by mean size. In the second column is an index of seasonality of employment for the years 1926–1936 (computed in the source[8]). In the last column the average proportion of the labor force who were clerks in 1939 is reported (computed here).

TABLE [14.]3 The relationship between mean size of firm, seasonality of employment, and the percentage of the labor force clerks, for branches of the construction industry[a]

Type of Contractor	Mean Size of Firms (1939)	Index of Seasonality of Employment (1926–1936)[b]	% of Clerks in Labor Force[c] (1939)
More than 8 employees per contractor			
Street, road, and sewer	12.3	73	4.8
Sand, gravel, excavation	9.9	43	7.6
Ventilating and heating	8.2	29	11.7
4–8 employees per contractor			
Brick, stone, and cement	5.5	47	3.3
General contracting	6.9	43	5.2
Sheet metal and roofing	4.9	29	11.7
Plumbing	5.1	20	10.9
Electrical	6.3	13	12.5
Less than 4 employees per contractor			
Painting and decorating	2.5	59	3.9

[a]Taken from Viva Boothe and Sam Arnold, *Seasonal Employment in Ohio* (Columbus: Ohio State University, 1944), Table 19, pp. 82–87. Plasterers are omitted from this table, because the number employed was not large enough to give a reliable figure on seasonality of clerks' work, the original purpose of the publication. There were less than 50 clerks in plastering enterprises in the state. Consequently the needed figure was not reported in the source. Plasterers' employment is very unstable, so the omission itself supports the trend.
[b]See [Note] 8.
[c]Excluding sales clerks.

The relationship between the development of clerical statuses in administration and the stability of the work flow is clear from Table [14.]3. The strength of the relationship within the industry can give us confidence in asserting that instability decreases bureaucratization. There are only two inversions, and these are of insignificant size: sheet metal and roofing should have been less bureaucratized than plumbing; and painters should have been less than brick, stone, and cement firms. This is a strong support for the hypothesis that the lack of bureaucratization in the construction industry is due to general instability.

We do not have space to document adequately the sources of variability in the work flow of construction administrations. The main elements may be outlined as follows:

1. Variations in the volume of work and in product mix in the course of the business cycle.[9]

2. Seasonal variations in both volume and product mix.[10]

3. The limitation of most construction administrations, especially in the specialty trades, to a small geographical radius. This smaller market magnifies

the variability facing particular firms according to well-known statistical principles (individual projects can form a large part of a local market).[11]

4. The organization of work at a particular site into stages (building "from the ground up"), with the resulting variability in the productive purpose of any particular site administration.[12]

Summary of Empirical Propositions

It now seems wise to review the argument thus far. We are trying to show that the professionalization of the manual work force persists partly because it is a cheaper form of administration for construction enterprises than the bureaucratic form.

First we argued that bureaucracy and professionalized work force were real alternatives, that: (a) decisions, which in mass production were made outside the work milieu and communicated bureaucratically, in construction work were actually part of the craftsman's culture and socialization, and were made at the level of the work crew, (b) the administrative status structure of construction showed signs of this difference in the communications structure by relative lack of clerks and professionals, and (c) the legitimate communications in construction (contracts and subcontracts) showed the expected differences in content from the orders and advice in a bureaucracy. Contracts contained specifications of the goals of work and prices; they did not contain the actual directives of work, which, it seemed to us, did not have to be there because they were already incorporated in the professionalized culture of the workers.

Secondly we argued that the bureaucratic alternative was too expensive and inefficient in construction because such administration requires continuous functioning in organizational statuses. But continuous functioning is prevented by the requirement that construction administrations adapt to variability in both volume and product mix. Using the employment of clerks as an index of bureaucratization, a close relation was found between seasonality in branches of construction and bureaucratization. This strong relationship was combined with knowledge of the general instability of construction to support the contention that bureaucracy was inefficient in construction.

THE IMPLICATIONS OF MARKETING REFORM

There is a good deal of careless talk about the bureaucratization of construction and the introduction of mass production by operative building of tract homes. The central innovation of operative building is in the field of marketing and finance rather than in the administration of production. The similarity of productive administration in operative building and in other large-scale building is well summarized by Sherman Maisel:

Many popular assumptions about subcontracting—that it lowers efficiency, raises costs, and leads to instability—are contradicted by our study in the Bay area of the reasons for subcontracting and its efficiency relative to its alternatives. Building appears to be one of the many industries where vertical disintegration increases efficiency and lowers costs without lessening stability. The fact that most large [operative housebuilding] firms have tried integrating various of the processes normally subcontracted but have usually returned to subcontracting them, is of great importance because it shows that the present prevalence of subcontracting is the result of a policy deliberately adopted by builders after testing alternative possibilities. . . .

The logic of trade contracting has developed as follows: (1) Efficiency reaches its maximum effectiveness under specialized labor. (2) Specialized labor reaches its maximum effectiveness when applied regularly on many units. . . . (3) The problem of sustaining specialized jobs as well as the coordination of the movement of men among them requires special supervision, usually performed by trade contractors. . . .

Given a need for specialized mechanisms, the builder gains greater flexibility and a decrease in the problems of supervision through subcontracting.[13]

The central limitation on supervision is the increase in overhead when mediated communication is introduced. "A disproportionate increase takes place [in overhead in the largest construction firms] because production has spread beyond the area of simple visual control by the owner or owners [of the firm]."[14]

In fact, the characteristic of mass production administration, increasing specialization of tools and other facilities at a planned work place, does not take place with increasing size. Most machinery added in large firms consists of hand power tools and materials-handling machinery.[15]

The low development of distinctively bureaucratic production-control mechanisms, such as cost accounting, detailed scheduling, regularized reporting of work progress, and standardized inspection of specific operations, is outlined by Maisel.[16] What happens instead of centralized planning and bureaucratic control of work is an increase in the fineness of stages on which crews of workers are put. This results in the development of more efficient, but still quite diversified, skills. And most important, these skills still form a component of a labor market rather than an organizational status system.

Operative decisions are still very important at the work level, rather than being concentrated in production engineering and cost-accounting departments. Modification of tools for special purposes is done by workers (e.g., the making of templates which provide guides for standardized cutting operations, or the construction of special scaffolds for the crew.) There is no large element in the administration with the specialized task of planning technological innovation in the work process. And stable communications between work crews and decision centers are poorly developed.

The central consideration is that variability of work load for the administration is not very much reduced, if at all, by operative building. And it is not necessarily economical to take advantage of what reduction there is, when the subcontracting system and structured labor market are already in existence.

What is changed, what makes the economies possible, is the place of the goal-setting function. The productive goals in the past were set by clients with architectural advice, who quite naturally did not set goals in such as way as to maximize productive efficiency. In operative building productive goals are set autonomously by the administration. This means that they can choose, among the products they might produce, those which are technically easier. The main reduction of costs, of course, comes from the planning of the construction site so as to minimize transportation and set-up costs. Sites next to each other minimize costs of moving men, materials, and equipment to the site. Warehousing of materials can be planned to fit the individual site, rather than burdening builders' supply places. Uniformity of design reduces the complexity of materials distribution, reduces design costs, and so forth.

The main innovation, then, is the planning of the *product* for ease of production, rather than in the planning of the *productive process*. This is the introduction of the conceptions of Eli Whitney on *standardized parts* into construction, rather than of Henry Ford's innovation of *standardized tasks*.

RATIONAL ADMINISTRATION AND BUREAUCRACY

Since Weber, there has been a tendency to regard rational administration as identical with bureaucratic administration. This tendency has been especially strong among sociologists. We have chosen to define bureaucracy as a special type of rational administration and to discuss the social sources of an alternative method of institutionalizing rationality, namely, professionalization.

The central point of this analysis is that the components of Weber's ideal type do not form an inherently connected set of variables. Some of the components of the ideal type are relatively uncorrelated with others, while some are highly correlated.

We have called craft production unbureaucratized, although it does involve "the principle of fixed and official jurisdictional areas, which are generally ordered by rules."[17] The rules in this case are to be found in the jurisdictional provisions of trade unions, in the introductory sections of collective contracts, and in state licensing laws for contractors. The duties in construction are "distributed in a fixed way as official duties"[18] through legally binding contracts. "The authority to give the commands required for the discharge of these duties is distributed in a stable way."[19] The sanctions, especially firing, are stably allocated to contractors and subcontractors on the particular project.

The principal difference comes in the criterion: "Methodical provision is made for the *regular and continuous* fulfillment of these duties and for the execution of the corresponding rights."[20] It is not the rules governing jurisdiction and authority which we take to be characteristic of bureaucracy, but the regularity and continuity of work and status within an administrative system. We have shown that regularity and continuity are in fact correlated with our operational criterion of bureaucratization, the proportion of clerks among administrators.

Secondly, we have argued that "the principles of office hierarchy . . . in which there is supervision of the lower officer by the higher ones,"[21] is dependent on stable communications structures, provided we differentiate *goal setting* from *supervision*. In construction there is no possibility of "appealing the decision of a lower office [subcontractor] to its higher authority [the general contractor or client]."[22] The goals of subcontractors are set by "higher authorities." But their work is not supervised, nor are their decisions appealable. Office hierarchy in the command-advice sense, then, is correlated with regularity and continuity in official statuses. Goal-setting arrangements can be changed drastically (e.g., from the client to the operative building corporation) without changing the administration of work in a bureaucratic direction.

The other main criterion Weber proposes concerns the stable structuring of communication (files), which we have taken as the empirical indicator of stable, rule-governed communication channels among official statuses.

These last three elements of Weber's ideal type (continuity, hierarchy, and files), then, are functionally interrelated; they are found together in mass-production administration but are absent in construction administration. But the first three elements (stable jurisdictions, official duties, and authority) are found in both construction and mass production, so they cannot be highly correlated with the elements of continuity, hierarchy, and files.

Weber draws from his ideal type certain implications concerning the position of the official. Some of these are derived from distinctive characteristics of bureaucracy as we have defined it, and some are derived from general requirements of rationality. Characteristics common to bureaucracies *and* nonbureaucratic rational administrations include:

1. Positions in the organization are separated from the household. Positions in construction as workers, foremen, and entrepreneurs involve the separation of work from home life, firm accounts from household accounts, firm and trade promotions from family ties.[23]

2. Rational administration requires the allocation of work to those who are competent. This often involves hiring on the basis of formal training, certification, and examination. Not only civil servants, but also craftsmen, and private legal and medical practitioners, have to pass examinations or possess certificates of formal training. The main difference is that professional examinations allocate work throughout a labor market, while civil service examinations recruit only to organizational statuses.

3. To a large extent pecuniary compensation, regulated by the status of the worker, characterizes rational administration, as well as bureaucracy. At least, wage rates for each occupational status in construction are negotiated.

A characteristic of bureaucratic officials not found in construction is permanent appointment. Authorities on a construction project are appointed by subcontracts only for the duration of the project. The basis of responsibility for leadership duties is the contract for specific work (and the contractors' reputations) rather than generalized loyalty to the administration. Payment to authorities is not salary determined by the status of the official but payment for performance set by competitive bidding. Finally the career of the worker in construction is structured not by administrative regulation but by status in a structured labor market. These differences also distinguish private professional practice from bureaucratic administration.

We would construct an ideal type of functionally interrelated characteristics of bureaucracy as follows: The defining criterion would be stable, rule-ordered communications channels from and to continuously occupied statuses. This criterion implies: (1) development of files and employment of clerks, (2) hierarchical command-advice authority structures, and (3) career commitment to an *organizational* rather than a labor market or *occupational* status system.

Bureaucracy thus defined is a subtype of rational administration. Rational administration requires the government of work activity by economic and technical standards and hence requires:

1. Differentiation of the work role from home life (and other deep interpersonal commitments).

2. The organization of work statuses into some sort of career, in which future rights and duties depend on present performance according to specified standards.

3. A stable allocation of work to persons formally identified as able and willing to work and subject to discipline by understood work standards, and payment by the administration only when such workers are "productive."

4. A stable legitimate way of communicating at least the goals to be reached by subordinates and of seeing that these goals are accomplished.

This means that we take Weber's observations on the "Presuppositions and Causes of Bureaucracy"[24] to be mainly about the presuppositions and causes of any kind of rational administration. The presuppositions of bureaucracy are conditions facilitating continuous operation of an organizational status system, either continuity of work load and returns or institutionalized legitimacy of the status system itself (e.g., the military).

Continuity in status in a labor market, instead of an organization, we take to be the defining characteristic of professional institutions. Both the traditional professions and crafts in construction have professional institutions in this sense. These are characterized by (roughly) occupationally homogeneous organizations seeking control of the rights and duties associated with doing work within a defined jurisdiction. By this control they assure competence discipline. Both professions and crafts, then, guarantee labor market rights and enforce labor market duties which make up a professional status.

CONCLUSION

Concepts in organizational theory, such as bureaucracy, tend to take on a nebulous character because research in this areas has consisted largely of case studies of particular organizations. An industrial firm engaged in mass production may certainly be bureaucratic, but not all the characteristics of the organization are distinctive of bureaucracy. Case studies cannot, ordinarily, sort out the inherent from the ephemeral connections among organizational characteristics. Systematic comparisons of different types of organizations, which we have attempted here, can refine our conceptual apparatus by defining complex concepts comprised of elements that hang together empirically.

The concept of bureaucracy developed here is not merely a descriptive one; it contains propositions about the connection between its elements. Such a concept can be refined either by proving new elements to be necessarily connected to those already incorporated or by disproving the hypothesized connection between elements. Similar definition is needed for other complex concepts in the social sciences; the city, sovereignty, the firm.

A definition of the firm, for example, should include those characteristics inevitably found in social units producing goods for markets. Such a definition of the firm would be not merely a category to put concrete organizations into, but a set of propositions about the relations between markets and social groups. Such propositional definitions can be best derived from the systematic comparative study of organizations.

NOTES

1. "Professionalized" here means that workers get technical socialization to achieve a publicly recognized occupational competence. "Public recognition" involves preferential hiring (ideally to the point of excluding all others) of workers who have proved their competence to an agency external to the hiring firm or consumer. Often this agency is a professional association composed exclusively of qualified persons and more or less exhaustive of the occupation. This professional association itself often enforces preferential hiring rights of its members. The professional's *permanent labor market status* is not to be confused with permanent firm status (preferential hiring or continued employment of the current employees of a firm). This definition, therefore, differs somewhat from that of Nelson Foote in The Professionalization of Labor in Detroit, *American Journal of Sociology,* 58 (1953), 371–380.

2. This account of mass production institutions is derived from Peter Drucker, *The New Society* (New York, 1950), and his *The Practice of Management* (New York, 1954), along with the work of David Granick, *Management of the Industrial Firm in the U.S.S.R.* (New York, 1954).

3. *Characteristics of the Population,* Part 1 (U.S. Summary) (*Census of the Population,* 2 [1950]), Table 134, pp. 290–291.

4. This takes one of Weber's criteria of bureaucratization as an empirical indicator, namely administration on the basis of files. I believe some of the other characteristics of bureaucracy named by Weber can be derived from this one, while some cannot. See Max Weber, *From Max Weber: Essays in Sociology,* tr. by H. H. Gerth and C. W. Mills (New York, 1946), pp. 196–198.

5. This step is omitted in the case of operative builders, but otherwise the authority structure is similar.

6. *The New Society,* p. 52 (our italics). Veblen said the same thing in a different moral vocabulary: "Under the changed circumstance [the replacement of the 'captain

of industry'] the spirit of venturesome enterprise is more than likely to foot up as a hunting of trouble, and wisdom in business enterprise has more and more settled down to the wisdom of 'watchful waiting.' Doubtless this form of words, 'watchful waiting,' will have been employed in the first instance to describe the frame of mind of a toad who had reached years of discretion . . . but by an easy turn of speech it has also been found suitable to describe the safe and sane strategy of that mature order of captains of industry who are governed by sound business principles" (Thorstein Veblen, *The Portable Veblen* [New York, 1950], pp. 385–386).

7. Also the class position of clerks makes it more difficult to hire temporary clerks.

8. The index of seasonality was computed in the source in the following way: The monthly index of employment in firms reporting was computed for each year of the ten-year period, to the base of the mean employment of that year. Then the ten indices (one index for each of the ten years) for each month were arrayed, and the median taken. The 12 monthly medians give an over-all picture of seasonality for the category for the ten years. Scatter diagrams of these monthly indices, standardized for the general level of employment during the year as outlined above, are presented in Viva Boothe and Sam Arnold, *Seasonal Employment in Ohio* (Columbus, 1944), Chart 16, pp. 83–86. Graphs of seasonality are presented by drawing lines through the median monthly indices. This procedure eliminates between-years (presumably cyclical) variations in employment level.

After this array of 12 monthly indices is found, the index of seasonality reported in Table [14.]3 is computed by the formula: [maximum − minimum/ maximum] × 100, where the maximum is the largest median monthly index, and minimum the smallest. This gives an index ranging from zero (no seasonality) to 100, which would be the result of no employment at all in the minimum month. From the scatter diagrams, this might result in an under-estimation of the short-time instability only for electrical contracting firms. But other evidence indicates that electrical construction firms have very stable employment. See W. Haber and H. Levinson, *Labor Relations and Productivity in the Building Trades* (Ann Arbor, 1956), p. 54. They rank construction occupations by percentage working a full year. Electricians work less than proprietors but more than any other occupation, including "foremen, all trades."

9. Miles L. Colean and Robinson Newcomb, *Stabilizing Construction* (New York, 1952), pp. 18–20, 49–50, and Appendix N, pp. 219–242. Also Clarence Long, *Building Cycles and the Theory of Investment* (Princeton, 1940).

10. The data reported from Boothe and Arnold show both great seasonality and differential seasonality by trade. Their data show construction to be one of the most seasonal industries (*op. cit.*, pp. 23–27).

11. *Cf.* Colean and Newcomb, *op. cit.*, pp. 250–251, for the ecological limitations on administrative scope. For data on variations in volume in local areas, see U.S. Bureau of Labor Statistics, *Construction during Five Decades* (Bulletin no. 1146 [July 1, 1953]), pp. 22–25.

12. *Cf.* Gordon W. Bertran and Sherman J. Maisel, *Industrial Relations in the Construction Industry* (Berkeley, 1955), pp. 3–5.

13. *Housebuilding in Transition* (Berkeley and Los Angeles, 1953), pp. 231–232.

14. *Ibid.*, p. 102.

15. *Ibid.*, p. 103.

16. *Ibid.*, pp. 123–130.

17. Max Weber, *op. cit.*, p. 196.

18. *Ibid.*

19. *Ibid.*

20. *Ibid.* (our italics).
21. *Ibid.*, p. 197.
22. *Ibid.*
23. Not that being a contractor's son doesn't give a competitive advantage; it is only that positions are not inherited, but awarded on a competitive basis. A contractor's son still has to meet occupational standards. On the advantage of sons of *Handwerker* in various trades in Germany, see Heinz Lamprecht, Über die soziale Herkunft der Handwerker, *Soziale Welt*, 3 (Oct., 1951), 42, 52.
24. *Op. cit.*, pp. 204–209.

EDITORS' NOTES ON FURTHER READING: STINCHCOMBE

For the background to this article, see the interview with Stinchcombe in Richard Swedberg's *Economics and Sociology: On Redefining Their Boundaries. Conversations with Economists and Sociologists* (1990), pp. 285–302. This interview also contains general information about Stinchcombe and references to his other important works in economic sociology, such as *Creating Efficient Industrial Administrations* (1974) and *Economic Sociology* (1983). The reader may also want to consult Stinchcombe's "Agricultural Enterprise and Rural Class Relations," *American Journal of Sociology* 67 (1961):165–176 and "Economic Sociology: Rationality and Subjectivity," pp. 133–147 in Ulf Himmelstrand, ed., *The Sociology of Structure and Action* (1986).

Stinchcombe's point of departure in his 1959 article on bureaucratic and craft administration was a confrontation with Weber's theory of bureaucracy. Weber had essentially argued that there exists *one* most efficient way of organizing activity— that of bureaucracy. For the classic text by Weber, see "Bureaucracy," pp. 196–244 in Hans Gerth and C. Wright Mills, eds., *From Max Weber: Essays in Sociology* (1946). (Taylorism offers another source for the idea that there exists one really efficient way of organizing work; see, e.g., David Stark, "Class Struggle and the Transformation of the Labour Process: A Relational Approach," *Theory and Society* 9 [1980]:89–103, 116–130.) Stinchcombe's argument that at least two equally efficient ways of organizing production exist has been very influential in industrial and economic sociology. Paul Hirsch's "Processing Fads and Fashions" (Chapter 15 in this anthology) makes this influence clear (see also the Editor's Notes on Further Reading to Hirsch's article [Chapter 15]). Another influential stream of thought in organization theory of this period that cast doubt on the "one best way" argument is exemplified by the "contingency theory" of Joan Woodward's *Industrial Organization: Theory and Practice*, 2d ed. (1980; 1st ed., 1965). Like Stinchcombe, but in fuller detail, Woodward argued that the best way of organizing production was contingent on the nature of the production technology and the market.

Stinchcombe's analysis of craft administration has not gone unchallenged. According to one author, Stinchcombe is wrong on a series of factual points, which raises questions about the validity of his entire argument. See Robert Eccles, "Bureaucratic Versus Craft Administration: The Relationship of Market Structure to the Construction Firm," *Administrative Science Quarterly* 26 (1981):449–469; see also Eccles, "The Quasifirm in the Construction Industry," *Journal of Economic Behavior and Organization* 2 (1981):335–357. The sharp distinction between craft industry and mass manufacturing, which underlies much of the argument in Stinchcombe's article, has also recently been questioned by some scholars who claim that craft production is much more common than we think. The best-known work along these lines is Michael Piore and Charles Sabel's *The Second Industrial Divide: Possibilities for Prosperity* (1984); see also Charles Sabel and Jonathan Zeitlin, "Historical Alternatives to Mass

Production and Technology in Nineteenth-Century Industrialization," *Past and Present* 108 (August 1985):133–176 and the November 1989 issue of *Economy and Society,* edited by Jonathan Zeitlin and devoted to local industrial strategies.

The related idea—that modern workplace organizations are always huge—is criticized in Mark Granovetter's "Small Is Bountiful: Labor Markets and Establishment Size," *American Sociological Review* 49 (1984):323–334. Finally, the notion that bureaucracies are so widespread because they are the most rational and efficient way of organizing production has been challenged in a classic article by John Meyer and Brian Rowan, "Institutionalized Organizations: Formal Structure as Myth and Ceremony," *American Journal of Sociology* 83 (1977):340–363. They argue that modern organizations must invoke rituals that present the *appearance* of rationality if they want to be taken seriously, which is quite different from actually becoming more rational and effective. For further elaborations on this theme, see also Paul DiMaggio and Walter Powell, "The Iron Cage Revisited: Institutional Isomorphism and Collective Rationality in Organizational Fields," *American Sociological Review* 48 (1983):147–160. On the reality of and conditions for survival despite poor performance, see Lynne Zucker and Marshall Meyer, *Permanently Failing Organizations* (1989).

15

Processing Fads and Fashions: An Organization-Set Analysis of Cultural Industry Systems[1]

PAUL M. HIRSCH

Some years ago I had the opportunity to study rather extensively and at first hand the women's fashion industry. I was forcibly impressed by the fact that the setting or determination of fashion takes place actually through an intense process of selection. At a seasonal opening of a major Parisian fashion house there may be presented a hundred or more designs of women's evening wear before an audience of from one to two hundred buyers. The managerial corps of the fashion house is able to indicate a group of about thirty designs of the entire lot, inside of which will fall the small number, usually about six to eight designs, that are chosen by the buyers, but the managerial staff is typically unable to predict this small number on which the choices converge. Now, these choices are made by the buyers—a highly competitive and secretive lot—independently of each other and without knowledge of each other's selections. Why should their choices converge on a few designs as they do? When the buyers were asked why they chose one dress in preference to another—between which my inexperienced eye could see no appreciable difference—the typical, honest, yet largely uninformative answer was that the dress was "stunning." [Blumer 1969, pp. 278–279]

The preselection of goods for potential consumption is a feature common to all industries. In order for new products or ideas to reach consumers, they must first be processed favorably through a system of organizations whose units filter out a large proportion of candidates before they arrive at the consumption stage (Barnett 1953). Much theory and research on complex organizations is concerned with isolated aspects of this process by which innovations flow through organization systems—such as the relation of research and development units to the industrial firm (Burns and Stalker 1961; Wilensky 1968); or problems encountered by public agencies attempting

From *American Journal of Sociology* 77 (January 1972):639–659. Reprinted by permission.

to implement new policy decisions (Selznick 1949; Bailey and Mosher 1968; Moynihan 1969).

Most studies of the "careers" of innovations, however, treat only the invention and the ultimate adoption stages as problematic. The "through-put" sector, comprised of organizations which filter the overflow of information and materials intended for consumers, is generally ignored.[2] Literature on the diffusion of innovations, for example, is concerned solely with the reception accorded a new product by consumers *subsequent* to its release into the marketplace by sponsoring organizations (Rogers 1962). From an organizational perspective, two questions pertaining to any innovation are logically prior to its experience in the marketplace: (1) by what criteria was it selected for sponsorship over available alternatives? and (2) might certain characteristics of its organizational sponsor, such as prestige or the size of an advertising budget, substantially aid in explaining the ultimate success or failure of the new product or idea?

In modern, industrial societies, the production and distribution of both fine art and popular culture entail relationships among a complex network of organizations which both facilitate and regulate the innovation process. Each object must be "discovered," sponsored, and brought to public attention by entrepreneurial organizations or nonprofit agencies before the originating artist or writer can be linked successfully to the intended audience. Decisions taken in organizations whose actions can block or facilitate communication, therefore, may wield great influence over the access of artist and audience to one another. The content of a nation's popular culture is especially subject to economic constraints due to the larger scale of capital investment required in this area to link creators and consumers effectively.[3]

This paper will outline the structure and operation of entrepreneurial organizations engaged in the production and mass distribution of three types of "cultural" items: books, recordings, and motion pictures. Entrepreneurial organizations in cultural industries confront a set of problems especially interesting to students of interorganizational relations, mainly: goal dissensus, boundary-spanning role occupants with nonorganizational norms, legal and value constraints against vertical integration, and, hence, dependence on autonomous agencies (especially mass-media gate-keepers) for linking the organization to its costumers. In response to environmental uncertainties, mainly a high-risk element and changing patterns of distribution, they have evolved a rich assortment of adaptive "coping" strategies and, thus, offer a promising arena in which to develop and apply tentative propositions derived from studies of other types of organizations and advanced in the field of organization studies. Our focal organizations (Evan 1963) are the commercial publishing house, the movie studio, and the record company. My description of their operation is based on information and impressions gathered from (1) an extensive sampling of trade papers directed at members of these industries, primarily: *Publishers' Weekly, Billboard* and *Variety;* (2) 53 open-ended interviews with individuals at all levels of the publishing, recording, and broadcasting industries;[4] and (3) a thorough review of available secondary sources.

DEFINITIONS AND CONCEPTUAL FRAMEWORK

Cultural products may be defined tentatively as "nonmaterial" goods directed at a public of consumers, for whom they generally serve an aesthetic or expressive, rather than a clearly utilitarian function. Insofar as one of its goals is to create and satisfy consumer demand for new fads and fashions, every consumer industry is engaged to some extent in the production of cultural goods, and any consumer good can thus be placed along the implied continuum between cultural and utilitarian products. The two poles, however, should be intuitively distinct. Movies, plays, books, art prints, phonograph records, and pro football games are predominantly cultural products; each is nonmaterial in the sense that it embodies a live, one-of-a-kind performance and/or contains a unique set of ideas. Foods and detergents, on the other hand, serve more obvious utilitarian needs. The term "cultural organization" refers here only to *profit-seeking firms producing cultural products for national distribution.* Noncommercial or strictly local organizations, such as university presses and athletic teams, respectively, are thus excluded from consideration. A fundamental difference between entrepreneurial organizations and non-profit agencies is summarized by Toffler (1965, pp. 181–82):

> In the non-profit sector the end-product is most frequently a live performance— a concert, a recital, a play. If for purposes of economic analysis we consider a live performance to be a commodity, we are immediately struck by the fact that, unlike most commodities offered for sale in our society, this commodity is not standardized. It is not machine made. It is a handicrafted item. . . . Contrast the output of the non-profit performing arts with that of the record manufacturer. He, too, sells what appears to be a performance. But it is not. It is a replica of a performance, a mass-produced embodiment of a performance. . . . The book publisher, in effect, does the same. The original manuscript of the poem or novel represents the author's work of art, the individual, the prototype. The book in which it is subsequently embodied is a [manufactured] replica of the original. Its form of production is fully in keeping with the level of technology in the surrounding society.

Our frame of reference is the cultural industry system, comprised of all organizations engaged in the process of filtering new products and ideas as they flow from "creative" personnel in the technical subsystem to the managerial, institutional, and societal levels of organization (Parsons 1960). Each industry system is seen as a single, concrete, and stable network of identifiable and interacting components. The concept of organization levels, proposed initially to analyze transactions within the boundaries of a single, large-scale organization, is easily applied to the analysis of interorganizational systems. Artist and mass audience are linked by an ordered sequence of events: before it can elicit any audience response, an art object first must succeed in (a) competition against others for selection and promotion by an entrepreneurial organization, and then in (b) receiving mass-media coverage in such forms as book reviews, radio-station air play, and film criticism. It must be ordered by retail outlets for display or exhibition to consumers and, ideally, its author or performer will appear on television talk shows[5] and be written up as an interesting news story. Drawing on a functionalist model of organizational control and facilitation of innovations proposed by Boskoff (1964), we view the mass media in their gatekeeping role as a primary "institutional regulator of innovation."

A number of concepts and assumptions implicit in this paper are taken from the developing field of interorganizational relations and elaborated on more fully by Thompson (1967).[6] Studies in this emerging tradition typically view all phenomena from the standpoint of the organization under analysis. It seldom inquires into the functions performed by the organization for the social system but asks rather, as a temporary partisan, how the goals of the organization may be constrained by society. The organization is assumed to act under norms of rationality, and the subject of analysis becomes its forms of adaptation to constraints imposed by its technology and "task environment." The term "organization-set" has been proposed by Evan (1963) as analogous to the role-set concept developed by Merton (1957) for analyzing role relationships.

> Instead of taking a particular status as the unit of analysis, as Merton does in his role-set analysis, I take . . . an organization, or a class of organizations, and trace its interactions with the network of organizations in its environment, i.e., with elements of its organization-set. As a partial social system, a focal organization depends on input organizations for various types of resources: personnel, matériel, capital, legality, and legitimacy. . . . The focal organization in turn produces a product or a service for a market, an audience, a client system, etc. [Evan 1963, pp. 177–79]

After examining transactions between the focal organization and elements of its task environment,[7] we will describe three adaptive strategies developed by cultural organizations to minimize uncertainty. Finally, variations within each industry will be reviewed.

INPUT AND OUTPUT ORGANIZATION-SETS

The publishing house, movie studio, and record company each invests entrepreneurial capital in the creations and services of affiliated organizations and individuals at its input (product selection) and output (marketing) boundaries. Each effects volume sales by linking individual creators and producer organizations with receptive consumers and mass-media gatekeepers. New material is sought constantly because of the rapid turnover of books, films, and recordings.

Cultural organizations constitute the managerial subsystems of the industry systems in which they must operate. From a universe of innovations proposed by "artists" in the "creative" (technical) subsystem, they select ("discover") a sample of cultural products for organizational sponsorship and promotion. A distinctive feature of cultural industry systems at the present time is the organizational segregation of functional units and subsystems. In the production sector, the technical and managerial levels of organization are linked by boundary-spanning talent scouts—for example, acquisitions editors, record "producers," and film directors—located on the input boundary of the focal organization.

To this point, cultural industries resemble the construction industry and other organization systems characterized by what Stinchcombe (1959) calls "craft administration of production." The location of professionals in the technical subsystem, and administrators in the managerial one, indicates that production may be organized along craft rather than bureaucratic lines (Stinchcombe 1959). In the cultural industry system, lower-level personnel (artists and talent scouts) are accorded professional status and seldom are associated with any one focal organization for long time periods. Although company executives may tamper with the final product of their collaborations, contracted artists and talent scouts are *delegated* the responsibility of producing marketable creations, with little or no interference from the front office beyond the setting of budgetary limits (Peterson and Berger 1971). Due to widespread uncertainty over the precise ingredients of a best-seller formula, administrators are forced to trust the professional judgment of their employees. Close supervision in the production sector is impeded by ignorance of relations between cause and effect.[8] A highly placed spokesman for the recording industry (Brief 1964, pp. 4–5) has stated the problem as follows:

> We have made records that appeared to have all the necessary ingredients—
> artist, song, arrangements, promotion, etc.—to guarantee they wind up as best
> sellers. . . . Yet they fell flat on their faces. On the other hand we have
> produced records for which only a modest success was anticipated that became
> runaway best sellers. . . . There are a large number of companies in our
> industry employing a large number of talented performers and creative producers
> who combine their talents, their ingenuity and their creativity to produce a
> record that each is sure will captivate the American public. The fact that only
> a small proportion of the output achieves hit status is not only true of our
> industry. . . . There are no formulas for producing a hit record . . . just as
> there are no pat answers for producing hit plays, or sell-out movies or best-
> selling books.

Stinchcombe's (1959, 1968) association of craft administration with a minimization of fixed overhead costs is supported in the case of cultural organizations. Here, we find, for example, artists (i.e., authors, singers, actors) contracted on a *royalty* basis and offered no tenure beyond the expiration of the contract. Remuneration (less advance payment on royalties) is contingent on the number of books, records, or theater tickets sold *after* the artist's product is released into the marketplace.[9] In addition, movie-production companies minimize overhead by hiring on a per-picture basis and renting sets and costumes as needed (Stinchcombe 1968), and publishers and record companies frequently subcontract out standardized printing and record-pressing jobs.

The organization of cultural industries' technical subsystems along craft lines is a function of (a) demand uncertainty and (b) a "cheap" technology.

Demand uncertainty is caused by: shifts in consumer taste preferences and patronage (Gans 1964; Meyersohn and Katz 1957); legal and normative constraints on vertical integration (Conant 1960; Brockway 1967); and widespread variability in the criteria employed by mass-media gatekeepers in selecting cultural items to be awarded coverage (Hirsch 1969). A cheap technology enables numerous cultural organizations to compete in producing a surplus of books, records, and low-budget films on relatively small capital investments. The cost of producing and manufacturing a new long-play record or hard-cover book for the general public is usually less than $25,000 (Brief 1964; Frase 1968). Once sales pass the break-even point (about 7,000 copies for books and 12,000 for records, *very roughly*), the new product begins to show a profit.[10] On reaching sales of 20,000 a new book is eligible for best-seller status; "hit records" frequently sell over several hundred thousand copies each. Mass media exposure and volume sales of a single item generally cover earlier losses and yield additional returns. Sponsoring organizations tend to judge the success of each new book or record on the basis of its performance in the marketplace during the first six weeks of its release. Movies require a far more substantial investment but follow a similar pattern.[11]

These sources of variance best account for the craft administration of production at the input boundary of the cultural organization. It is interesting to note that in an earlier, more stable environment, that is, less heterogeneous markets and few constraints on vertical integration, the production of both films and popular records was administered more bureaucratically: lower-level personnel were delegated less responsibility, overhead costs were less often minimized, and the status of artists resembled more closely the salaried employee's than the free-lance professional's (Coser 1965; Brown 1968; Powdermaker 1950; Rosten 1941; Hughes 1959; Montagu 1964; Peterson and Berger 1971).

At their output boundaries, cultural organizations confront high levels of uncertainty concerning the commercial prospects of goods shipped out to national networks of promoters and distributors. Stratification within each industry is based partly on each firm's ability to control the distribution of marginally differentiated products. Competitive advantage lies with firms best able to link available input to reliable and established distribution channels. In the book industry, distribution "for the great majority of titles is limited, ineffective, and costly. In part this weakness in distribution is a direct consequence of the strength of the industry in issuing materials. . . . If it were harder to get a book published, it would be easier to get it distributed" (Lacy 1963, pp. 53–54).[12]

The mass distribution of cultural items requires more *bureaucratic* organizational arrangements than the administration of production, for example, a higher proportion of salaried clerks to process information, greater continuity of personnel and ease of supervision, less delegation of responsibility, and higher fixed overhead (Stinchcombe 1959). Whereas the building contractor produces custom goods to meet the specifications of a clearly defined client-set, cultural organizations release a wide variety of items which must be publicized and made attractive to thousands of consumers in order to succeed. Larger organizations generally maintain their own sales forces, which may contract with smaller firms to distribute their output as well as the parent company's.

The more highly bureaucratized distribution sector of cultural industries is characterized by more economic concentration than the craft-administered production sector, where lower costs pose fewer barriers to entry. Although heavy expenditures required for product promotion and marketing may be reduced by contracting with independent sales organizations on a commission basis, this practice is engaged in primarily by smaller, weaker, and poorly capitalized firms. As one publishing company executive explains:

> If a company does not have a big sales force, it's far more difficult for them to have a best seller. But unless a firm does $7,500,000 worth of trade book business a year, they can't afford to maintain an adequate sales force. Many publishing houses, consequently, do not have any sales force at all. They rely on middlemen—jobbers—to get their books into bookstores. But jobbers, of course, don't attend sales conferences. They handle so many books for so many publishers that they can't be expected to "push" certain books from a certain house. [Mann 1967, p. 14]

Contracting with autonomous sales organizations places the entrepreneurial firm in a position of dependence on outsiders, with the attendant risk of having cultural products regarded highly by the sponsoring organization assigned a low priority by its distributor. In the absence of media coverage and/or advertising by the sponsoring organization, retail outlets generally fail to stock new books or records.

A functional equivalent of direct advertising for cultural organizations is provided by the selective coverage afforded new styles and titles in books, recordings, and movies by the mass media. Cultural products provide "copy" and "programming" for newspapers, magazines, radio stations, and television programs; in exchange, they receive "free" publicity. The presence or absence of coverage, rather than its favorable or unfavorable interpretation, is the important variable here. Public awareness of the existence and availability of a new cultural product often is contingent on feature stories in newspapers and national magazines, review columns, and broadcast talk shows, and, for recordings, radio-station air play. While the total number of products to be awarded media coverage may be predicted in the aggregate, the estimation of *which ones* will be selected from the potential universe is problematic.

The organizational segregation of the producers of cultural items from their disseminators places definite restrictions on the forms of power which cultural organizations may exercise over mass-media gatekeepers to effect the selection of particular items for coverage. Widely shared social norms mandate the independence of book-review editors, radio-station personnel, film critics, and other arbiters of coverage from the special needs and commercial interests of cultural organizations.[13] Thus, autonomous gatekeepers present the producer organization with the "control" problem of favorably influencing the probability that a given new release will be selected for exposure to consumers.

For publishing houses and record firms, especially, it would be uneconomical to engage in direct, large-scale advertising campaigns to bring more than a few releases to public attention.[14]

> The fact that each one of the thousands of titles every year must be separately advertised imposes almost insuperable obstacles in the way of effective national advertising. It is as though General Motors for each tenth Chevrolet had to change the name, design, and characteristics of the car and launch a new national advertising campaign to sell the next ten cars. . . . The advertising problem . . . is thus wholly different from that of the advertiser of a single brand that remains on sale indefinitely. [Lacy 1963, pp. 54–55]

> The publisher's advertising problem is greatly aggravated by what we have all agreed is true—too many books are published, most of them doomed in advance to a short and inglorious life. . . . Many a novel is dead the day it is published, many others survive a month or two or three. The sales of such books are always small, and what little advertising they get may be rendered doubly useless by the fact that the bookseller tends to return to the publisher his stock of slow-moving books before they have had time to be exposed to very many potential customers. . . . Well then, what does make a book sell? Charles Darwin gave the right answer to Samuel Butler when he was asked this question: "Getting talked about is what makes a book sell." [Knopf 1964, p. 17]

> Record companies are dependent on radio . . . to introduce new artists as well as to introduce new records of all artists and to get them exposed to the public. . . . [We] cannot expose their performances because it's just on grooves and the public will not know what they sound like. (Q.) "Would it be fair to say that radio accounts for 75, or 90 percent of the promotion of new releases?" (A.) I think your figures are probably accurate, yes. [Davis 1967, p. 5]

For book publishers, record companies, and, to a lesser extent, movie studios, then, the crucial target audience for promotional campaigns consists of autonomous gatekeepers, or "surrogate consumers" such as disk jockeys, film critics, and book reviewers, employed by mass-media organizations to serve as fashion experts and opinion leaders for their respective constituencies.

The mass media constitute the institutional subsystem of the cultural industry. *The diffusion of particular fads and fashions is either blocked or facilitated at this strategic checkpoint.* Cultural innovations are seen as originating in the technical subsystem. A sample selected for sponsorship by cultural organizations in the managerial subsystem is introduced into the marketplace. This output is filtered by mass-media gatekeepers serving as "institutional regulators of innovation" (Boskoff 1964). Organizations in the managerial subsystem are highly responsive to feedback from institutional regulators: styles afforded coverage are imitated and reproduced on a large scale until the fad has "run its course" (Boskoff 1964; Meyersohn and Katz 1957).[15]

We see the consumer's role in this process as essentially one of rank ordering cultural styles and items "preselected" for consideration by role occupants in the managerial and institutional subsystems. Feedback from consumers, in the form of sales figures and box-office receipts, cues producers and disseminators of cultural innovations as to which experiments may be imitated profitably and which should probably be dropped.[16] This process is analogous to the preselection of electoral candidates by political parties, followed by voter feedback at the ballot box. The orderly sequence of events and the possibility of only two outcomes at each checkpoint resemble a Markov process.

This model assumes a surplus of available "raw material" at the outset (e.g., writers, singers, politicians) and pinpoints a number of strategic checkpoints at which the oversupply is filtered out. It is "value added" in the sense that no product can enter the societal subsystem (e.g., retail outlets) until it has been processed favorably through each of the preceding levels of organization, respectively.[17]

ORGANIZATIONAL RESPONSE TO TASK-ENVIRONMENT UNCERTAINTIES

Our analysis suggests that organizations at the managerial level of cultural industry systems are confronted by (1) constraints on output distribution imposed by mass-media gatekeepers, and (2) contingencies in recruiting creative "raw materials" for organizational sponsorship. To minimize dependence on these elements of their task environments, publishing houses, record companies, and movie studios have developed three proactive strategies: (1) the allocation of numerous personnel to boundary-spanning roles; (2) overproduction and differential promotion of new items; and (3) cooptation of mass-media gatekeepers.

Proliferation of Contact Men

Entrepreneurial organizations in cultural industries require competent intelligence agents and representatives to actively monitor developments at their input and output boundaries. Inability to locate and successfully market new cultural items leads to organizational failure: new manuscripts must be located, new singers recorded, and new movies produced. Boundary-spanning units have therefore been established, and a large proportion of personnel allocated to serve as "contact men" (Wilensky 1956), with titles such as talent scout, promoter, press coordinator, and vice-president in charge of public relations. The centrality of information on boundary developments to managers and executives in cultural organizations is suggested in these industries' trade papers: coverage of artist relations and selections by mass-media gatekeepers far exceeds that of matters managed more easily in a standardized manner, such as inflation in warehousing, shipping, and physical production costs.

Contact men linking the cultural organization to the artist community contract for creative raw material on behalf of the organization and supervise its production. Much of their work is performed in the field. In publishing, for example:

> "You have to get out to lunch to find out what's going on out there—and what's going on out there is where an editor's books come from," says James Silberman, editor-in-chief of Random House. "Over the years, I've watched people in the book business stop having lunch, and they stop getting books."

> There are, in general, three kinds of publishing lunches. The first, and most common, takes place between editor and agent: its purpose is to generate book ideas for the agent's clients; also, it provides an opportunity for the agent to grow to like the editor enough to send him completed manuscripts. The second kind is set up by publicists with whomever they want to push their books: television people, critics, book-review editors. . . .

> The third kind takes place between authors and editors, and it falls into three phases: the precontract phase, where the editor woos the author with good food and book ideas; the postcontract phase, where the author is given assistance on his manuscript and the impetus to go on; and the postpublication phase, where the editor explains to the author why the publishing house took so few advertisements for his book. [Ephron 1969, p. 8]

Professional agents on the input boundary must be allowed a great deal of discretion in their activities on behalf of the cultural organization. Successful editors, record "producers," and film directors and producers thus pose control problems for the focal organization. In fields characterized by uncertainty over cause/effect relations, their talent has been "validated" by the successful marketplace performance of "their discoveries"—providing high visibility and opportunities for mobility outside a single firm. Their value to the cultural organization as recruiters and intelligence agents is indicated by high salaries, commissions, and prestige within the industry system.

Cultural organizations deploy additional contact men at their output boundaries, linking the organization to (1) retail outlets and (2) surrogate consumers in mass-media organizations. The tasks of promoting and distributing new cultural items are analytically distinct, although boundary units combining both functions may be established. Transactions between retailers and boundary personnel at the wholesale level are easily programmed and supervised. In terms of Thompson's (1962) typology of output transactions, the retailer's "degree of nonmember discretion" is limited to a small number of fixed options concerning such matters as discount schedules and return privileges.[18] In contrast, where organizations are dependent on "surrogate consumers" for coverage of new products, the latter enjoy a high degree of discretion: tactics employed by contact men at this boundary entail more "personal influence"; close supervision by the organization is more difficult and may be politically inexpedient. Further development of Thompson's typology would facilitate tracing the flow of innovations through organization systems by extending the analysis of transactions "at the end of the line"—that is, between salesmen and consumers or bureaucrats and clients—to encompass boundary transactions at all levels of organization through which new products are processed.

A high ratio of promotional personnel to surrogate consumers appears to be a structural feature of any industry system in which (a) goods are marginally differentiated; (b) producers' access to consumer markets is regulated by independent gatekeepers; and (c) large-scale, *direct* advertising campaigns are uneconomical or prohibited by law. Cultural products are advertised *indirectly* to independent gatekeepers within the industry system in order to reduce demand uncertainty over which products will be selected for exposure to consumers. Where independent gatekeepers neither filter information nor mediate between producer and consumer, the importance of contact men at the organization's output boundary is correspondingly diminished. In industry systems where products are advertised more directly to consumers, the contact man is superseded by full-page advertisements and sponsored commercials, purchased outright by the producer organization and directed at the lay consumer.

Overproduction and Differential Promotion of Cultural Items

Differential promotion of new items, in conjunction with overproduction, is a second proactive strategy employed by cultural organizations to overcome dependence on mass-media gatekeepers. Overproduction is a rational organizational response in an environment of low capital investments and demand uncertainty. "Fortunately, from a cultural point of view if not from the publisher's, the market is full of uncertainties. . . . A wise publisher will hedge his bets" (Bailey 1970, pp. 144, 170).

Under these conditions it apparently is more efficient to produce many "failures" for each success than to sponsor fewer items and pretest each on a massive scale to increase media coverage and consumer sales. The number of books, records, and low-budget films released annually far exceeds coverage capacity and consumer demand for these products.[19] The publisher's "books cannibalize one another. And even if he hasn't deliberately lowered his editorial standards (and he almost certainly has) he is still publishing more books than he can possibly do justice to" (Knopf 1964, p. 18). While over 15,000 new titles are issued annually, the probability of any one appearing in a given bookstore is only 10% (Lacy 1963). Similarly, fewer than 20% of over 6,000 (45 rpm) "singles" appear in retail record outlets (Shemel and Krasilovsky 1964). Movie theaters exhibit a larger proportion of approximately 400 feature films released annually, fewer than half of which, however, are believed to recoup the initial investment. The production of a surplus is facilitated further by contracts negotiated with artists on a royalty basis and other cost-minimizing features of the craft administration of production.

Cultural organizations ideally maximize profits by mobilizing promotional resources in support of volume sales for a small number of items. These resources are not divided equally among each firm's new releases. Only a small proportion of all new books and records "sponsored" by cultural organizations is selected by company policy makers for large-scale promotion within the industry system. In the record industry:

> The strategy of massive promotion is employed by policymakers in an attempt to influence the coverage of their product by media over which they exert little control. They must rely on independently owned trade papers to bring new records to the attention of radio programmers and disk jockeys, and upon radio airplay and journalists to reach the consumer market. For this reason, selected artists are sent to visit key radio stations, and parties are arranged in cities throughout the country to bring together the artist and this advanced audience. It seems likely that if . . . policymakers could better predict exposure for particular releases, then fewer would be recorded. . . . Records are released (1) with no advance publicity, (2) with minimal fanfare, or (3) only after a large-scale advance promotional campaign. The extent of a record's promotion informs the policymakers' immediate audience of regional promoters and Top 40 programmers of their expectations for, and evaluation of, their product. In this way the company rank orders its own material. The differential promotion of records serves to sensitize Top 40 programmers to the names of certain songs and artists. Heavily promoted records are publicized long before their release through full-page advertisements in the trade press, special mailings, and personal appearances by the recording's artists. The program director is made familiar with the record long before he receives it. It is "expected" to be a hit. In this way, though radio stations receive records gratis, anticipation and "demand" for selected releases are created. . . . The best indicator of a record's potential for becoming a hit at this stage is the amount of promotion it is allocated. [Hirsch 1969, pp. 34, 36]

Similarly, in the publishing industry:

> Publishers' advertising has several subsidiary functions to perform besides that of selling books, or even making readers. Among them are:
>
> 1. Influencing the "trade"—that is impressing book jobbers and retail booksellers with the fact that the publisher is actively backing a certain title and that it would be good business for them to stock and push it.
> 2. Influencing authors and their agents. Many an author has left one publisher for another because he felt that the first publisher was not giving his book enough advertising support.
> 3. Influencing reviewers. The implication here is not that any reputable reviewer can be "bought" by the use of his paper's advertising columns, but reviewers are apt to watch publishers' announcements (particularly those that appear in the trade papers) for information which will aid them in selecting books for review, and in deciding which ones to feature or to review at length.
> 4. Influencing the sale of book club, reprint, and other subsidiary rights. Publishers sometimes advertise solely to keep a book on the best-seller list while a projected movie sale is in prospect. Occasionally this works the

other way round: movie producers have been known to contribute generously to the ad budget of the initial hardcover edition so as to reap the benefit of the best-seller publicity for their film when it finally appears. [Spier 1967, pp. 155–56]

Most cultural items are allocated minimal amounts for promotion and are "expected" to fail (recall the description of postpublication author-editor luncheons cited earlier). Such long shots constitute a pool of "understudies," from which substitutes may be drawn in the event that either mass-media gatekeepers or consumers reject more heavily plugged items.[20] We see the strategy of differential promotion as an attempt by cultural organizations to "buffer" their technical core from demand uncertainties by smoothing out output transactions (Thompson 1967).

Cooptation of "Institutional Regulators"

Mass-media gatekeepers report a wide variety of mechanisms developed by cultural organizations to influence and manipulate their coverage decisions. These range from "indications" by the sponsoring organization of high expectations for particular new "discoveries" (e.g., full-page advertisements in the trade press, parties arranged to introduce the artist to recognized opinion leaders) to personal requests and continuous barrages of indirect advertising, encouraging and cajoling the gatekeeper to "cover," endorse, and otherwise contribute toward the fulfillment of the organization's prophesy of great success for its new product.

The goals of cultural and mass-media organizations come into conflict over two issues. First, public opinion, professional ethics, and, to a lesser extent, job security, all require that institutional gatekeepers maintain independent standards of judgment and quality rather than endorse only those items which cultural organizations elect to promote. Second, the primary goal of commercial mass-media organizations is to maximize revenue by "delivering" audiences for sponsored messages rather than to serve as promotional vehicles for particular cultural items. Hit records, for example, are featured by commercial radio stations primarily to sell advertising:

Q. Do you play this music because it is the most popular?
A. Exactly for that reason. . . . We use the entertainment part of our programming, which is music, essentially, to attract the largest possible audience, so that what else we have to say . . . in terms of advertising message . . . [is] exposed to the largest number of people possible—and the way to get the largest number to tune in is to play the kind of music they like . . . so that you have a mass audience at the other end.

Q. If, let's say that by some freak of nature, a year from now the most popular music was chamber music, would you be playing that?
A. Absolutely . . . , and the year after that, if it's Chinese madrigals, we'll be playing them. [Strauss 1966, p. 3][21]

Goal conflict and value dissensus are reflected in frequent disputes among cultural organizations, mass-media gatekeepers, and public representatives concerning the legitimacy (or legality) of promoters' attempts to acquire power over the decision autonomy of surrogate consumers.

Cultural organizations strive to control gatekeepers' decision autonomy to the extent that coverage for new items is (a) crucial for building consumer demand, and (b) problematic. Promotional campaigns aimed at coopting institutional gatekeepers are most likely to require proportionately large budgets and illegitimate tactics when consumers' awareness of the product hinges almost exclusively on coverage by these personnel. As noted earlier, cultural organizations are less likely to deploy boundary agents or sanction high-pressure tactics for items whose sale is less contingent on gatekeepers' actions.

VARIABILITY WITHIN CULTURAL INDUSTRIES

Up to this point, we have tended to minimize variability among cultural organizations, cultural products, and the markets at which they are directed. Our generalizations apply mainly to the most *speculative* and entrepreneurial segments of the publishing, recording, and motion picture industries, that is, adult trade books, popular records, and low-budget movies.[22] Within each of these categories, organizations subscribe, in varying degrees, to normative as well as to the more economic goals we have assumed thus far. Certain publishing houses, record companies, and movie producers command high prestige within each industry system for financing cultural products of high quality but of doubtful commercial value. To the extent they do *not* conform to economic norms of rationality, these organizations should be considered separately from the more dominant pattern of operations described above.[23]

Whether our generalizations might also characterize less-uncertain industry segments, such as educational textbook and children's-book publishing divisions, or classical record production is also subject to question. In each of these instances, cost factors and/or degree of demand uncertainty may be quite different, which, in turn, would affect the structure and operation of the producer organizations. Textbook publishers, for example, face a more predictable market than do publishers (or divisions) specializing in trade books: more capital investment is required, and larger sales forces must be utilized for school-to-school canvassing (Brammer 1967). In the case of children's books, some differences might be expected in that libraries rather than retail stores account for 80% of sales (Lacy 1968).

Within the adult-trade-book category, coverage in book-review columns is more crucial to the success of literary novels than to detective stories or science-fiction books (Blum 1959). Review coverage is also problematic: "Even *The New York Times*, which reviews many more books than any other journal addressed to the general public, covers only about 20 percent of the annual output. Many books of major importance in specialized fields go entirely unnoticed in such general media, and it is by no means unknown for even National Book Award winners to go unreviewed in the major national journals" (Lacy 1963, p. 55). We would therefore expect publishers' agents to push novels selected for national promotion more heavily than either detective stories or science-fiction works. Serious novels should be promoted more differentially than others.

Similarly, coverage in the form of radio-station air play is far more crucial in building consumer demand for recordings of popular music than for classical selections. Control over the selection of new "pop" releases by radio-station programmers and disk jockeys is highly problematic. Record companies are dependent on radio air play as the *only* effective vehicle of exposure for new pop records. In this setting—where access to consumers hinges almost exclusively on coverage decisions by autonomous gatekeepers—institutionalized side payments ("payola") emerged as a central tactic in the overall strategy of cooptation employed by producer organizations to assure desired coverage.

Radio air play for classical records is less crucial for building consumer demand; the probability of obtaining coverage for classical releases is also easier to estimate. Whereas producers and consumers of pop records are often unsure about a song's likely sales appeal or musical worth, criteria of both musical merit and consumer demand are comparatively clear in the classical field. Record companies, therefore, allocate proportionately fewer promotional resources to assure coverage of classical releases by mass-media gatekeepers, and record-company agents promoting classical releases employ more legitimate tactics to influence coverage decisions than promoters of pop records employ to coopt the decision autonomy of institutional regulators.

Thompson (1967, p. 36) has proposed that "when support capacity is concentrated but demand dispersed, the weaker organization will attempt to handle its dependence through coopting." In our analysis, cultural organizations represent a class of weaker organizations, dependent on support capacity concentrated in mass-media organizations; demand is dispersed among retail outlets and consumers. While all cultural organizations attempt to coopt autonomous consumer surrogates, the intensity of the tactics employed tends to vary with degree of dependence. Thus, cultural organizations most dependent on mass-media gatekeepers (i.e., companies producing pop records) resorted to the most costly and illegitimate tactics; the institution of payola may be seen as an indication of their weaker power position.

CONCLUSION

This paper has outlined the structure of entrepreneurial organizations engaged in the production and distribution of cultural items and has examined three adaptive strategies employed to minimize dependence on elements of their task environments: the deployment of contact men to organizational boundaries, overproduction and differential promotion of new items, and the cooptation of mass-media gatekeepers. It is suggested that in order for new products or ideas to reach a public of consumers, they first must be processed favorably through a system of organizations whose units filter out large numbers of candidates before they arrive at the consumption stage. The concept of an industry system is proposed as a useful frame of reference in which to (1) trace the flow of new products and ideas as they are filtered at each level or organization, and (2) examine relations among organizations.

NOTES

1. This paper was developed in connection with a study of the popular music industry and its audience conducted at the Survey Research Center, University of Michigan, under the supervision of Dr. Stephen B. Withey and supported by grant numbers 1-RO1-MH17064-01 and 1-FO1-MH48847-01 from the National Institute of Mental Health. I wish to thank Edward O. Laumann, Albert J. Reiss, Jr., Randall Collins, Theodore L. Reed, David R. Segal, and an anonymous reviewer for critical comments on an earlier version of this paper, presented at the sixty-fifth annual meeting of the American Sociological Association, August 1970.

2. A notable exception is Alfred Chandler's classic study of corporate innovation (1962). In the areas of fine art and popular culture, this problem has been noted by Albrecht (1968), Barnett (1959), Baumol and Bowen (1968), and Gans (1966).

3. As Lane (1970a, p. 240) puts it, a central sociological question is the extent to which sponsoring organizations "manage and control values and knowledge rather than simply purvey." An organizational approach to the study of American mass culture suggests that changes in content can be caused by shrinking markets only partially due to shifts in consumer taste preferences. Industry observers see increased public access since 1955 to "art" films (Houston 1963; Gubeck 1969) and popular-song lyrics with protest themes (Carey 1969) as reflecting the near-total loss of a once-dependable audience, whose unchanged predispositions now receive confirmation from television fare. The advent of television forced movie exhibitors and radio-station managers to relinquish the majority audience and alter program content to attract minority subcultures *previously neglected for economic reasons.* The production of "rock 'n' roll" records and films by independent producers was stimulated by unprecedented opportunity for radio air play and exhibition (Hirsch 1971). While the altered content represents the best market share now available to many producers and distributors, it is directed at the teenage and intellectual markets, respectively, and not to former patrons.

4. Large firms and record-industry personnel are disproportionately represented.

5. An excellent, first-person account of this experience is provided by Cowan (1970).

6. For a more far-ranging consideration of the genesis and life cycle of fads and fashions from the standpoint of classic sociological theories, see Meyersohn and Katz (1957), Blumer (1968), and Denzin (1970).

7. A focal organization's task environment consists of other organizations located on its input and output boundaries.

8. "Production" here refers to the performances or manuscripts created by artists and talent scouts for later replication in the form of books, film-negative prints, and phonograph records. The physical manufacture of these goods is sufficiently amenable to control as to be nearly irrelevant to our discussion.

9. Royalty payments in the motion-picture industry are an alternative to costly, long-term contracts with established movie stars and permit producers to partially defer expenditures until the picture is in exhibition. Contracts specifying royalties (in addition to negotiated fees) are limited to well-known actors with proven "track records." Author-publisher contracts are more uniform, specifying royalties of at least 10% to all authors. Record companies seldom provide royalties higher than 3%–5% of sales. Since popular records are frequently purchased in greater quantities than best-selling books, however, musicians' royalties may equal or exceed those of authors.

10. The cost of producing and manufacturing (45 rpm) record "singles" averages only $2,500 (Brief 1964).

11. Low-budget feature films range in cost from $100,000 to $2 million each. The break-even point for movies is believed to be $4 in box-office receipts for each dollar invested in the film. A recent film, *Easy Rider*, produced on a low budget of $360,000 is reported to have earned $50 million in box-office receipts and netted its producers approximately $10 million. "Rather than make one expensive film, with all the correct box-office insurance in the way of story and star-casting, and see the whole thing go down the drain," many producers have tried putting "the same kind of money into three or four cheap films by young directors, gambling that at least one of them would prove [to be a smash]" (Houston 1963, p. 101). Houston's description of French filmmaking has since come to characterize its American counterpart.

12. Prior to implementation of a (1948) judgment by the U.S. Supreme Court, independent and foreign film-production companies without powerful distribution arms were blocked most effectively from access to consumers through movie exhibition. The *Paramount Decrees* divested movie-theater-chain ownership from nine major film producers and distributors (Conant 1960).

13. Public reaction to the "payola" scandals in the late 1950s demonstrated a widespread belief that the disseminators of mass culture should be independent of its producers. Disk jockeys, book reviewers, and film critics are expected to remain free from the influence or manipulations of record companies, book publishers, and movie studios, respectively. This feeling is shared generally by members of each industry system as well as embodied in our legal system.

14. New movies, faced with fewer competitors and representing far greater investment per capita, are advertised more heavily directly.

15. Boskoff (1964, p. 224) sees the sources of innovations within any social system as the technical and/or managerial levels of organization, or external sources. . . . By its very nature, the institutional level is uncongenial to innovative roles for itself." Changes occur at an increasing rate when "the institutional level is ineffective in controlling the cumulation of variations. . . . This may be called change by institutional default." Changes in pop-culture content consistently follow this pattern.

16. Two interesting formal models of aspects of this process are presented by McPhee (1963).

17. For a more detailed discussion of the *role-set* engaged in the processing of fads and fashions, with particular application to "hit" records, see Hirsch (1969).

18. Sponsoring organizations without access to established channels of distribution, however, experience great difficulty in obtaining orders for their products from retail outlets and consumers. Thompson's (1962) typology of interaction between organization members and nonmembers consists of two dimensions: Degree of nonmember discretion, and specificity of organizational control over members in output roles. Output roles are defined as those which arrange for the distribution of an organization's ultimate product (or service) to other agents in society.

19. This is not to say that "uneconomical" selections may not appeal to a fair number of consumers. Each industry defines consumer demand according to its own costs and convenience. Thus, a network television program with only 14 million viewers fails for inadequate consumer demand.

20. Two recent successful long shots are the best-selling reissue of turn-of-the-century Sears Roebuck catalogs and the film *Endless Summer*. For a discussion of criteria employed to choose pop records for differential promotion, see Hirsch 1969.

21. Similarly, the recent demise of the *Saturday Evening Post* was precipitated by an inability to attract sufficient advertising revenue: too many of its 6 million subscribers lived in rural areas and fell into low-income categories (Friedrich 1970).

22. Adult trade books account for less than 10% of all sales in the book-publishing industry, excluding book-club sales (Bowker 1969). Records of popular music (subsuming folk and country and western categories) provide the majority of sales in the record industry (Brief 1964). Figures on the contribution of low-budget films to movie industry sales were not obtained. Low-budget films are more speculative than high-budget "blockbusters" on a *per picture* basis only, where their probability of box-office success as well as their costs appear to be lower.

23. Lane (1970b) presents a valuable portrait of one such publishing house; Miller (1949) provides an excellent study of cross-pressures within the book industry.

REFERENCES

Albrecht, Milton C. 1968. "Art as an Institution." *American Sociological Review* 33 (June):383–96.

Bailey, Herbert S. 1970. *The Art and Science of Book Publishing*. New York: Harper & Row.

Bailey, Stephen K., and Edith K. Mosher. 1968. *ESEA: The Office of Education Administers a Law*. Syracuse, N.Y.: Syracuse University Press.

Barnett, H. G. 1953. *Innovation: The Basis of Cultural Change*. New York: McGraw-Hill.

Barnett, James H. 1959. "The Sociology of Art." In *Sociology Today*, edited by Robert K. Merton, Leonard Broom, and Leonard S. Cottrell, Jr. New York: Basic.

Baumol, William J., and William G. Bowen. 1968. *Performing Arts: The Economic Dilemma*. Cambridge, Mass.: M.I.T. Press.

Blum, Eleanor. 1959. "Paperback Book Publishing: A Survey of Content." *Journalism Quarterly* 36 (Fall):447–54.

Blumer, Herbert. 1968. "Fashion." In *International Encyclopedia of the Social Sciences*. 2d ed. New York: Macmillan.

———. 1969. "Fashion: From Class Differentiation to Collective Selection." *Sociological Quarterly* 10 (Summer):275–91.

Boskoff, Alvin. 1964. "Functional Analysis as a Source of a Theoretical Repertory and Research Tasks in the Study of Social Change." In *Explorations in Social Change*, edited by George K. Zollschan and Walter Hirsch. Boston: Houghton Mifflin.

Bowker, R. R., Co. 1969. *The Bowker Annual of Library and Book Trade Information*. New York: R. R. Bowker Co.

Brammer, Mauck. 1967. "Textbook Publishing." In *What Happens in Book Publishing*, edited by Chandler B. Grannis. 2d ed. New York: Columbia University Press.

Brief, Henry. 1964. *Radio and Records: A Presentation by the Record Industry Association of America at the 1964 Regional Meetings of the National Association of Broadcasters*. New York: Record Industry Association of America.

Brockway, George P. 1967. "Business Management and Accounting." In *What Happens in Book Publishing*, edited by Chandler B. Grannis. 2d ed. New York: Columbia University Press.

Brown, Roger L. 1968. "The Creative Process in the Popular Arts." *International Social Science Journal* 20 (4):613–24.

Burns, Tom, and G. M. Stalker. 1961. *The Management of Innovation*. London: Tavistock.

Carey, James T. 1969. "Changing Courtship Patterns in the Popular Song." *American Journal of Sociology* 74 (May):720–31.

Chandler, Alfred D., Jr. 1962. *Strategy and Structure: Chapters in the History of the American Industrial Enterprise*. Cambridge, Mass.: M.I.T. Press.

Conant, Michael. 1960. *Antitrust in the Motion Picture Industry*. Berkeley: University of California Press.

Coser, Lewis A. 1965. *Men of Ideas*. New York: Free Press.

Cowan, Paul. 1970. "Electronic Vaudeville Tour: Miking of an Un-American." *Village Voice*, April 16, 1970, p. 5.

Davis, Clive. 1967. "The Truth About Radio: A WNEW Inquiry." Transcript of interview with general manager CBS Records. Mimeographed. New York: WNEW.

Denzin, Norman K. 1970. "Problems in Analyzing Elements of Mass Culture. Notes on the Popular Song and Other Artistic Productions." *American Journal of Sociology* 75 (May):1035–38.

Ephron, Nora. 1969. "Where Bookmen Meet to Eat." *New York Times Book Review*, June 22, 1969, pp. 8–12.

Evan, William M. 1963. "Toward a Theory of Inter-Organizational Relations." *Management Science* 11:B217–30. Reprinted in *Approaches to Organizational Design*, edited by James D. Thompson. Pittsburgh: University of Pittsburgh Press, 1966.

Frase, Robert W. 1968. "The Economics of Publishing." In *Trends in American Publishing*, edited by Kathryn L. Henderson. Champaign: Graduate School of Library Science, University of Illinois.

Friedrich, Otto. 1970. *Decline and Fall*. New York: Harper & Row.

Gans, Herbert J. 1964. "The Rise of the Problem Film." *Social Problems* 11 (Spring):327–36.

———. 1966. "Popular Culture in America: Social Problem in a Mass Society or Social Asset in a Pluralist Society?" In *Social Problems: A Modern Approach*, edited by Howard S. Becker. New York: Wiley.

Guback, Thomas H. 1969. *The International Film Industry: Western Europe and American Since 1945*. Bloomington: Indiana University Press.

Hirsch, Paul M. 1969. *The Structure of the Popular Music Industry*. Ann Arbor: Survey Research Center, University of Michigan.

———. 1971. "Sociological Approaches to the Pop Music Phenomenon." *American Behavioral Scientist* 14 (January):371–88.

Houston, Penelope. 1963. *The Contemporary Cinema: 1945–1963*. Baltimore: Penguin.

Hughes, Richard, ed. 1959. *Film: The Audience and the Filmmaker*. Vol. 1. New York: Grove.

Knopf, Alfred A. 1964. "Publishing Then and Now, 1912–1964." Twenty-first of the R. R. Bowker Memorial Lectures. New York: New York Public Library.

Lacy, Dan. 1963. "The Economics of Publishing, or Adam Smith and Literature." In "The American Reading Public," edited by Stephen R. Graubard. *Daedalus* (Winter), pp. 42–62.

———. 1968. "Major Trends in American Book Publishing." In *Trends in American Book Publishing*, edited by Kathryn L. Henderson. Champaign: Graduate School of Library Science, University of Illinois.

Lane, Michael. 1970*a*. "Books and Their Publishers." In *Media Sociology*, edited by Jeremy Tunstall. Urbana: University of Illinois Press.

———. 1970*b*. "Publishing Managers, Publishing House Organization and Role Conflict," *Sociology* 4:367–83.

McPhee, William. 1963. "Survival Theory in Culture," and "Natural Exposure and the Theory of Popularity." In *Formal Theories of Mass Behavior*. Glencoe, Ill.: Free Press.

Mann, Peggy. 1967. "A Dual Portrait and Market Report: Harper and Row." *Writer's Yearbook* 37:10–17.

Merton, Robert K. 1957. *Social Theory and Social Structure*. Rev. ed. Glencoe, Ill.: Free Press.

Meyersohn, Rolf, and Elihu Katz. 1957. "Notes on a Natural History of Fads." *American Journal of Sociology* 62 (May):594–601.

Miller, William. 1949. *The Book Industry: A Report of the Public Library Inquiry of the Social Science Research Council*. New York: Columbia University Press.

Montagu, Ivor. 1964. *Film World*. Baltimore: Penguin.

Moynihan, Daniel P. 1969. *Maximum Feasible Misunderstanding*. New York: Free Press.

Parsons, Talcott. 1960. *Structure and Process in Modern Societies*. Glencoe, Ill.: Free Press.

Peterson, Richard, and David Berger. 1971. "Entrepreneurship in Organizations: Evidence from the Popular Music Industry." *Administrative Science* Quarterly 16 (March): 97–107.

Powdermaker, Hortense. 1950. *Hollywood: The Dream Factory*. New York: Grosset & Dunlap.

Rogers, Everett. 1962. *Diffusion of Innovations*. Glencoe, Ill.: Free Press.

Rosten, Leo. 1941. *Hollywood*. New York: Harcourt Brace.

Selznick, Phillip. 1949. *TVA and the Grass Roots*. Berkeley: University of California Press.

Shemel, Sidney, and M. William Krasilovsky. 1964. *This Business of Music*. New York: Billboard.

Spier, Franklin. 1967. "Book Advertising." In *What Happens in Book Publishing*, edited by Chandler B. Grannis, 2d ed. New York: Columbia University Press.

Stinchcombe, Arthur L. 1959. "Bureaucratic and Craft Administration of Production: A Comparative Study." *Administrative Science Quarterly* 4 (September): 168–87.

———. 1968. *Constructing Social Theories*. New York: Harcourt, Brace & World.

Strauss, R. Peter. 1966. "The Truth About Radio: A WNEW Inquiry." Transcript of interview. Mimeographed. New York: WNEW.

Thompson, James D. 1962. "Organizations and Output Transactions." *American Journal of Sociology* 68 (November):309–24.

———. 1967. *Organizations in Action*. New York: McGraw-Hill.

Toffler, Alvin. 1965. *The Culture Consumers*. Baltimore: Penguin.

Wilensky, Harold. 1956. *Intellectuals in Labor Unions*. Glencoe, Ill.: Free Press.

———. 1968. "Organizational Intelligence." In *International Encyclopedia of the Social Sciences*. 2d ed. New York: Macmillan.

EDITORS' NOTES ON FURTHER READING: HIRSCH

In this article, as in several others, Paul M. Hirsch analyzes the sequence of organizations involved in the process that starts with the production of a certain product and ends with it being sold. This article was one of the first sociological treatments of the interaction of the various organizations that form an industry. The different mechanisms involved here are well emphasized in Jeffrey Bradach and Robert Eccles's "Price, Authority, and Trust: From Ideal Types to Plural Forms," *Annual Review of Sociology* 15 (1989):97–118. Hirsch's approach has a definite affinity to Stinchcombe's in "Bureaucratic and Craft Administration of Production" (Chapter 14) in that he looks at organizations that differ from the familiar hierarchical-bureaucratic ones.

As opposed to such students of organizational variation as Stinchcombe and Eccles, however, who are mainly interested in the interactions within and between firms, Hirsch focuses on industries that sell mass-produced goods directly to the general public. Hirsch draws intellectual inspiration from a particular branch of organization theory, which emphasizes the importance of the environment of organizations, as formulated, for example, in Paul Lawrence and Jay Lorsch's *Organizations and Environment: Managing Differentiation and Integration* (1967). (See also the overview of organization theory in Howard Aldrich and Peter Marsden's "Environments and Organizations," pp. 361–392 in Neil Smelser, ed., *Handbook of Sociology* [1988] and chapter 6 of Charles Perrow's *Complex Organizations* [1986], which includes a summary and critique of research on the popular music industry.)

Other sociological studies of culturally oriented industries are Lewis Coser, Charles Kadushin, and Walter Powell's *Books: The Culture and Commerce of Publishing* (1982); Walter Powell's *Getting into Print* (1985); Robert Faulkner's *Music on Demand: Composers and Careers in the Hollywood Film Industry* (1983); and Robert Faulkner and Andy Anderson's "Short-term Projects and Emergent Careers: Evidence from Hollywood," *American Journal of Sociology* 92 (1987):879–909. An attempt to formulate what all these industries have in common can be found in Walter Powell's "Neither Market Nor Hierarchy: Network Forms of Organization," *Research in Organizational Behavior* 12 (1990):295–336. Hirsch himself has also analyzed the record industry in *The Structure of the Popular Music Industry: An Examination of the Filtering Process by Which Records Are Preselected for Public Consumption* (1969); and he has compared it to the pharmaceutical manufacturing industry in "Organizational Effectiveness and the Institutional Environment," *Administrative Science Quarterly* 20 (1975):327–344.

About the Book and Editors

In recent years sociologists have taken up a fruitful examination of such institutions as capital, labor, and product markets, industrial organization, and stock exchanges. Compared to earlier traditions of economic sociology, recent work shows more interest in phenomena usually studied exclusively by economists while at the same time challenging the adequacy of the neoclassical model.

Incorporating classic and contemporary readings in economic sociology as well as offerings from related disciplines, this book provides students with a broad understanding of the dimensions of economic life. A major introduction by the editors traces the history of thought in the field and assesses recent advances and future trends.

Mark Granovetter is professor of sociology at the State University of New York–Stony Brook. He received the American Sociological Association's Theory Prize in 1985 for his paper "Economic Action and Social Structure: The Problem of Embeddedness." **Richard Swedberg,** associate professor of sociology at the University of Stockholm, Sweden, is the author of several books in economic sociology, including *Economics and Sociology* (1990) and *Schumpeter: A Biography* (1991).

Index

Abraham, Katharine, 250
Absolutism, 93
Accounting. *See* Capital accounting; Cost(s), accounting
Actes de la Recherche en Sciences Sociales, 16
Administration, 345–358. *See also* Craft administration; Management
Advertising, 369, 370, 374–375
Agency theory, 312
Agriculture, 90, 96, 213(n26). *See also* Societies, agrarian
Akerlof, George, 2, 3, 7, 247
Allis Chalmers Manufacturing Company, 268
Altruism, 171, 234, 298
Aluminum, 142
American Business Creed, The (Sutton et al.), 5
Anthropology, 5, 40, 181, 225–226
formalists vs. substantivists, 5, 51, 54, 225. *See also* Economics, as formal vs. substantive
Ariès, Philippe, 300(nn 14, 15)
Aristotle, 37, 42
Armenians, 42
Arrow, Kenneth, 60
Art, 364
Arthur, Brian, 17, 22(n5)
Assistant-to, role of, 341–342
Assyria, 47
Atomization, 7, 9, 54, 55, 56, 58, 59, 63, 70, 73, 74, 233–234, 239, 243, 244, 254
Auctions, 49
Audits, 69, 75
Austria, 3, 119, 122
Austrian-Hungarian Empire, 119, 122
Authority, 181–182, 196, 197, 199–208, 210, 220, 316–320, 341, 346, 347–348, 355, 356

Authors, 372
Automobiles, 142, 145, 150, 152, 154, 155, 165, 166, 208
Aztecs, 43

Babylonia, 47, 87, 91
Backwardness. *See* Economies, backward
Bailyn, Bernard, 14
Baker, Wayne, 5
Bakke, E. W., 235
Balances of opposites, 98–99
Baltimore, 289
Banking, 10–11, 11–12, 115–119, 122, 123–124, 128, 131, 133, 154, 166, 185, 186, 187, 201, 202, 211(n3), 290, 300(n18)
Bankruptcy, 122, 191, 193
Bargaining, 38, 162, 170, 228, 229, 231, 270, 280, 293. *See also* Higgling-haggling
Barley, 47
Barnard, Chester, 77(n5)
Bartel, Ann, 241
Barter, 35, 36, 46, 49
Battle of the forms, 270–271
Bazaars, 225–231
Becker, Gary, 1–2, 5, 57, 171, 257, 295
Beecher, Henry Ward, 292, 295
Beer, 144
Belgium, 117, 119
Belongingness, 182
Bendix, Reinhard, 199, 200
Benevolence, 159, 169, 170. *See also* Goodwill
Bengal, 107(n22)
Ben-Porath, Yoram, 62
Berger, Peter, 17
Bessemer steel process, 142, 157(n7)
Best sellers, 367, 368
Billboard, 364

Mostacci-Calzavara, Liviana, 242
Motion pictures, 364–378, 378(n3), 379(nn 9, 11, 12), 380(n22)
Motives/motivations, 41–42, 234, 256, 298, 312
Motor vehicles and equipment, 346. *See also* Automobiles
Multinationals, 134, 135(fig.), 147, 148(table)
Music, classical, 377. *See* Recording industry
Myers, Ramon, 192, 202

Nakamura, Takafusa, 194
Nakane, Chie, 195
Nakatani, I., 168
Napoleon III, 115–116, 124
Natural selection, 234. *See also* Darwinism
Networks, 9, 10–12, 18, 19, 60, 61–62, 66, 71, 72, 76, 80, 165, 185, 188, 192, 206, 211(nn 2, 3), 246, 248, 249, 256. *See also* Embeddedness; Labor, and personal contacts; Social relations; *under* Marketing
New Christianity, 125
New England Merchants, The (Bailyn), 14
New Guinea, 36
New Institutional Economics, 9, 13–16, 54, 59, 62, 64, 74, 80–81, 235–236
New Sociology of Economic Life. *See* Sociology, New Economic
New York (city), 289
New York Life Insurance Co., 291
New York Times, The, 376
Nishiwake, Japan, 161, 164, 165
Nobel Explosives, 151
Non-profit agencies, 365
North, Douglass, 13, 14, 15
Numeracy, 162

Obedience, 70, 77(n5), 199–200. *See also* Authority
Oberschall, Anthony, 16
Obligations, 163, 165, 167–168, 169, 170, 173, 174, 177, 277
Okumura, H., 165
Okun, Arthur, 12–13, 176, 243–244
Oligopolies, 141, 142, 150, 152, 176
Operative building. *See under* Construction industry

Opportunism, 58, 60, 61, 64, 162–163, 190
Order/disorder, 59, 61, 63, 71, 72
Organizations, 361
  economic, 181–210
  industrial, patterns of, 185–188
  interorganizational relations, 366
  levels, 365
  and mass culture studies, 378
  multifunctional/multinational, 132(fig.), 134, 135(fig.)
  organization-sets, 366–371
  patterns/structures, 185–210, 209(table)
  theory, 357–358, 360, 383
  See also Business firms; Corporations; Cultural organizations
Organ transplants, 286, 299(n8)
Orient, 95
Ouchi, William, 195, 212(n16)
Over- and undersocialized conceptions, 54–58, 59, 60, 65, 70, 77(n2)

Packaging/packaged goods, 144, 153, 154–155
Palestine, 42
Paramount Decrees, 379(n12)
Parsons, Talcott, 5, 55, 86, 87, 169, 286, 293, 298, 300(n19)
Passions, 75
Passions and the Interests, The (Hirschman), 7, 59
Path-dependent development, 17–18, 22(n5)
Patrimonialism, 93, 94
Payments, 45–46, 56
Payola, 377, 379(n13)
Peasants, 101, 113, 120, 121, 127, 128, 129. *See also* Serfdom
Pereire brothers, 116, 117, 124
Perishables, 144
Perrow, Charles, 16, 200
Peter the Great, 120
Petroleum, 141–142, 145
Pfeffer, Jeffrey, 251, 255
Philadelphia, 289
Philosophie des Geldes (Simmel), 285
Phoenicians, 42
Piore, Michael, 57, 236, 248, 253
Planning, 346, 347, 348, 354, 355. *See also under* Contracts
Plastics, 192